THE WALKING DEAD

BOOK TWO

a continuing story of survival horror.

created by Robert Kirkman

image comics presents

The Walking Dead
book two

ROBERT KIRKMAN
creator, writer, letterer

CHARLIE ADLARD
penciler, inker, cover

CLIFF RATHBURN
gray tones

RUS WOOTON
letterer (chapter 4)

Original series covers by
TONY MOORE

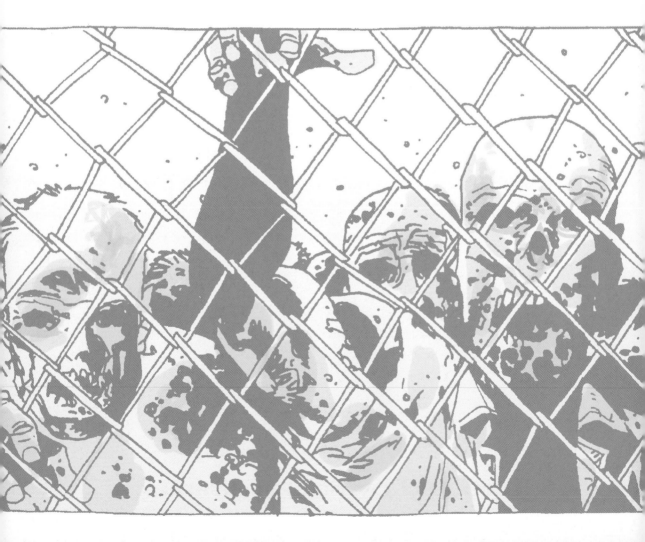

for image comics:

Erik Larsen
Publisher

Todd McFarlane
President

Marc Silvestri
CEO

Jim Valentino
Vice-President

Eric Stephenson
Executive Director

Joe Keatinge
PR & Marketing Coordinator

Branywn Bigglestone
Accounts Manager

Traci Hui
Traffic Manager

Allen Hui
Production Manager

Jonathan Chan
Production Artist

Drew Gill
Production Artist

www.imagecomics.com

THE WALKING DEAD, BOOK TWO. Second Printing. Published by Image Comics, Inc., Office of publication: 1942 University Avenue, Suite 305, Berkeley, California 94704. Copyright © 2008 Robert Kirkman. Originally published in single magazine form as THE WALKING DEAD #13-24. All rights reserved. THE WALKING DEAD™ (including all prominent characters featured herein), its logo and all character likenesses are trademarks of Robert Kirkman, unless otherwise noted. Image Comics® is a trademark of Image Comics, Inc. All rights reserved. No part of this publication may be reproduced or transmitted, in any form or by any means (except for short excerpts for review purposes) without the express written permission of Image Comics, Inc. All names, characters, events and locales in this publication are entirely fictional. Any resemblance to actual persons (living and/or dead), events or places, without satiric intent, is coincidental. PRINTED IN CHINA.

ISBN: 978-1-58240-759-3

Chapter Three:
Safety Behind Bars

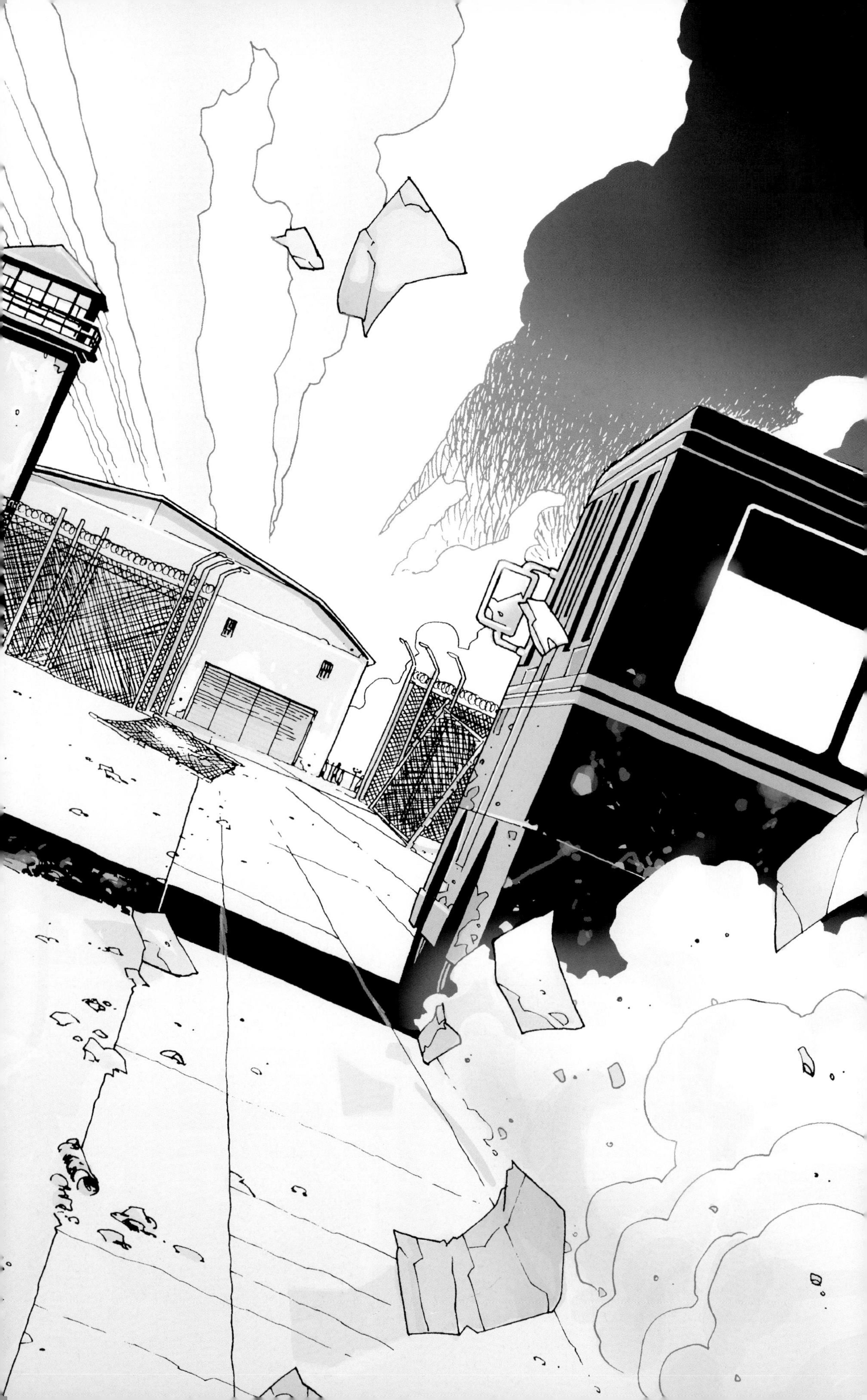

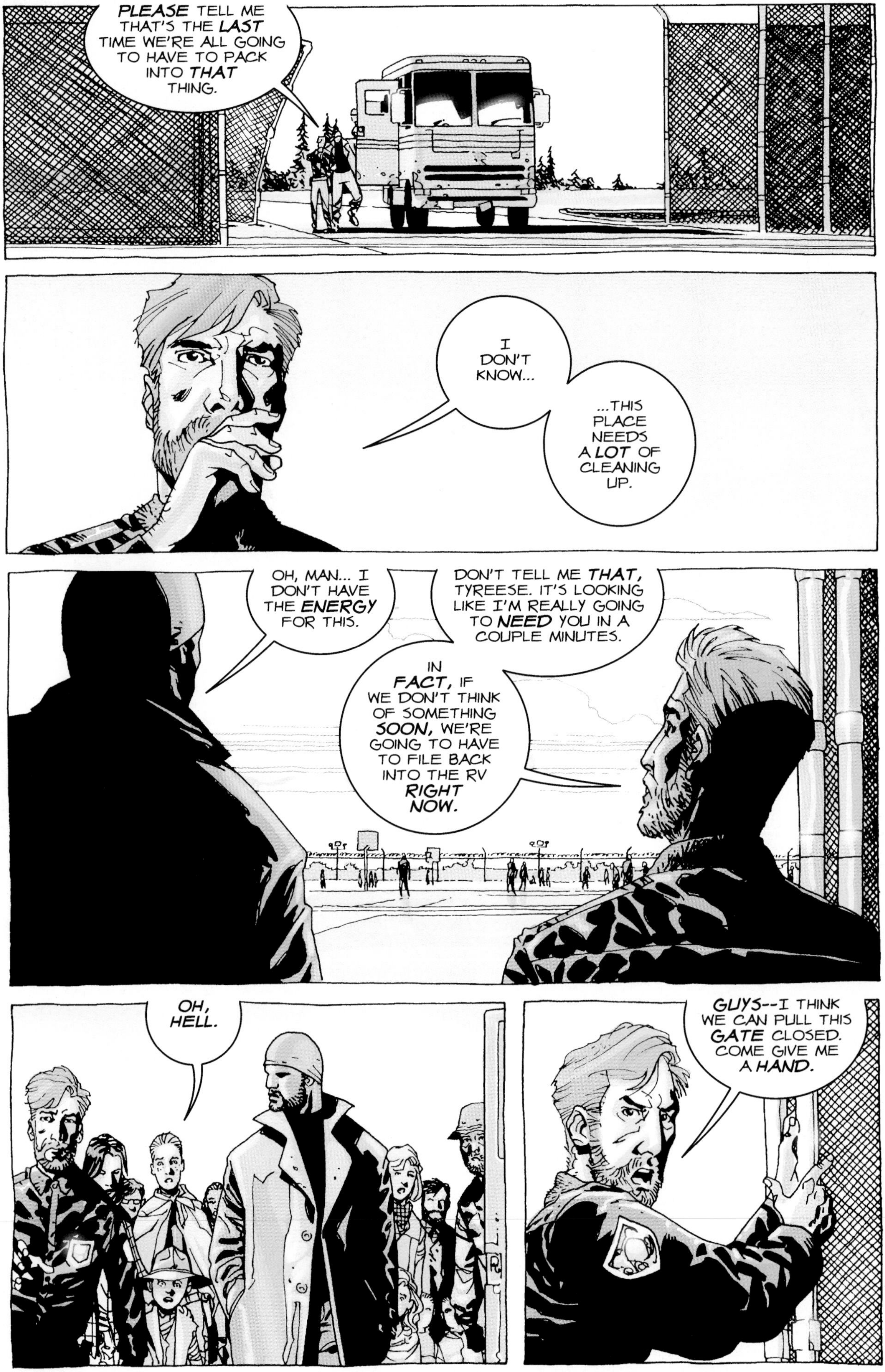
PLEASE TELL ME THAT'S THE LAST TIME WE'RE ALL GOING TO HAVE TO PACK INTO THAT THING.
I DON'T KNOW...
...THIS PLACE NEEDS A LOT OF CLEANING UP.
OH, MAN... I DON'T HAVE THE ENERGY FOR THIS.
DON'T TELL ME THAT, TYREESE. IT'S LOOKING LIKE I'M REALLY GOING TO NEED YOU IN A COUPLE MINUTES.
IN FACT, IF WE DON'T THINK OF SOMETHING SOON, WE'RE GOING TO HAVE TO FILE BACK INTO THE RV RIGHT NOW.
OH, HELL.
GUYS--I THINK WE CAN PULL THIS GATE CLOSED. COME GIVE ME A HAND.

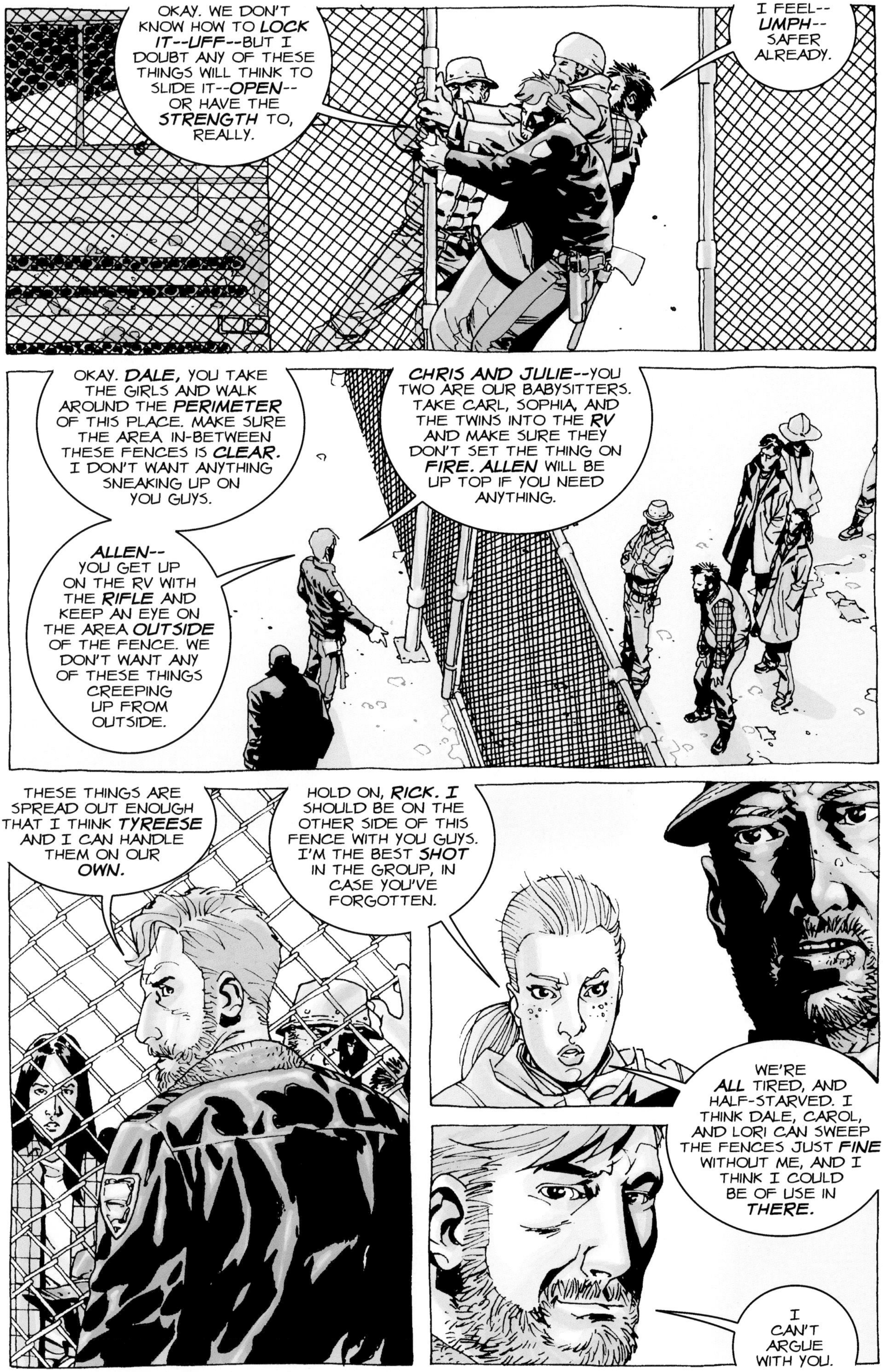
OKAY. WE DON'T KNOW HOW TO LOCK IT--UFF--BUT I DOUBT ANY OF THESE THINGS WILL THINK TO SLIDE IT--OPEN--OR HAVE THE STRENGTH TO, REALLY.
I FEEL--UMPH--SAFER ALREADY.
OKAY. DALE, YOU TAKE THE GIRLS AND WALK AROUND THE PERIMETER OF THIS PLACE. MAKE SURE THE AREA IN-BETWEEN THESE FENCES IS CLEAR. I DON'T WANT ANYTHING SNEAKING UP ON YOU GUYS.
ALLEN--YOU GET UP ON THE RV WITH THE RIFLE AND KEEP AN EYE ON THE AREA OUTSIDE OF THE FENCE. WE DON'T WANT ANY OF THESE THINGS CREEPING UP FROM OUTSIDE.
CHRIS AND JULIE--YOU TWO ARE OUR BABYSITTERS. TAKE CARL, SOPHIA, AND THE TWINS INTO THE RV AND MAKE SURE THEY DON'T SET THE THING ON FIRE. ALLEN WILL BE UP TOP IF YOU NEED ANYTHING.
THESE THINGS ARE SPREAD OUT ENOUGH THAT I THINK TYREESE AND I CAN HANDLE THEM ON OUR OWN.
HOLD ON, RICK. I SHOULD BE ON THE OTHER SIDE OF THIS FENCE WITH YOU GUYS. I'M THE BEST SHOT IN THE GROUP, IN CASE YOU'VE FORGOTTEN.
WE'RE ALL TIRED, AND HALF-STARVED. I THINK DALE, CAROL, AND LORI CAN SWEEP THE FENCES JUST FINE WITHOUT ME, AND I THINK I COULD BE OF USE IN THERE.
I CAN'T ARGUE WITH YOU.

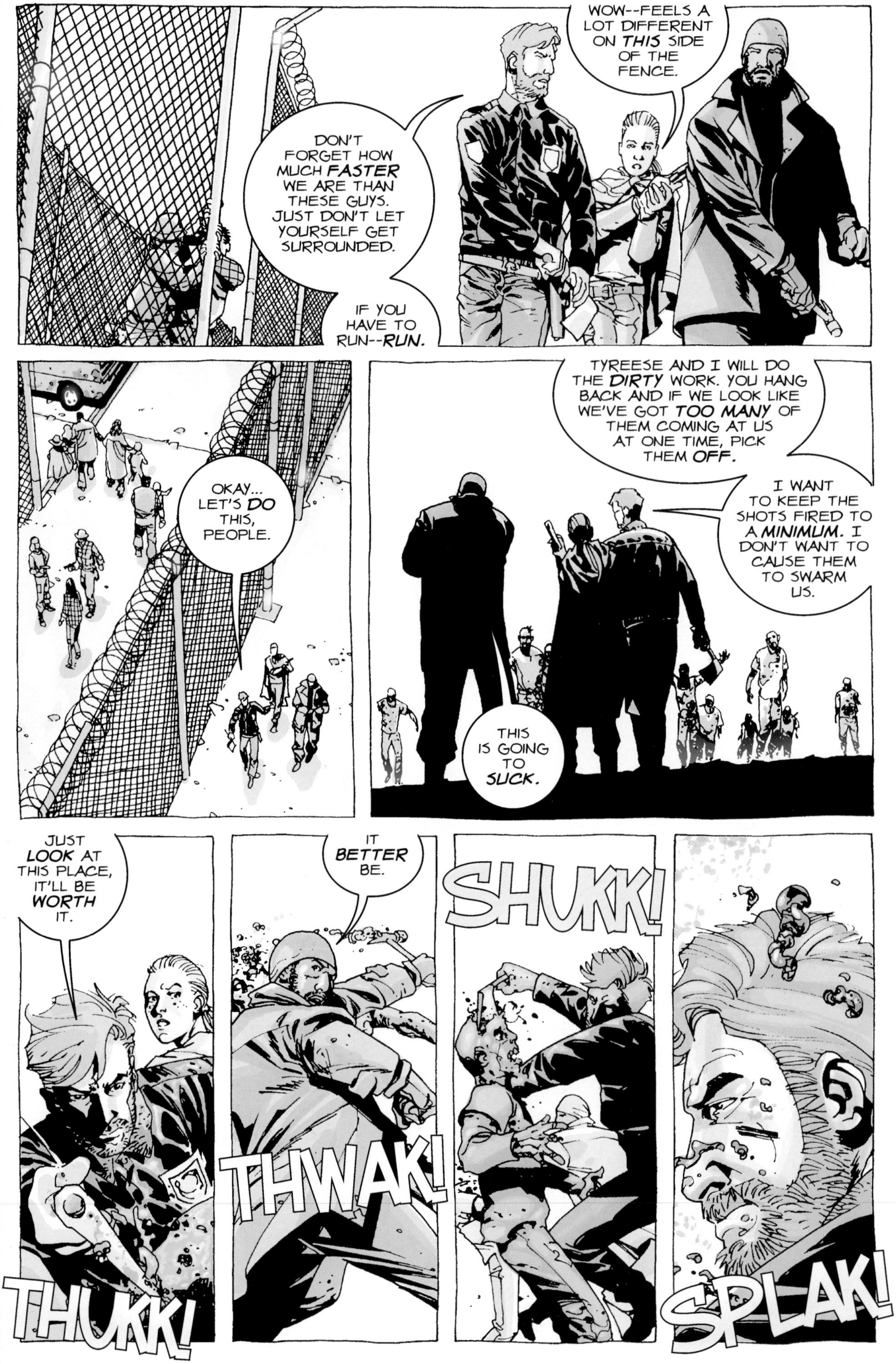
WOW--FEELS A LOT DIFFERENT ON THIS SIDE OF THE FENCE.
DON'T FORGET HOW MUCH FASTER WE ARE THAN THESE GUYS. JUST DON'T LET YOURSELF GET SURROUNDED.
IF YOU HAVE TO RUN--RUN.
OKAY... LET'S DO THIS, PEOPLE.
TYREESE AND I WILL DO THE DIRTY WORK. YOU HANG BACK AND IF WE LOOK LIKE WE'VE GOT TOO MANY OF THEM COMING AT US AT ONE TIME, PICK THEM OFF.
I WANT TO KEEP THE SHOTS FIRED TO A MINIMUM. I DON'T WANT TO CAUSE THEM TO SWARM US.
THIS IS GOING TO SUCK.
JUST LOOK AT THIS PLACE, IT'LL BE WORTH IT.
THUKK!
IT BETTER BE.
THWAK!
SHUKK!
SPLAK!

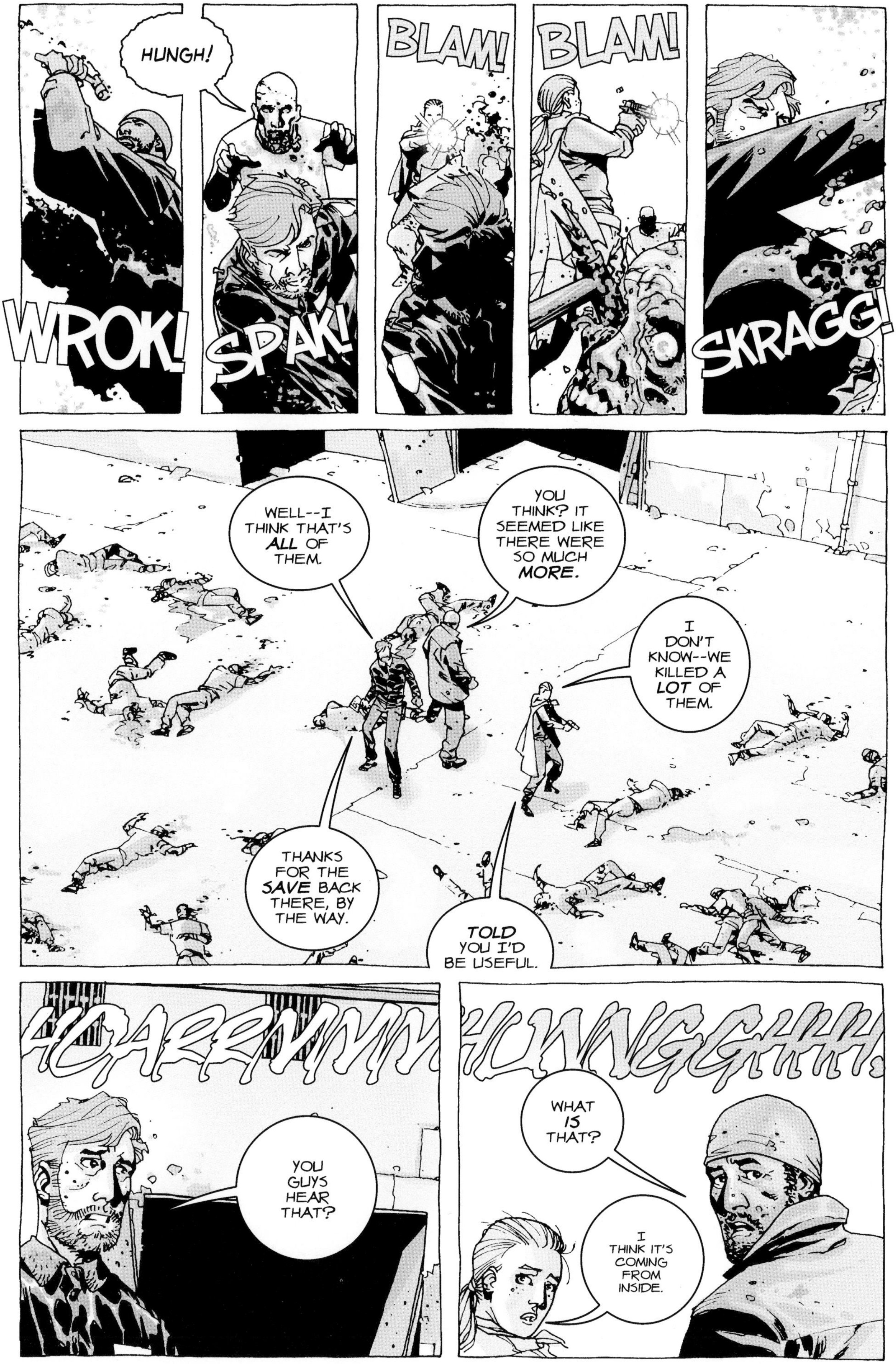
WROK!
HUNGH!
SPAK!
BLAM!
BLAM!
SKRAGG!
WELL--I THINK THAT'S ALL OF THEM.
YOU THINK? IT SEEMED LIKE THERE WERE SO MUCH MORE.
I DON'T KNOW--WE KILLED A LOT OF THEM.
THANKS FOR THE SAVE BACK THERE, BY THE WAY.
TOLD YOU I'D BE USEFUL.
HGARRMMMHUNNGGHHH.
YOU GUYS HEAR THAT?
WHAT IS THAT?
I THINK IT'S COMING FROM INSIDE.

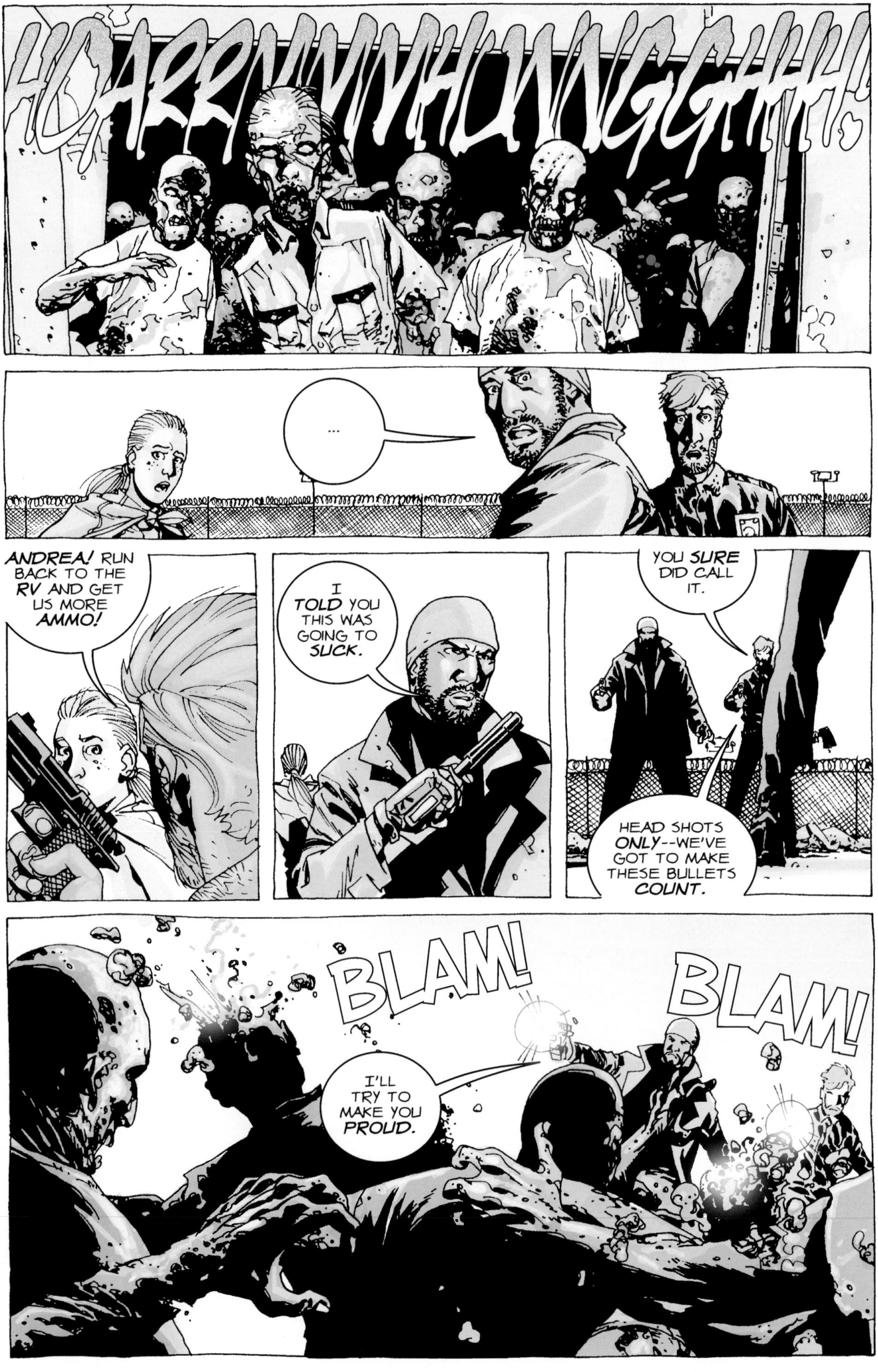
...
ANDREA! RUN BACK TO THE RV AND GET US MORE AMMO!
I TOLD YOU THIS WAS GOING TO SUCK.
YOU SURE DID CALL IT.
HEAD SHOTS ONLY--WE'VE GOT TO MAKE THESE BULLETS COUNT.
BLAM!
I'LL TRY TO MAKE YOU PROUD.
BLAM!

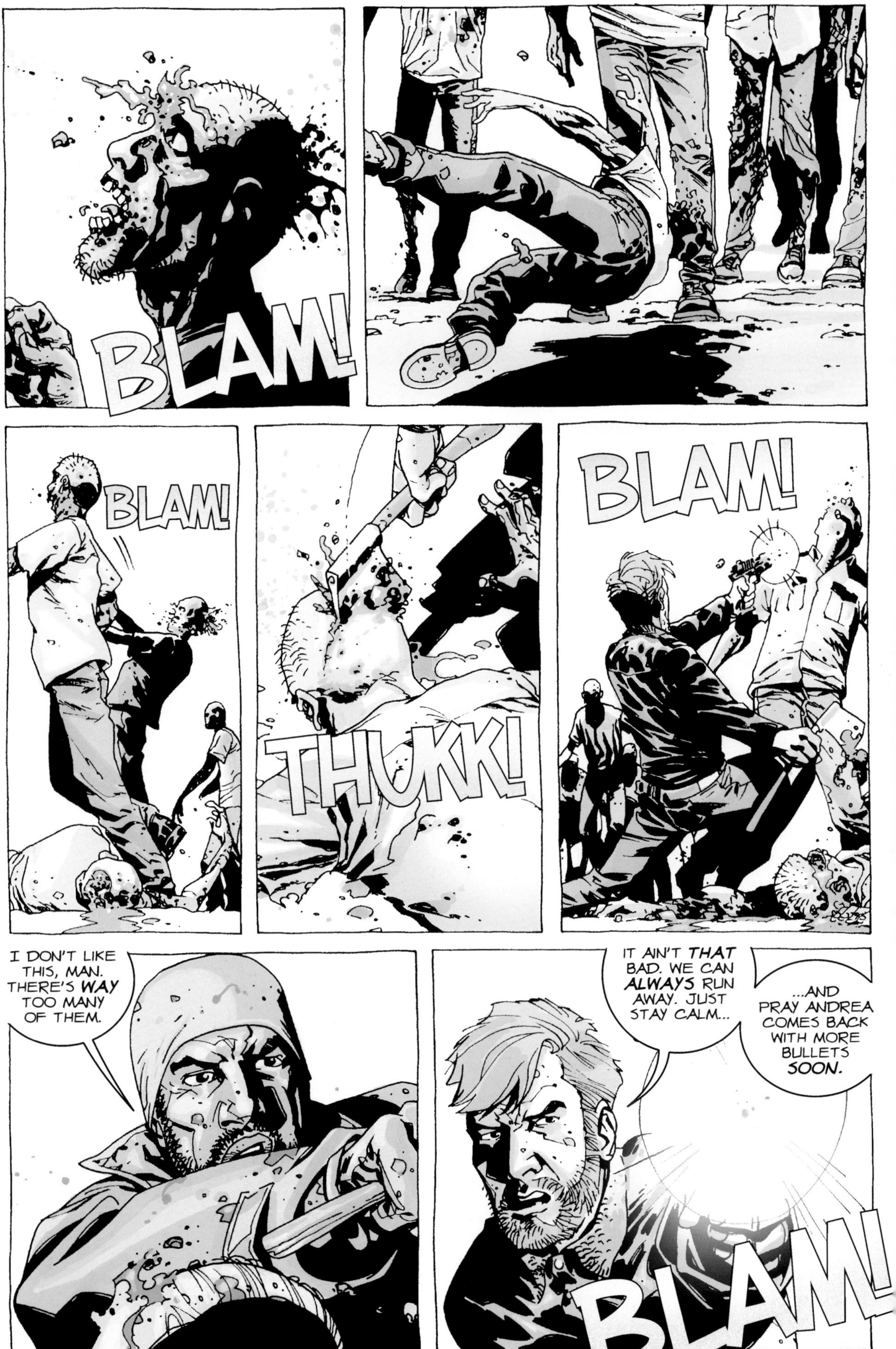
BLAM!
BLAM!
THUKK!
BLAM!
I DON'T LIKE THIS, MAN. THERE'S WAY TOO MANY OF THEM.
IT AIN'T THAT BAD. WE CAN ALWAYS RUN AWAY. JUST STAY CALM...
...AND PRAY ANDREA COMES BACK WITH MORE BULLETS SOON.
BLAM!

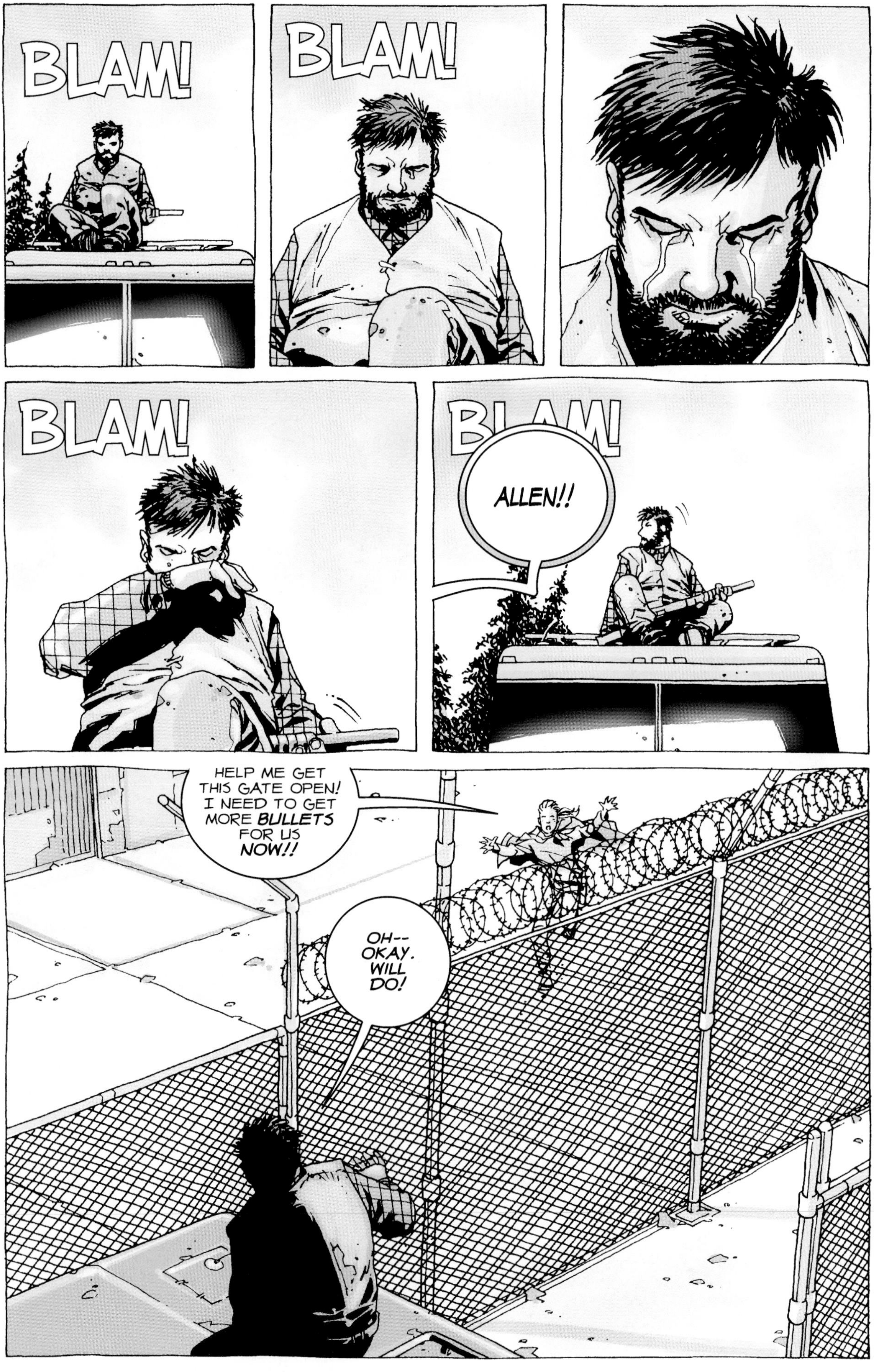
BLAM!
BLAM!
BLAM!
BLAM!
ALLEN!!
HELP ME GET THIS GATE OPEN! I NEED TO GET MORE BULLETS FOR US NOW!!
OH-- OKAY. WILL DO!

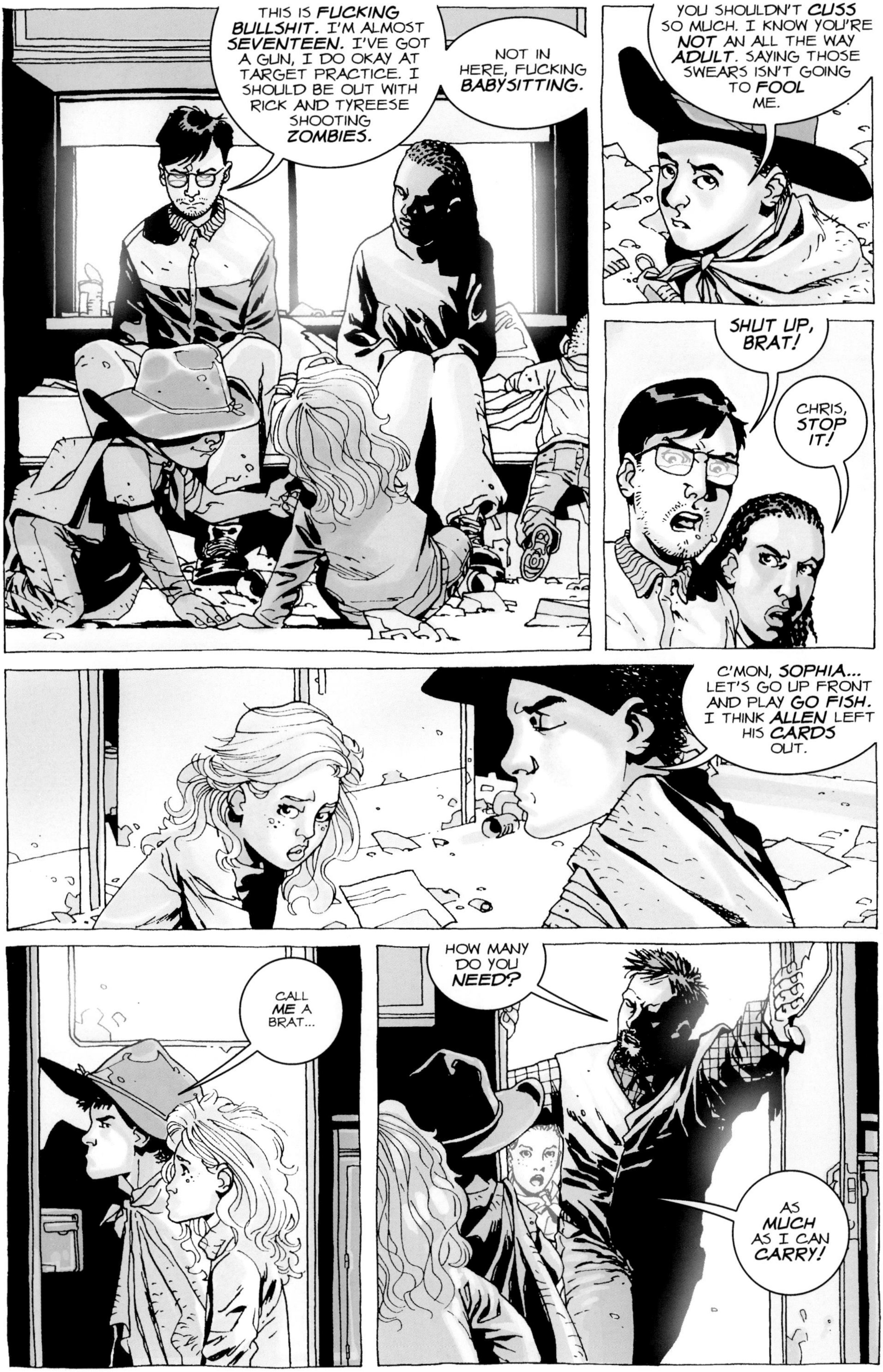
THIS IS FUCKING BULLSHIT. I'M ALMOST SEVENTEEN. I'VE GOT A GUN, I DO OKAY AT TARGET PRACTICE. I SHOULD BE OUT WITH RICK AND TYREESE SHOOTING ZOMBIES.
NOT IN HERE, FUCKING BABYSITTING.
YOU SHOULDN'T CUSS SO MUCH. I KNOW YOU'RE NOT AN ALL THE WAY ADULT. SAYING THOSE SWEARS ISN'T GOING TO FOOL ME.
SHUT UP, BRAT!
CHRIS, STOP IT!
C'MON, SOPHIA... LET'S GO UP FRONT AND PLAY GO FISH. I THINK ALLEN LEFT HIS CARDS OUT.
CALL ME A BRAT...
HOW MANY DO YOU NEED?
AS MUCH AS I CAN CARRY!

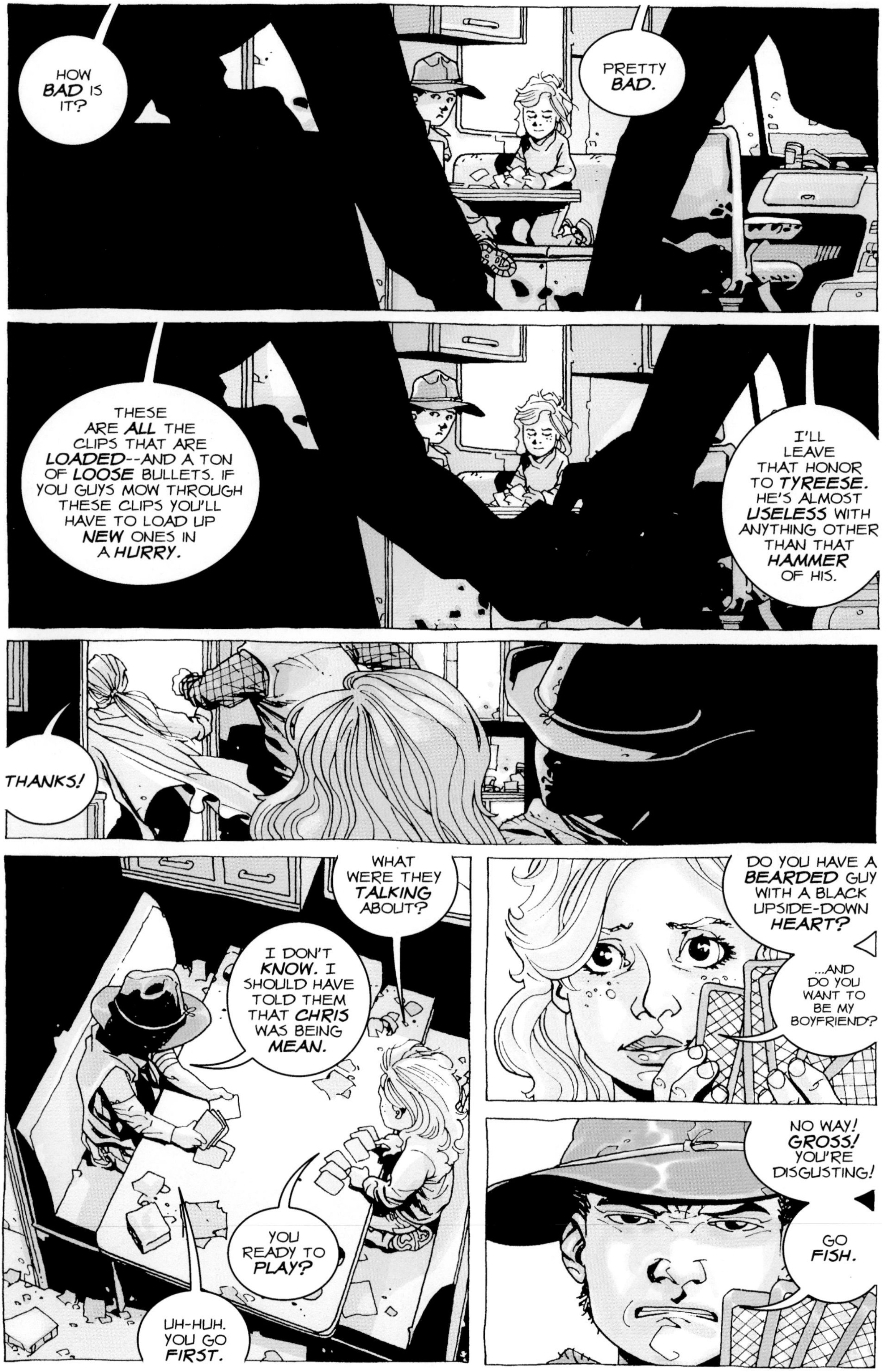
HOW BAD IS IT?
PRETTY BAD.
THESE ARE ALL THE CLIPS THAT ARE LOADED--AND A TON OF LOOSE BULLETS. IF YOU GUYS MOW THROUGH THESE CLIPS YOU'LL HAVE TO LOAD UP NEW ONES IN A HURRY.
I'LL LEAVE THAT HONOR TO TYREESE. HE'S ALMOST USELESS WITH ANYTHING OTHER THAN THAT HAMMER OF HIS.
THANKS!
WHAT WERE THEY TALKING ABOUT?
I DON'T KNOW. I SHOULD HAVE TOLD THEM THAT CHRIS WAS BEING MEAN.
YOU READY TO PLAY?
UH-HUH. YOU GO FIRST.
DO YOU HAVE A BEARDED GUY WITH A BLACK UPSIDE-DOWN HEART?
...AND DO YOU WANT TO BE MY BOYFRIEND?
NO WAY! GROSS! YOU'RE DISGUSTING!
GO FISH.

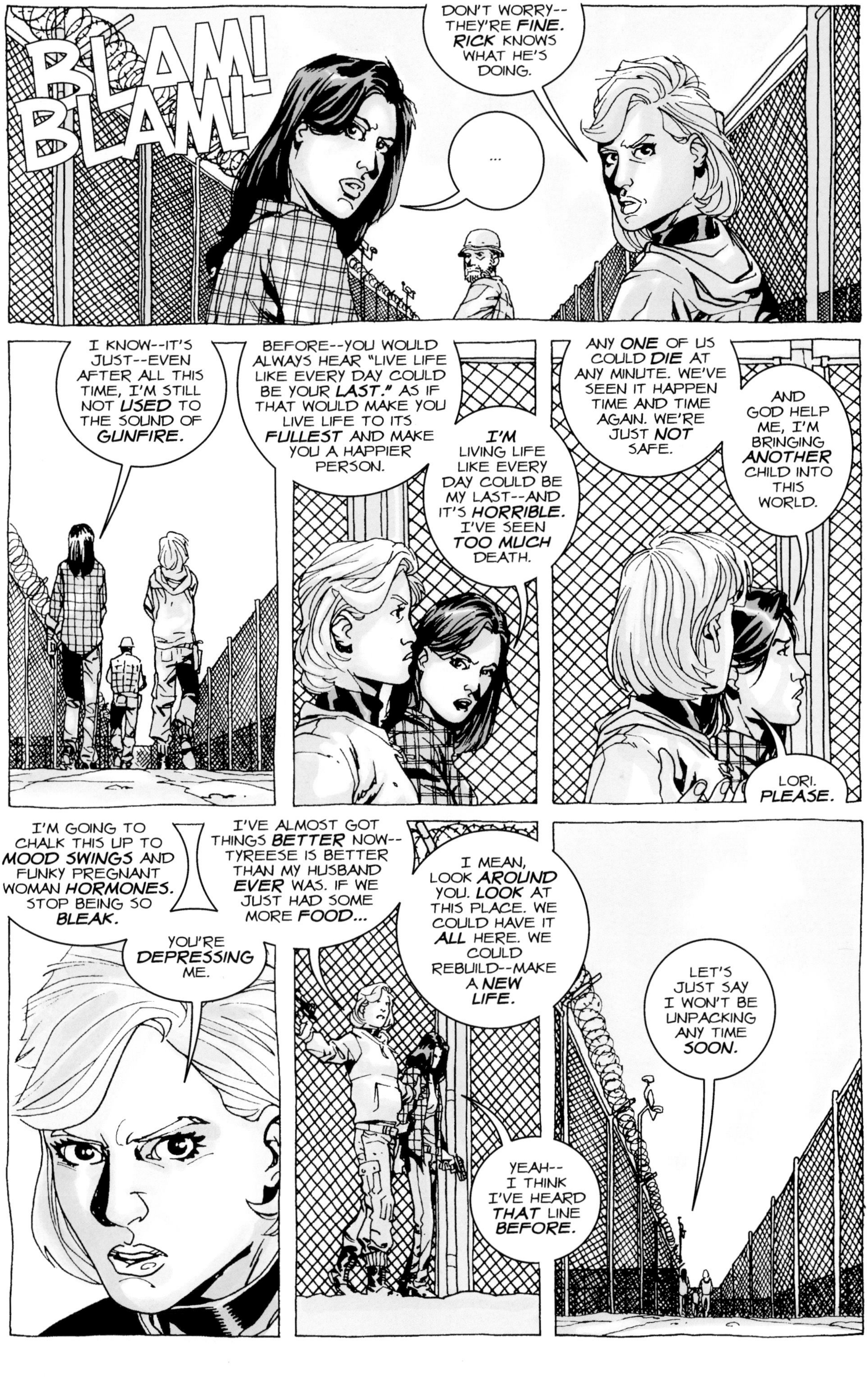

BLAM! BLAM!
DON'T WORRY-- THEY'RE FINE. RICK KNOWS WHAT HE'S DOING.
...
I KNOW--IT'S JUST--EVEN AFTER ALL THIS TIME, I'M STILL NOT USED TO THE SOUND OF GUNFIRE.
BEFORE--YOU WOULD ALWAYS HEAR "LIVE LIFE LIKE EVERY DAY COULD BE YOUR LAST." AS IF THAT WOULD MAKE YOU LIVE LIFE TO ITS FULLEST AND MAKE YOU A HAPPIER PERSON.
I'M LIVING LIFE LIKE EVERY DAY COULD BE MY LAST--AND IT'S HORRIBLE. I'VE SEEN TOO MUCH DEATH.
ANY ONE OF US COULD DIE AT ANY MINUTE. WE'VE SEEN IT HAPPEN TIME AND TIME AGAIN. WE'RE JUST NOT SAFE.
AND GOD HELP ME, I'M BRINGING ANOTHER CHILD INTO THIS WORLD.
LORI. PLEASE.
I'M GOING TO CHALK THIS UP TO MOOD SWINGS AND FUNKY PREGNANT WOMAN HORMONES. STOP BEING SO BLEAK.
YOU'RE DEPRESSING ME.
I'VE ALMOST GOT THINGS BETTER NOW-- TYREESE IS BETTER THAN MY HUSBAND EVER WAS. IF WE JUST HAD SOME MORE FOOD...
I MEAN, LOOK AROUND YOU. LOOK AT THIS PLACE. WE COULD HAVE IT ALL HERE. WE COULD REBUILD--MAKE A NEW LIFE.
YEAH-- I THINK I'VE HEARD THAT LINE BEFORE.
LET'S JUST SAY I WON'T BE UNPACKING ANY TIME SOON.

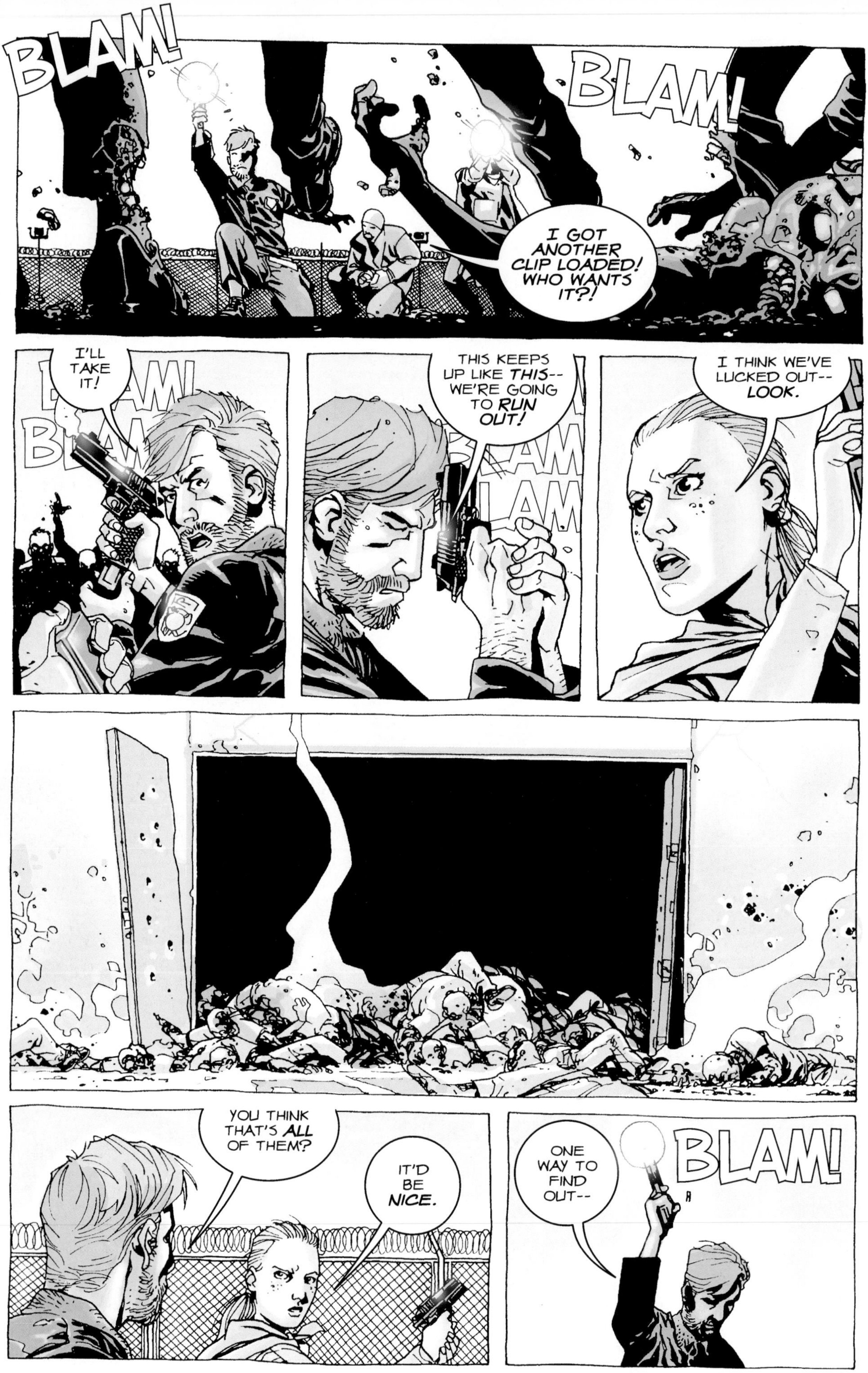
BLAM!
BLAM!
I GOT ANOTHER CLIP LOADED! WHO WANTS IT?!
I'LL TAKE IT!
BLAM!
BLAM
THIS KEEPS UP LIKE THIS-- WE'RE GOING TO RUN OUT!
I THINK WE'VE LUCKED OUT-- LOOK.
YOU THINK THAT'S ALL OF THEM?
IT'D BE NICE.
ONE WAY TO FIND OUT--
BLAM!

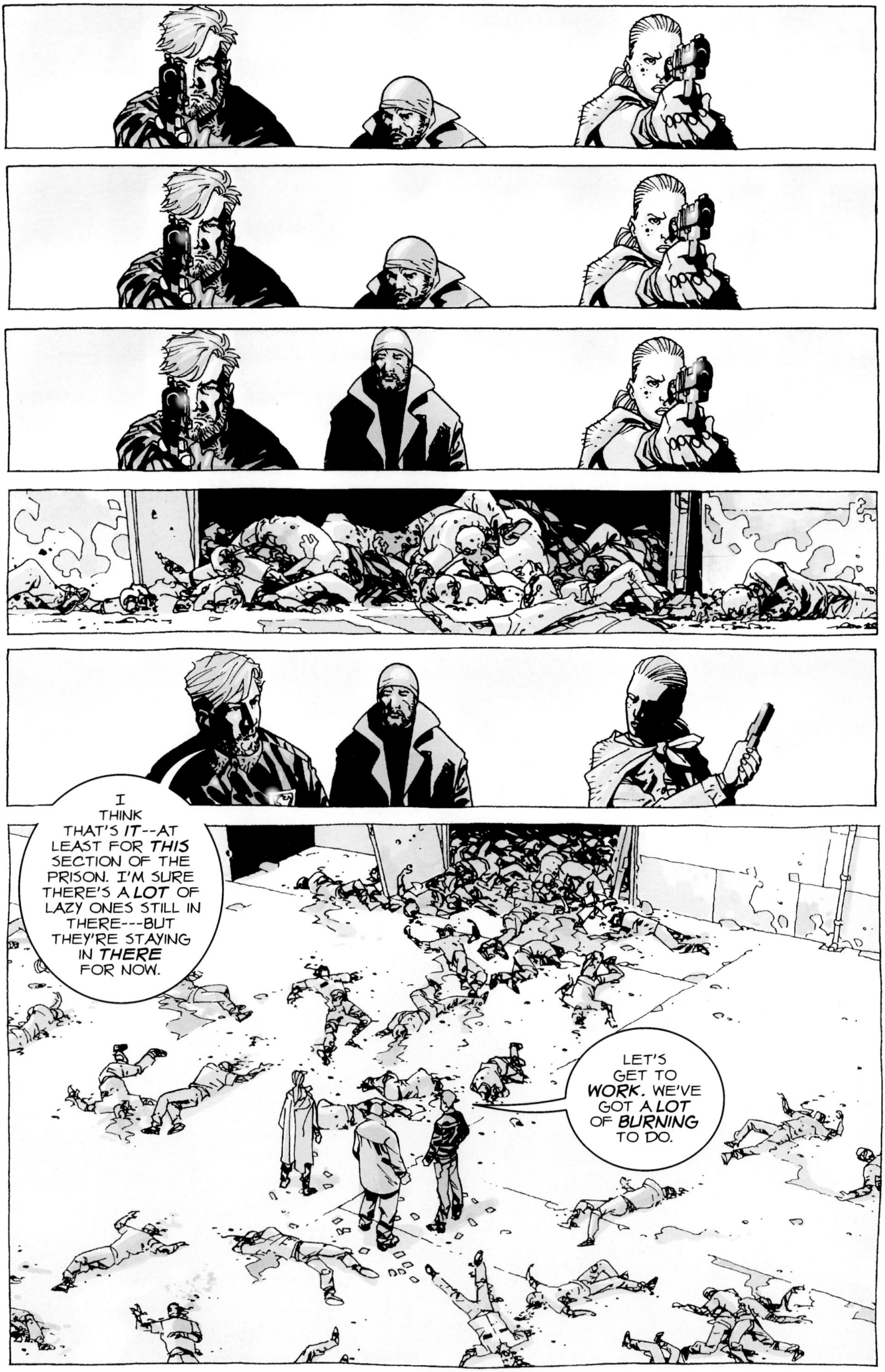
I THINK THAT'S IT--AT LEAST FOR THIS SECTION OF THE PRISON. I'M SURE THERE'S A LOT OF LAZY ONES STILL IN THERE---BUT THEY'RE STAYING IN THERE FOR NOW.
LET'S GET TO WORK. WE'VE GOT A LOT OF BURNING TO DO.

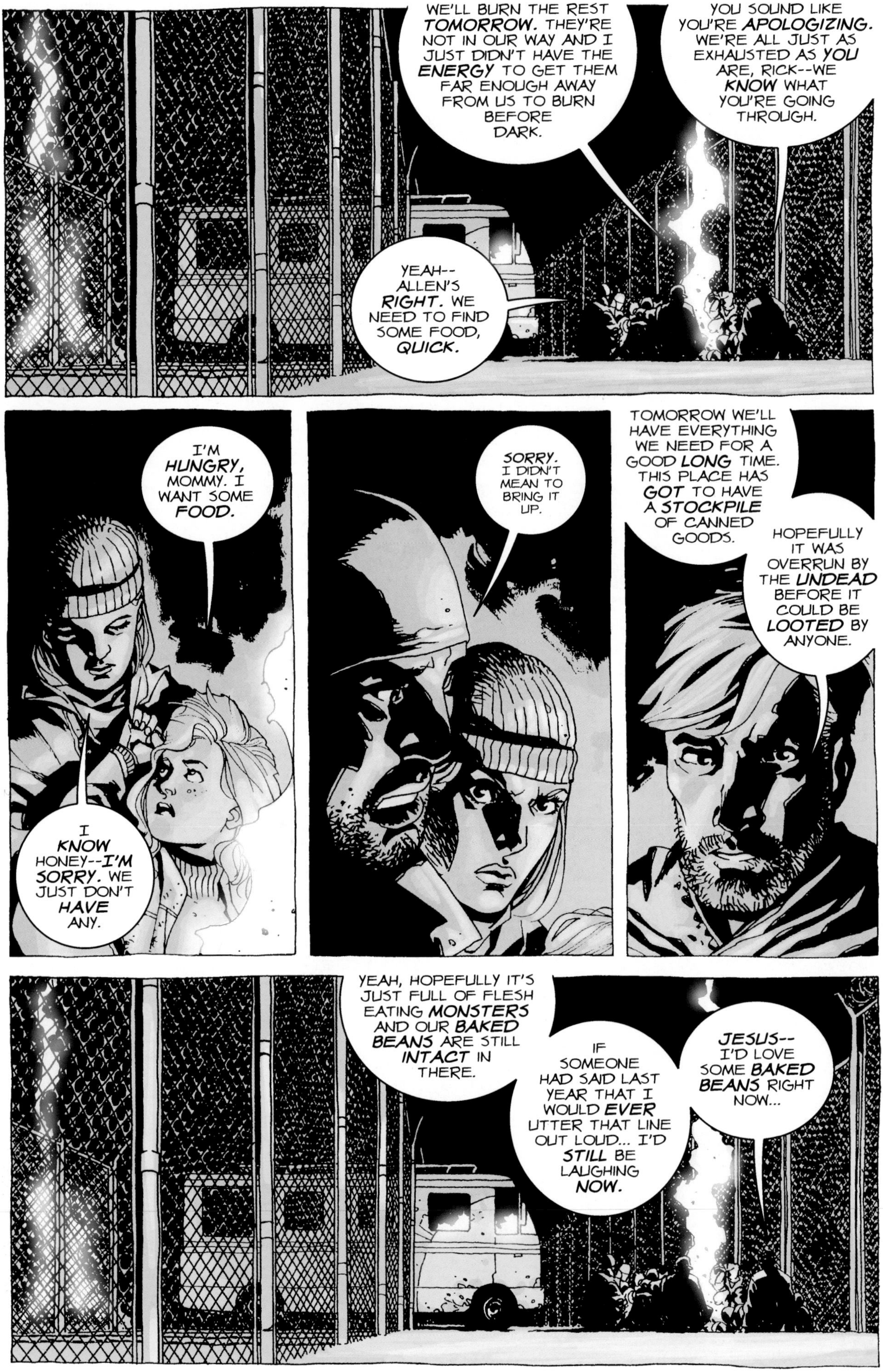

WE'LL BURN THE REST TOMORROW. THEY'RE NOT IN OUR WAY AND I JUST DIDN'T HAVE THE ENERGY TO GET THEM FAR ENOUGH AWAY FROM US TO BURN BEFORE DARK.
YOU SOUND LIKE YOU'RE APOLOGIZING. WE'RE ALL JUST AS EXHAUSTED AS YOU ARE, RICK--WE KNOW WHAT YOU'RE GOING THROUGH.
YEAH--ALLEN'S RIGHT. WE NEED TO FIND SOME FOOD, QUICK.
I'M HUNGRY, MOMMY. I WANT SOME FOOD.
I KNOW HONEY--I'M SORRY. WE JUST DON'T HAVE ANY.
SORRY. I DIDN'T MEAN TO BRING IT UP.
TOMORROW WE'LL HAVE EVERYTHING WE NEED FOR A GOOD LONG TIME. THIS PLACE HAS GOT TO HAVE A STOCKPILE OF CANNED GOODS.
HOPEFULLY IT WAS OVERRUN BY THE UNDEAD BEFORE IT COULD BE LOOTED BY ANYONE.
YEAH, HOPEFULLY IT'S JUST FULL OF FLESH EATING MONSTERS AND OUR BAKED BEANS ARE STILL INTACT IN THERE.
IF SOMEONE HAD SAID LAST YEAR THAT I WOULD EVER UTTER THAT LINE OUT LOUD... I'D STILL BE LAUGHING NOW.
JESUS--I'D LOVE SOME BAKED BEANS RIGHT NOW...

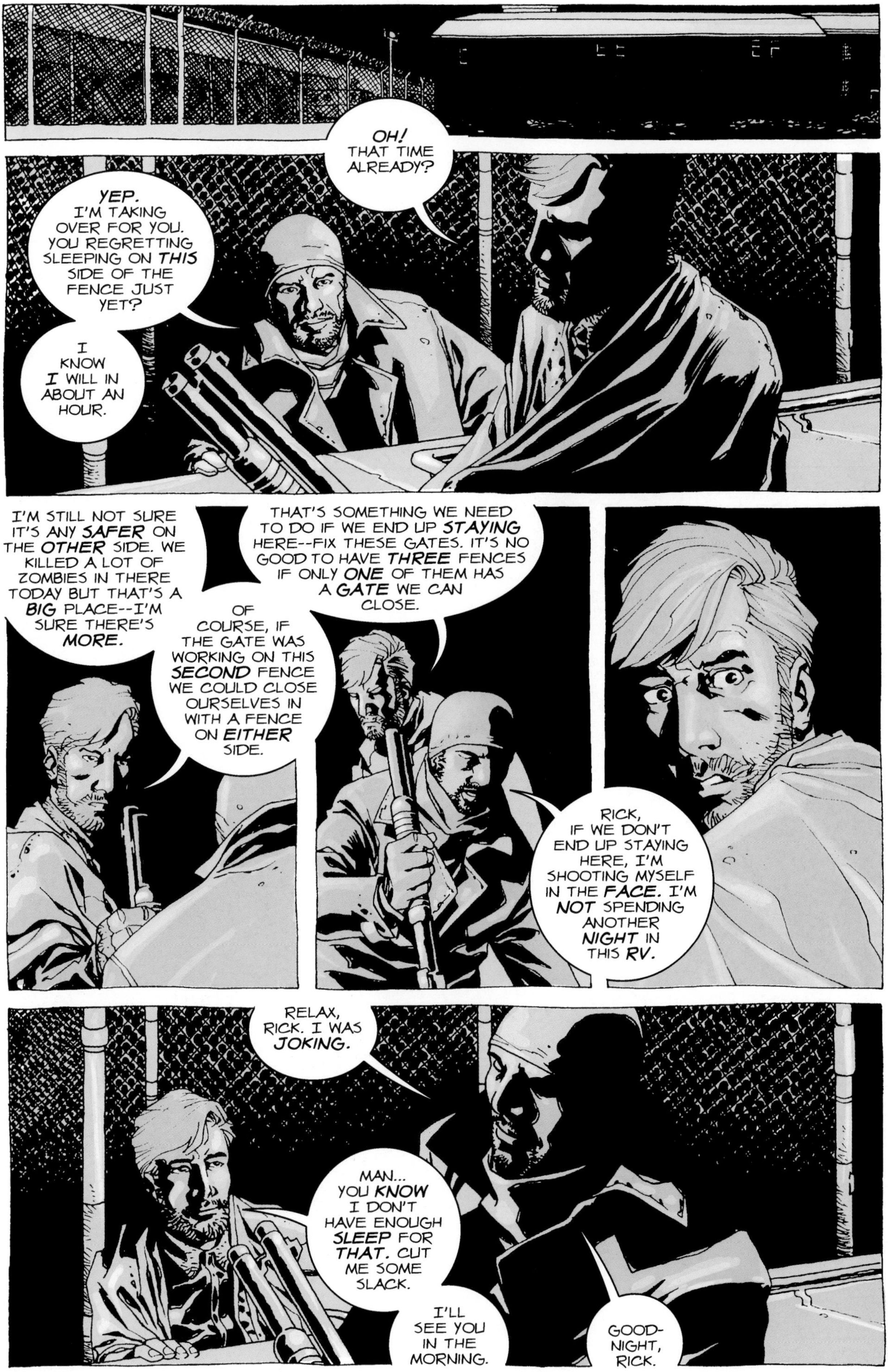
OH! THAT TIME ALREADY?
YEP. I'M TAKING OVER FOR YOU. YOU REGRETTING SLEEPING ON THIS SIDE OF THE FENCE JUST YET?
I KNOW I WILL IN ABOUT AN HOUR.
I'M STILL NOT SURE IT'S ANY SAFER ON THE OTHER SIDE. WE KILLED A LOT OF ZOMBIES IN THERE TODAY BUT THAT'S A BIG PLACE--I'M SURE THERE'S MORE.
OF COURSE, IF THE GATE WAS WORKING ON THIS SECOND FENCE WE COULD CLOSE OURSELVES IN WITH A FENCE ON EITHER SIDE.
THAT'S SOMETHING WE NEED TO DO IF WE END UP STAYING HERE--FIX THESE GATES. IT'S NO GOOD TO HAVE THREE FENCES IF ONLY ONE OF THEM HAS A GATE WE CAN CLOSE.
RICK, IF WE DON'T END UP STAYING HERE, I'M SHOOTING MYSELF IN THE FACE. I'M NOT SPENDING ANOTHER NIGHT IN THIS RV.
RELAX, RICK. I WAS JOKING.
MAN... YOU KNOW I DON'T HAVE ENOUGH SLEEP FOR THAT. CUT ME SOME SLACK.
I'LL SEE YOU IN THE MORNING.
GOOD-NIGHT, RICK.

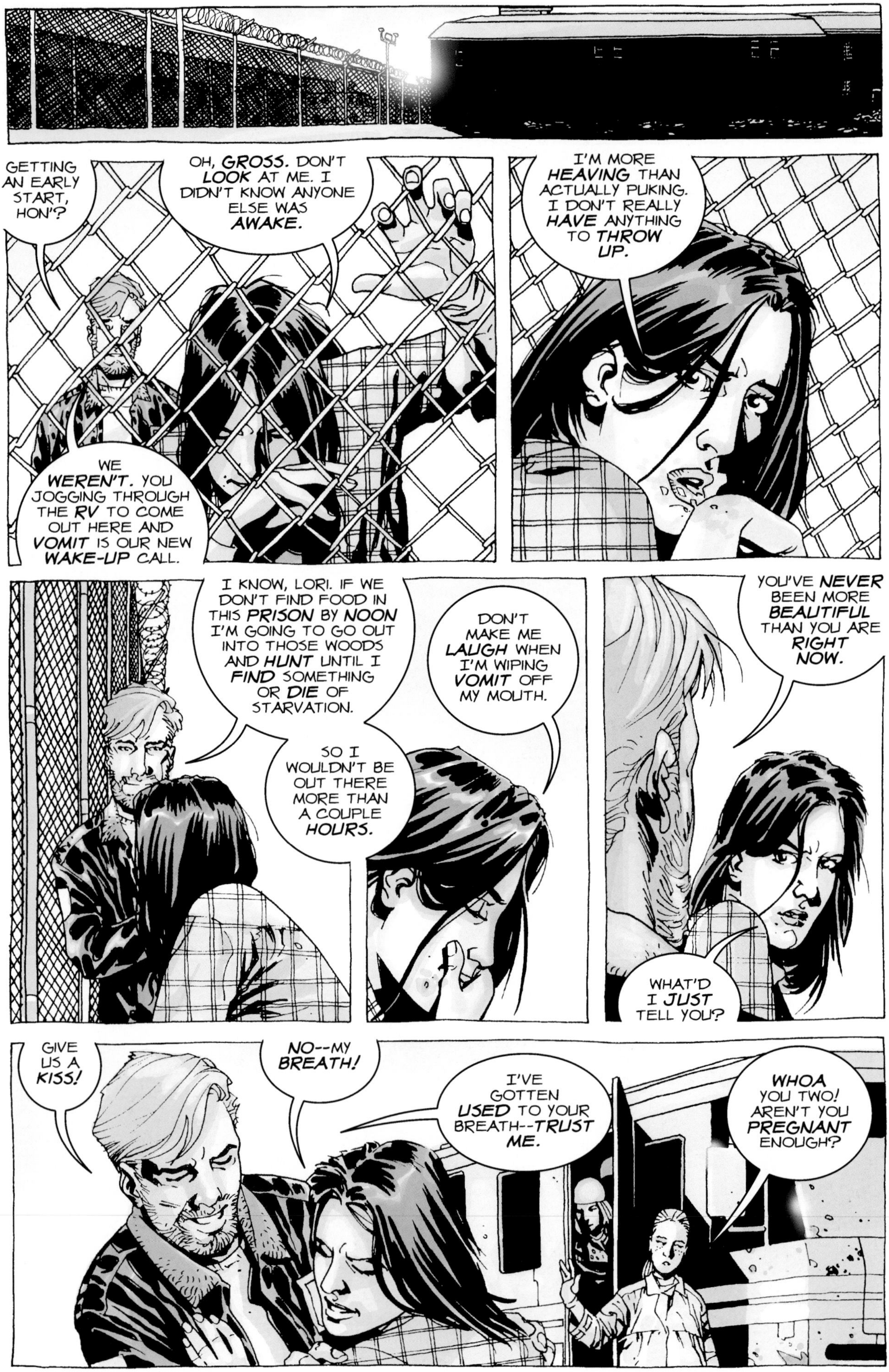
GETTING AN EARLY START, HON'?
OH, GROSS. DON'T LOOK AT ME. I DIDN'T KNOW ANYONE ELSE WAS AWAKE.
WE WEREN'T. YOU JOGGING THROUGH THE RV TO COME OUT HERE AND VOMIT IS OUR NEW WAKE-UP CALL.
I'M MORE HEAVING THAN ACTUALLY PUKING. I DON'T REALLY HAVE ANYTHING TO THROW UP.
I KNOW, LORI. IF WE DON'T FIND FOOD IN THIS PRISON BY NOON I'M GOING TO GO OUT INTO THOSE WOODS AND HUNT UNTIL I FIND SOMETHING OR DIE OF STARVATION.
SO I WOULDN'T BE OUT THERE MORE THAN A COUPLE HOURS.
DON'T MAKE ME LAUGH WHEN I'M WIPING VOMIT OFF MY MOUTH.
YOU'VE NEVER BEEN MORE BEAUTIFUL THAN YOU ARE RIGHT NOW.
WHAT'D I JUST TELL YOU?
GIVE US A KISS!
NO--MY BREATH!
I'VE GOTTEN USED TO YOUR BREATH--TRUST ME.
WHOA YOU TWO! AREN'T YOU PREGNANT ENOUGH?

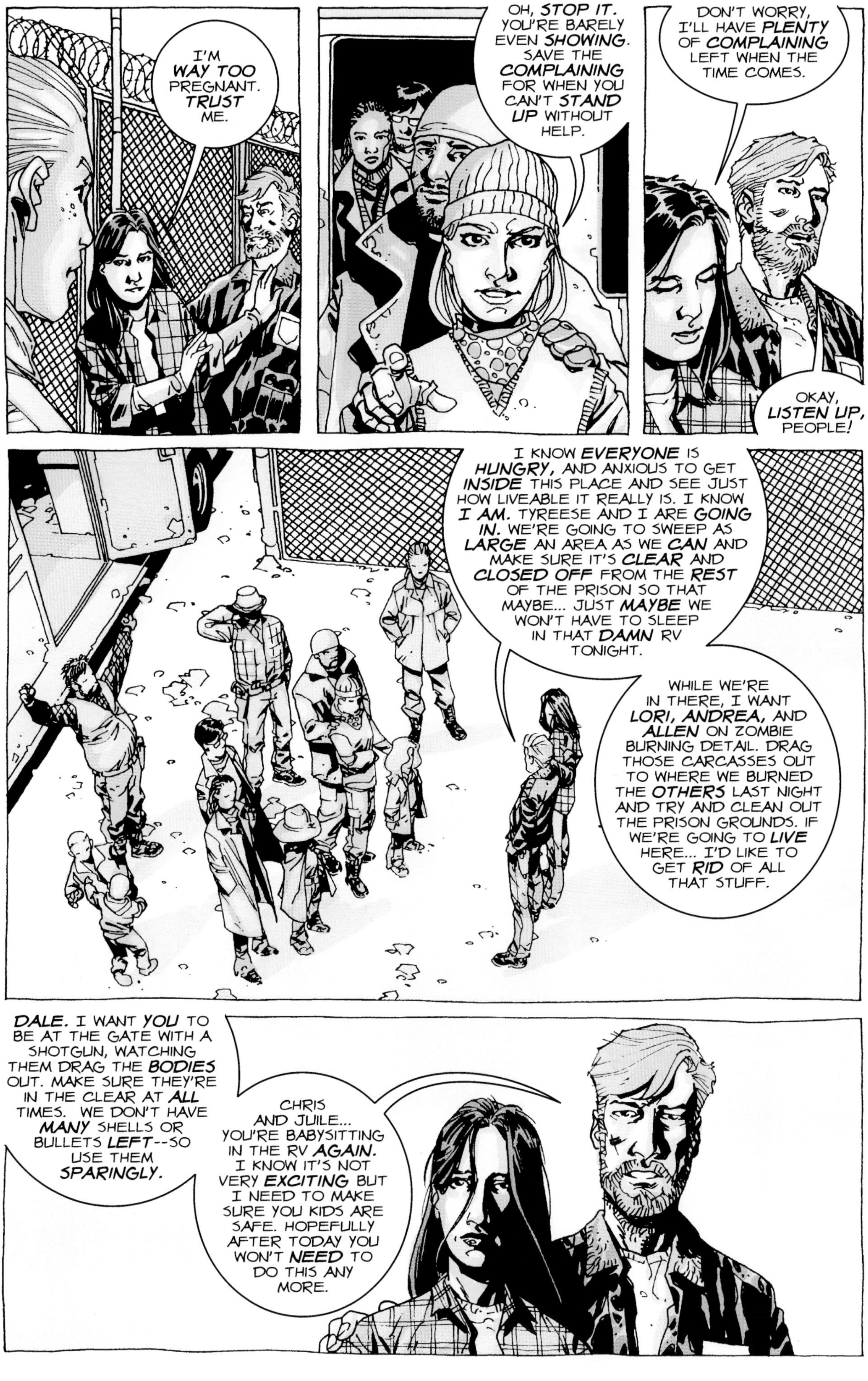

I'M WAY TOO PREGNANT. TRUST ME.
OH, STOP IT. YOU'RE BARELY EVEN SHOWING. SAVE THE COMPLAINING FOR WHEN YOU CAN'T STAND UP WITHOUT HELP.
DON'T WORRY, I'LL HAVE PLENTY OF COMPLAINING LEFT WHEN THE TIME COMES.
OKAY, LISTEN UP, PEOPLE!
I KNOW EVERYONE IS HUNGRY, AND ANXIOUS TO GET INSIDE THIS PLACE AND SEE JUST HOW LIVEABLE IT REALLY IS. I KNOW I AM. TYREESE AND I ARE GOING IN. WE'RE GOING TO SWEEP AS LARGE AN AREA AS WE CAN AND MAKE SURE IT'S CLEAR AND CLOSED OFF FROM THE REST OF THE PRISON SO THAT MAYBE... JUST MAYBE WE WON'T HAVE TO SLEEP IN THAT DAMN RV TONIGHT.
WHILE WE'RE IN THERE, I WANT LORI, ANDREA, AND ALLEN ON ZOMBIE BURNING DETAIL. DRAG THOSE CARCASSES OUT TO WHERE WE BURNED THE OTHERS LAST NIGHT AND TRY AND CLEAN OUT THE PRISON GROUNDS. IF WE'RE GOING TO LIVE HERE... I'D LIKE TO GET RID OF ALL THAT STUFF.
DALE. I WANT YOU TO BE AT THE GATE WITH A SHOTGUN, WATCHING THEM DRAG THE BODIES OUT. MAKE SURE THEY'RE IN THE CLEAR AT ALL TIMES. WE DON'T HAVE MANY SHELLS OR BULLETS LEFT--SO USE THEM SPARINGLY.
CHRIS AND JUILE... YOU'RE BABYSITTING IN THE RV AGAIN. I KNOW IT'S NOT VERY EXCITING BUT I NEED TO MAKE SURE YOU KIDS ARE SAFE. HOPEFULLY AFTER TODAY YOU WON'T NEED TO DO THIS ANY MORE.

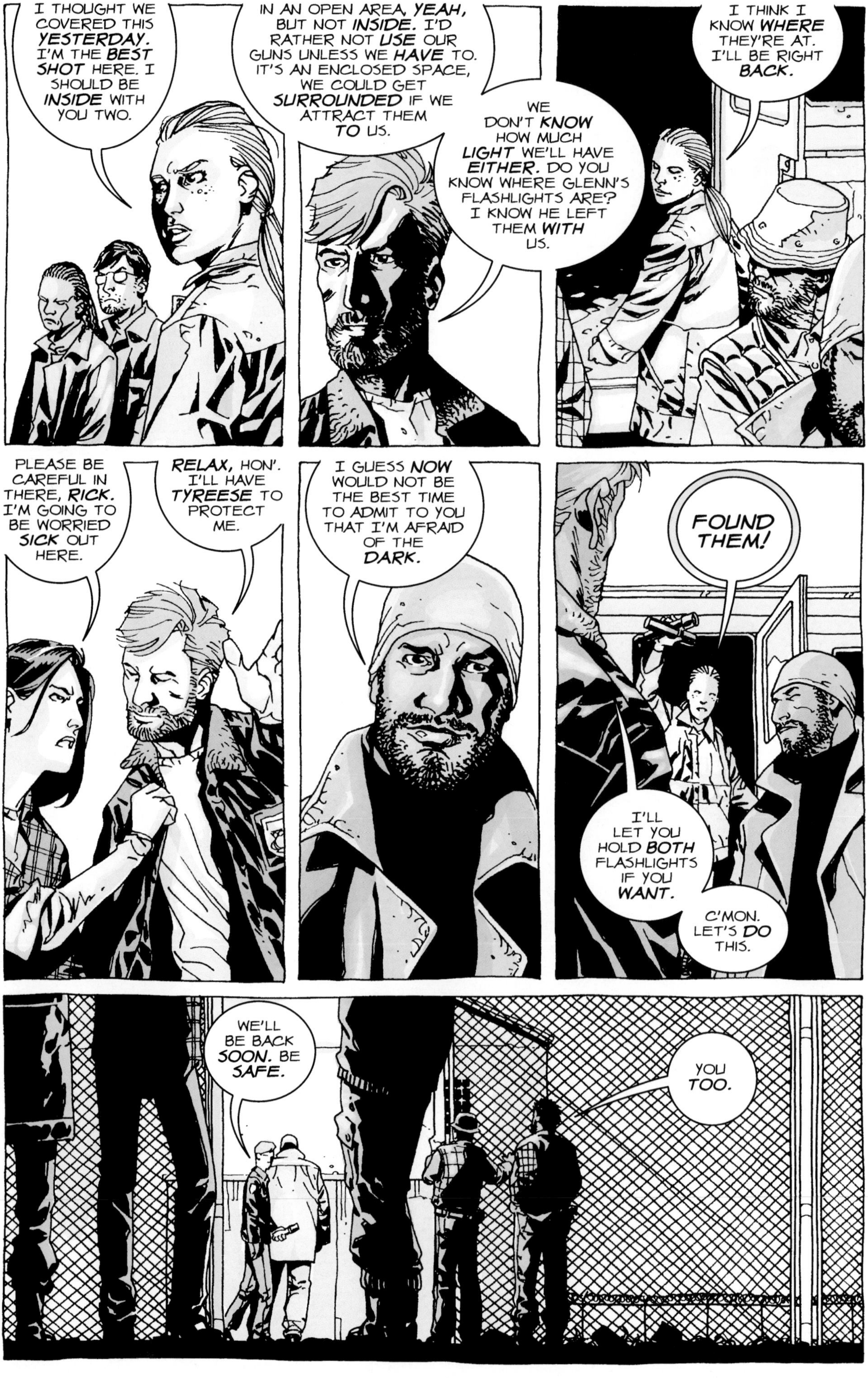
I THOUGHT WE COVERED THIS YESTERDAY. I'M THE BEST SHOT HERE. I SHOULD BE INSIDE WITH YOU TWO.
IN AN OPEN AREA, YEAH, BUT NOT INSIDE. I'D RATHER NOT USE OUR GUNS UNLESS WE HAVE TO. IT'S AN ENCLOSED SPACE, WE COULD GET SURROUNDED IF WE ATTRACT THEM TO US.
WE DON'T KNOW HOW MUCH LIGHT WE'LL HAVE EITHER. DO YOU KNOW WHERE GLENN'S FLASHLIGHTS ARE? I KNOW HE LEFT THEM WITH US.
I THINK I KNOW WHERE THEY'RE AT. I'LL BE RIGHT BACK.
PLEASE BE CAREFUL IN THERE, RICK. I'M GOING TO BE WORRIED SICK OUT HERE.
RELAX, HON'. I'LL HAVE TYREESE TO PROTECT ME.
I GUESS NOW WOULD NOT BE THE BEST TIME TO ADMIT TO YOU THAT I'M AFRAID OF THE DARK.
FOUND THEM!
I'LL LET YOU HOLD BOTH FLASHLIGHTS IF YOU WANT.
C'MON. LET'S DO THIS.
WE'LL BE BACK SOON. BE SAFE.
YOU TOO.

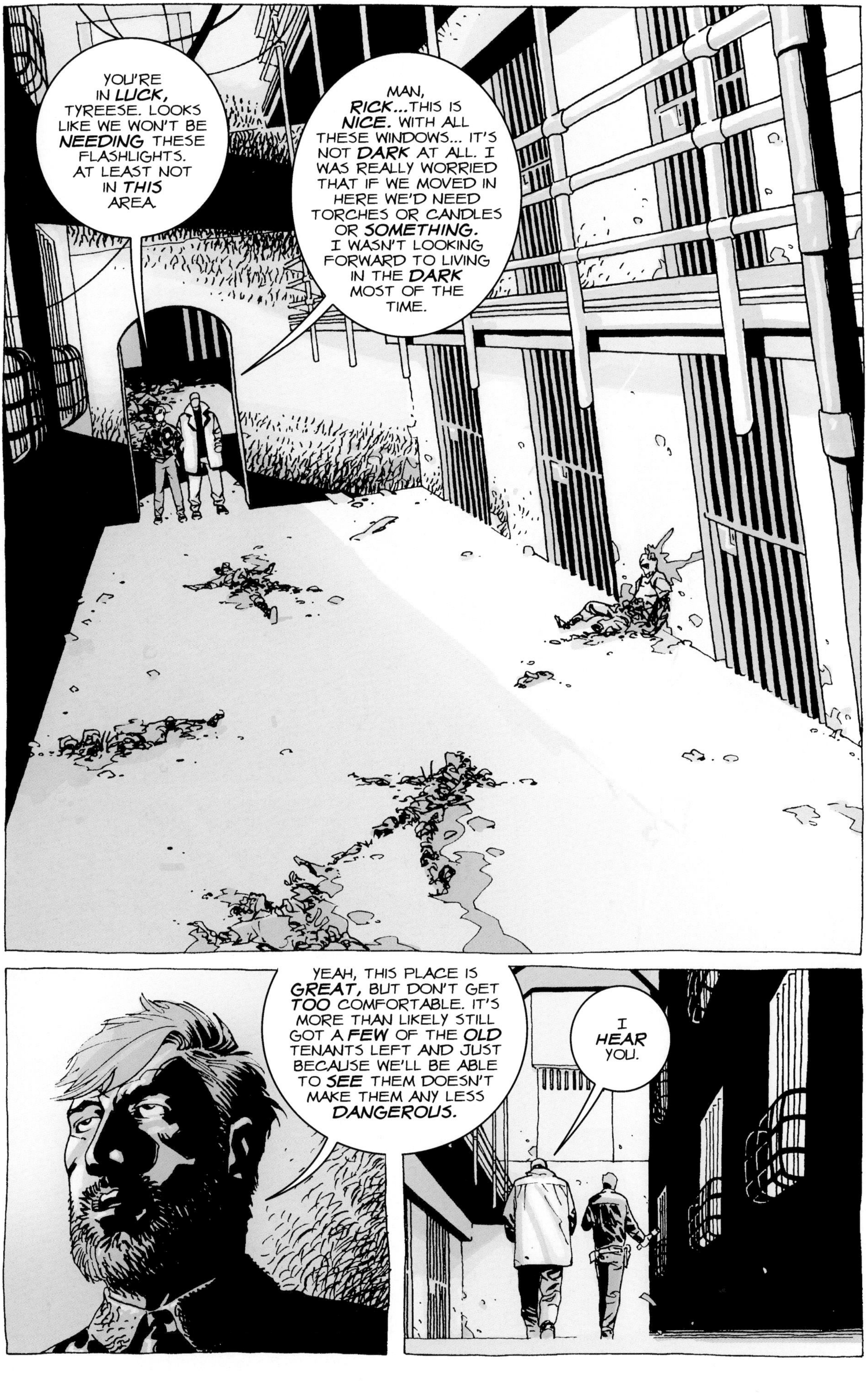
YOU'RE IN LUCK, TYREESE. LOOKS LIKE WE WON'T BE NEEDING THESE FLASHLIGHTS. AT LEAST NOT IN THIS AREA.
MAN, RICK... THIS IS NICE. WITH ALL THESE WINDOWS... IT'S NOT DARK AT ALL. I WAS REALLY WORRIED THAT IF WE MOVED IN HERE WE'D NEED TORCHES OR CANDLES OR SOMETHING. I WASN'T LOOKING FORWARD TO LIVING IN THE DARK MOST OF THE TIME.
YEAH, THIS PLACE IS GREAT, BUT DON'T GET TOO COMFORTABLE. IT'S MORE THAN LIKELY STILL GOT A FEW OF THE OLD TENANTS LEFT AND JUST BECAUSE WE'LL BE ABLE TO SEE THEM DOESN'T MAKE THEM ANY LESS DANGEROUS.
I HEAR YOU.

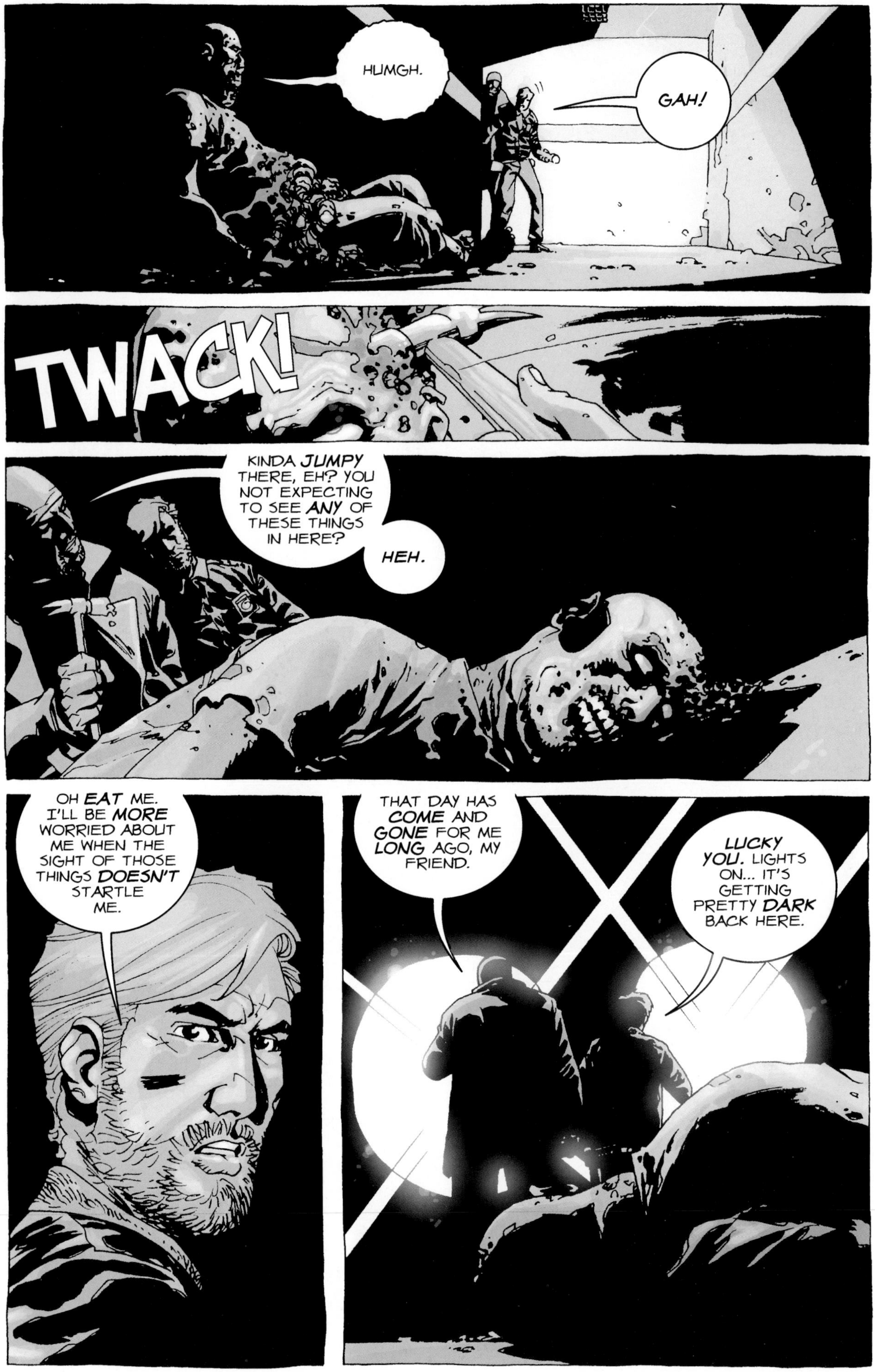
HUMGH.
GAH!
TWACK!
KINDA JUMPY THERE, EH? YOU NOT EXPECTING TO SEE ANY OF THESE THINGS IN HERE?
HEH.
OH EAT ME. I'LL BE MORE WORRIED ABOUT ME WHEN THE SIGHT OF THOSE THINGS DOESN'T STARTLE ME.
THAT DAY HAS COME AND GONE FOR ME LONG AGO, MY FRIEND.
LUCKY YOU. LIGHTS ON... IT'S GETTING PRETTY DARK BACK HERE.

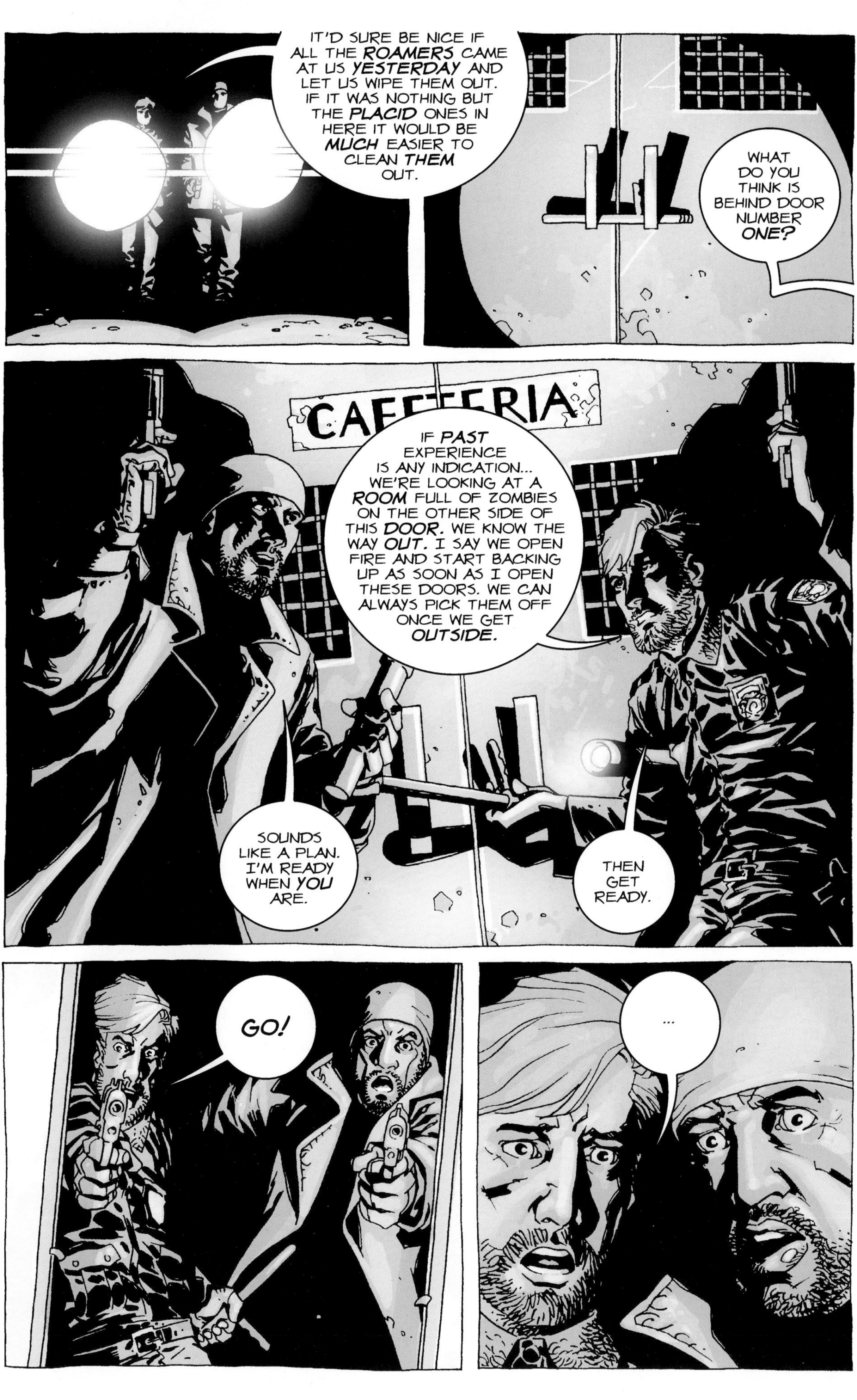

IT'D SURE BE NICE IF ALL THE ROAMERS CAME AT US YESTERDAY AND LET US WIPE THEM OUT. IF IT WAS NOTHING BUT THE PLACID ONES IN HERE IT WOULD BE MUCH EASIER TO CLEAN THEM OUT.
WHAT DO YOU THINK IS BEHIND DOOR NUMBER ONE?
CAFETERIA
IF PAST EXPERIENCE IS ANY INDICATION... WE'RE LOOKING AT A ROOM FULL OF ZOMBIES ON THE OTHER SIDE OF THIS DOOR. WE KNOW THE WAY OUT. I SAY WE OPEN FIRE AND START BACKING UP AS SOON AS I OPEN THESE DOORS. WE CAN ALWAYS PICK THEM OFF ONCE WE GET OUTSIDE.
SOUNDS LIKE A PLAN. I'M READY WHEN YOU ARE.
THEN GET READY.
GO!
...

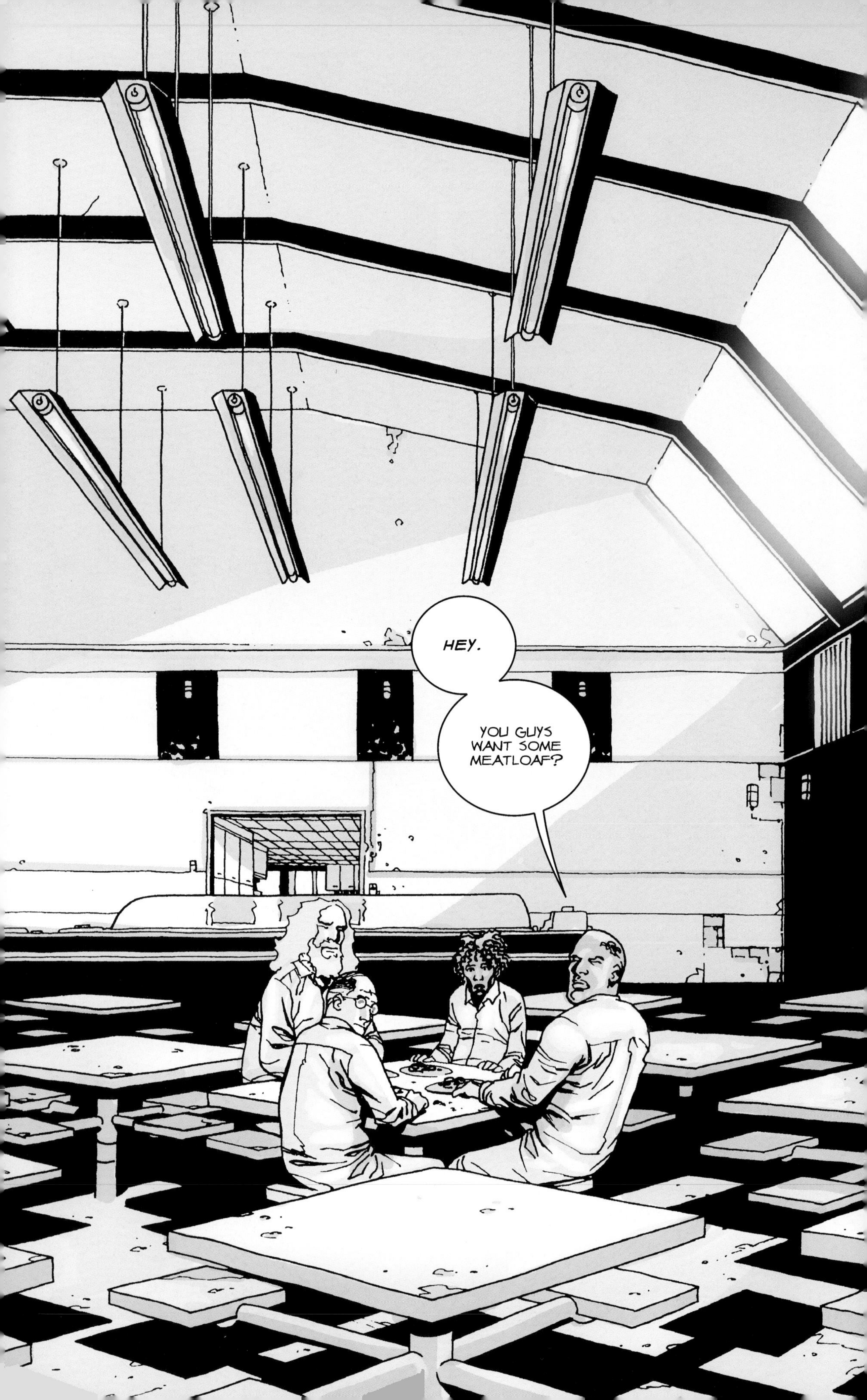
HEY.
YOU GUYS WANT SOME MEATLOAF?

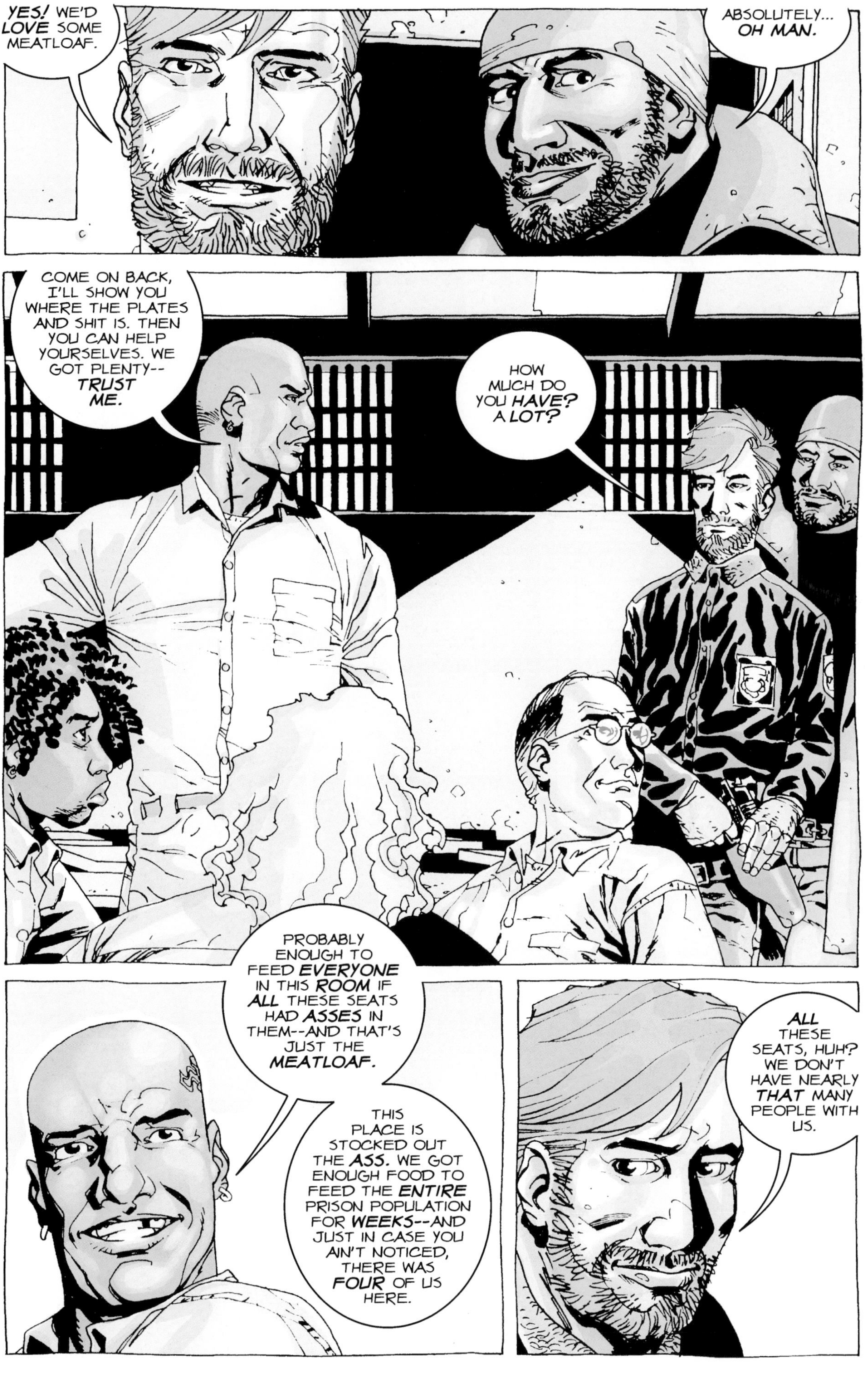
YES! WE'D LOVE SOME MEATLOAF.
ABSOLUTELY... OH MAN.
COME ON BACK, I'LL SHOW YOU WHERE THE PLATES AND SHIT IS. THEN YOU CAN HELP YOURSELVES. WE GOT PLENTY-- TRUST ME.
HOW MUCH DO YOU HAVE? A LOT?
PROBABLY ENOUGH TO FEED EVERYONE IN THIS ROOM IF ALL THESE SEATS HAD ASSES IN THEM--AND THAT'S JUST THE MEATLOAF.
THIS PLACE IS STOCKED OUT THE ASS. WE GOT ENOUGH FOOD TO FEED THE ENTIRE PRISON POPULATION FOR WEEKS--AND JUST IN CASE YOU AIN'T NOTICED, THERE WAS FOUR OF US HERE.
ALL THESE SEATS, HUH? WE DON'T HAVE NEARLY THAT MANY PEOPLE WITH US.

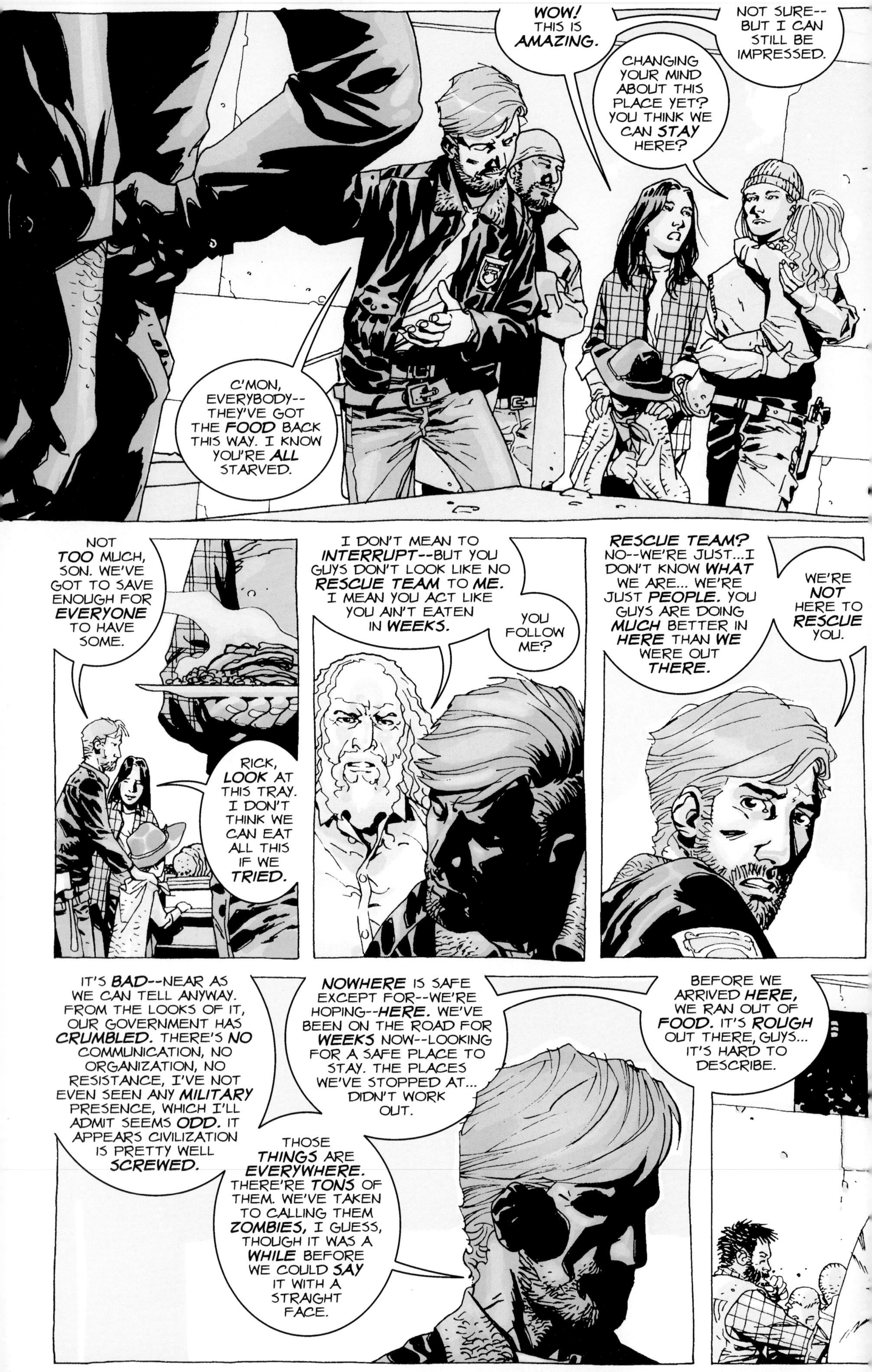
WOW! THIS IS AMAZING.
NOT SURE-- BUT I CAN STILL BE IMPRESSED.
CHANGING YOUR MIND ABOUT THIS PLACE YET? YOU THINK WE CAN STAY HERE?
C'MON, EVERYBODY-- THEY'VE GOT THE FOOD BACK THIS WAY. I KNOW YOU'RE ALL STARVED.
NOT TOO MUCH, SON. WE'VE GOT TO SAVE ENOUGH FOR EVERYONE TO HAVE SOME.
RICK, LOOK AT THIS TRAY. I DON'T THINK WE CAN EAT ALL THIS IF WE TRIED.
I DON'T MEAN TO INTERRUPT--BUT YOU GUYS DON'T LOOK LIKE NO RESCUE TEAM TO ME. I MEAN YOU ACT LIKE YOU AIN'T EATEN IN WEEKS.
YOU FOLLOW ME?
RESCUE TEAM? NO--WE'RE JUST...I DON'T KNOW WHAT WE ARE... WE'RE JUST PEOPLE. YOU GUYS ARE DOING MUCH BETTER IN HERE THAN WE WERE OUT THERE.
WE'RE NOT HERE TO RESCUE YOU.
IT'S BAD--NEAR AS WE CAN TELL ANYWAY. FROM THE LOOKS OF IT, OUR GOVERNMENT HAS CRUMBLED. THERE'S NO COMMUNICATION, NO ORGANIZATION, NO RESISTANCE, I'VE NOT EVEN SEEN ANY MILITARY PRESENCE, WHICH I'LL ADMIT SEEMS ODD. IT APPEARS CIVILIZATION IS PRETTY WELL SCREWED.
NOWHERE IS SAFE EXCEPT FOR--WE'RE HOPING--HERE. WE'VE BEEN ON THE ROAD FOR WEEKS NOW--LOOKING FOR A SAFE PLACE TO STAY. THE PLACES WE'VE STOPPED AT... DIDN'T WORK OUT.
THOSE THINGS ARE EVERYWHERE. THERE'RE TONS OF THEM. WE'VE TAKEN TO CALLING THEM ZOMBIES, I GUESS, THOUGH IT WAS A WHILE BEFORE WE COULD SAY IT WITH A STRAIGHT FACE.
BEFORE WE ARRIVED HERE, WE RAN OUT OF FOOD. IT'S ROUGH OUT THERE, GUYS... IT'S HARD TO DESCRIBE.

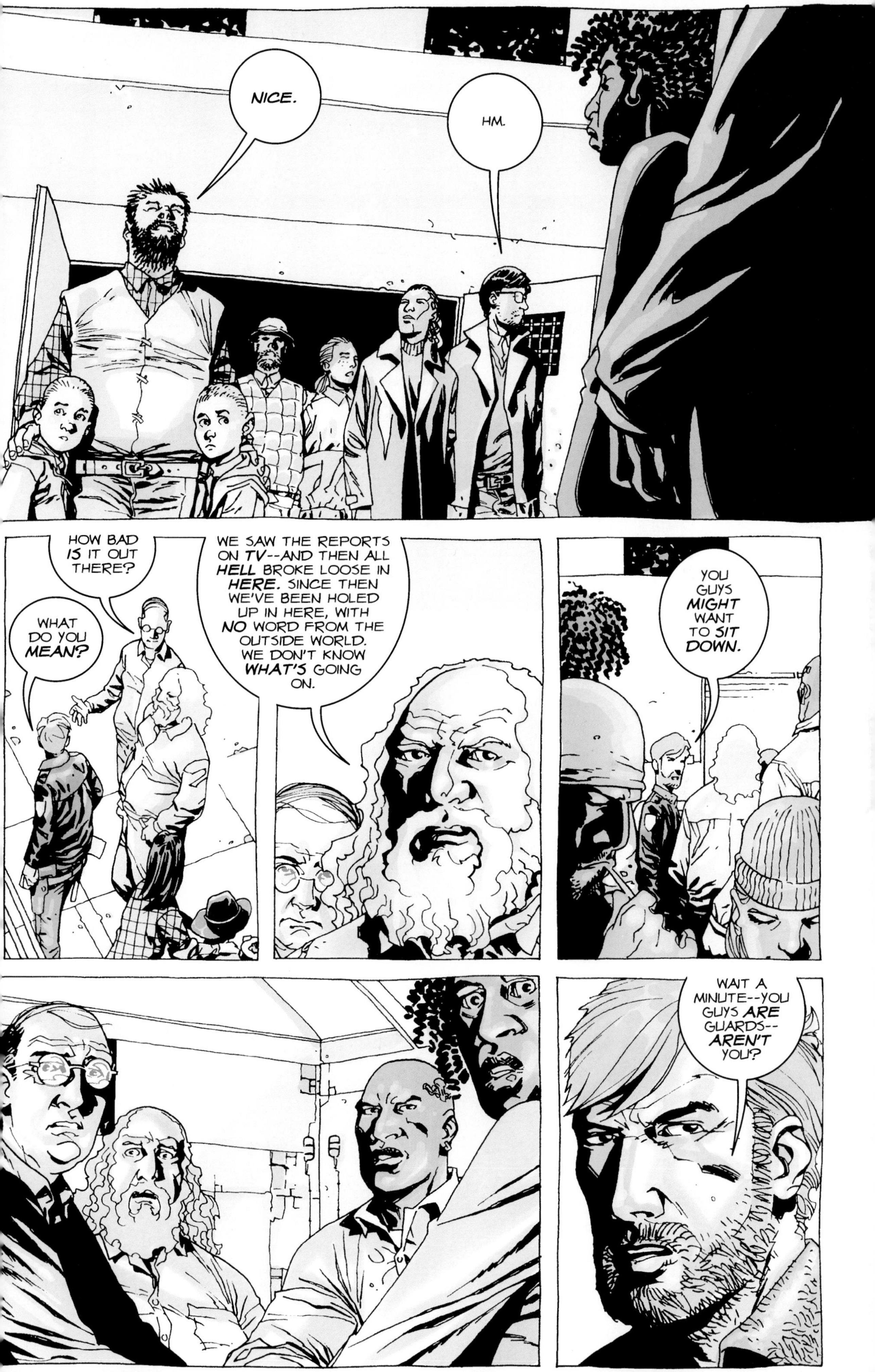
NICE.
HM.
HOW BAD IS IT OUT THERE?
WHAT DO YOU MEAN?
WE SAW THE REPORTS ON TV--AND THEN ALL HELL BROKE LOOSE IN HERE. SINCE THEN WE'VE BEEN HOLED UP IN HERE, WITH NO WORD FROM THE OUTSIDE WORLD. WE DON'T KNOW WHAT'S GOING ON.
YOU GUYS MIGHT WANT TO SIT DOWN.
WAIT A MINUTE--YOU GUYS ARE GUARDS--AREN'T YOU?

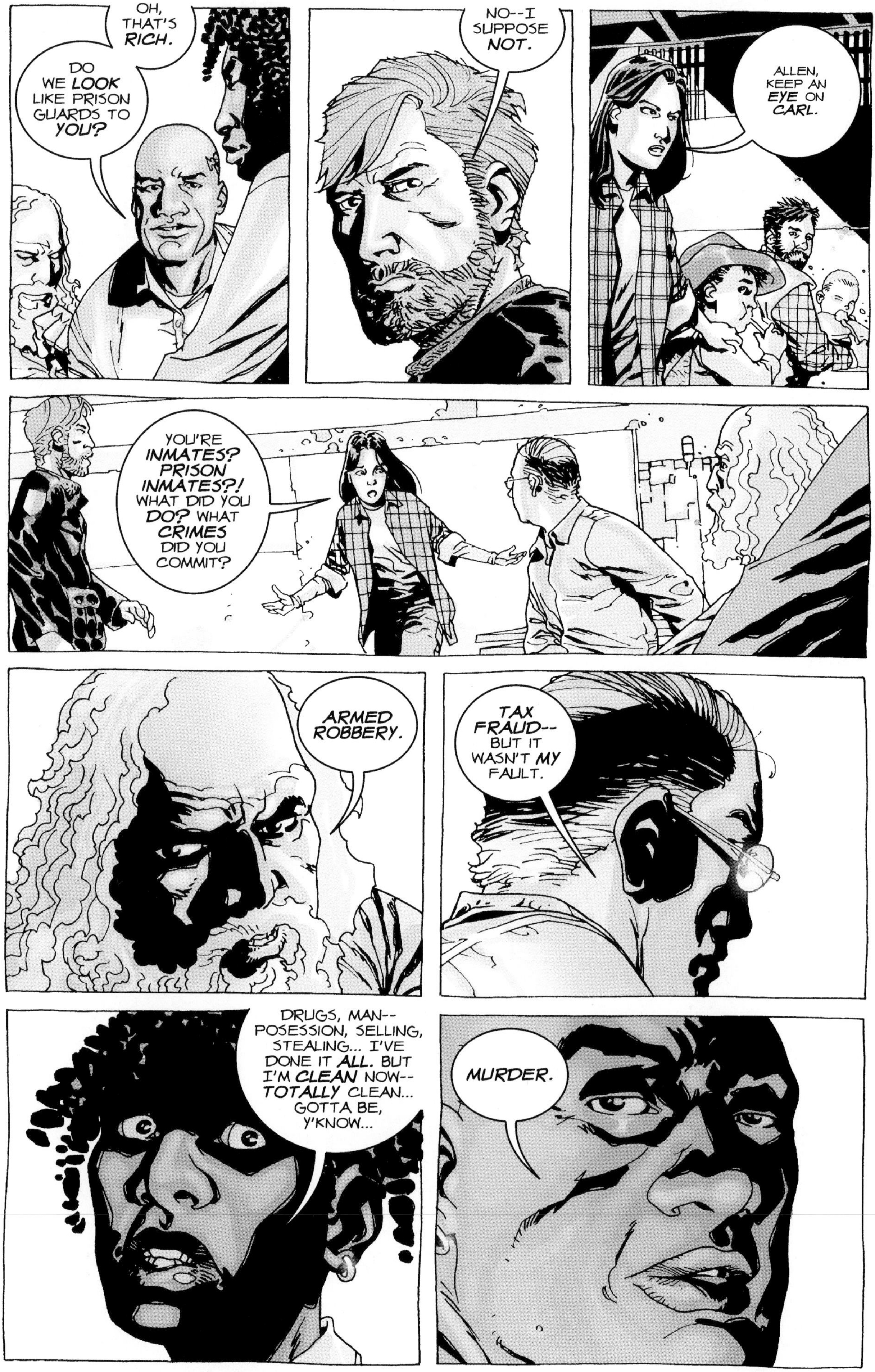
OH, THAT'S RICH.
DO WE LOOK LIKE PRISON GUARDS TO YOU?
NO--I SUPPOSE NOT.
ALLEN, KEEP AN EYE ON CARL.
YOU'RE INMATES? PRISON INMATES?! WHAT DID YOU DO? WHAT CRIMES DID YOU COMMIT?
ARMED ROBBERY.
TAX FRAUD-- BUT IT WASN'T MY FAULT.
DRUGS, MAN-- POSESSION, SELLING, STEALING... I'VE DONE IT ALL. BUT I'M CLEAN NOW-- TOTALLY CLEAN... GOTTA BE, Y'KNOW...
MURDER.

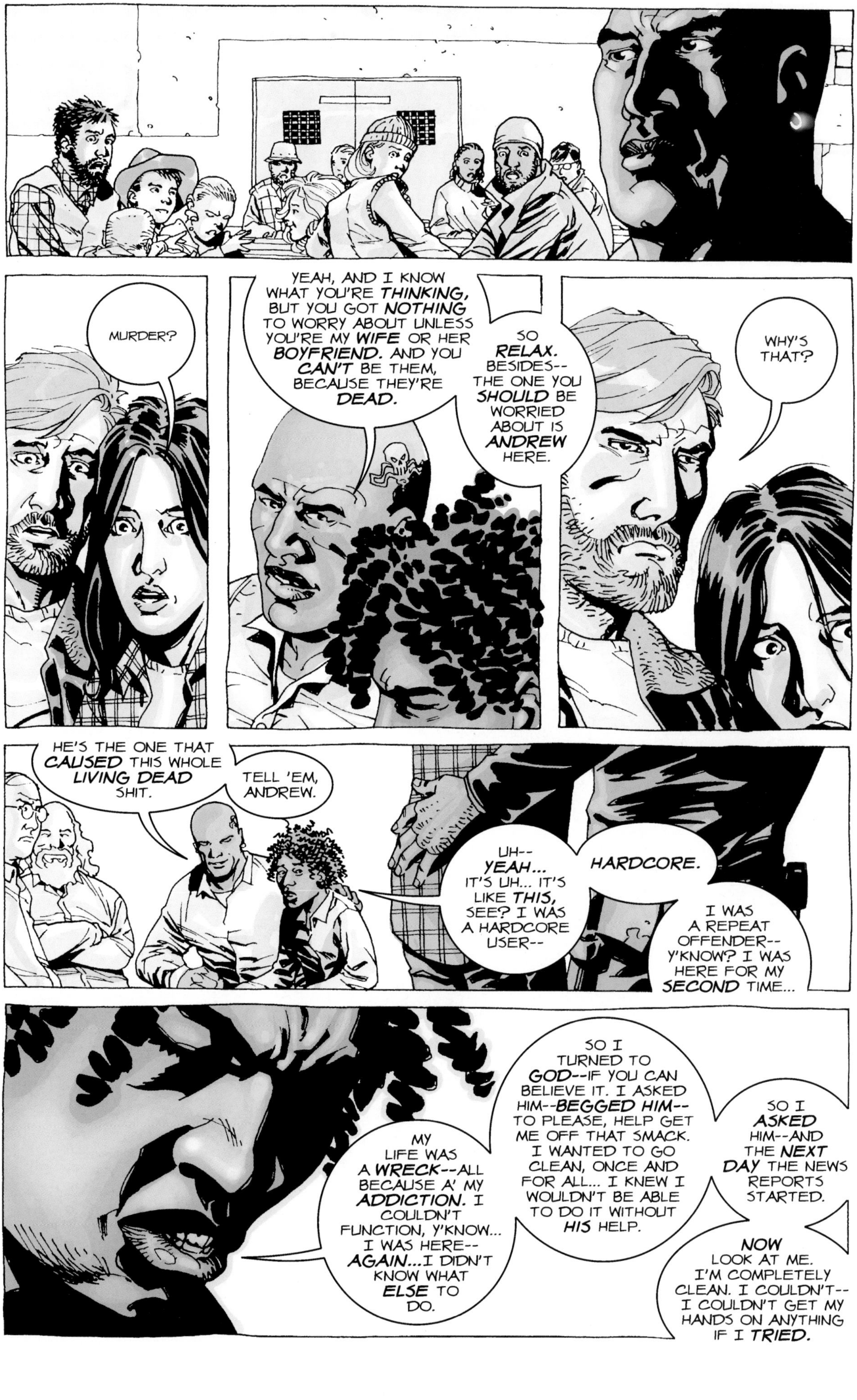
MURDER?
YEAH, AND I KNOW WHAT YOU'RE THINKING, BUT YOU GOT NOTHING TO WORRY ABOUT UNLESS YOU'RE MY WIFE OR HER BOYFRIEND. AND YOU CAN'T BE THEM, BECAUSE THEY'RE DEAD.
SO RELAX. BESIDES-- THE ONE YOU SHOULD BE WORRIED ABOUT IS ANDREW HERE.
WHY'S THAT?
HE'S THE ONE THAT CAUSED THIS WHOLE LIVING DEAD SHIT.
TELL 'EM, ANDREW.
UH-- YEAH... IT'S UH... IT'S LIKE THIS, SEE? I WAS A HARDCORE USER--
HARDCORE.
I WAS A REPEAT OFFENDER-- Y'KNOW? I WAS HERE FOR MY SECOND TIME...
MY LIFE WAS A WRECK--ALL BECAUSE A' MY ADDICTION. I COULDN'T FUNCTION, Y'KNOW... I WAS HERE-- AGAIN...I DIDN'T KNOW WHAT ELSE TO DO.
SO I TURNED TO GOD--IF YOU CAN BELIEVE IT. I ASKED HIM--BEGGED HIM-- TO PLEASE, HELP GET ME OFF THAT SMACK. I WANTED TO GO CLEAN, ONCE AND FOR ALL... I KNEW I WOULDN'T BE ABLE TO DO IT WITHOUT HIS HELP.
SO I ASKED HIM--AND THE NEXT DAY THE NEWS REPORTS STARTED.
NOW LOOK AT ME. I'M COMPLETELY CLEAN. I COULDN'T-- I COULDN'T GET MY HANDS ON ANYTHING IF I TRIED.

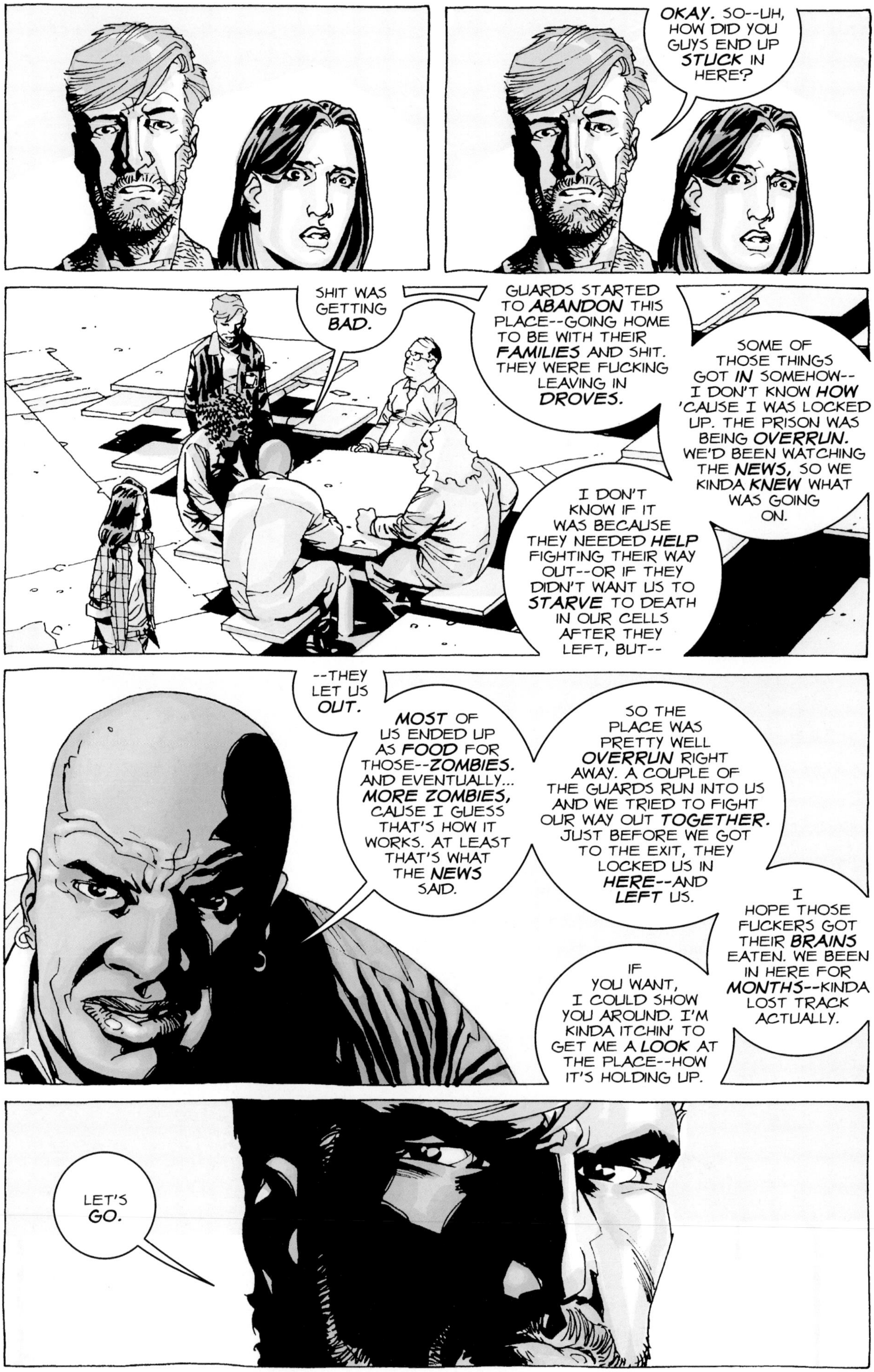
OKAY. SO--UH, HOW DID YOU GUYS END UP STUCK IN HERE?
SHIT WAS GETTING BAD.
GUARDS STARTED TO ABANDON THIS PLACE--GOING HOME TO BE WITH THEIR FAMILIES AND SHIT. THEY WERE FUCKING LEAVING IN DROVES.
SOME OF THOSE THINGS GOT IN SOMEHOW-- I DON'T KNOW HOW 'CAUSE I WAS LOCKED UP. THE PRISON WAS BEING OVERRUN. WE'D BEEN WATCHING THE NEWS, SO WE KINDA KNEW WHAT WAS GOING ON.
I DON'T KNOW IF IT WAS BECAUSE THEY NEEDED HELP FIGHTING THEIR WAY OUT--OR IF THEY DIDN'T WANT US TO STARVE TO DEATH IN OUR CELLS AFTER THEY LEFT, BUT--
--THEY LET US OUT.
MOST OF US ENDED UP AS FOOD FOR THOSE--ZOMBIES. AND EVENTUALLY... MORE ZOMBIES, CAUSE I GUESS THAT'S HOW IT WORKS. AT LEAST THAT'S WHAT THE NEWS SAID.
SO THE PLACE WAS PRETTY WELL OVERRUN RIGHT AWAY. A COUPLE OF THE GUARDS RUN INTO US AND WE TRIED TO FIGHT OUR WAY OUT TOGETHER. JUST BEFORE WE GOT TO THE EXIT, THEY LOCKED US IN HERE--AND LEFT US.
I HOPE THOSE FUCKERS GOT THEIR BRAINS EATEN. WE BEEN IN HERE FOR MONTHS--KINDA LOST TRACK ACTUALLY.
IF YOU WANT, I COULD SHOW YOU AROUND. I'M KINDA ITCHIN' TO GET ME A LOOK AT THE PLACE--HOW IT'S HOLDING UP.
LET'S GO.

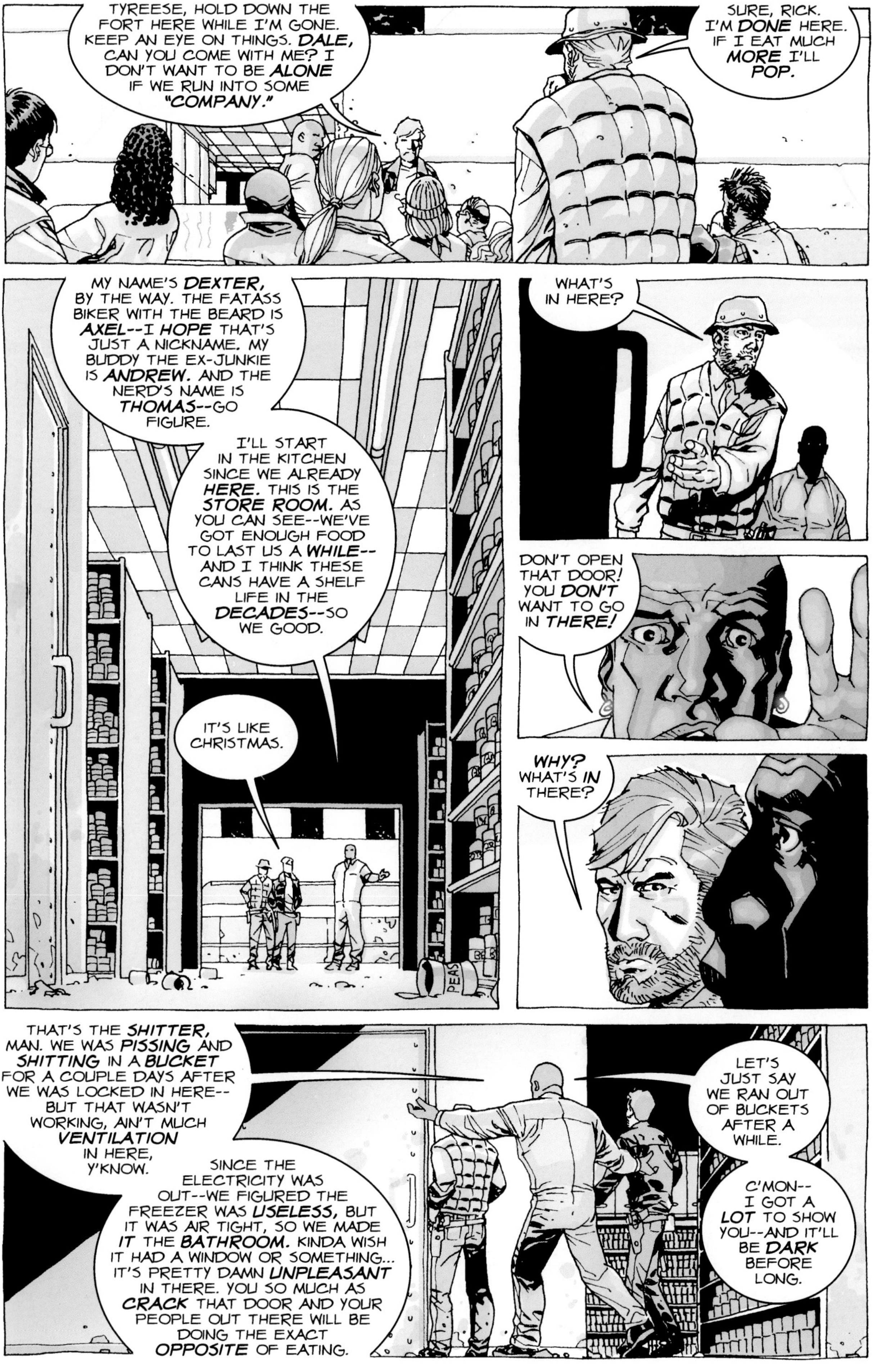
TYREESE, HOLD DOWN THE FORT HERE WHILE I'M GONE. KEEP AN EYE ON THINGS. DALE, CAN YOU COME WITH ME? I DON'T WANT TO BE ALONE IF WE RUN INTO SOME "COMPANY."
SURE, RICK. I'M DONE HERE. IF I EAT MUCH MORE I'LL POP.
MY NAME'S DEXTER, BY THE WAY. THE FATASS BIKER WITH THE BEARD IS AXEL--I HOPE THAT'S JUST A NICKNAME. MY BUDDY THE EX-JUNKIE IS ANDREW. AND THE NERD'S NAME IS THOMAS--GO FIGURE.
I'LL START IN THE KITCHEN SINCE WE ALREADY HERE. THIS IS THE STORE ROOM. AS YOU CAN SEE--WE'VE GOT ENOUGH FOOD TO LAST US A WHILE--AND I THINK THESE CANS HAVE A SHELF LIFE IN THE DECADES--SO WE GOOD.
IT'S LIKE CHRISTMAS.
WHAT'S IN HERE?
DON'T OPEN THAT DOOR! YOU DON'T WANT TO GO IN THERE!
WHY? WHAT'S IN THERE?
THAT'S THE SHITTER, MAN. WE WAS PISSING AND SHITTING IN A BUCKET FOR A COUPLE DAYS AFTER WE WAS LOCKED IN HERE--BUT THAT WASN'T WORKING, AIN'T MUCH VENTILATION IN HERE, Y'KNOW.
SINCE THE ELECTRICITY WAS OUT--WE FIGURED THE FREEZER WAS USELESS, BUT IT WAS AIR TIGHT, SO WE MADE IT THE BATHROOM. KINDA WISH IT HAD A WINDOW OR SOMETHING... IT'S PRETTY DAMN UNPLEASANT IN THERE. YOU SO MUCH AS CRACK THAT DOOR AND YOUR PEOPLE OUT THERE WILL BE DOING THE EXACT OPPOSITE OF EATING.
LET'S JUST SAY WE RAN OUT OF BUCKETS AFTER A WHILE.
C'MON--I GOT A LOT TO SHOW YOU--AND IT'LL BE DARK BEFORE LONG.

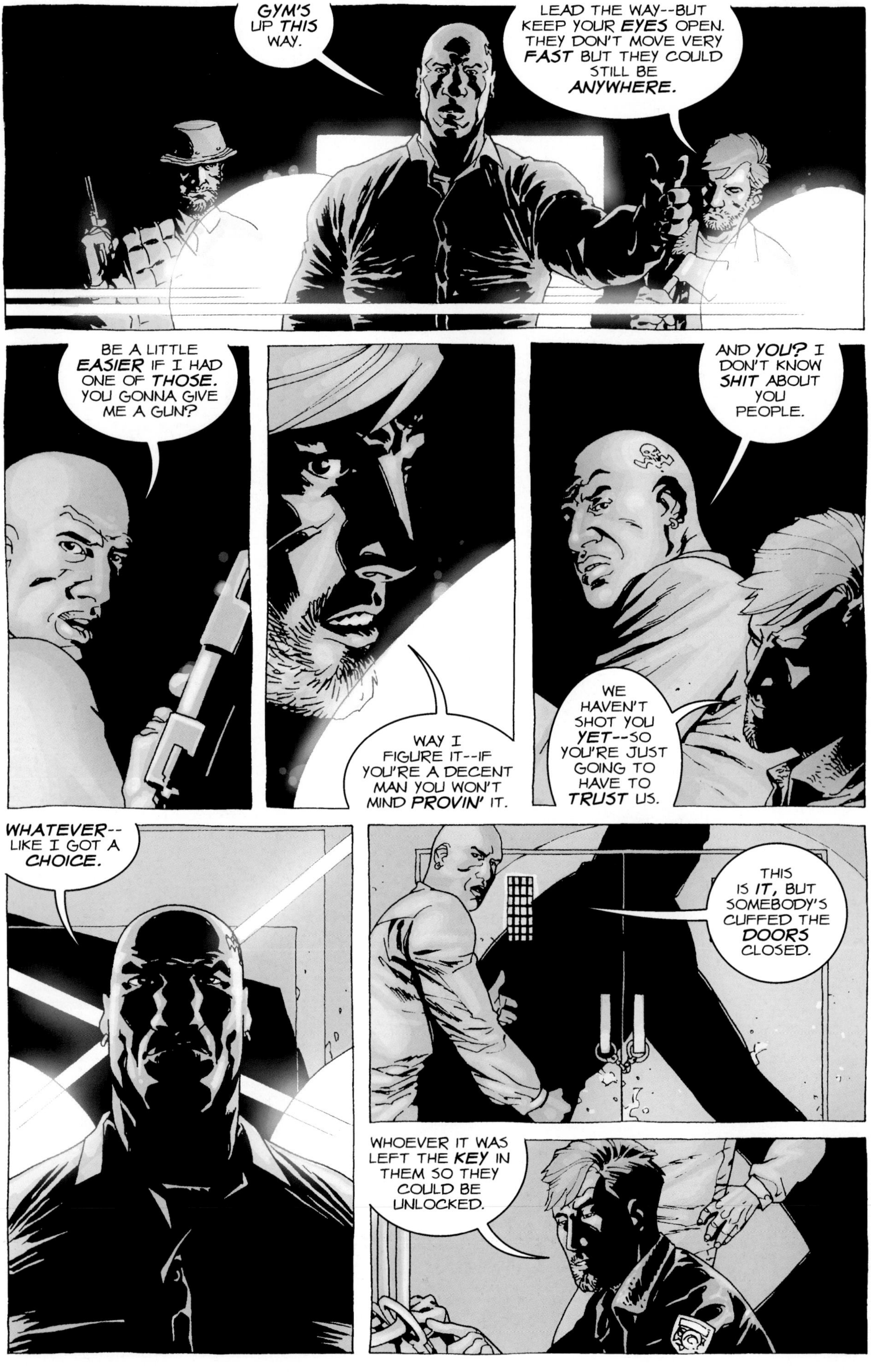
GYM'S UP THIS WAY.
LEAD THE WAY--BUT KEEP YOUR EYES OPEN. THEY DON'T MOVE VERY FAST BUT THEY COULD STILL BE ANYWHERE.
BE A LITTLE EASIER IF I HAD ONE OF THOSE. YOU GONNA GIVE ME A GUN?
WAY I FIGURE IT--IF YOU'RE A DECENT MAN YOU WON'T MIND PROVIN' IT.
AND YOU? I DON'T KNOW SHIT ABOUT YOU PEOPLE.
WE HAVEN'T SHOT YOU YET--SO YOU'RE JUST GOING TO HAVE TO TRUST US.
WHATEVER-- LIKE I GOT A CHOICE.
THIS IS IT, BUT SOMEBODY'S CUFFED THE DOORS CLOSED.
WHOEVER IT WAS LEFT THE KEY IN THEM SO THEY COULD BE UNLOCKED.

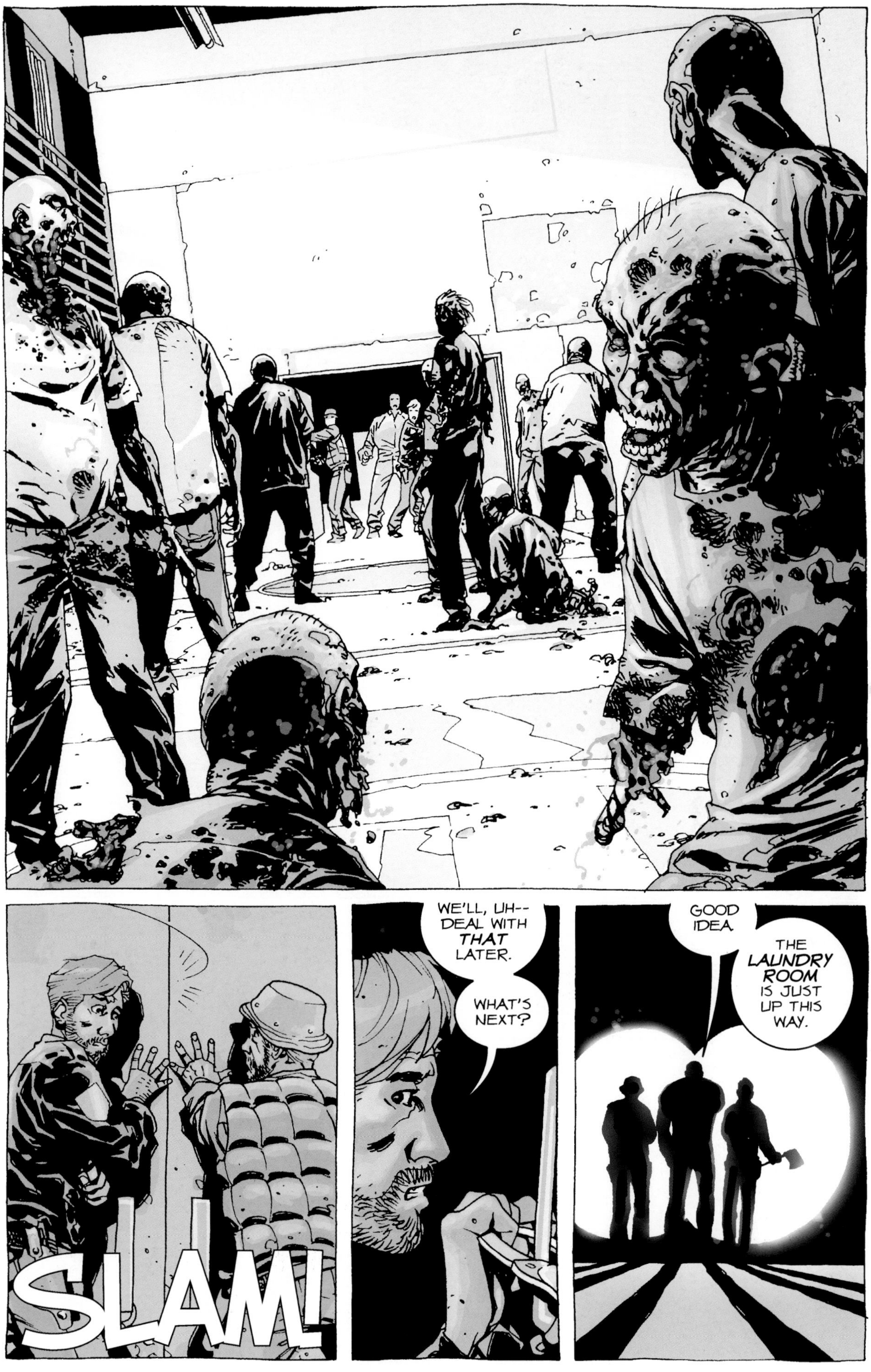
SLAM!
WE'LL, UH-- DEAL WITH THAT LATER.
WHAT'S NEXT?
GOOD IDEA.
THE LAUNDRY ROOM IS JUST UP THIS WAY.

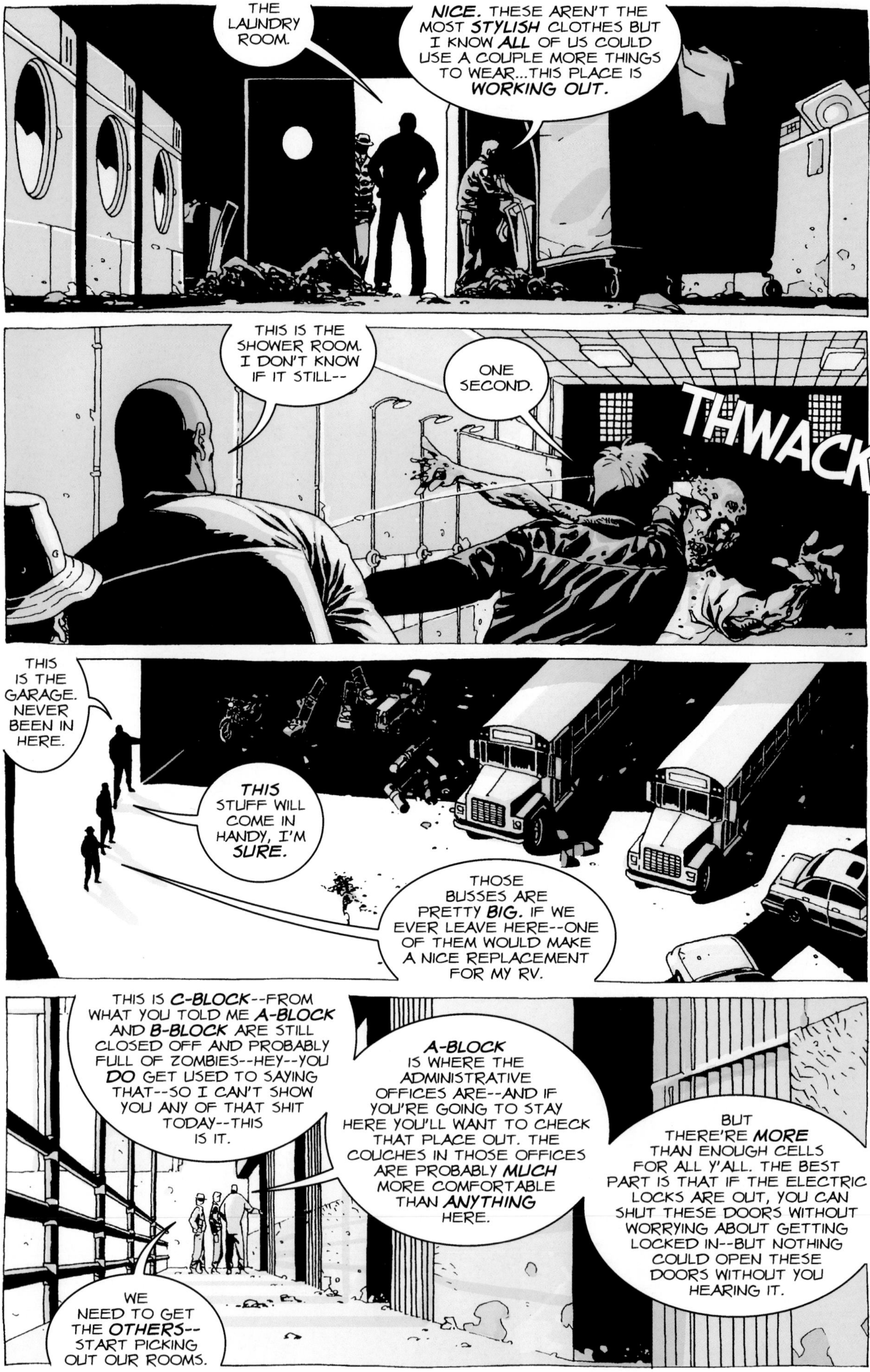
THE LAUNDRY ROOM.
NICE. THESE AREN'T THE MOST STYLISH CLOTHES BUT I KNOW ALL OF US COULD USE A COUPLE MORE THINGS TO WEAR...THIS PLACE IS WORKING OUT.
THIS IS THE SHOWER ROOM. I DON'T KNOW IF IT STILL--
ONE SECOND.
THWACK!
THIS IS THE GARAGE. NEVER BEEN IN HERE.
THIS STUFF WILL COME IN HANDY, I'M SURE.
THOSE BUSSES ARE PRETTY BIG. IF WE EVER LEAVE HERE--ONE OF THEM WOULD MAKE A NICE REPLACEMENT FOR MY RV.
THIS IS C-BLOCK--FROM WHAT YOU TOLD ME A-BLOCK AND B-BLOCK ARE STILL CLOSED OFF AND PROBABLY FULL OF ZOMBIES--HEY--YOU DO GET USED TO SAYING THAT--SO I CAN'T SHOW YOU ANY OF THAT SHIT TODAY--THIS IS IT.
A-BLOCK IS WHERE THE ADMINISTRATIVE OFFICES ARE--AND IF YOU'RE GOING TO STAY HERE YOU'LL WANT TO CHECK THAT PLACE OUT. THE COUCHES IN THOSE OFFICES ARE PROBABLY MUCH MORE COMFORTABLE THAN ANYTHING HERE.
BUT THERE'RE MORE THAN ENOUGH CELLS FOR ALL Y'ALL. THE BEST PART IS THAT IF THE ELECTRIC LOCKS ARE OUT, YOU CAN SHUT THESE DOORS WITHOUT WORRYING ABOUT GETTING LOCKED IN--BUT NOTHING COULD OPEN THESE DOORS WITHOUT YOU HEARING IT.
WE NEED TO GET THE OTHERS-- START PICKING OUT OUR ROOMS.

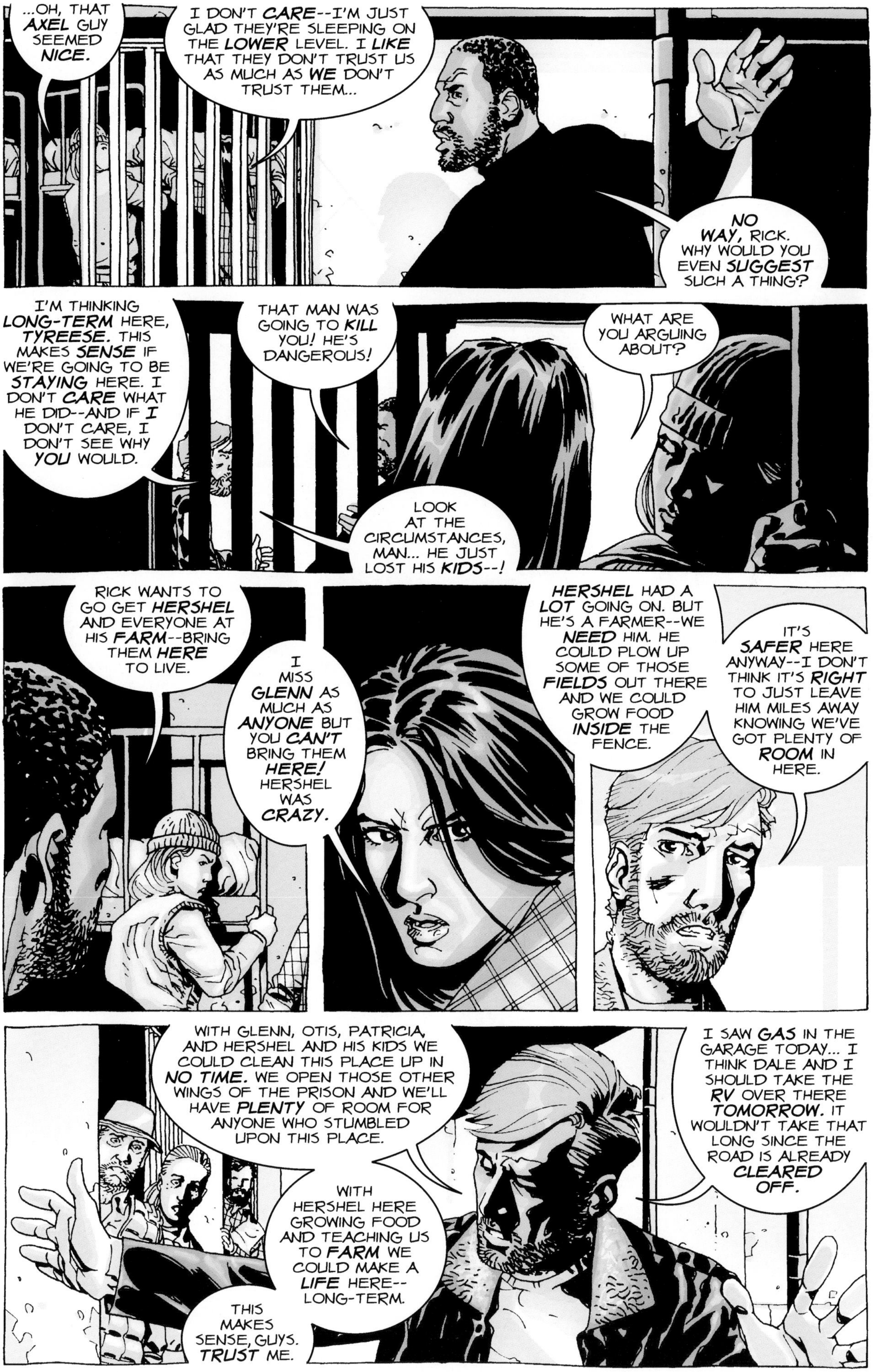
...OH, THAT AXEL GUY SEEMED NICE.
I DON'T CARE--I'M JUST GLAD THEY'RE SLEEPING ON THE LOWER LEVEL. I LIKE THAT THEY DON'T TRUST US AS MUCH AS WE DON'T TRUST THEM...
NO WAY, RICK. WHY WOULD YOU EVEN SUGGEST SUCH A THING?
I'M THINKING LONG-TERM HERE, TYREESE. THIS MAKES SENSE IF WE'RE GOING TO BE STAYING HERE. I DON'T CARE WHAT HE DID--AND IF I DON'T CARE, I DON'T SEE WHY YOU WOULD.
THAT MAN WAS GOING TO KILL YOU! HE'S DANGEROUS!
WHAT ARE YOU ARGUING ABOUT?
LOOK AT THE CIRCUMSTANCES, MAN... HE JUST LOST HIS KIDS--!
RICK WANTS TO GO GET HERSHEL AND EVERYONE AT HIS FARM--BRING THEM HERE TO LIVE.
I MISS GLENN AS MUCH AS ANYONE BUT YOU CAN'T BRING THEM HERE! HERSHEL WAS CRAZY.
HERSHEL HAD A LOT GOING ON. BUT HE'S A FARMER--WE NEED HIM. HE COULD PLOW UP SOME OF THOSE FIELDS OUT THERE AND WE COULD GROW FOOD INSIDE THE FENCE.
IT'S SAFER HERE ANYWAY--I DON'T THINK IT'S RIGHT TO JUST LEAVE HIM MILES AWAY KNOWING WE'VE GOT PLENTY OF ROOM IN HERE.
WITH GLENN, OTIS, PATRICIA, AND HERSHEL AND HIS KIDS WE COULD CLEAN THIS PLACE UP IN NO TIME. WE OPEN THOSE OTHER WINGS OF THE PRISON AND WE'LL HAVE PLENTY OF ROOM FOR ANYONE WHO STUMBLED UPON THIS PLACE.
WITH HERSHEL HERE GROWING FOOD AND TEACHING US TO FARM WE COULD MAKE A LIFE HERE-- LONG-TERM.
THIS MAKES SENSE, GUYS. TRUST ME.
I SAW GAS IN THE GARAGE TODAY... I THINK DALE AND I SHOULD TAKE THE RV OVER THERE TOMORROW. IT WOULDN'T TAKE THAT LONG SINCE THE ROAD IS ALREADY CLEARED OFF.

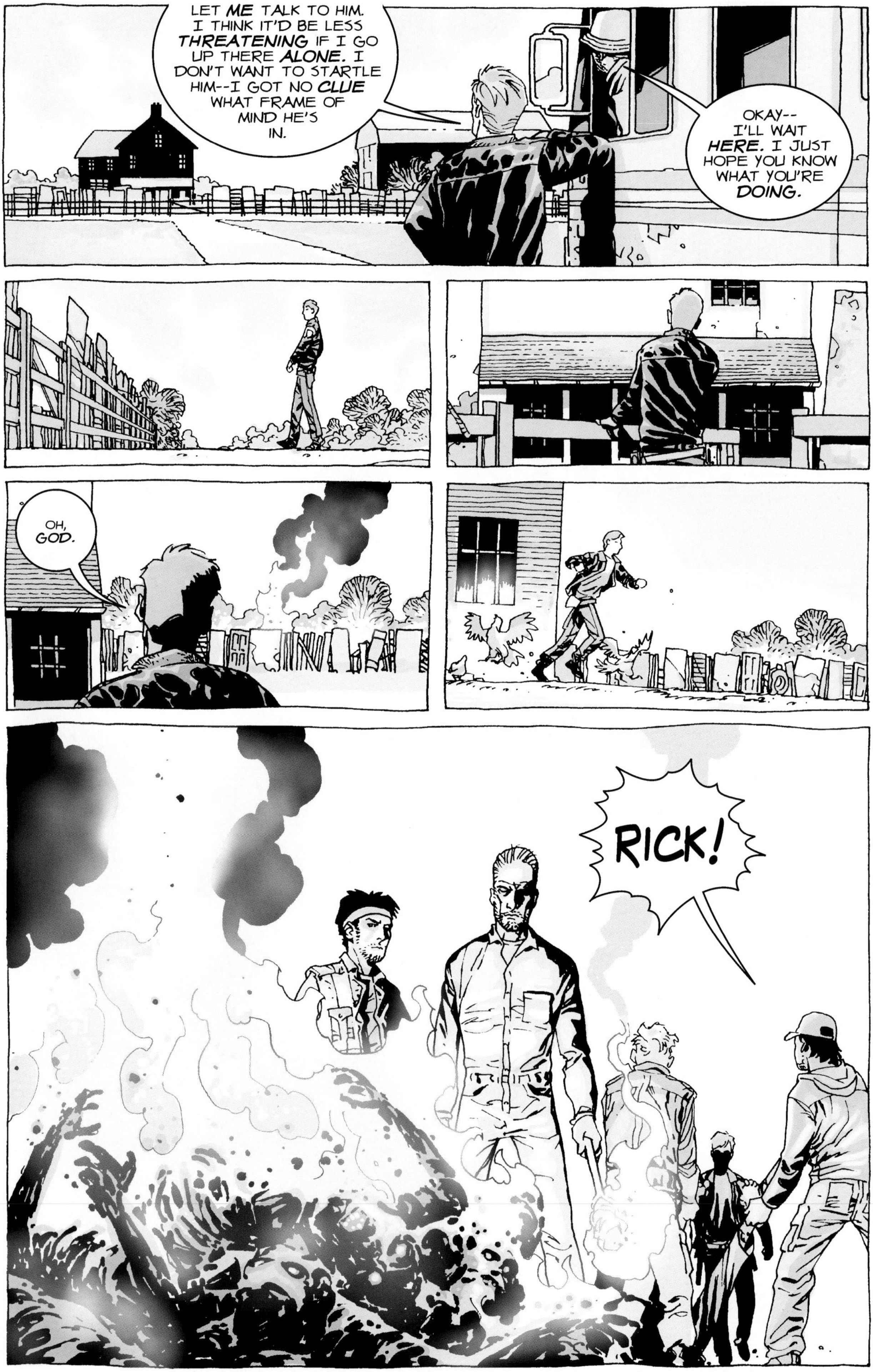
LET ME TALK TO HIM. I THINK IT'D BE LESS THREATENING IF I GO UP THERE ALONE. I DON'T WANT TO STARTLE HIM--I GOT NO CLUE WHAT FRAME OF MIND HE'S IN.
OKAY-- I'LL WAIT HERE. I JUST HOPE YOU KNOW WHAT YOU'RE DOING.
OH, GOD.
RICK!

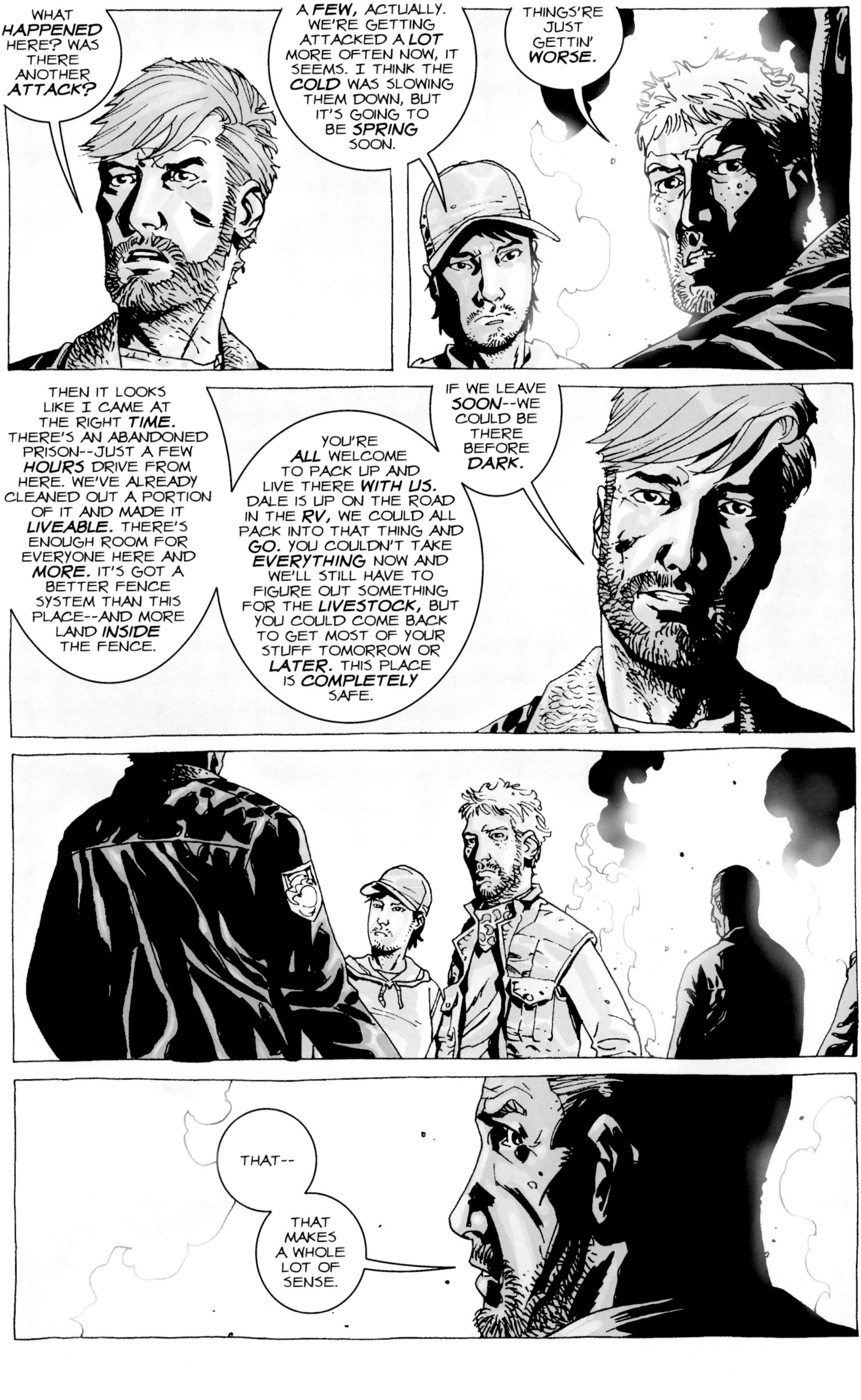
WHAT HAPPENED HERE? WAS THERE ANOTHER ATTACK?
A FEW, ACTUALLY. WE'RE GETTING ATTACKED A LOT MORE OFTEN NOW, IT SEEMS. I THINK THE COLD WAS SLOWING THEM DOWN, BUT IT'S GOING TO BE SPRING SOON.
THINGS'RE JUST GETTIN' WORSE.
THEN IT LOOKS LIKE I CAME AT THE RIGHT TIME. THERE'S AN ABANDONED PRISON--JUST A FEW HOURS DRIVE FROM HERE. WE'VE ALREADY CLEANED OUT A PORTION OF IT AND MADE IT LIVEABLE. THERE'S ENOUGH ROOM FOR EVERYONE HERE AND MORE. IT'S GOT A BETTER FENCE SYSTEM THAN THIS PLACE--AND MORE LAND INSIDE THE FENCE.
YOU'RE ALL WELCOME TO PACK UP AND LIVE THERE WITH US. DALE IS UP ON THE ROAD IN THE RV, WE COULD ALL PACK INTO THAT THING AND GO. YOU COULDN'T TAKE EVERYTHING NOW AND WE'LL STILL HAVE TO FIGURE OUT SOMETHING FOR THE LIVESTOCK, BUT YOU COULD COME BACK TO GET MOST OF YOUR STUFF TOMORROW OR LATER. THIS PLACE IS COMPLETELY SAFE.
IF WE LEAVE SOON--WE COULD BE THERE BEFORE DARK.
THAT--
THAT MAKES A WHOLE LOT OF SENSE.

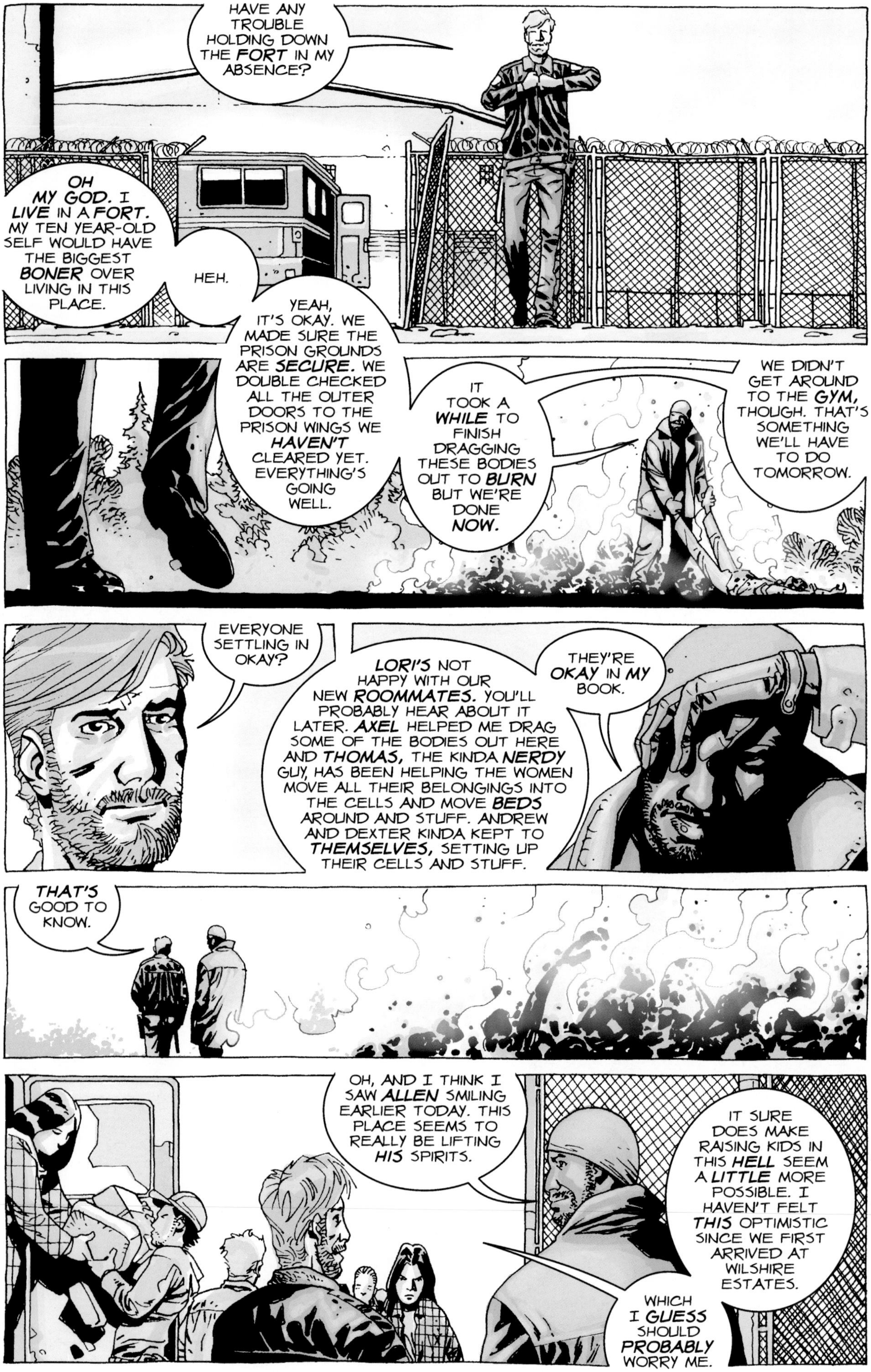
HAVE ANY TROUBLE HOLDING DOWN THE FORT IN MY ABSENCE?
OH MY GOD. I LIVE IN A FORT. MY TEN YEAR-OLD SELF WOULD HAVE THE BIGGEST BONER OVER LIVING IN THIS PLACE.
HEH.
YEAH, IT'S OKAY. WE MADE SURE THE PRISON GROUNDS ARE SECURE. WE DOUBLE CHECKED ALL THE OUTER DOORS TO THE PRISON WINGS WE HAVEN'T CLEARED YET. EVERYTHING'S GOING WELL.
IT TOOK A WHILE TO FINISH DRAGGING THESE BODIES OUT TO BURN BUT WE'RE DONE NOW.
WE DIDN'T GET AROUND TO THE GYM, THOUGH. THAT'S SOMETHING WE'LL HAVE TO DO TOMORROW.
EVERYONE SETTLING IN OKAY?
LORI'S NOT HAPPY WITH OUR NEW ROOMMATES. YOU'LL PROBABLY HEAR ABOUT IT LATER. AXEL HELPED ME DRAG SOME OF THE BODIES OUT HERE AND THOMAS, THE KINDA NERDY GUY, HAS BEEN HELPING THE WOMEN MOVE ALL THEIR BELONGINGS INTO THE CELLS AND MOVE BEDS AROUND AND STUFF. ANDREW AND DEXTER KINDA KEPT TO THEMSELVES, SETTING UP THEIR CELLS AND STUFF.
THEY'RE OKAY IN MY BOOK.
THAT'S GOOD TO KNOW.
OH, AND I THINK I SAW ALLEN SMILING EARLIER TODAY. THIS PLACE SEEMS TO REALLY BE LIFTING HIS SPIRITS.
IT SURE DOES MAKE RAISING KIDS IN THIS HELL SEEM A LITTLE MORE POSSIBLE. I HAVEN'T FELT THIS OPTIMISTIC SINCE WE FIRST ARRIVED AT WILSHIRE ESTATES.
WHICH I GUESS SHOULD PROBABLY WORRY ME.

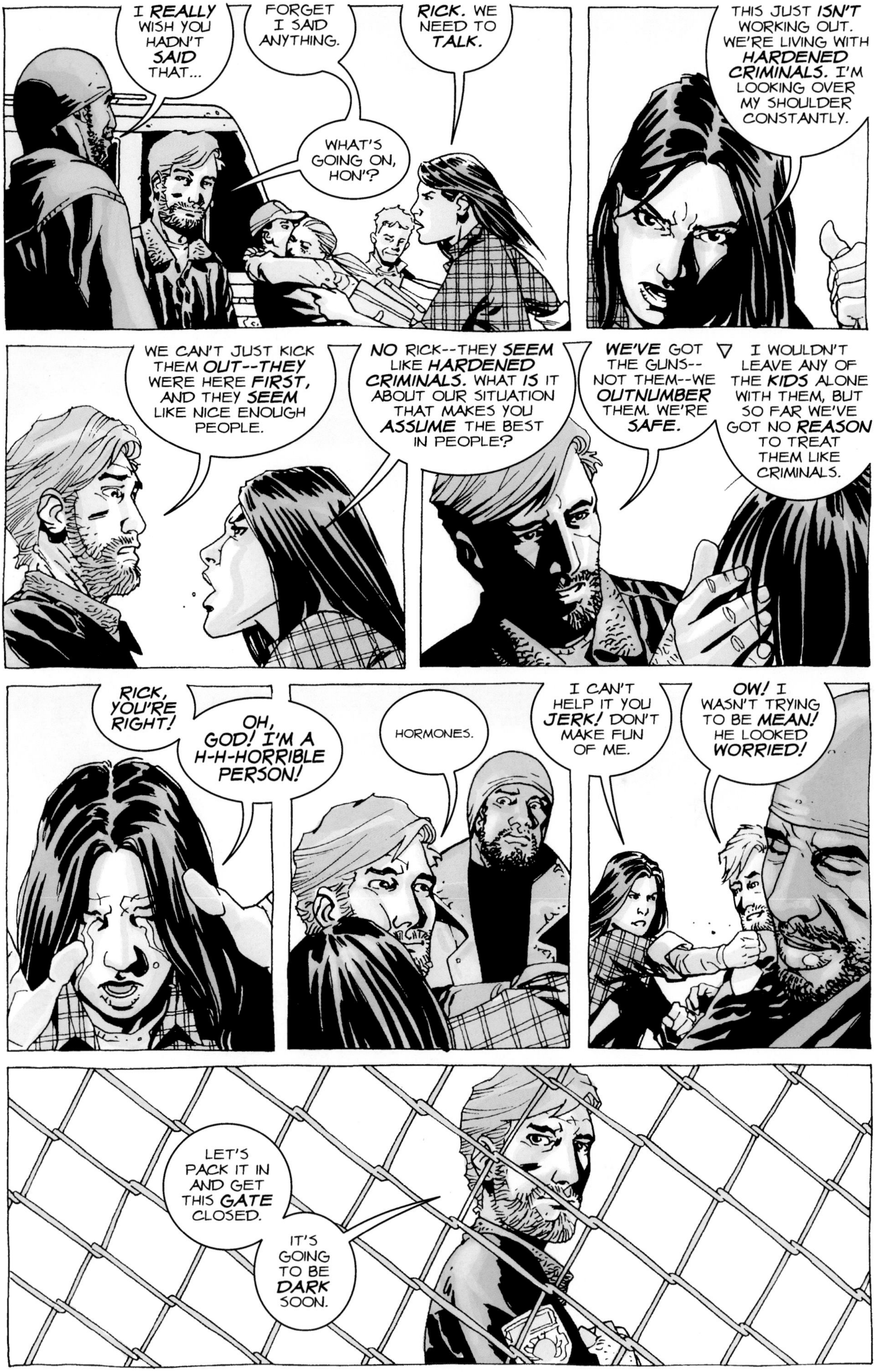
I REALLY WISH YOU HADN'T SAID THAT...
FORGET I SAID ANYTHING.
RICK. WE NEED TO TALK.
WHAT'S GOING ON, HON'?
THIS JUST ISN'T WORKING OUT. WE'RE LIVING WITH HARDENED CRIMINALS. I'M LOOKING OVER MY SHOULDER CONSTANTLY.
WE CAN'T JUST KICK THEM OUT--THEY WERE HERE FIRST, AND THEY SEEM LIKE NICE ENOUGH PEOPLE.
NO RICK--THEY SEEM LIKE HARDENED CRIMINALS. WHAT IS IT ABOUT OUR SITUATION THAT MAKES YOU ASSUME THE BEST IN PEOPLE?
WE'VE GOT THE GUNS--NOT THEM--WE OUTNUMBER THEM. WE'RE SAFE.
I WOULDN'T LEAVE ANY OF THE KIDS ALONE WITH THEM, BUT SO FAR WE'VE GOT NO REASON TO TREAT THEM LIKE CRIMINALS.
RICK, YOU'RE RIGHT!
OH, GOD! I'M A H-H-HORRIBLE PERSON!
HORMONES.
I CAN'T HELP IT YOU JERK! DON'T MAKE FUN OF ME.
OW! I WASN'T TRYING TO BE MEAN! HE LOOKED WORRIED!
LET'S PACK IT IN AND GET THIS GATE CLOSED.
IT'S GOING TO BE DARK SOON.

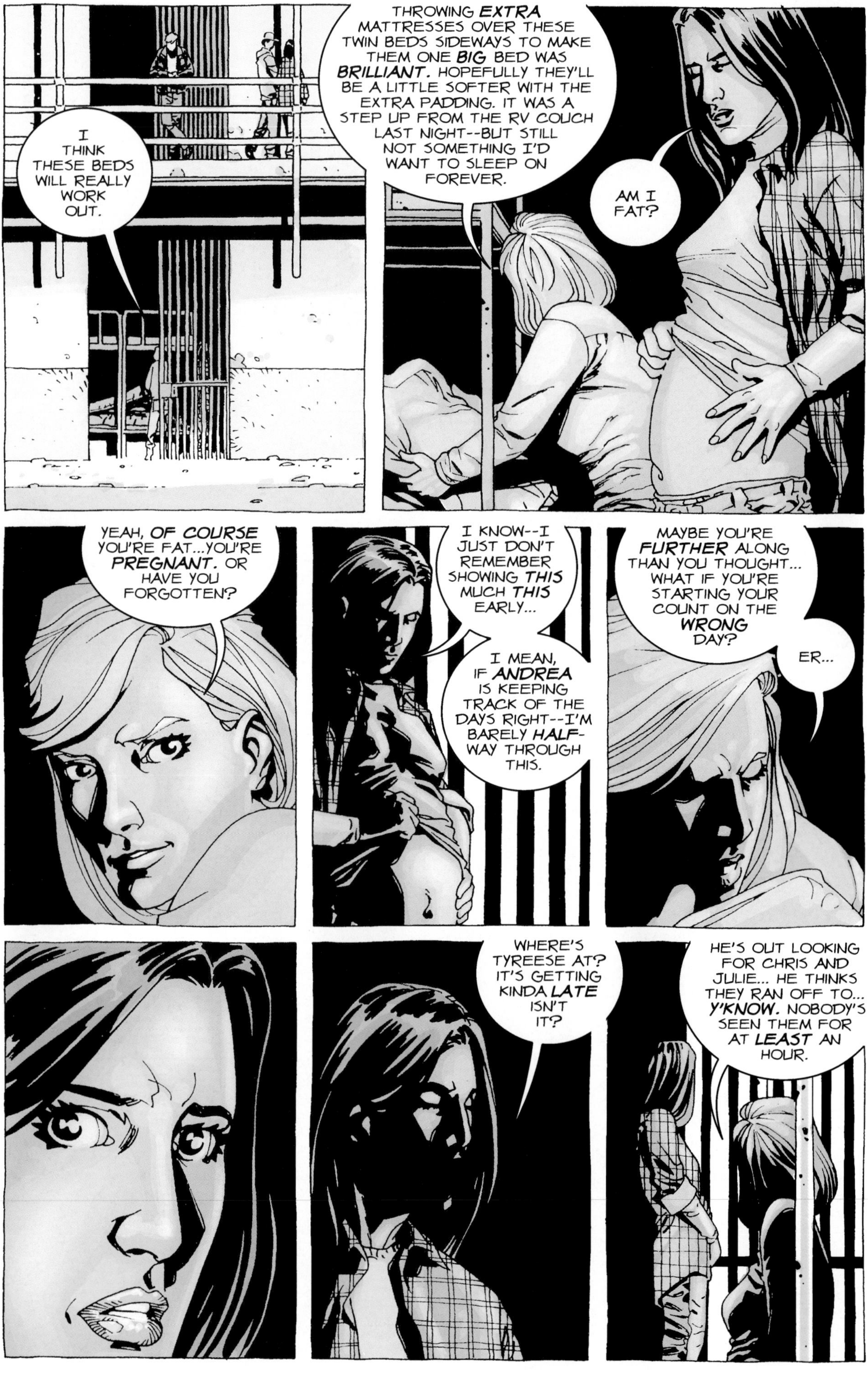
I THINK THESE BEDS WILL REALLY WORK OUT.
THROWING EXTRA MATTRESSES OVER THESE TWIN BEDS SIDEWAYS TO MAKE THEM ONE BIG BED WAS BRILLIANT. HOPEFULLY THEY'LL BE A LITTLE SOFTER WITH THE EXTRA PADDING. IT WAS A STEP UP FROM THE RV COUCH LAST NIGHT--BUT STILL NOT SOMETHING I'D WANT TO SLEEP ON FOREVER.
AM I FAT?
YEAH, OF COURSE YOU'RE FAT...YOU'RE PREGNANT. OR HAVE YOU FORGOTTEN?
I KNOW--I JUST DON'T REMEMBER SHOWING THIS MUCH THIS EARLY...
I MEAN, IF ANDREA IS KEEPING TRACK OF THE DAYS RIGHT--I'M BARELY HALF-WAY THROUGH THIS.
MAYBE YOU'RE FURTHER ALONG THAN YOU THOUGHT... WHAT IF YOU'RE STARTING YOUR COUNT ON THE WRONG DAY?
ER...
WHERE'S TYREESE AT? IT'S GETTING KINDA LATE ISN'T IT?
HE'S OUT LOOKING FOR CHRIS AND JULIE... HE THINKS THEY RAN OFF TO... Y'KNOW. NOBODY'S SEEN THEM FOR AT LEAST AN HOUR.

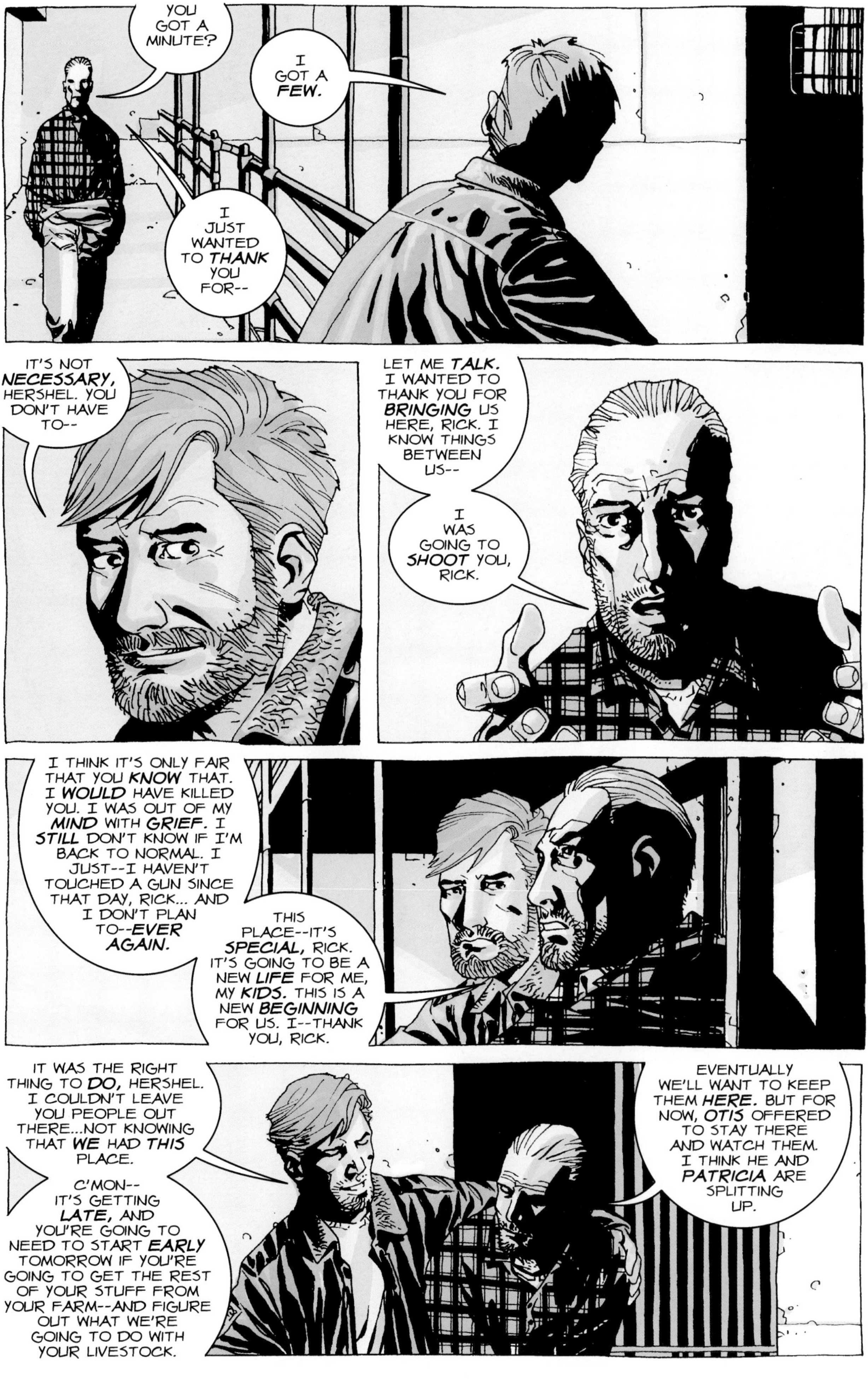

YOU GOT A MINUTE?
I GOT A FEW.
I JUST WANTED TO THANK YOU FOR--
IT'S NOT NECESSARY, HERSHEL. YOU DON'T HAVE TO--
LET ME TALK. I WANTED TO THANK YOU FOR BRINGING US HERE, RICK. I KNOW THINGS BETWEEN US--
I WAS GOING TO SHOOT YOU, RICK.
I THINK IT'S ONLY FAIR THAT YOU KNOW THAT. I WOULD HAVE KILLED YOU. I WAS OUT OF MY MIND WITH GRIEF. I STILL DON'T KNOW IF I'M BACK TO NORMAL. I JUST--I HAVEN'T TOUCHED A GUN SINCE THAT DAY, RICK... AND I DON'T PLAN TO--EVER AGAIN.
THIS PLACE--IT'S SPECIAL, RICK. IT'S GOING TO BE A NEW LIFE FOR ME, MY KIDS. THIS IS A NEW BEGINNING FOR US. I--THANK YOU, RICK.
IT WAS THE RIGHT THING TO DO, HERSHEL. I COULDN'T LEAVE YOU PEOPLE OUT THERE...NOT KNOWING THAT WE HAD THIS PLACE.
C'MON-- IT'S GETTING LATE, AND YOU'RE GOING TO NEED TO START EARLY TOMORROW IF YOU'RE GOING TO GET THE REST OF YOUR STUFF FROM YOUR FARM--AND FIGURE OUT WHAT WE'RE GOING TO DO WITH YOUR LIVESTOCK.
EVENTUALLY WE'LL WANT TO KEEP THEM HERE. BUT FOR NOW, OTIS OFFERED TO STAY THERE AND WATCH THEM. I THINK HE AND PATRICIA ARE SPLITTING UP.

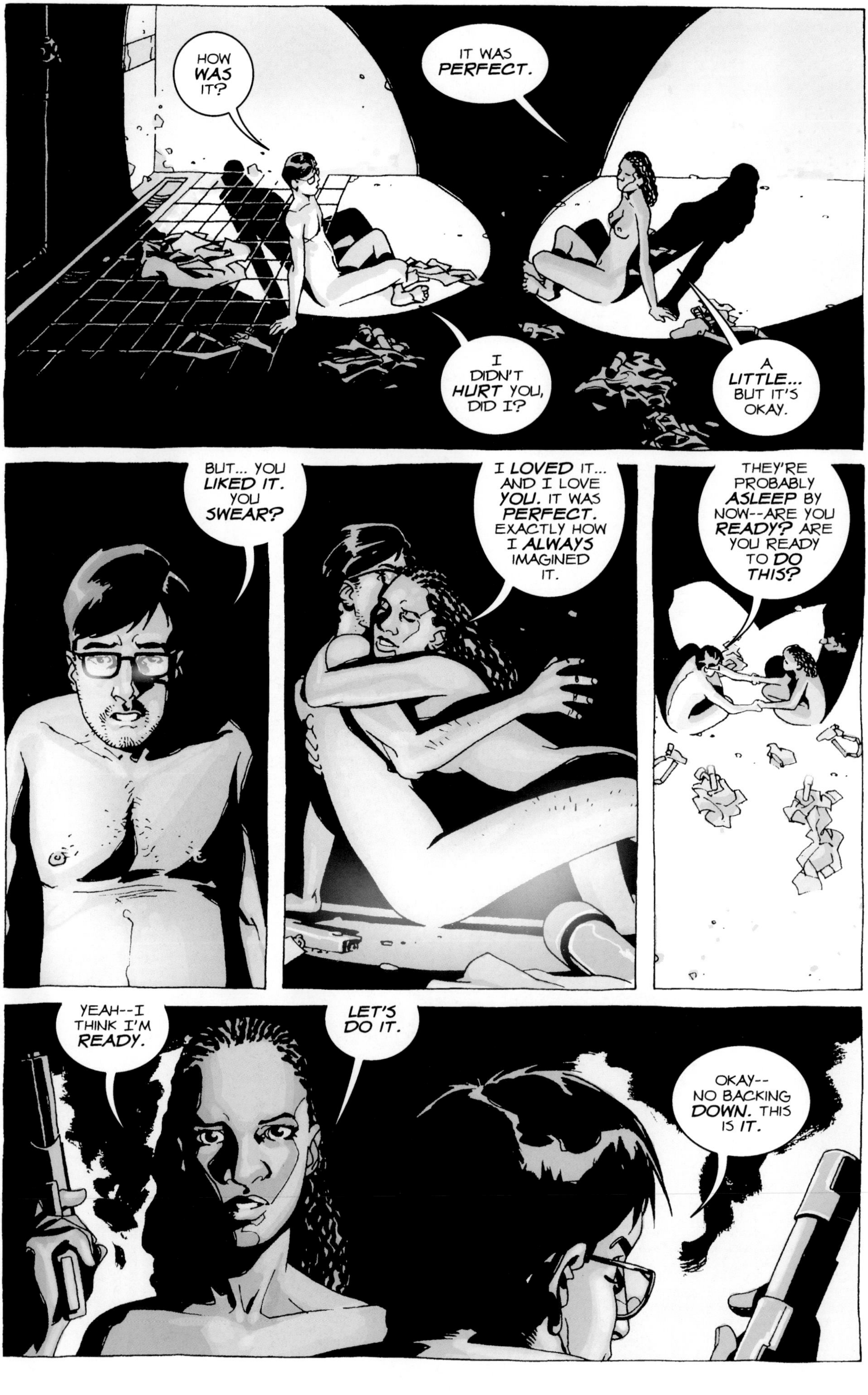
HOW WAS IT?
IT WAS PERFECT.
I DIDN'T HURT YOU, DID I?
A LITTLE... BUT IT'S OKAY.
BUT... YOU LIKED IT. YOU SWEAR?
I LOVED IT... AND I LOVE YOU. IT WAS PERFECT. EXACTLY HOW I ALWAYS IMAGINED IT.
THEY'RE PROBABLY ASLEEP BY NOW--ARE YOU READY? ARE YOU READY TO DO THIS?
YEAH--I THINK I'M READY.
LET'S DO IT.
OKAY-- NO BACKING DOWN. THIS IS IT.

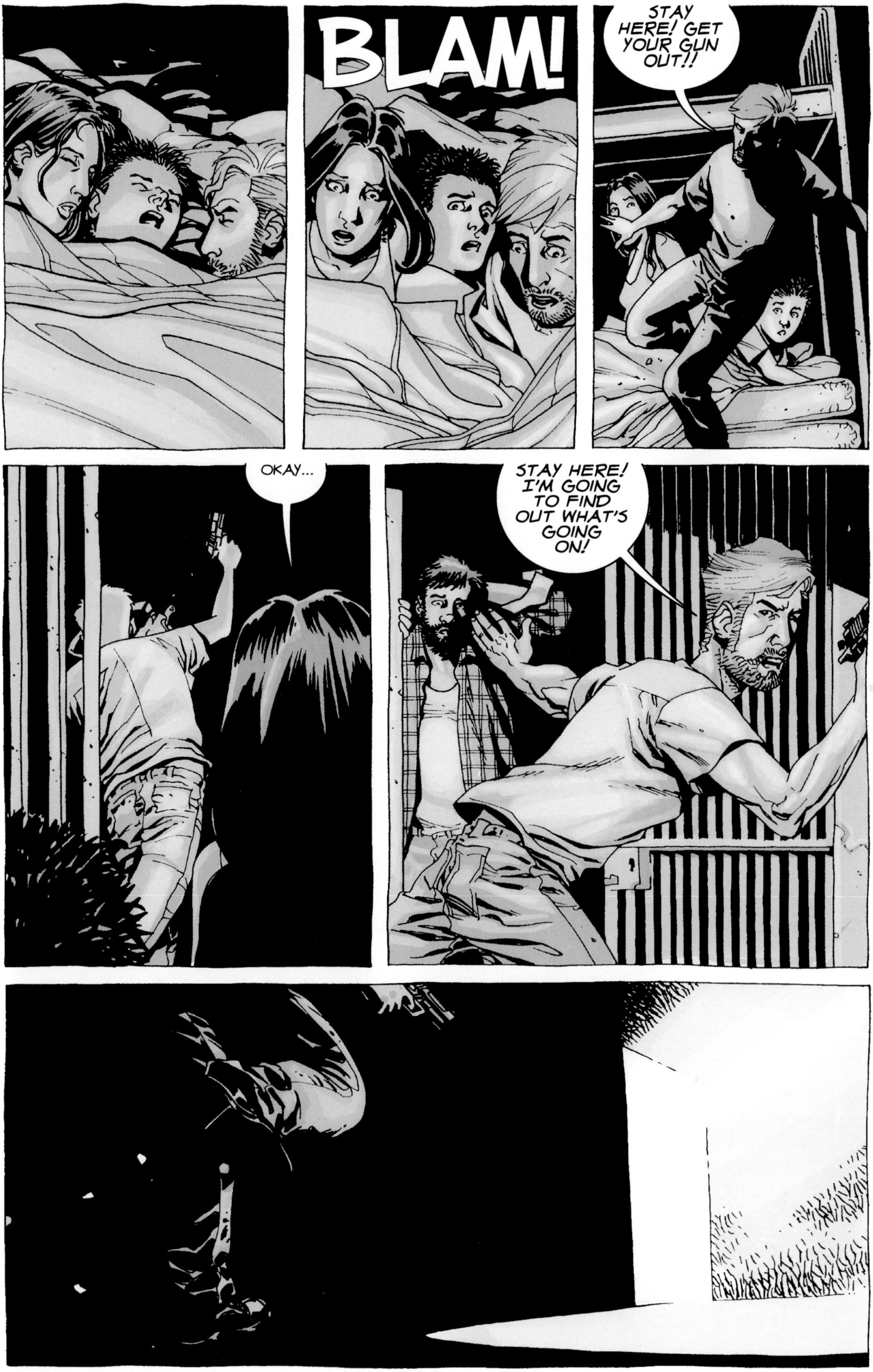
BLAM!
STAY HERE! GET YOUR GUN OUT!!
OKAY...
STAY HERE! I'M GOING TO FIND OUT WHAT'S GOING ON!

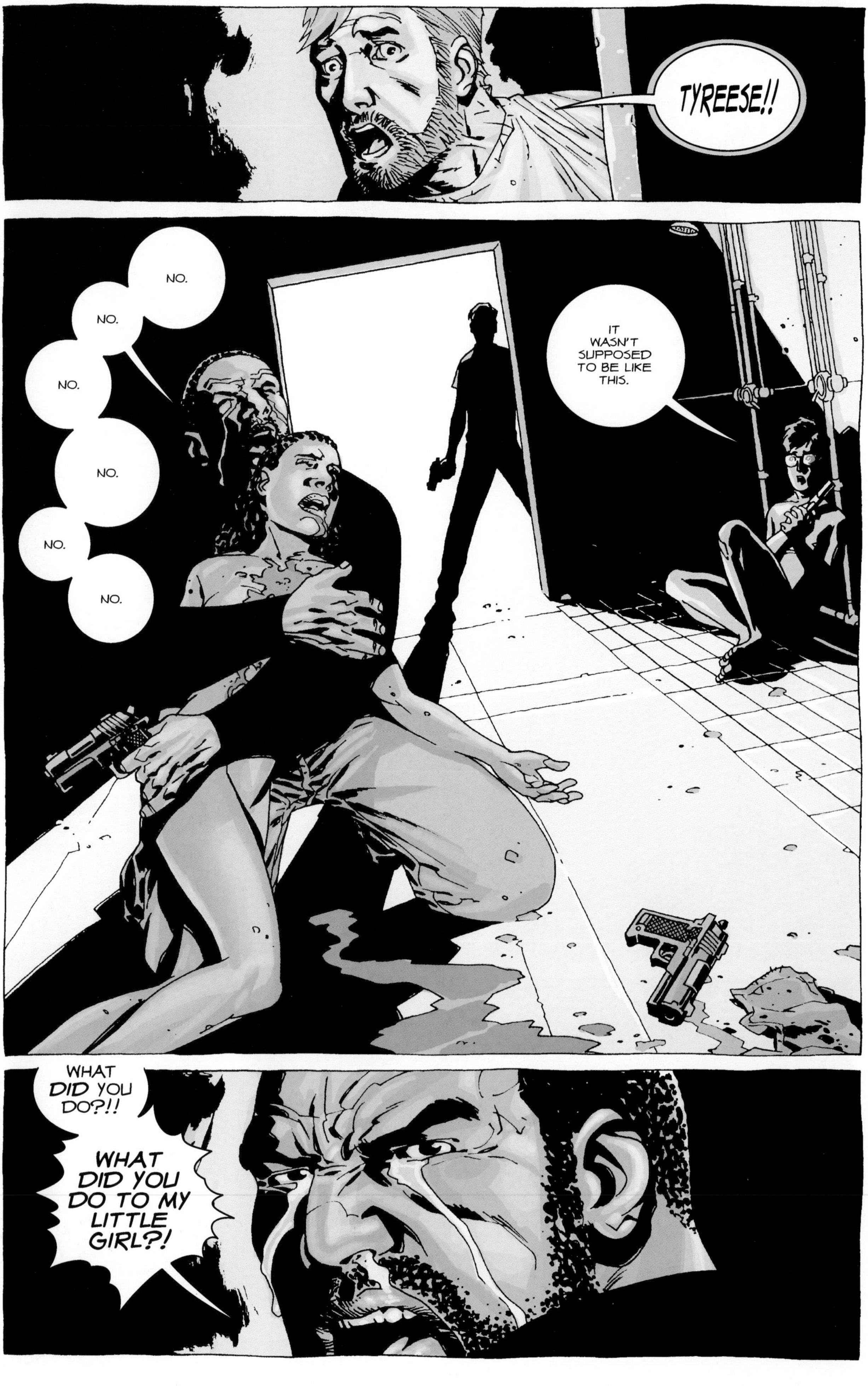
TYREESE!!
NO.
NO.
NO.
NO.
NO.
NO.
IT WASN'T SUPPOSED TO BE LIKE THIS.
WHAT DID YOU DO?!!
WHAT DID YOU DO TO MY LITTLE GIRL?!

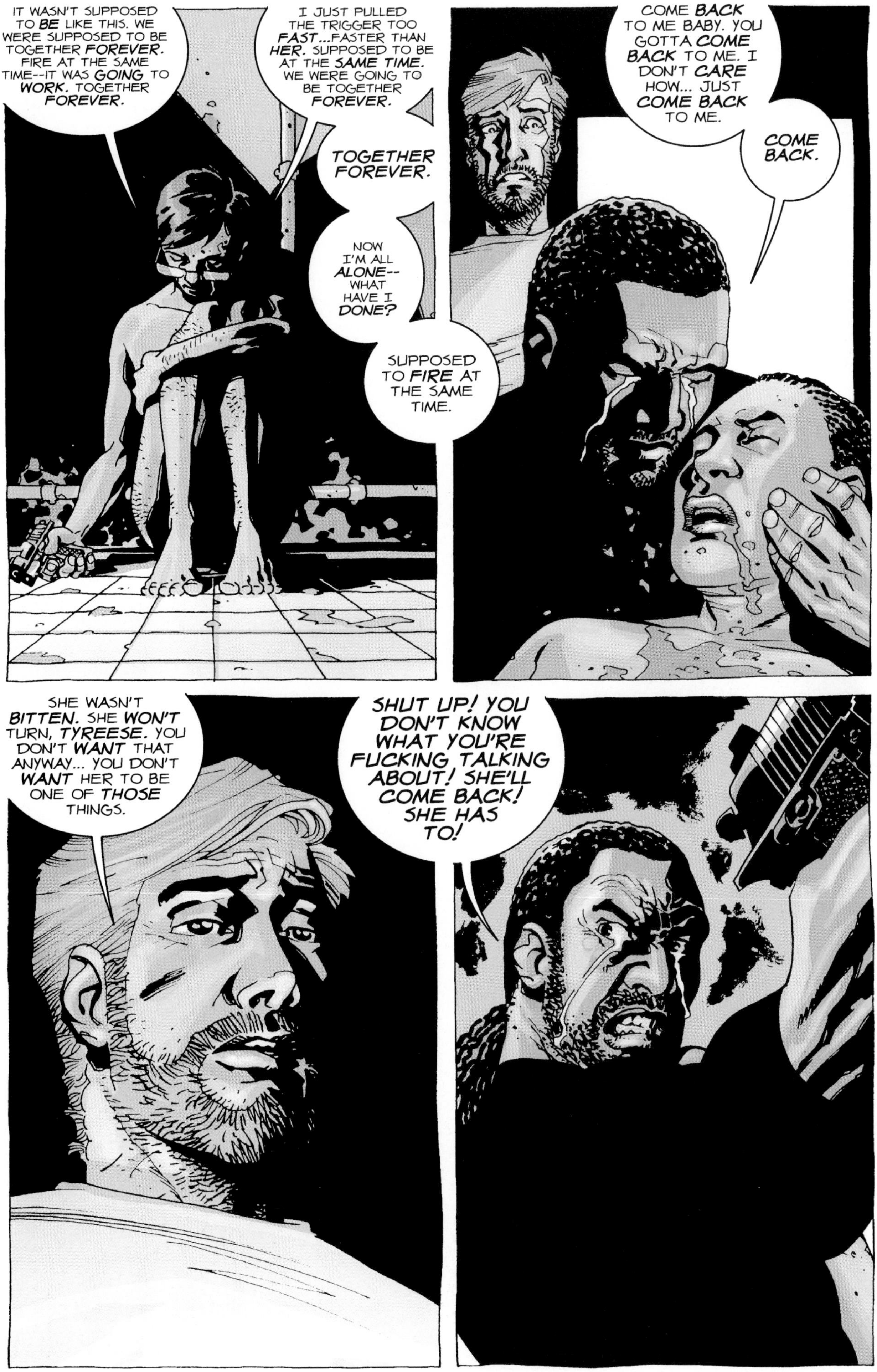
IT WASN'T SUPPOSED TO BE LIKE THIS. WE WERE SUPPOSED TO BE TOGETHER FOREVER. FIRE AT THE SAME TIME--IT WAS GOING TO WORK. TOGETHER FOREVER.
I JUST PULLED THE TRIGGER TOO FAST...FASTER THAN HER. SUPPOSED TO BE AT THE SAME TIME. WE WERE GOING TO BE TOGETHER FOREVER.
TOGETHER FOREVER.
NOW I'M ALL ALONE-- WHAT HAVE I DONE?
SUPPOSED TO FIRE AT THE SAME TIME.
COME BACK TO ME BABY. YOU GOTTA COME BACK TO ME. I DON'T CARE HOW... JUST COME BACK TO ME.
COME BACK.
SHE WASN'T BITTEN. SHE WON'T TURN, TYREESE. YOU DON'T WANT THAT ANYWAY... YOU DON'T WANT HER TO BE ONE OF THOSE THINGS.
SHUT UP! YOU DON'T KNOW WHAT YOU'RE FUCKING TALKING ABOUT! SHE'LL COME BACK! SHE HAS TO!

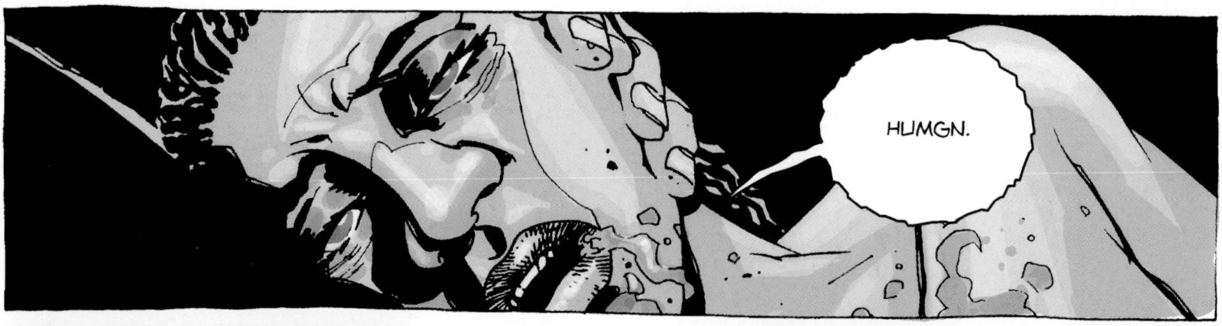
HUMGN.

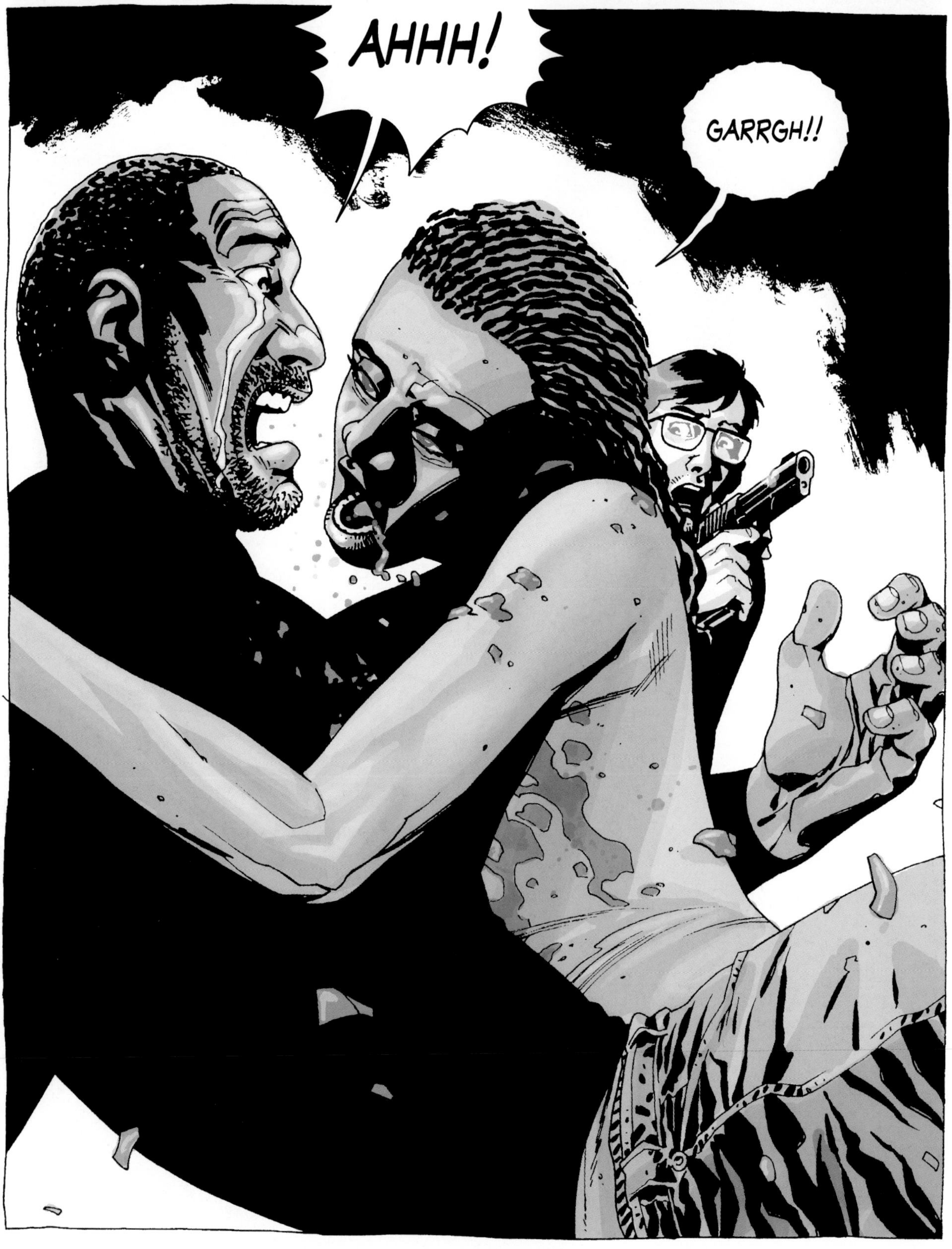
AHHH!
GARRGH!!

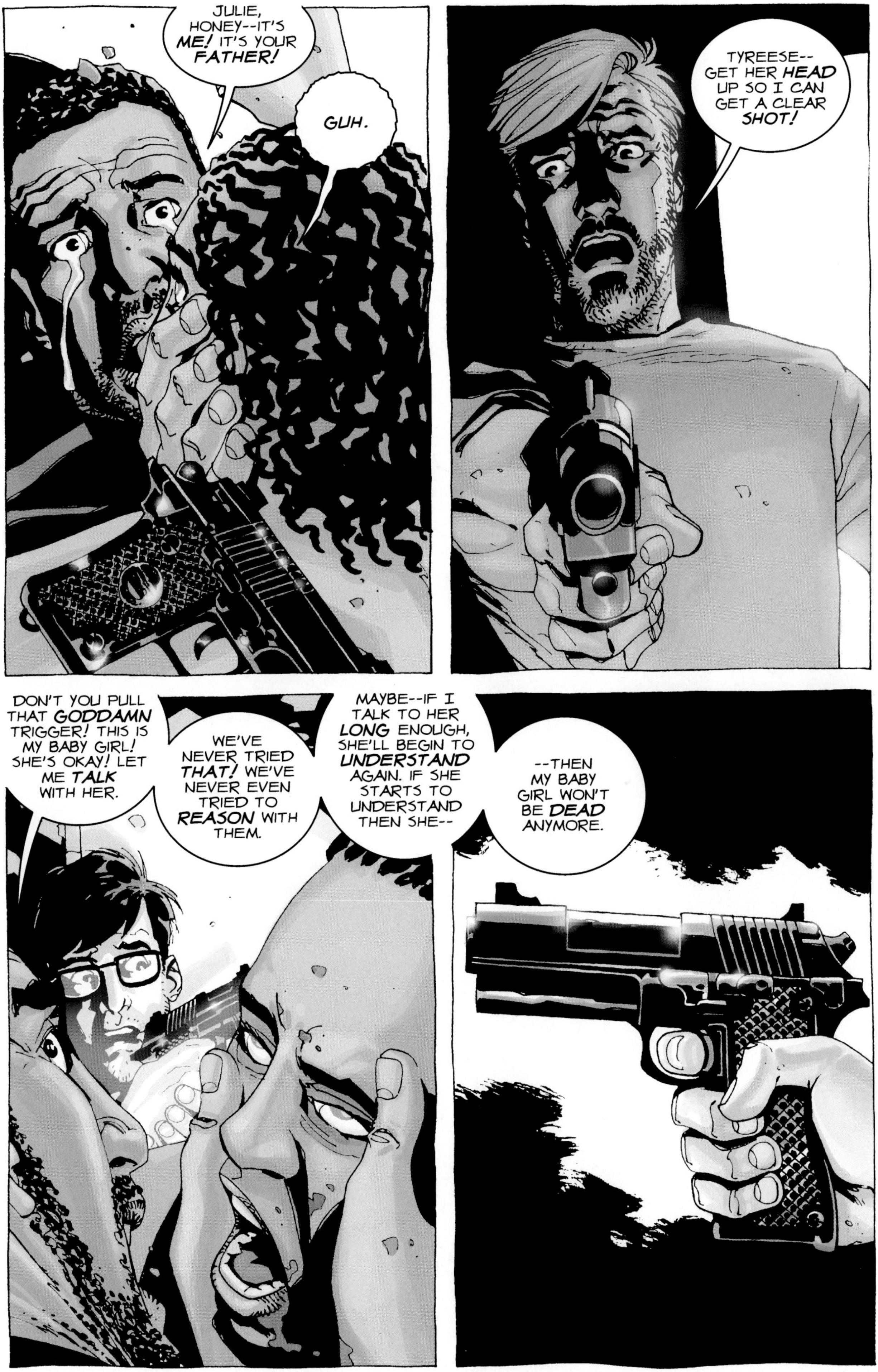
JULIE, HONEY--IT'S ME! IT'S YOUR FATHER!
GUH.
TYREESE--GET HER HEAD UP SO I CAN GET A CLEAR SHOT!
DON'T YOU PULL THAT GODDAMN TRIGGER! THIS IS MY BABY GIRL! SHE'S OKAY! LET ME TALK WITH HER.
WE'VE NEVER TRIED THAT! WE'VE NEVER EVEN TRIED TO REASON WITH THEM.
MAYBE--IF I TALK TO HER LONG ENOUGH, SHE'LL BEGIN TO UNDERSTAND AGAIN. IF SHE STARTS TO UNDERSTAND THEN SHE--
--THEN MY BABY GIRL WON'T BE DEAD ANYMORE.

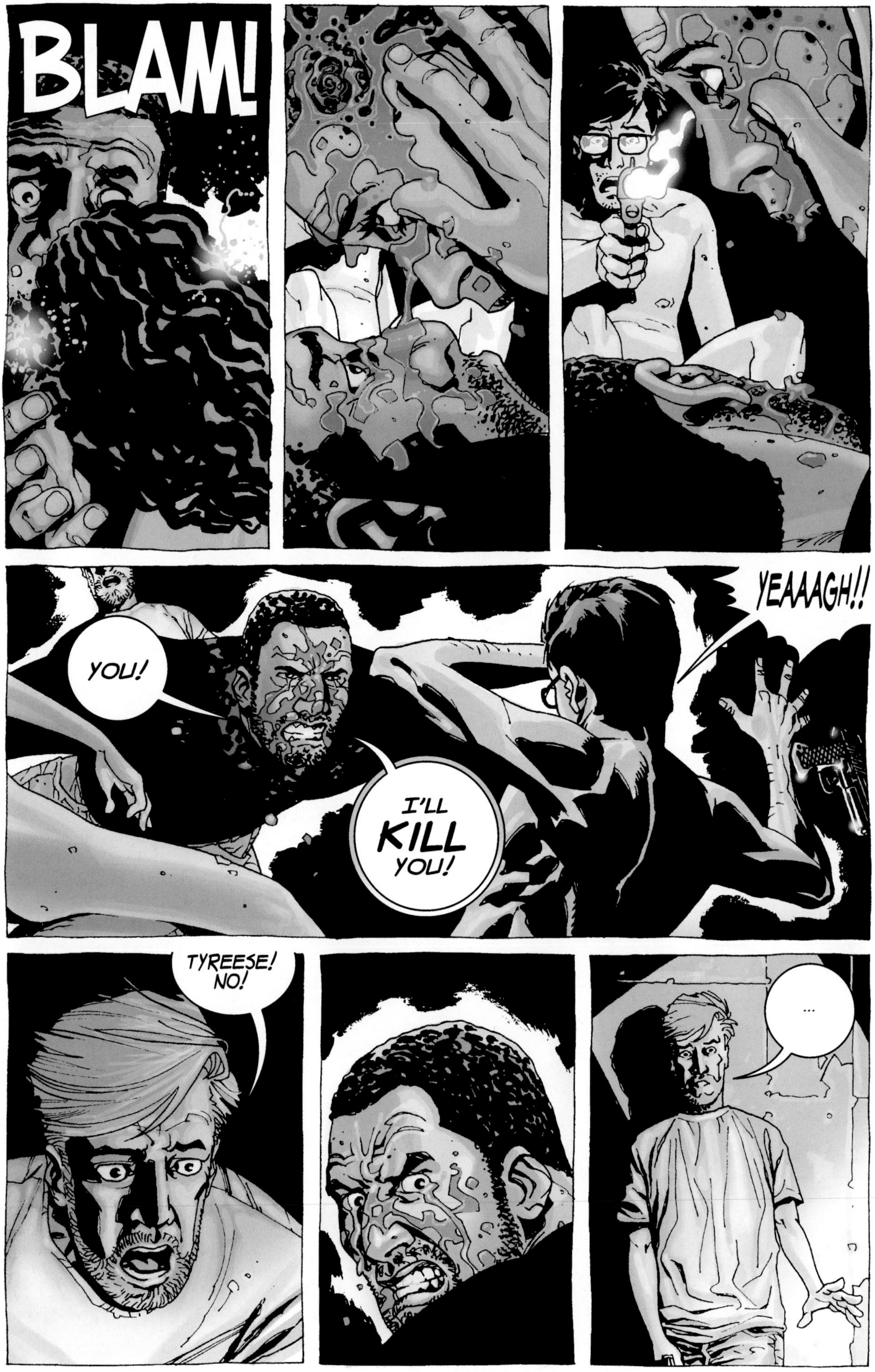
BLAM!
YOU!
I'LL KILL YOU!
YEAAAGH!!
TYREESE! NO!
...

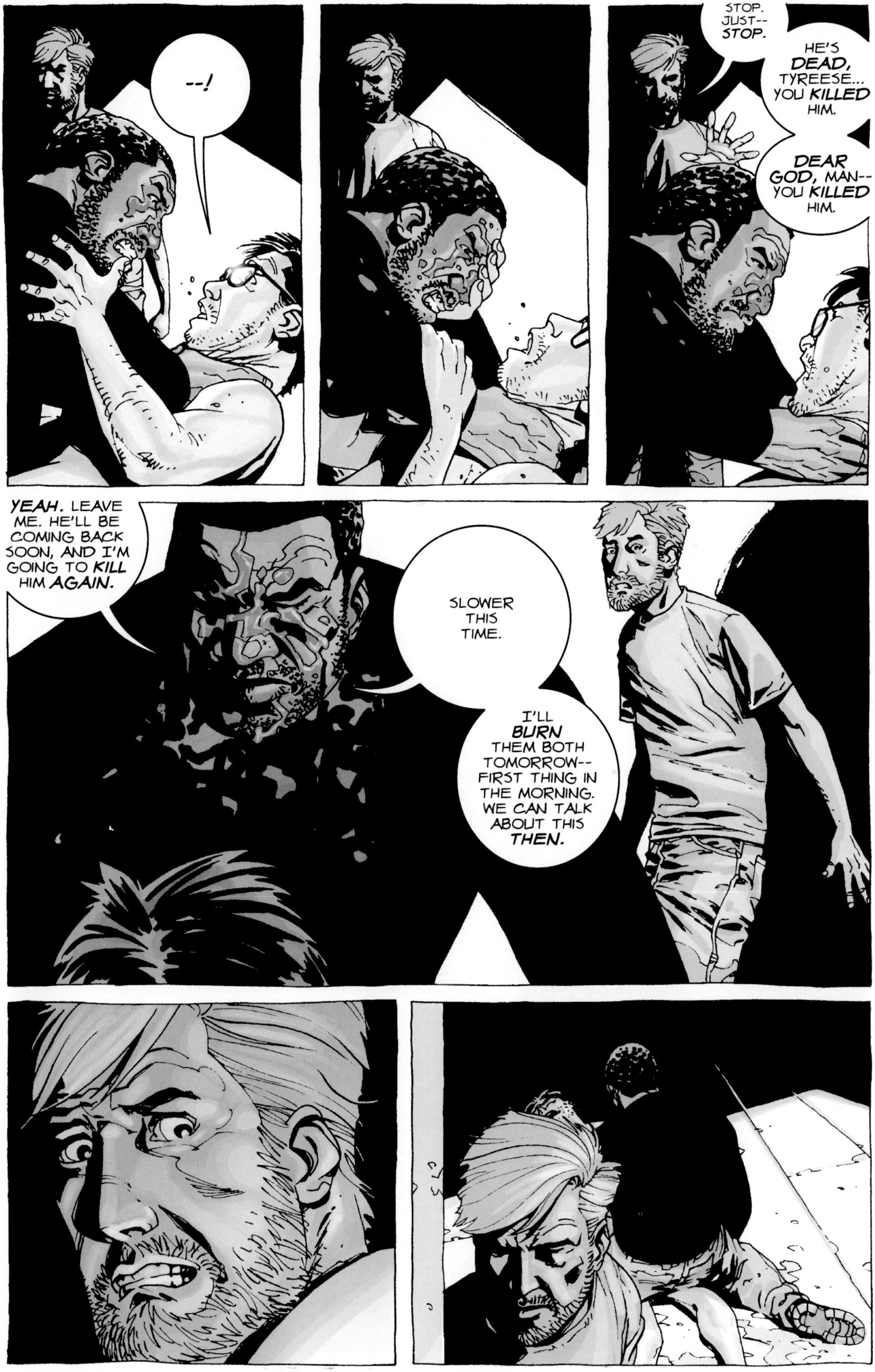
--!
STOP. JUST-- STOP.
HE'S DEAD, TYREESE... YOU KILLED HIM.
DEAR GOD, MAN-- YOU KILLED HIM.
YEAH. LEAVE ME. HE'LL BE COMING BACK SOON, AND I'M GOING TO KILL HIM AGAIN.
SLOWER THIS TIME.
I'LL BURN THEM BOTH TOMORROW-- FIRST THING IN THE MORNING. WE CAN TALK ABOUT THIS THEN.

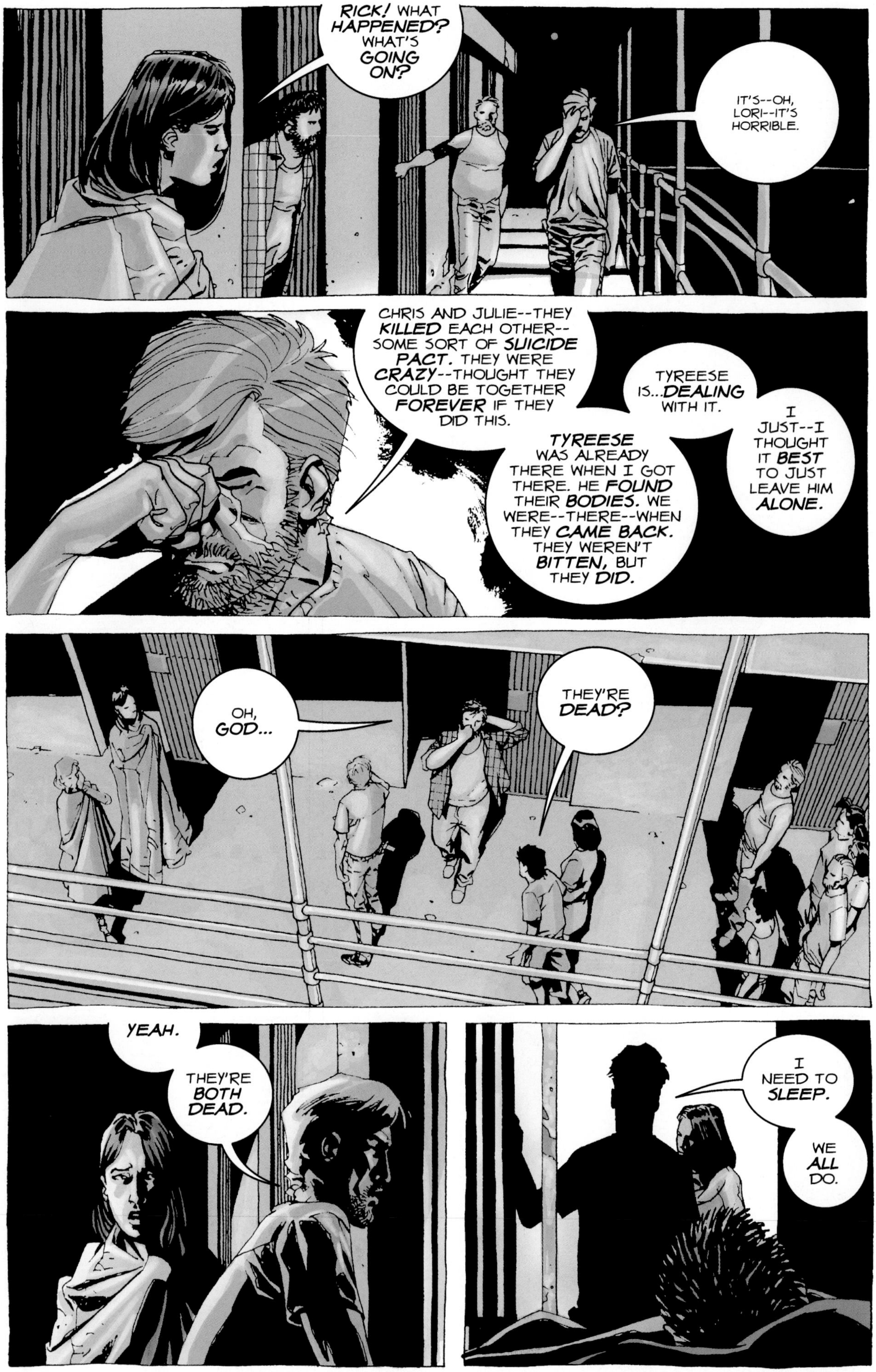
RICK! WHAT HAPPENED? WHAT'S GOING ON?
IT'S--OH, LORI--IT'S HORRIBLE.
CHRIS AND JULIE--THEY KILLED EACH OTHER--SOME SORT OF SUICIDE PACT. THEY WERE CRAZY--THOUGHT THEY COULD BE TOGETHER FOREVER IF THEY DID THIS.
TYREESE WAS ALREADY THERE WHEN I GOT THERE. HE FOUND THEIR BODIES. WE WERE--THERE--WHEN THEY CAME BACK. THEY WEREN'T BITTEN, BUT THEY DID.
TYREESE IS...DEALING WITH IT.
I JUST--I THOUGHT IT BEST TO JUST LEAVE HIM ALONE.
OH, GOD...
THEY'RE DEAD?
YEAH.
THEY'RE BOTH DEAD.
I NEED TO SLEEP.
WE ALL DO.

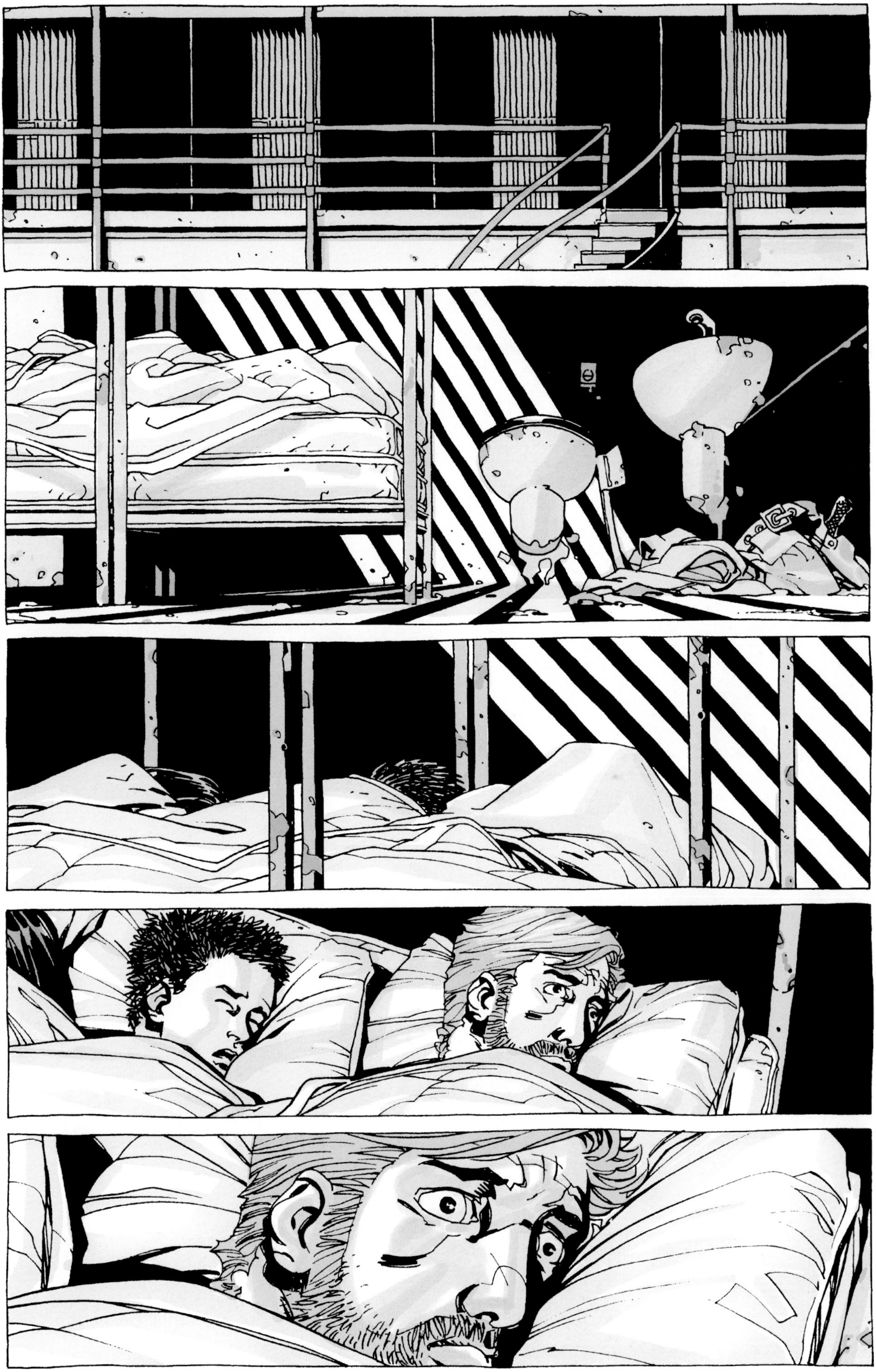

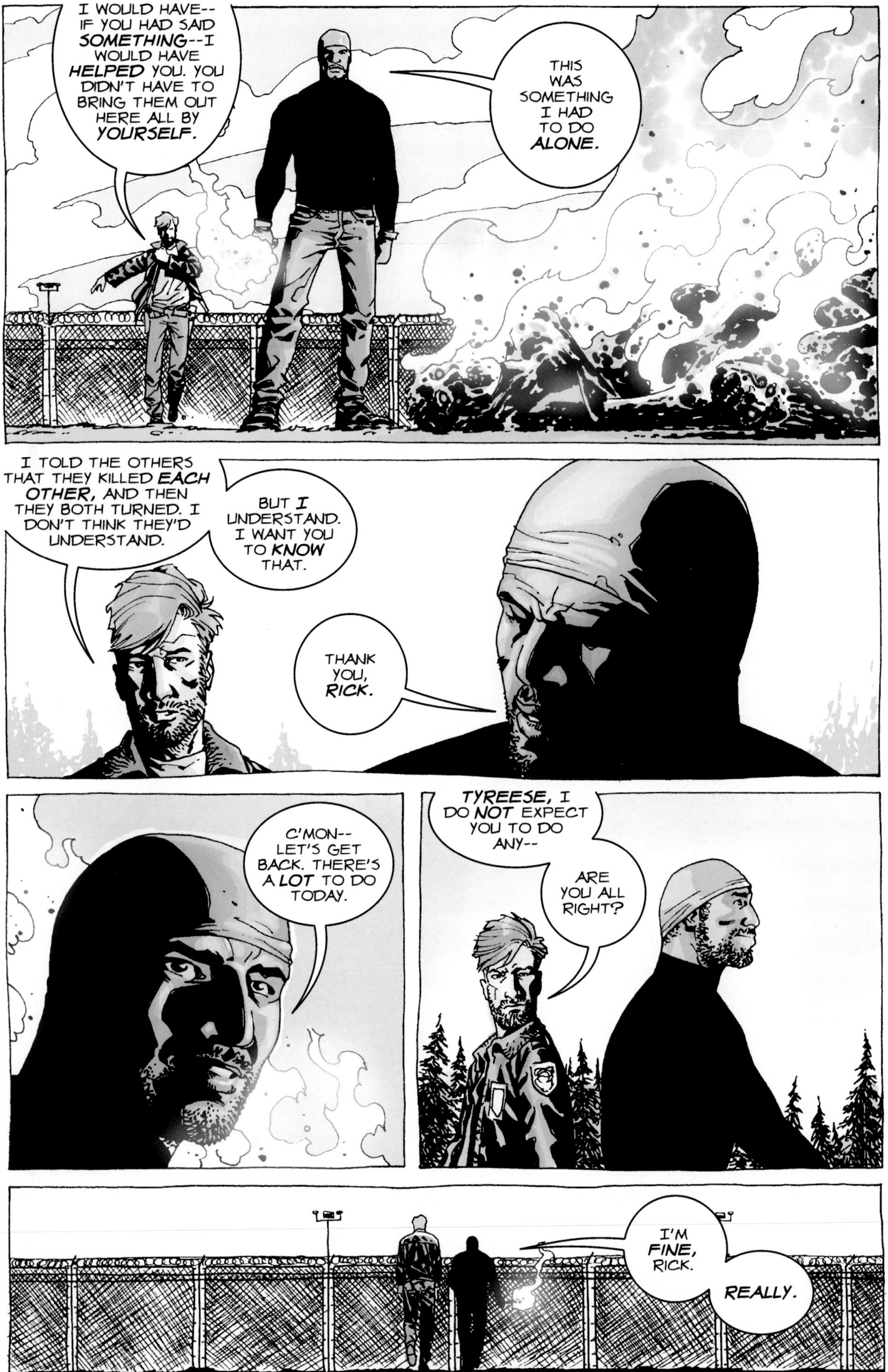
I WOULD HAVE-- IF YOU HAD SAID SOMETHING--I WOULD HAVE HELPED YOU. YOU DIDN'T HAVE TO BRING THEM OUT HERE ALL BY YOURSELF.
THIS WAS SOMETHING I HAD TO DO ALONE.
I TOLD THE OTHERS THAT THEY KILLED EACH OTHER, AND THEN THEY BOTH TURNED. I DON'T THINK THEY'D UNDERSTAND.
BUT I UNDERSTAND. I WANT YOU TO KNOW THAT.
THANK YOU, RICK.
C'MON-- LET'S GET BACK. THERE'S A LOT TO DO TODAY.
TYREESE, I DO NOT EXPECT YOU TO DO ANY--
ARE YOU ALL RIGHT?
I'M FINE, RICK.
REALLY.

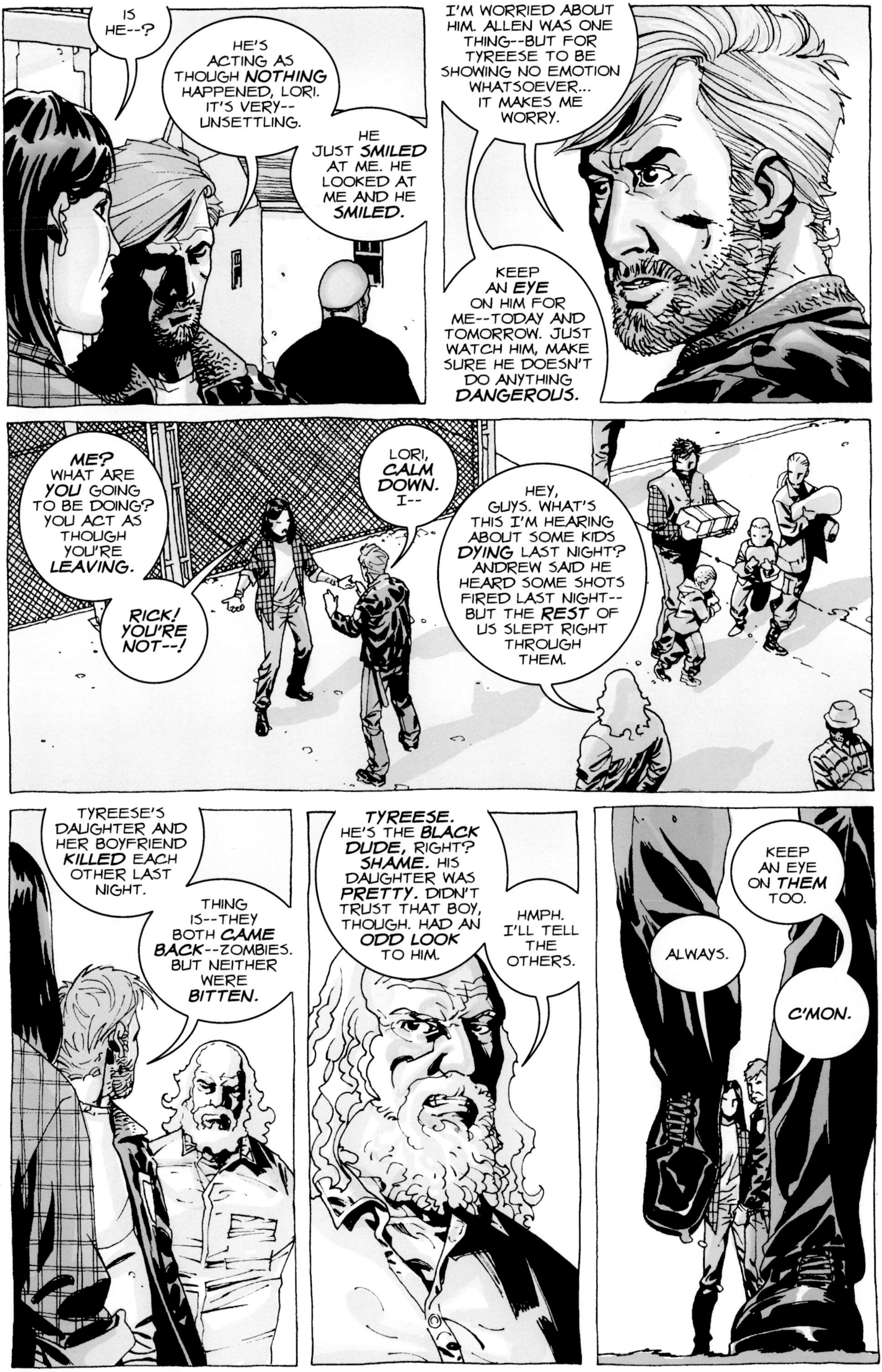
IS HE--?
HE'S ACTING AS THOUGH NOTHING HAPPENED, LORI. IT'S VERY-- UNSETTLING.
HE JUST SMILED AT ME. HE LOOKED AT ME AND HE SMILED.
I'M WORRIED ABOUT HIM. ALLEN WAS ONE THING--BUT FOR TYREESE TO BE SHOWING NO EMOTION WHATSOEVER... IT MAKES ME WORRY.
KEEP AN EYE ON HIM FOR ME--TODAY AND TOMORROW. JUST WATCH HIM, MAKE SURE HE DOESN'T DO ANYTHING DANGEROUS.
ME? WHAT ARE YOU GOING TO BE DOING? YOU ACT AS THOUGH YOU'RE LEAVING.
RICK! YOU'RE NOT--!
LORI, CALM DOWN. I--
HEY, GUYS. WHAT'S THIS I'M HEARING ABOUT SOME KIDS DYING LAST NIGHT? ANDREW SAID HE HEARD SOME SHOTS FIRED LAST NIGHT--BUT THE REST OF US SLEPT RIGHT THROUGH THEM.
TYREESE'S DAUGHTER AND HER BOYFRIEND KILLED EACH OTHER LAST NIGHT.
THING IS--THEY BOTH CAME BACK--ZOMBIES. BUT NEITHER WERE BITTEN.
TYREESE. HE'S THE BLACK DUDE, RIGHT? SHAME. HIS DAUGHTER WAS PRETTY. DIDN'T TRUST THAT BOY, THOUGH. HAD AN ODD LOOK TO HIM.
HMPH. I'LL TELL THE OTHERS.
KEEP AN EYE ON THEM TOO.
ALWAYS.
C'MON.

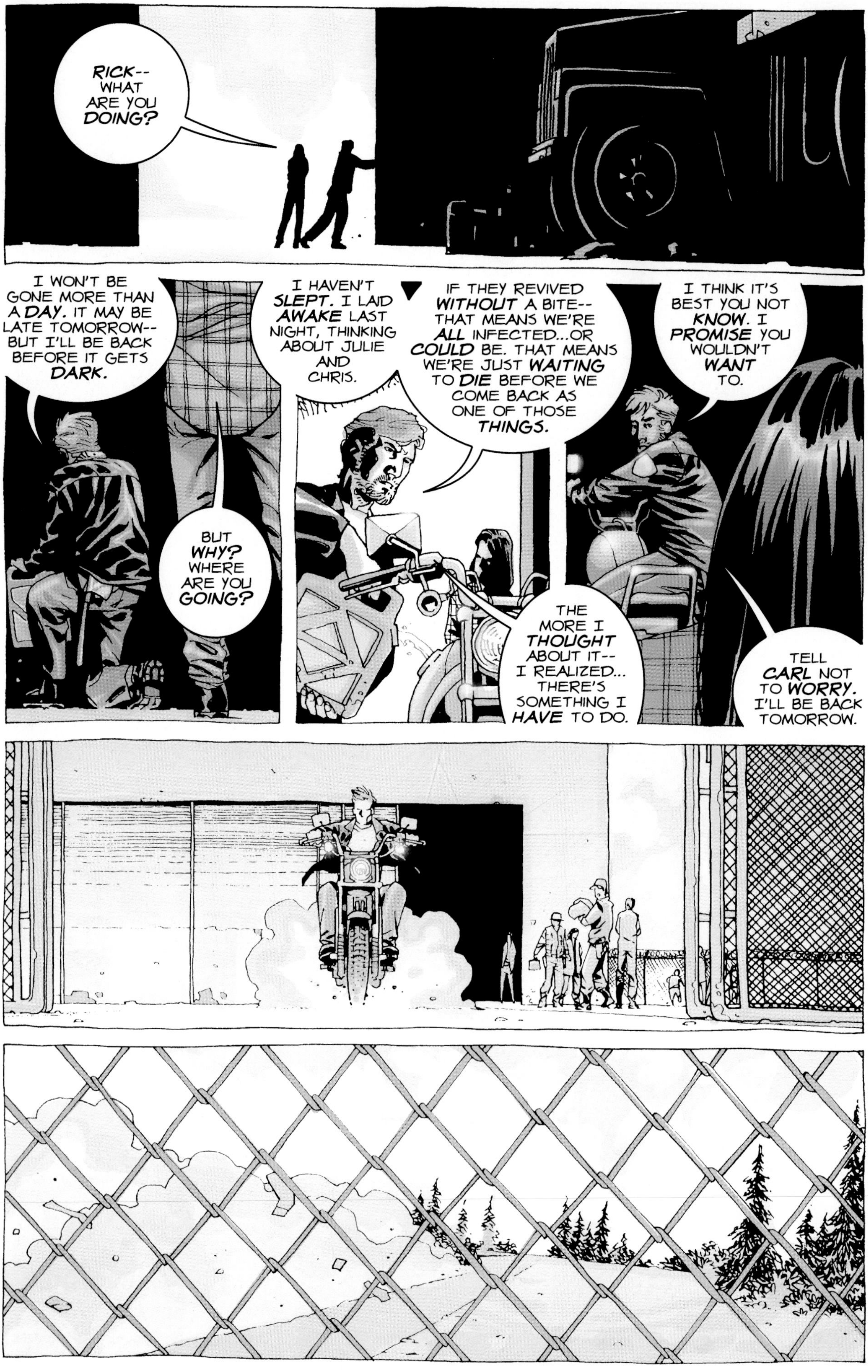
RICK-- WHAT ARE YOU DOING?
I WON'T BE GONE MORE THAN A DAY. IT MAY BE LATE TOMORROW-- BUT I'LL BE BACK BEFORE IT GETS DARK.
BUT WHY? WHERE ARE YOU GOING?
I HAVEN'T SLEPT. I LAID AWAKE LAST NIGHT, THINKING ABOUT JULIE AND CHRIS.
IF THEY REVIVED WITHOUT A BITE-- THAT MEANS WE'RE ALL INFECTED...OR COULD BE. THAT MEANS WE'RE JUST WAITING TO DIE BEFORE WE COME BACK AS ONE OF THOSE THINGS.
THE MORE I THOUGHT ABOUT IT-- I REALIZED... THERE'S SOMETHING I HAVE TO DO.
I THINK IT'S BEST YOU NOT KNOW. I PROMISE YOU WOULDN'T WANT TO.
TELL CARL NOT TO WORRY. I'LL BE BACK TOMORROW.

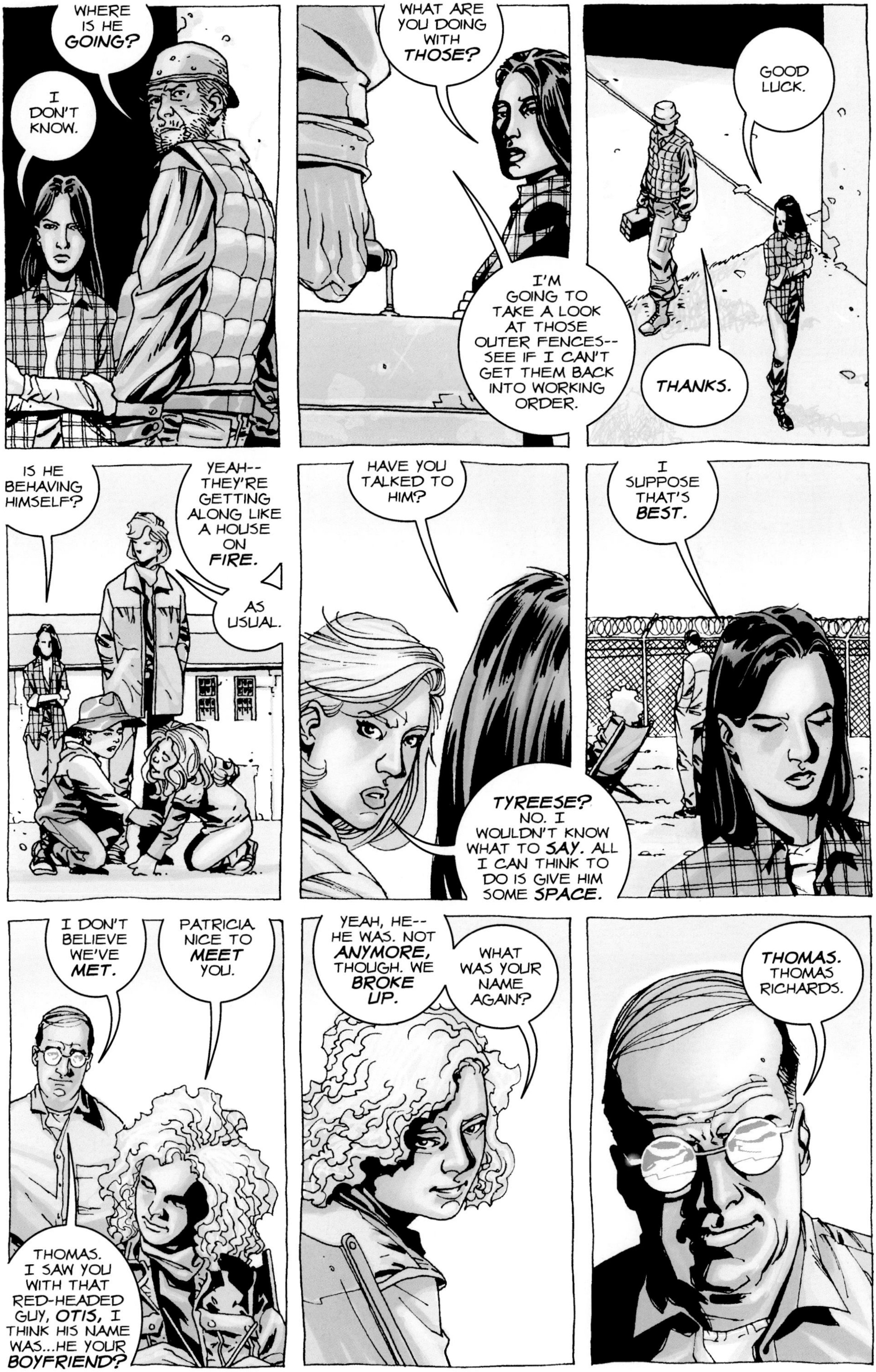
WHERE IS HE GOING?
I DON'T KNOW.
WHAT ARE YOU DOING WITH THOSE?
I'M GOING TO TAKE A LOOK AT THOSE OUTER FENCES-- SEE IF I CAN'T GET THEM BACK INTO WORKING ORDER.
GOOD LUCK.
THANKS.
IS HE BEHAVING HIMSELF?
YEAH-- THEY'RE GETTING ALONG LIKE A HOUSE ON FIRE.
AS USUAL.
HAVE YOU TALKED TO HIM?
TYREESE? NO. I WOULDN'T KNOW WHAT TO SAY. ALL I CAN THINK TO DO IS GIVE HIM SOME SPACE.
I SUPPOSE THAT'S BEST.
I DON'T BELIEVE WE'VE MET.
PATRICIA. NICE TO MEET YOU.
THOMAS. I SAW YOU WITH THAT RED-HEADED GUY, OTIS, I THINK HIS NAME WAS...HE YOUR BOYFRIEND?
YEAH, HE-- HE WAS. NOT ANYMORE, THOUGH. WE BROKE UP.
WHAT WAS YOUR NAME AGAIN?
THOMAS. THOMAS RICHARDS.

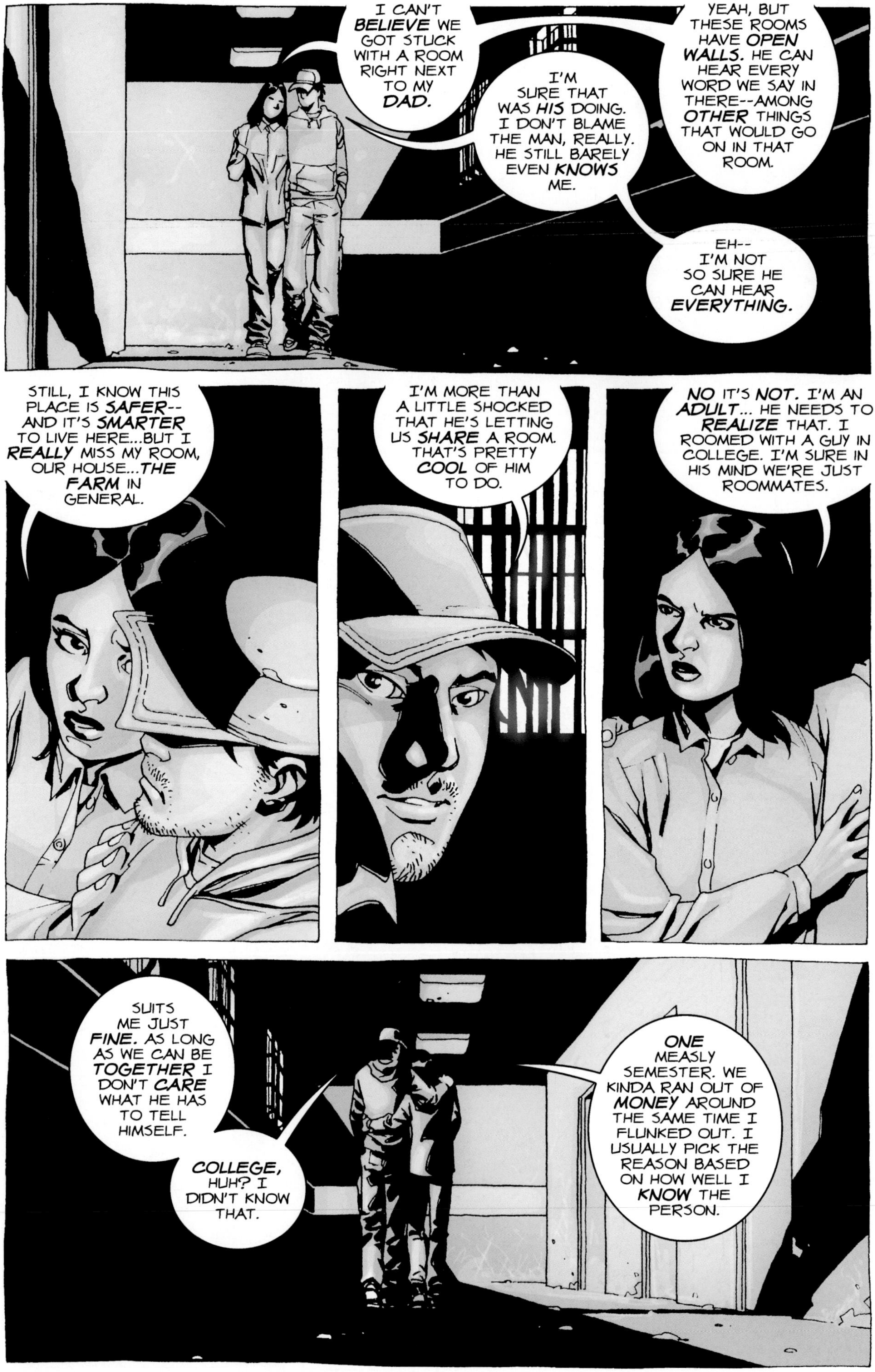
I CAN'T BELIEVE WE GOT STUCK WITH A ROOM RIGHT NEXT TO MY DAD.
I'M SURE THAT WAS HIS DOING. I DON'T BLAME THE MAN, REALLY. HE STILL BARELY EVEN KNOWS ME.
YEAH, BUT THESE ROOMS HAVE OPEN WALLS. HE CAN HEAR EVERY WORD WE SAY IN THERE--AMONG OTHER THINGS THAT WOULD GO ON IN THAT ROOM.
EH-- I'M NOT SO SURE HE CAN HEAR EVERYTHING.
STILL, I KNOW THIS PLACE IS SAFER--AND IT'S SMARTER TO LIVE HERE...BUT I REALLY MISS MY ROOM, OUR HOUSE...THE FARM IN GENERAL.
I'M MORE THAN A LITTLE SHOCKED THAT HE'S LETTING US SHARE A ROOM. THAT'S PRETTY COOL OF HIM TO DO.
NO IT'S NOT. I'M AN ADULT... HE NEEDS TO REALIZE THAT. I ROOMED WITH A GUY IN COLLEGE. I'M SURE IN HIS MIND WE'RE JUST ROOMMATES.
SUITS ME JUST FINE. AS LONG AS WE CAN BE TOGETHER I DON'T CARE WHAT HE HAS TO TELL HIMSELF.
COLLEGE, HUH? I DIDN'T KNOW THAT.
ONE MEASLY SEMESTER. WE KINDA RAN OUT OF MONEY AROUND THE SAME TIME I FLUNKED OUT. I USUALLY PICK THE REASON BASED ON HOW WELL I KNOW THE PERSON.

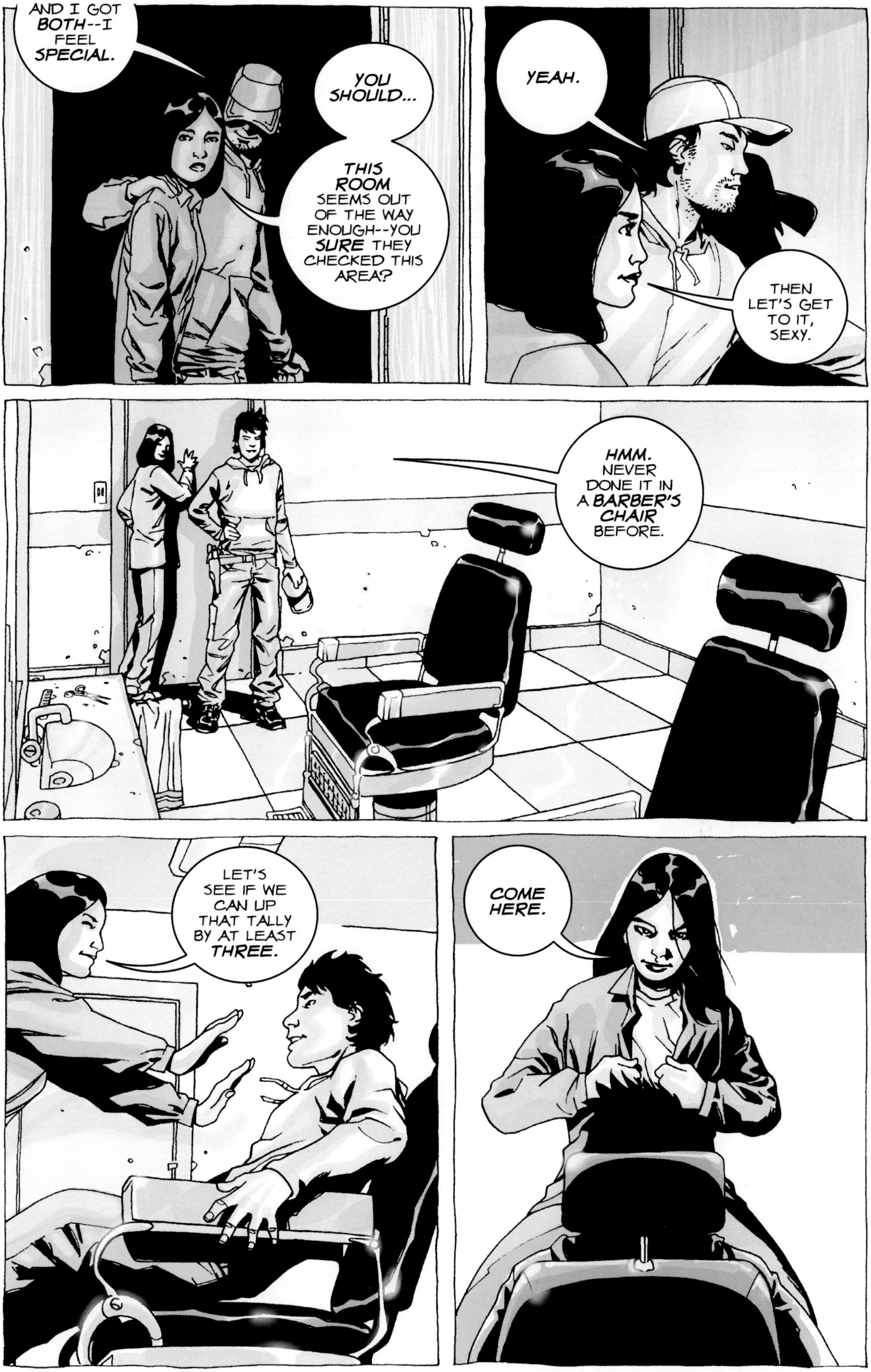
AND I GOT BOTH--I FEEL SPECIAL.
YOU SHOULD...
THIS ROOM SEEMS OUT OF THE WAY ENOUGH--YOU SURE THEY CHECKED THIS AREA?
YEAH.
THEN LET'S GET TO IT, SEXY.
HMM. NEVER DONE IT IN A BARBER'S CHAIR BEFORE.
LET'S SEE IF WE CAN UP THAT TALLY BY AT LEAST THREE.
COME HERE.

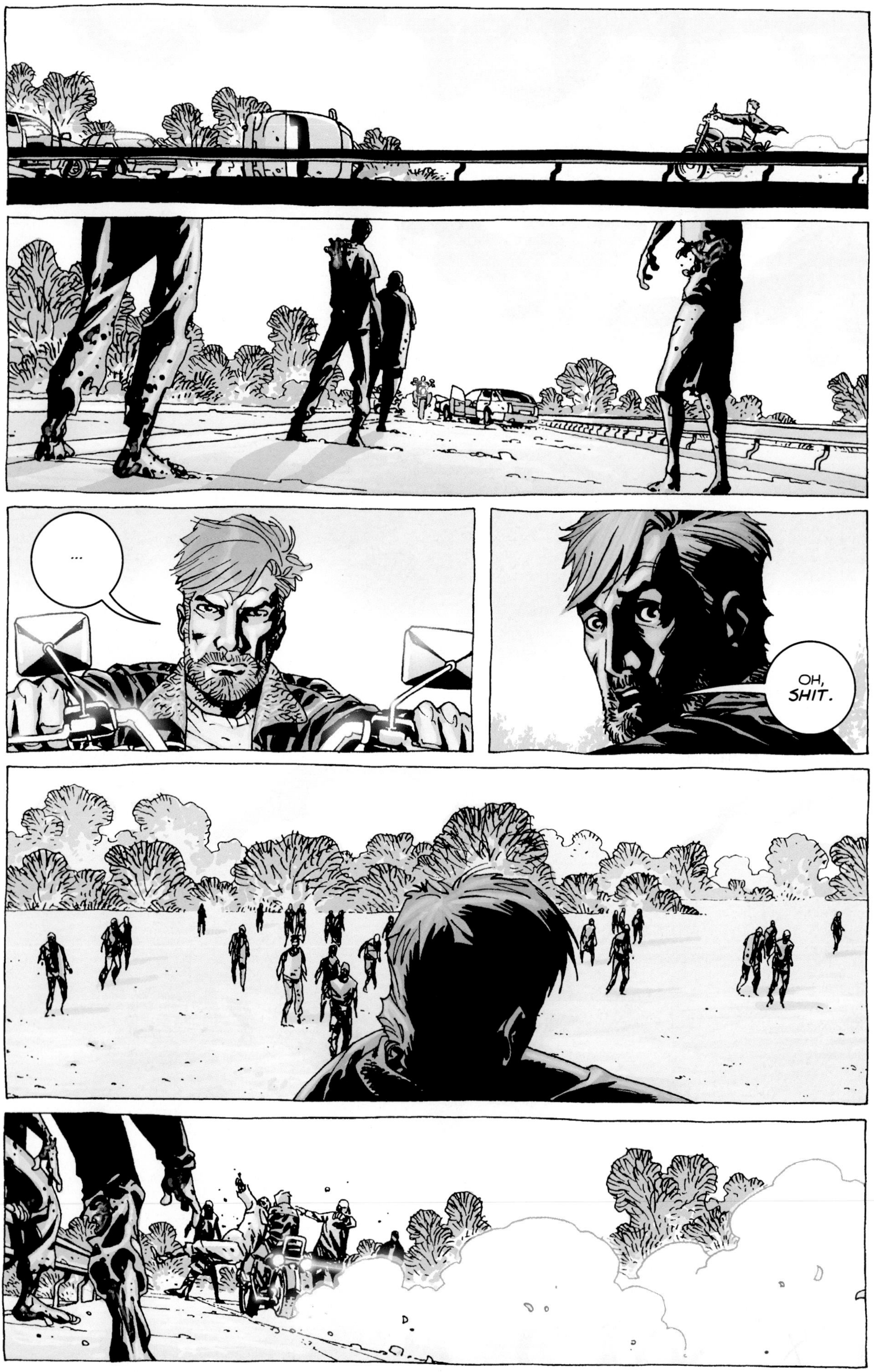
...
OH, SHIT.

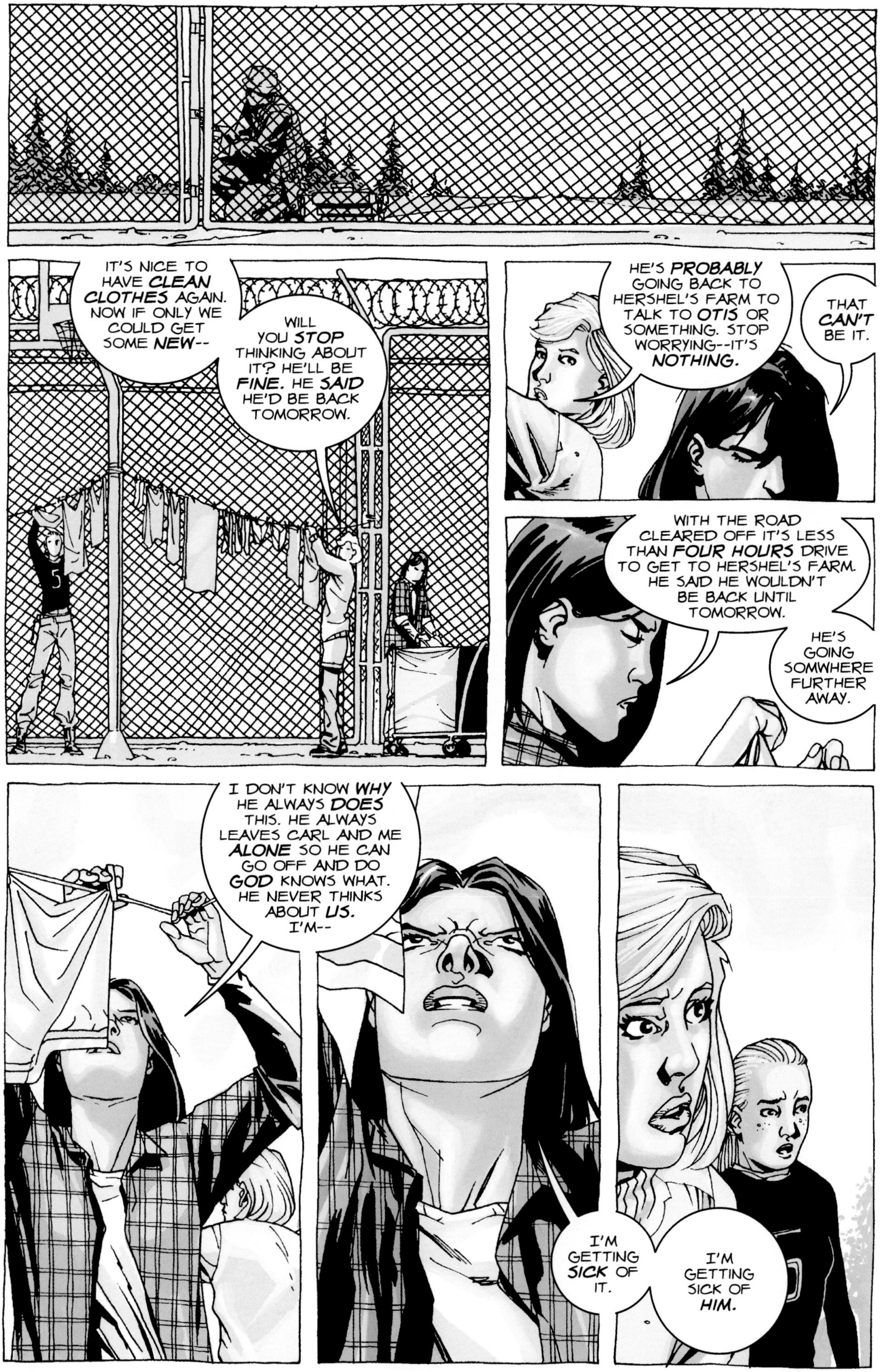
IT'S NICE TO HAVE CLEAN CLOTHES AGAIN. NOW IF ONLY WE COULD GET SOME NEW--
WILL YOU STOP THINKING ABOUT IT? HE'LL BE FINE. HE SAID HE'D BE BACK TOMORROW.
HE'S PROBABLY GOING BACK TO HERSHEL'S FARM TO TALK TO OTIS OR SOMETHING. STOP WORRYING--IT'S NOTHING.
THAT CAN'T BE IT.
WITH THE ROAD CLEARED OFF IT'S LESS THAN FOUR HOURS DRIVE TO GET TO HERSHEL'S FARM. HE SAID HE WOULDN'T BE BACK UNTIL TOMORROW.
HE'S GOING SOMWHERE FURTHER AWAY.
I DON'T KNOW WHY HE ALWAYS DOES THIS. HE ALWAYS LEAVES CARL AND ME ALONE SO HE CAN GO OFF AND DO GOD KNOWS WHAT. HE NEVER THINKS ABOUT US. I'M--
I'M GETTING SICK OF IT.
I'M GETTING SICK OF HIM.

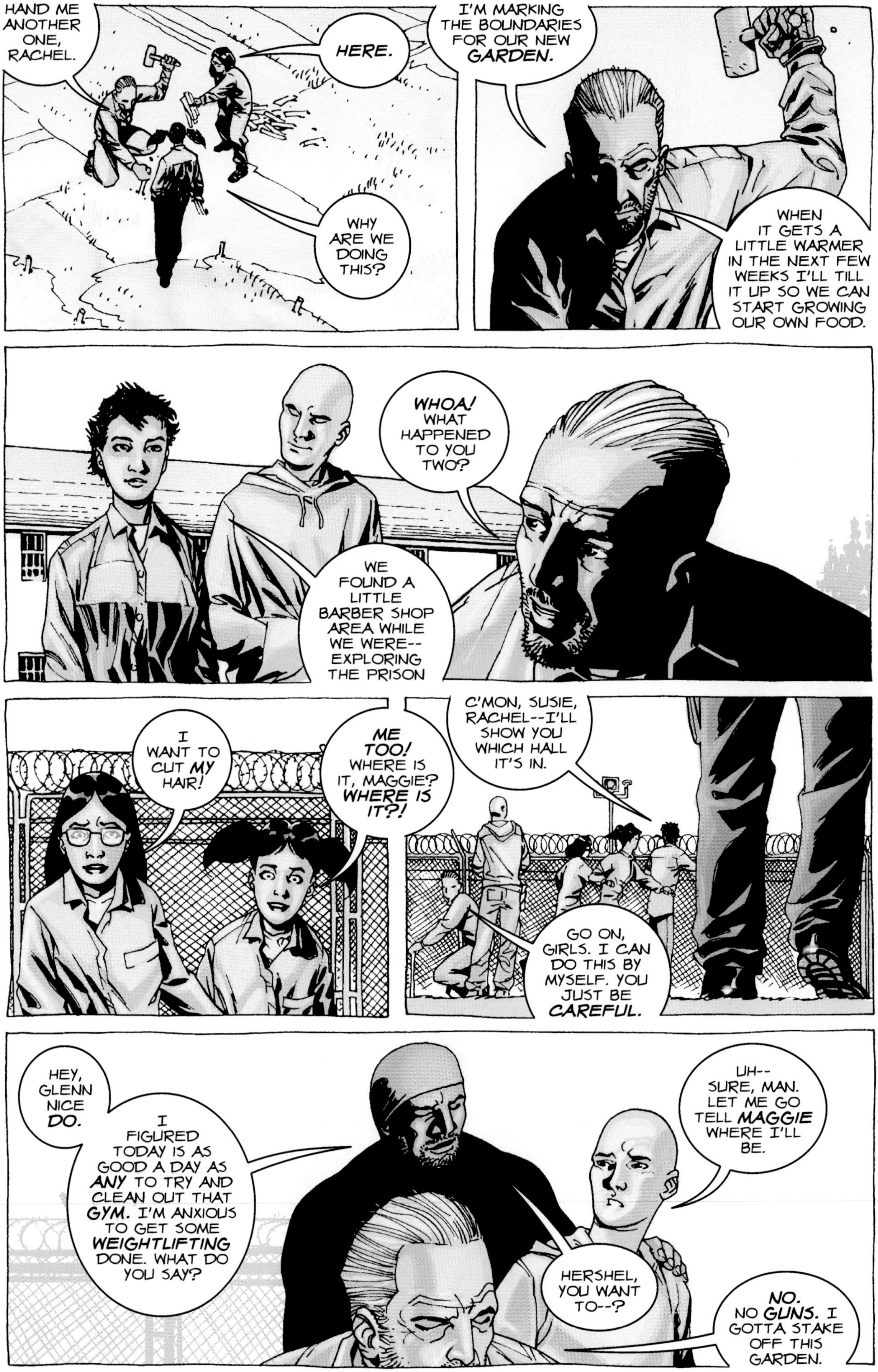
HAND ME ANOTHER ONE, RACHEL.
HERE.
WHY ARE WE DOING THIS?
I'M MARKING THE BOUNDARIES FOR OUR NEW GARDEN.
WHEN IT GETS A LITTLE WARMER IN THE NEXT FEW WEEKS I'LL TILL IT UP SO WE CAN START GROWING OUR OWN FOOD.
WHOA! WHAT HAPPENED TO YOU TWO?
WE FOUND A LITTLE BARBER SHOP AREA WHILE WE WERE-- EXPLORING THE PRISON
I WANT TO CUT MY HAIR!
ME TOO! WHERE IS IT, MAGGIE? WHERE IS IT?!
C'MON, SUSIE, RACHEL--I'LL SHOW YOU WHICH HALL IT'S IN.
GO ON, GIRLS. I CAN DO THIS BY MYSELF. YOU JUST BE CAREFUL.
HEY, GLENN NICE DO.
I FIGURED TODAY IS AS GOOD A DAY AS ANY TO TRY AND CLEAN OUT THAT GYM. I'M ANXIOUS TO GET SOME WEIGHTLIFTING DONE. WHAT DO YOU SAY?
UH-- SURE, MAN. LET ME GO TELL MAGGIE WHERE I'LL BE.
HERSHEL, YOU WANT TO--?
NO. NO GUNS. I GOTTA STAKE OFF THIS GARDEN.

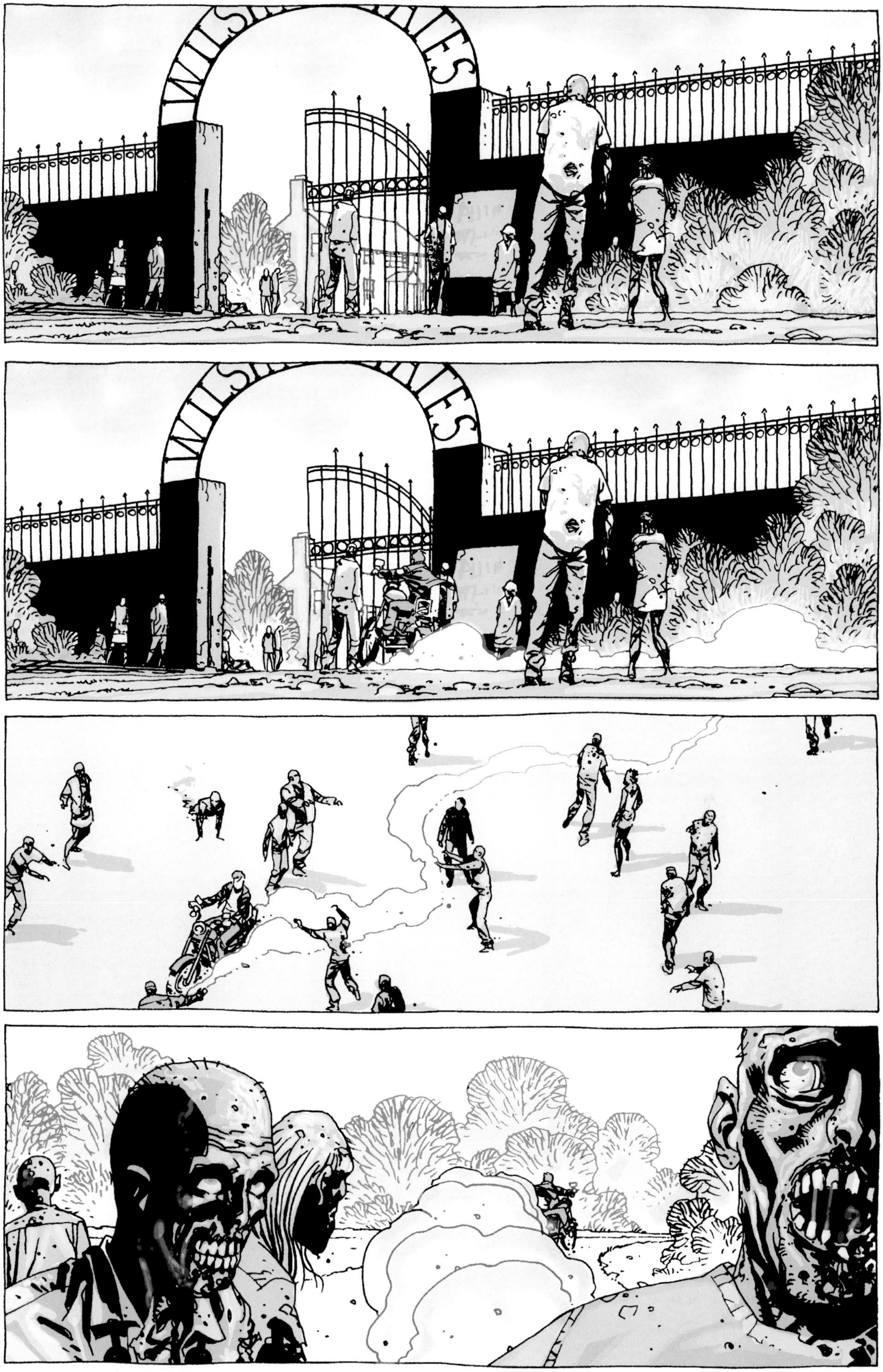

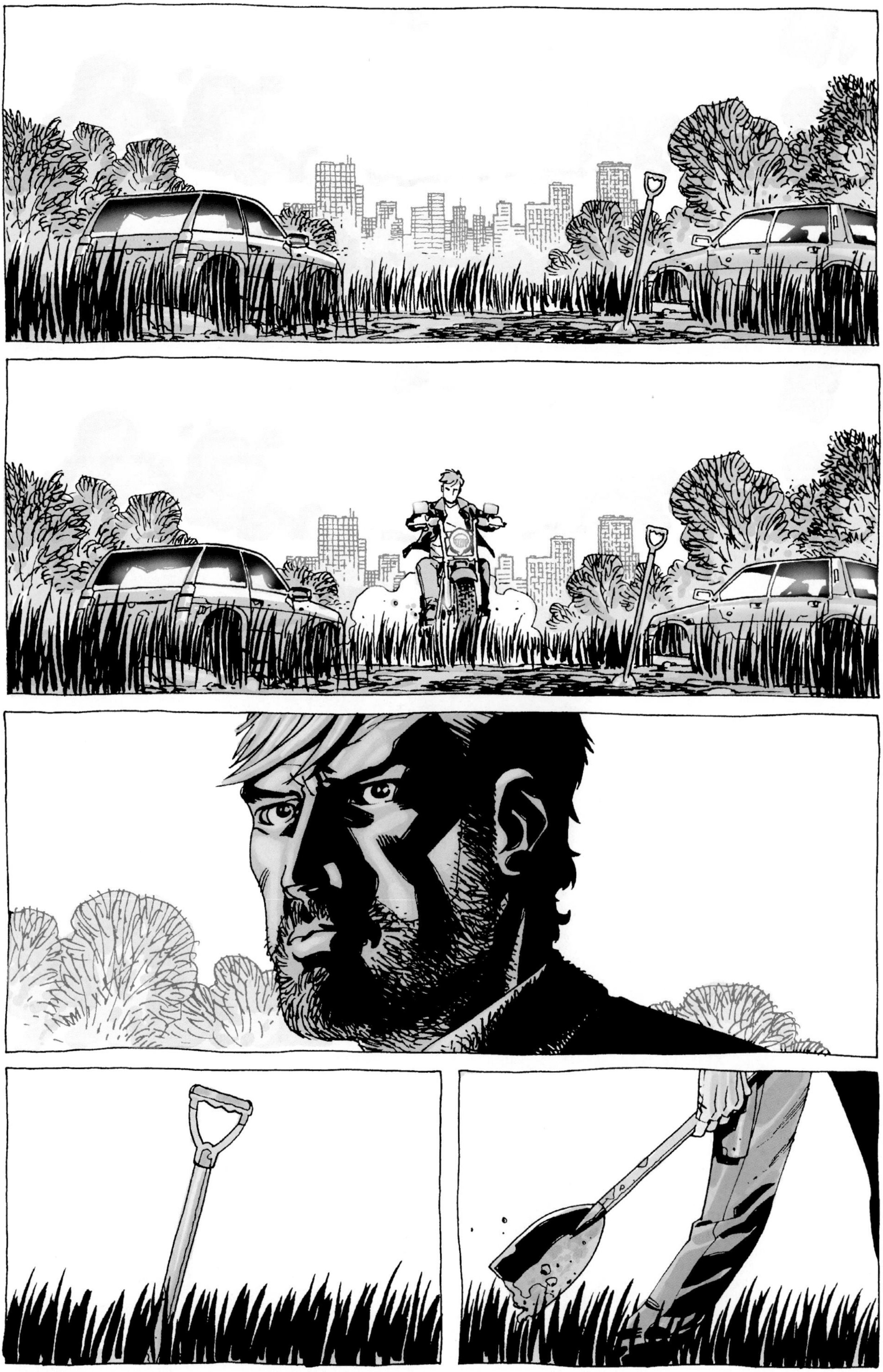

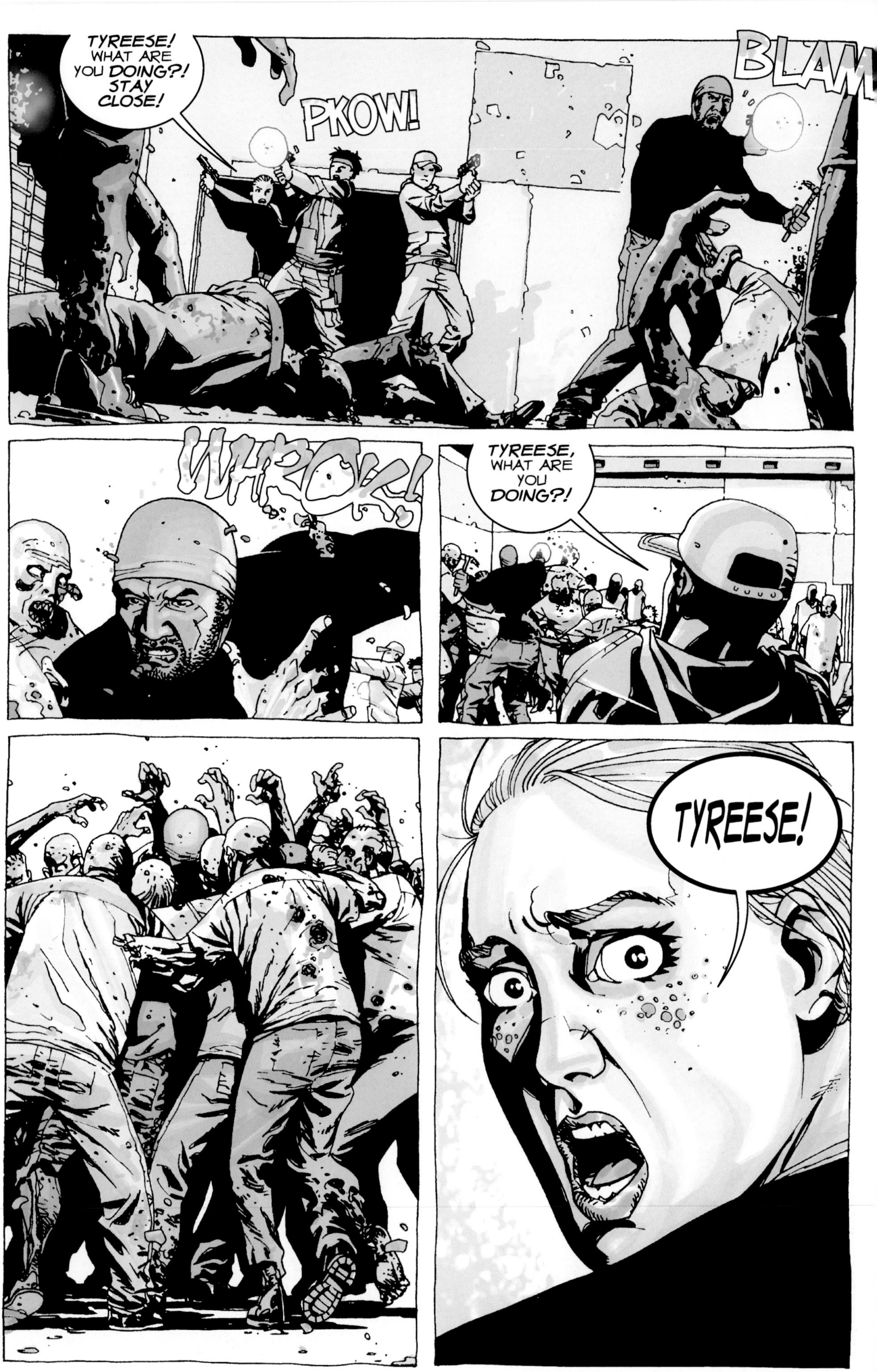

TYREESE! WHAT ARE YOU DOING?! STAY CLOSE!
PKOW!
BLAM
WHROK!
TYREESE, WHAT ARE YOU DOING?!
TYREESE!

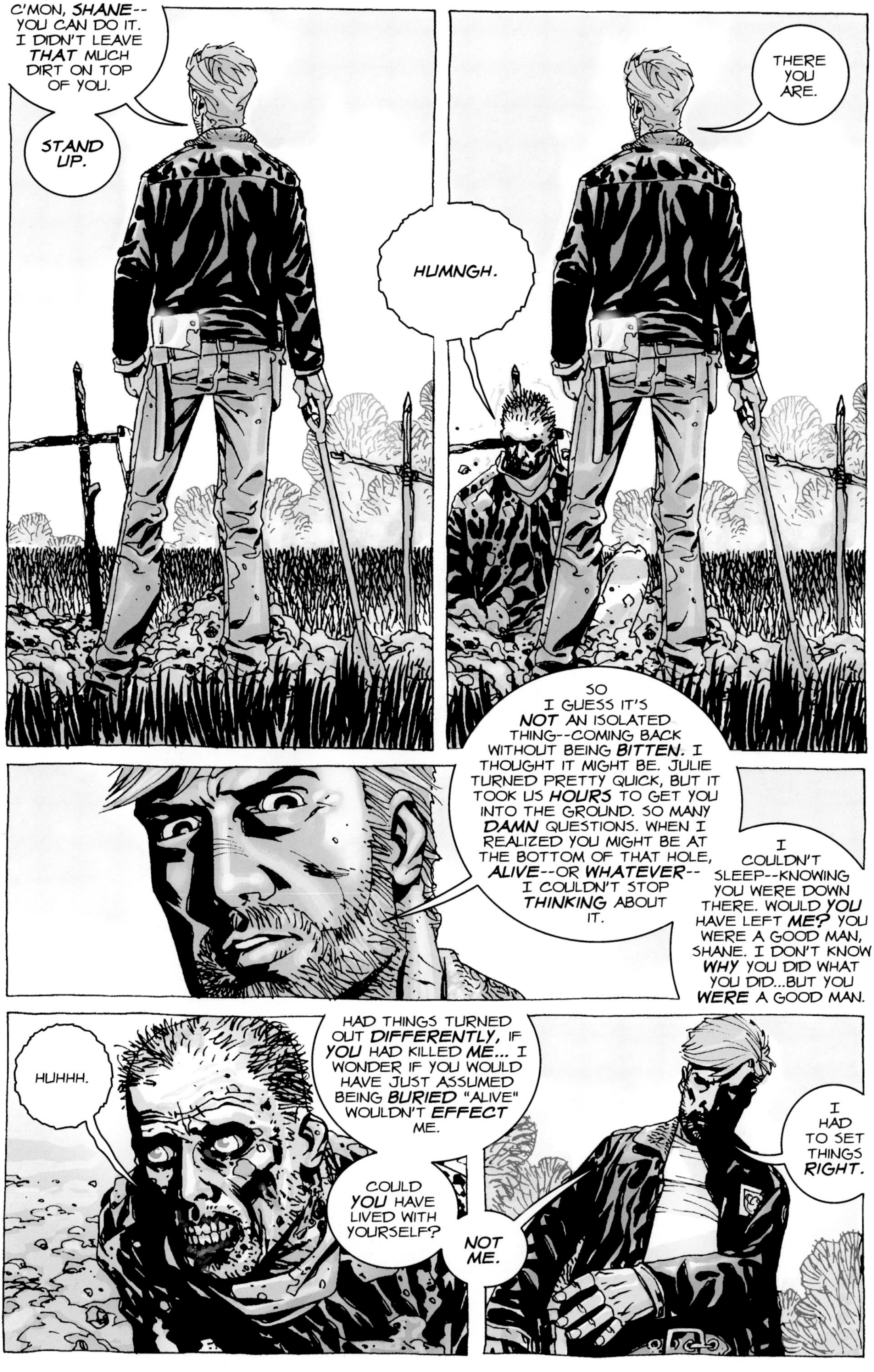

C'MON, SHANE--YOU CAN DO IT. I DIDN'T LEAVE THAT MUCH DIRT ON TOP OF YOU.
STAND UP.
THERE YOU ARE.
HUMNGH.
SO I GUESS IT'S NOT AN ISOLATED THING--COMING BACK WITHOUT BEING BITTEN. I THOUGHT IT MIGHT BE. JULIE TURNED PRETTY QUICK, BUT IT TOOK US HOURS TO GET YOU INTO THE GROUND. SO MANY DAMN QUESTIONS. WHEN I REALIZED YOU MIGHT BE AT THE BOTTOM OF THAT HOLE, ALIVE--OR WHATEVER--I COULDN'T STOP THINKING ABOUT IT.
I COULDN'T SLEEP--KNOWING YOU WERE DOWN THERE. WOULD YOU HAVE LEFT ME? YOU WERE A GOOD MAN, SHANE. I DON'T KNOW WHY YOU DID WHAT YOU DID...BUT YOU WERE A GOOD MAN.
HUHHH.
HAD THINGS TURNED OUT DIFFERENTLY, IF YOU HAD KILLED ME... I WONDER IF YOU WOULD HAVE JUST ASSUMED BEING BURIED "ALIVE" WOULDN'T EFFECT ME.
COULD YOU HAVE LIVED WITH YOURSELF?
NOT ME.
I HAD TO SET THINGS RIGHT.

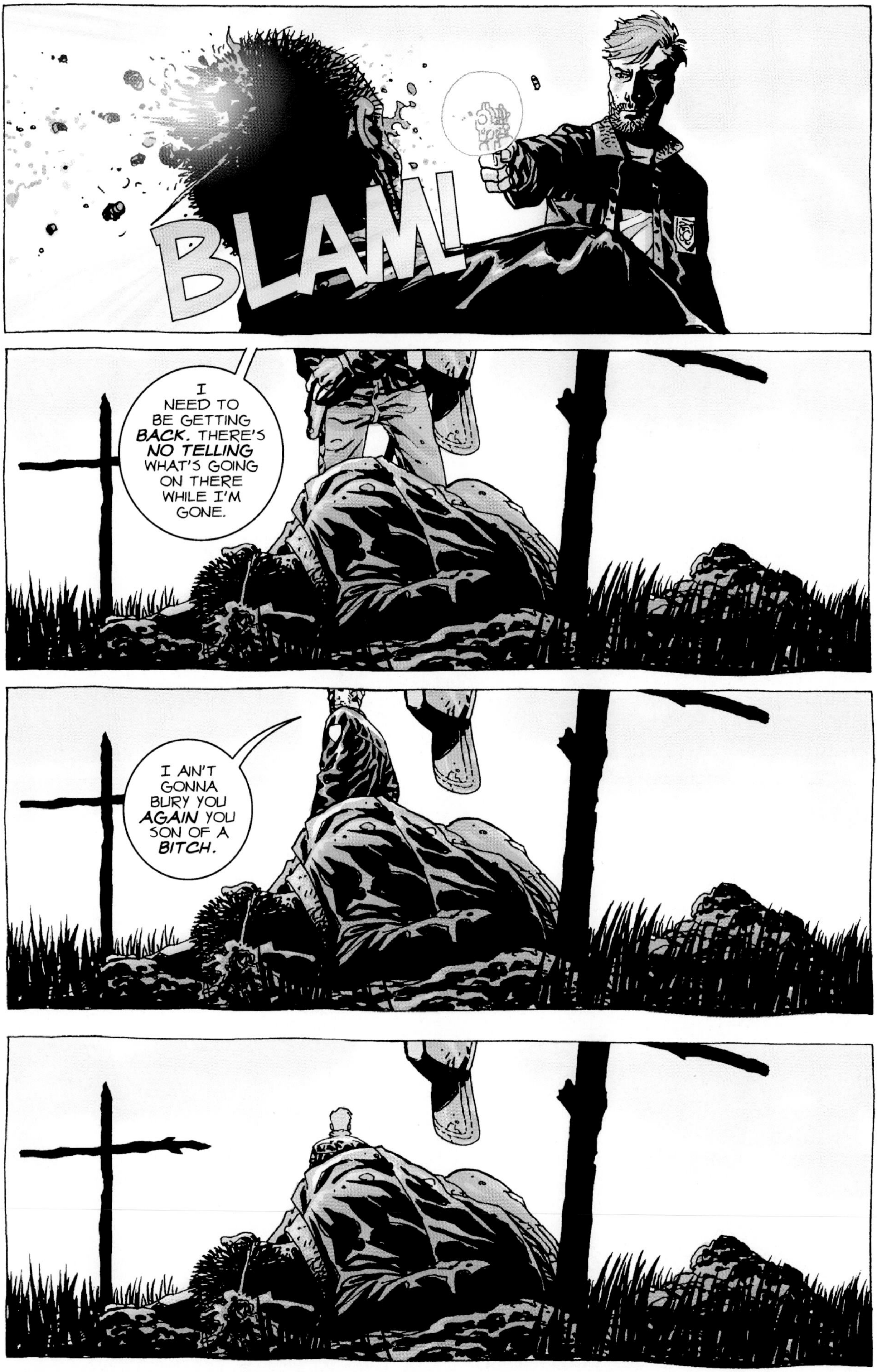
BLAM!
I NEED TO BE GETTING BACK. THERE'S NO TELLING WHAT'S GOING ON THERE WHILE I'M GONE.
I AIN'T GONNA BURY YOU AGAIN YOU SON OF A BITCH.

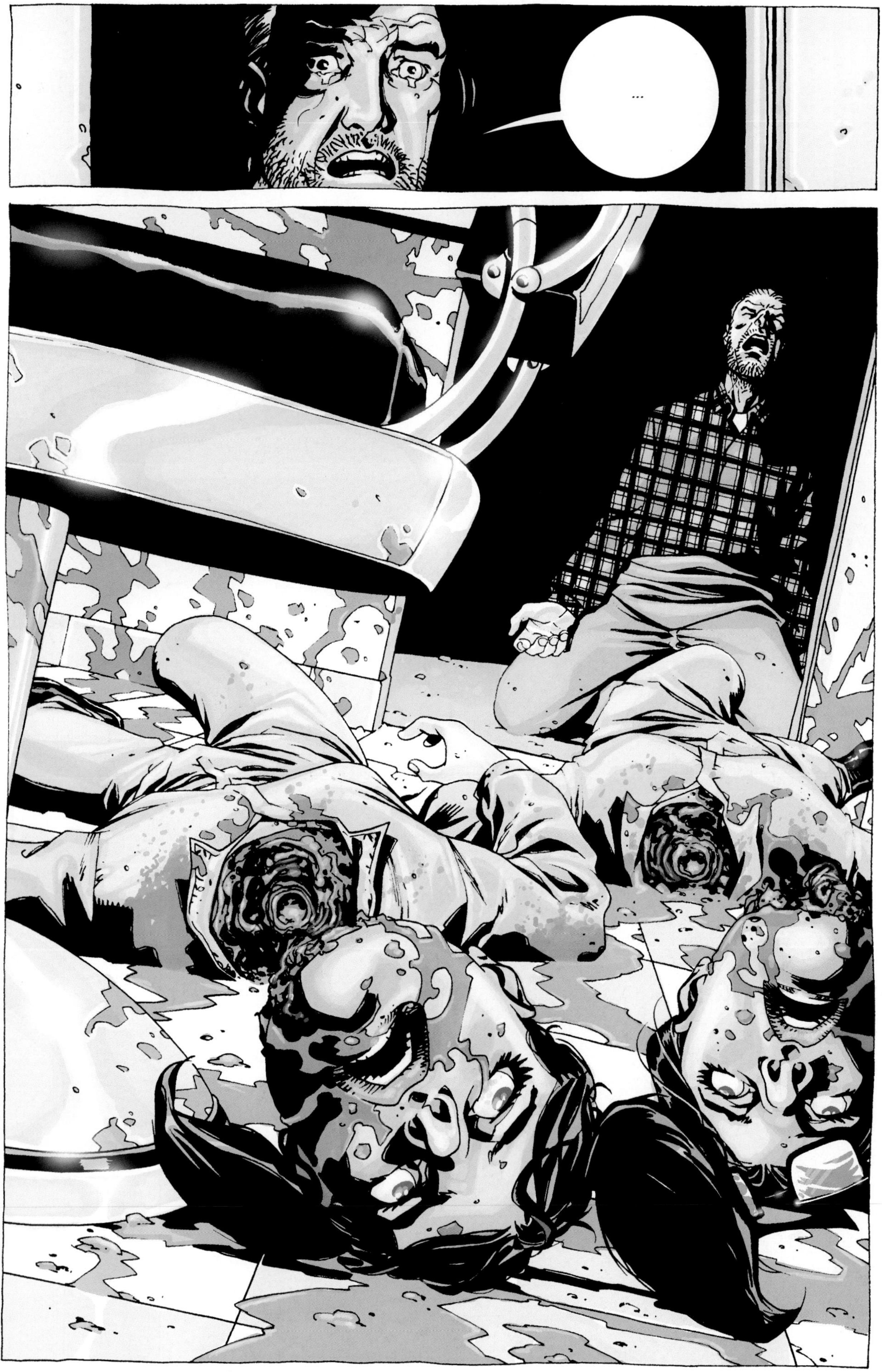
...

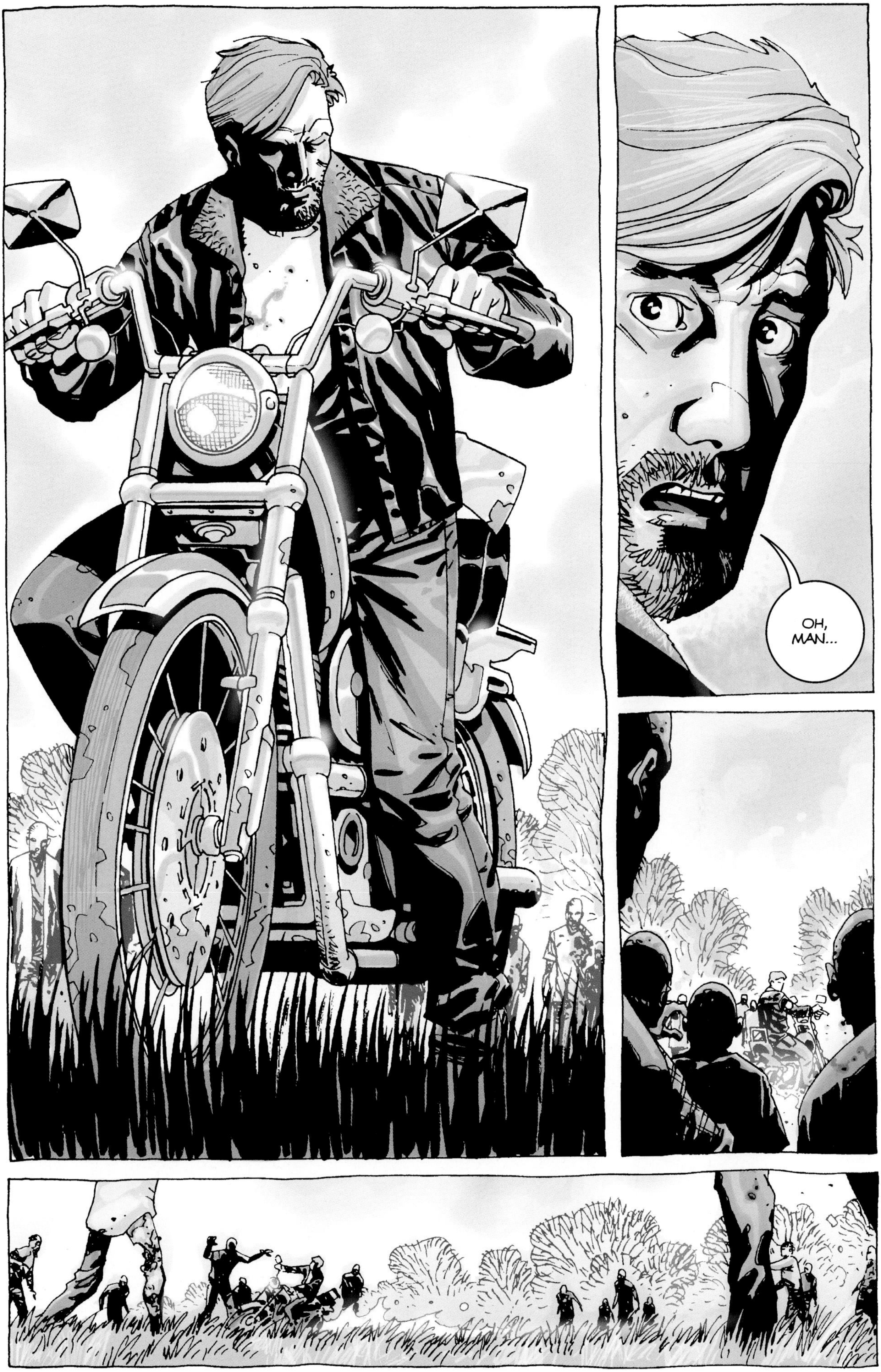
OH, MAN...

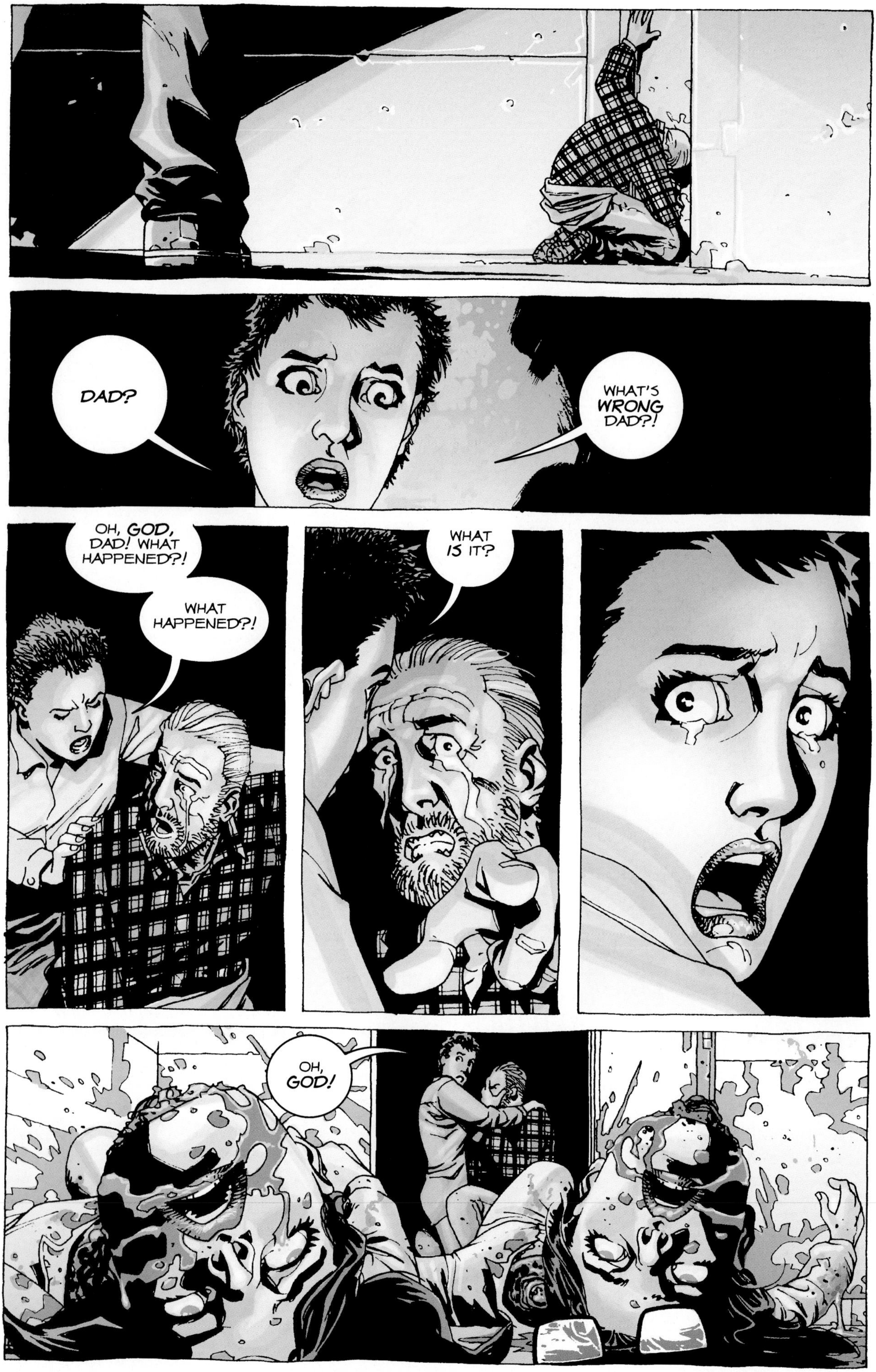
DAD?
WHAT'S WRONG DAD?!
OH, GOD, DAD! WHAT HAPPENED?!
WHAT HAPPENED?!
WHAT IS IT?
OH, GOD!

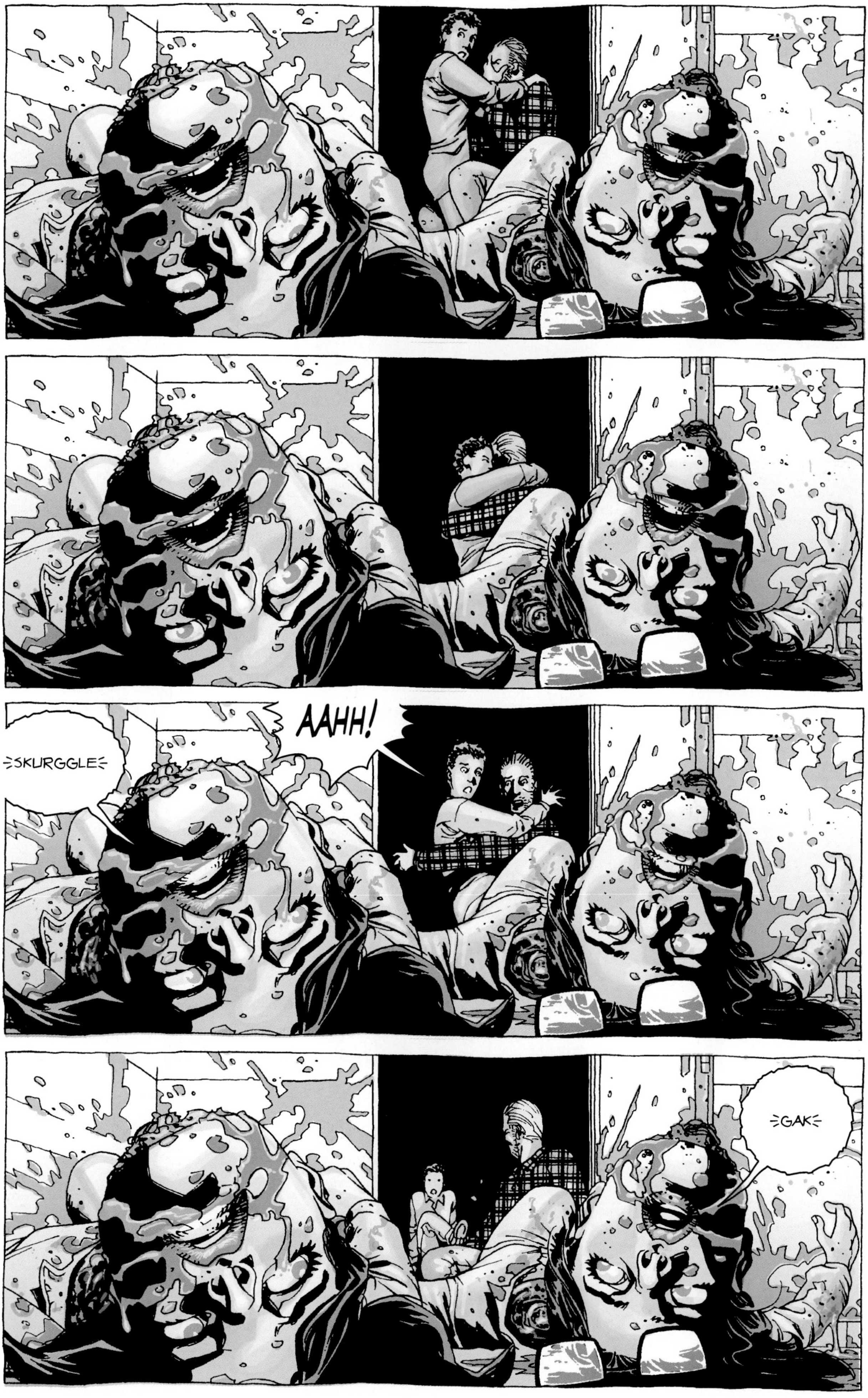
SKURGGLE
AAHH!
GAK

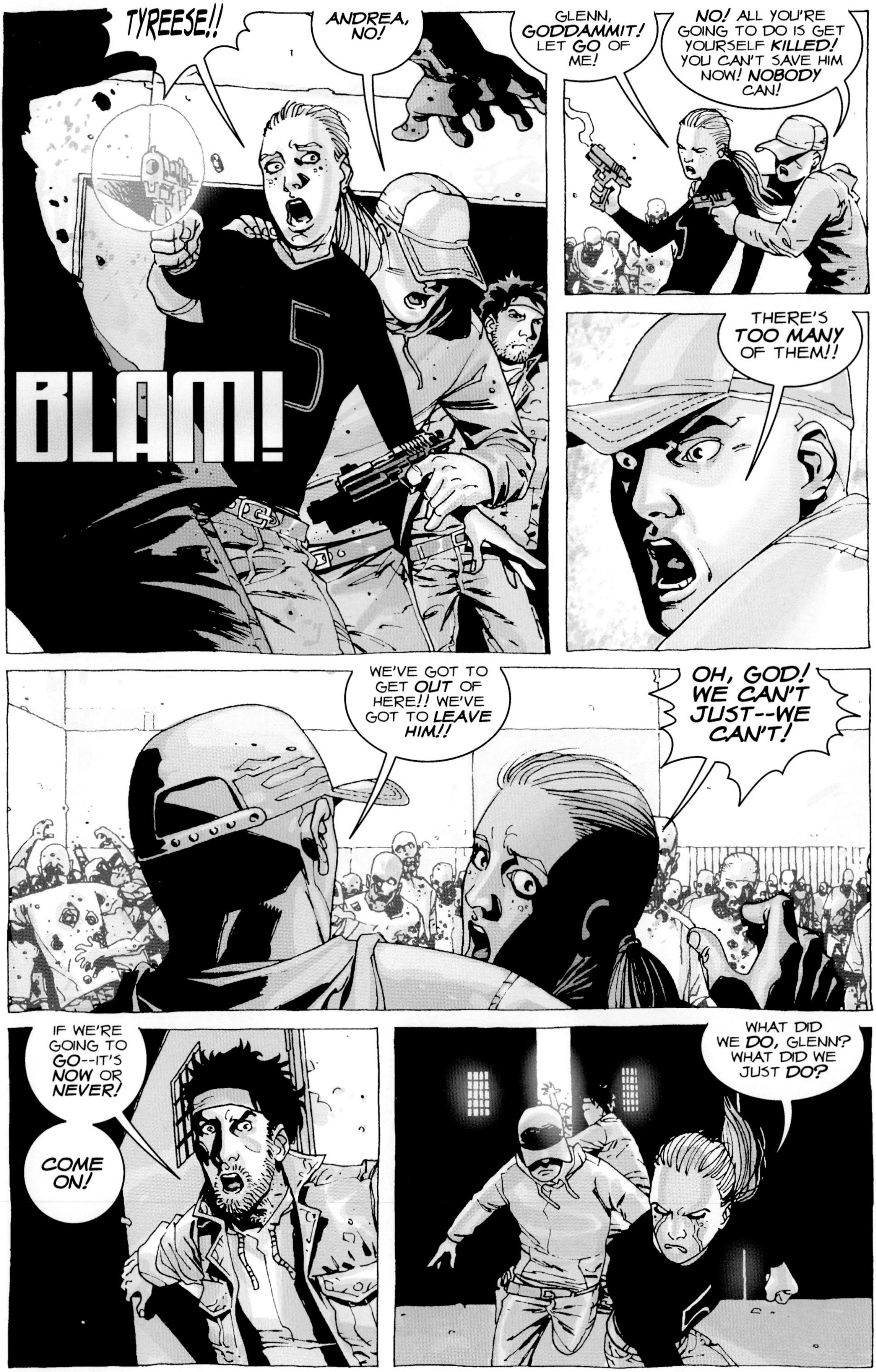

TYREESE!!
ANDREA, NO!
BLAM!
GLENN, GODDAMMIT! LET GO OF ME!
NO! ALL YOU'RE GOING TO DO IS GET YOURSELF KILLED! YOU CAN'T SAVE HIM NOW! NOBODY CAN!
THERE'S TOO MANY OF THEM!!
WE'VE GOT TO GET OUT OF HERE!! WE'VE GOT TO LEAVE HIM!!
OH, GOD! WE CAN'T JUST--WE CAN'T!
IF WE'RE GOING TO GO--IT'S NOW OR NEVER!
COME ON!
WHAT DID WE DO, GLENN? WHAT DID WE JUST DO?

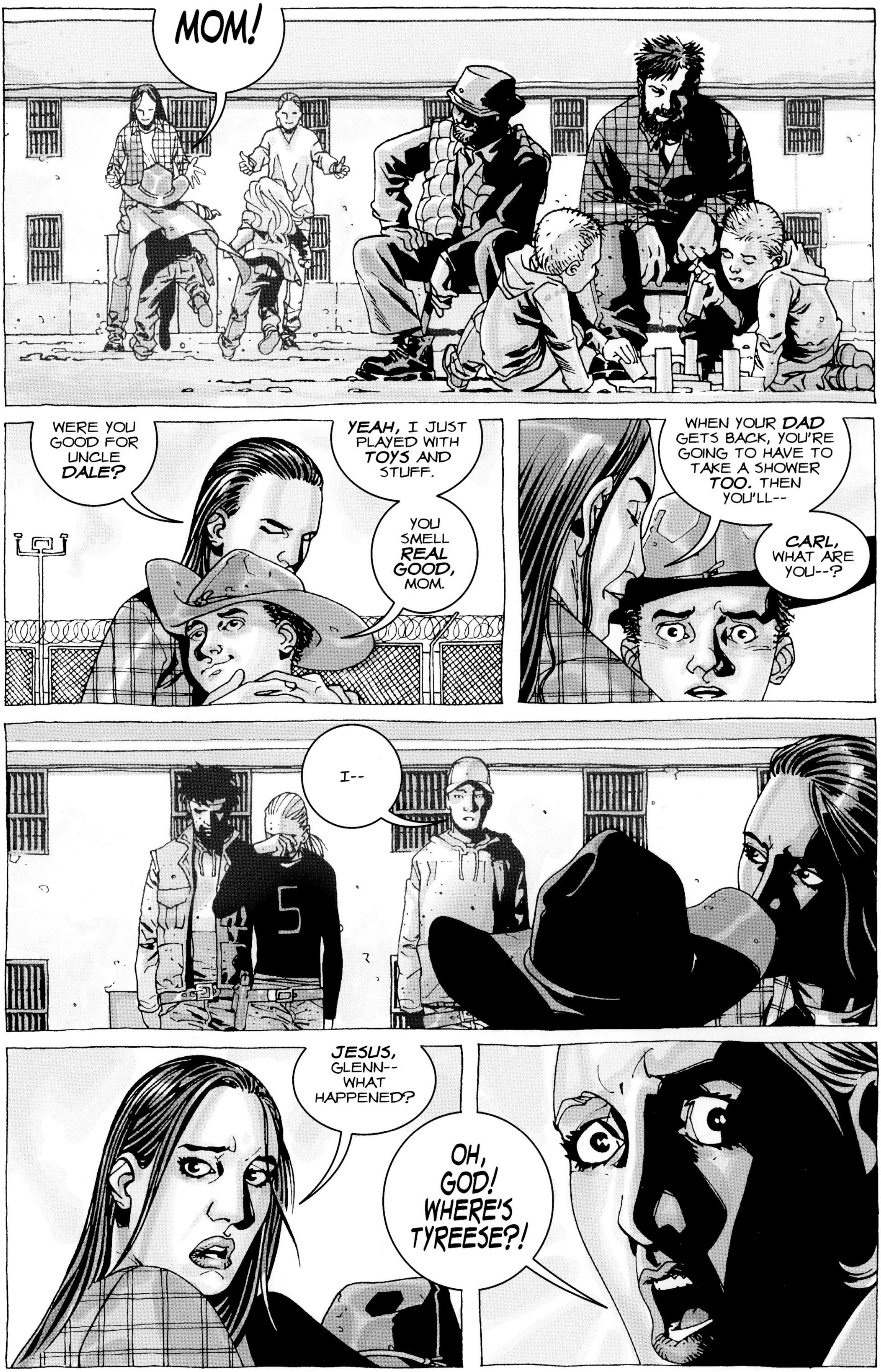
MOM!
WERE YOU GOOD FOR UNCLE DALE?
YEAH, I JUST PLAYED WITH TOYS AND STUFF.
YOU SMELL REAL GOOD, MOM.
WHEN YOUR DAD GETS BACK, YOU'RE GOING TO HAVE TO TAKE A SHOWER TOO. THEN YOU'LL--
CARL, WHAT ARE YOU--?
I--
JESUS, GLENN-- WHAT HAPPENED?
OH, GOD! WHERE'S TYREESE?!

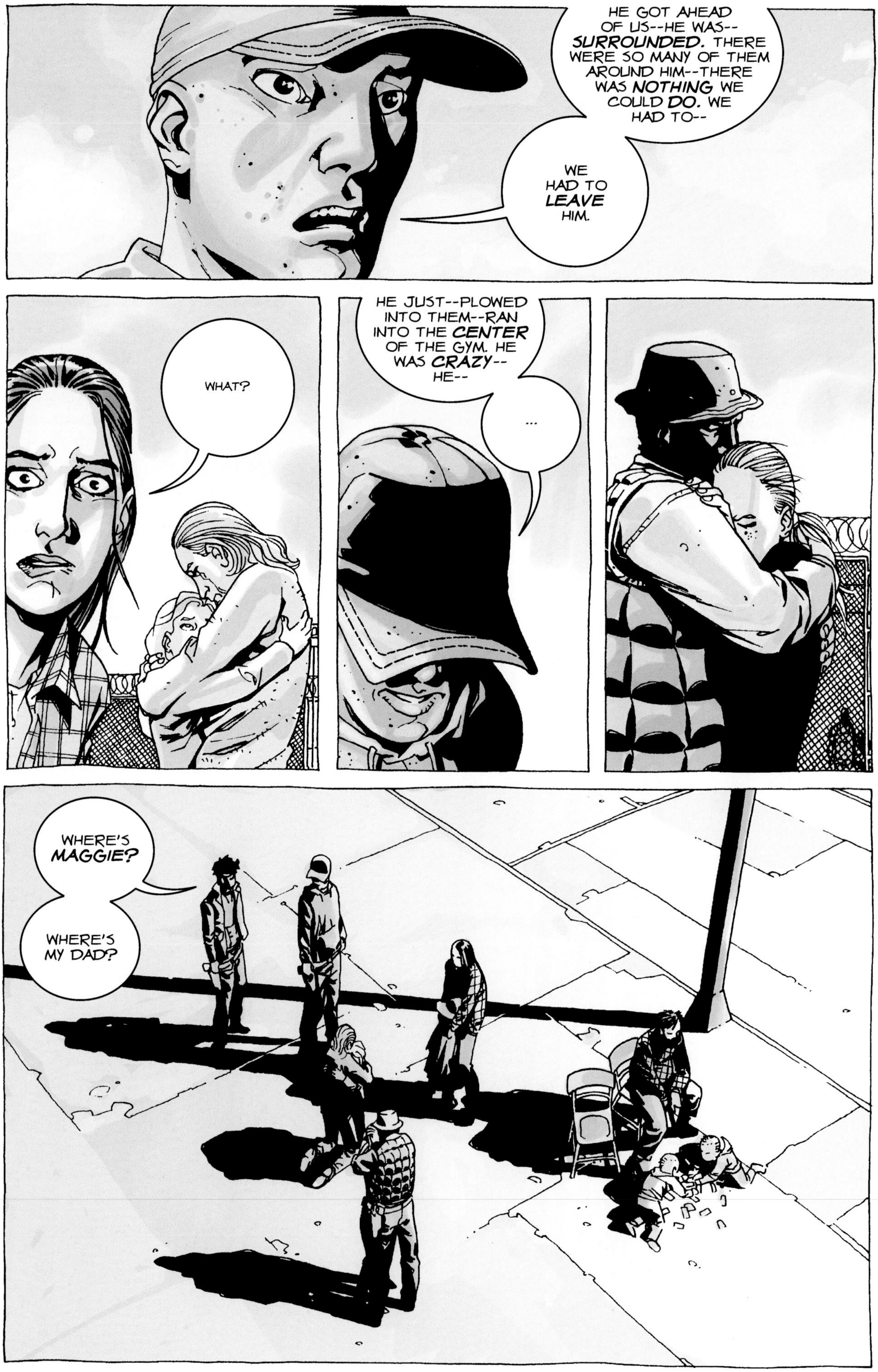
HE GOT AHEAD OF US--HE WAS-- SURROUNDED. THERE WERE SO MANY OF THEM AROUND HIM--THERE WAS NOTHING WE COULD DO. WE HAD TO--
WE HAD TO LEAVE HIM.
WHAT?
HE JUST--PLOWED INTO THEM--RAN INTO THE CENTER OF THE GYM. HE WAS CRAZY-- HE--
...
WHERE'S MAGGIE?
WHERE'S MY DAD?

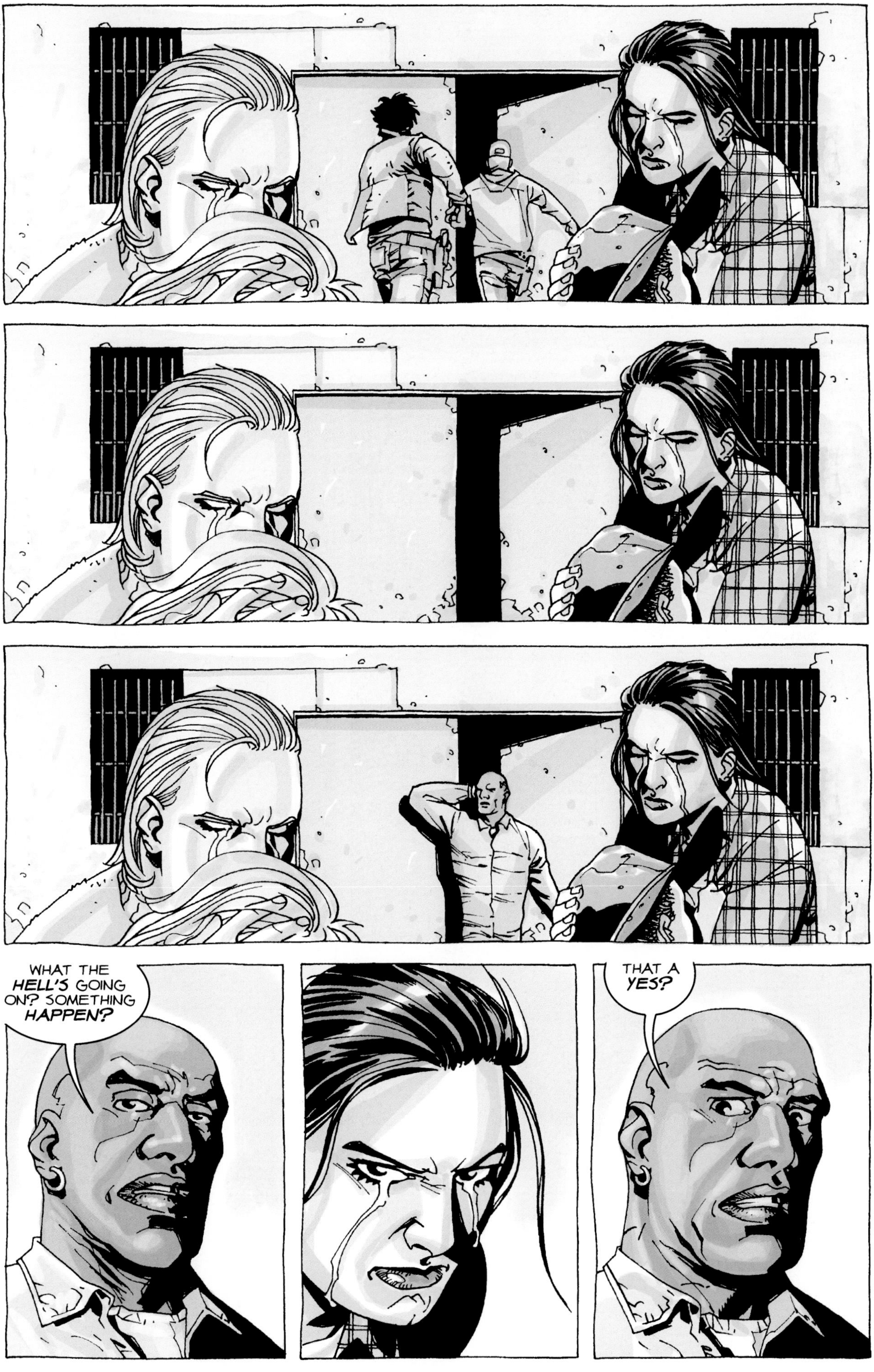
WHAT THE HELL'S GOING ON? SOMETHING HAPPEN?
THAT A YES?

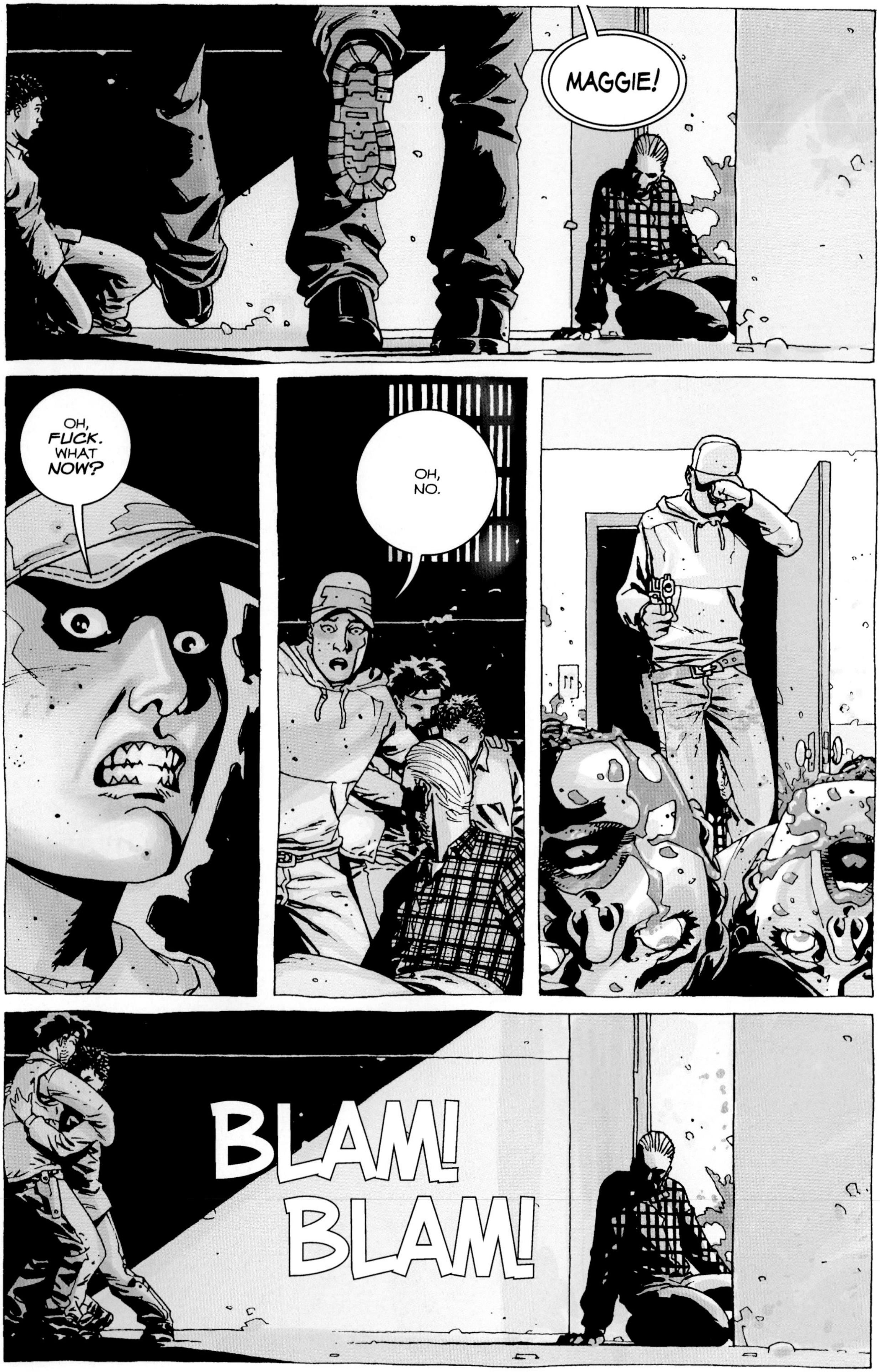
MAGGIE!
OH, FUCK. WHAT NOW?
OH, NO.
BLAM! BLAM!

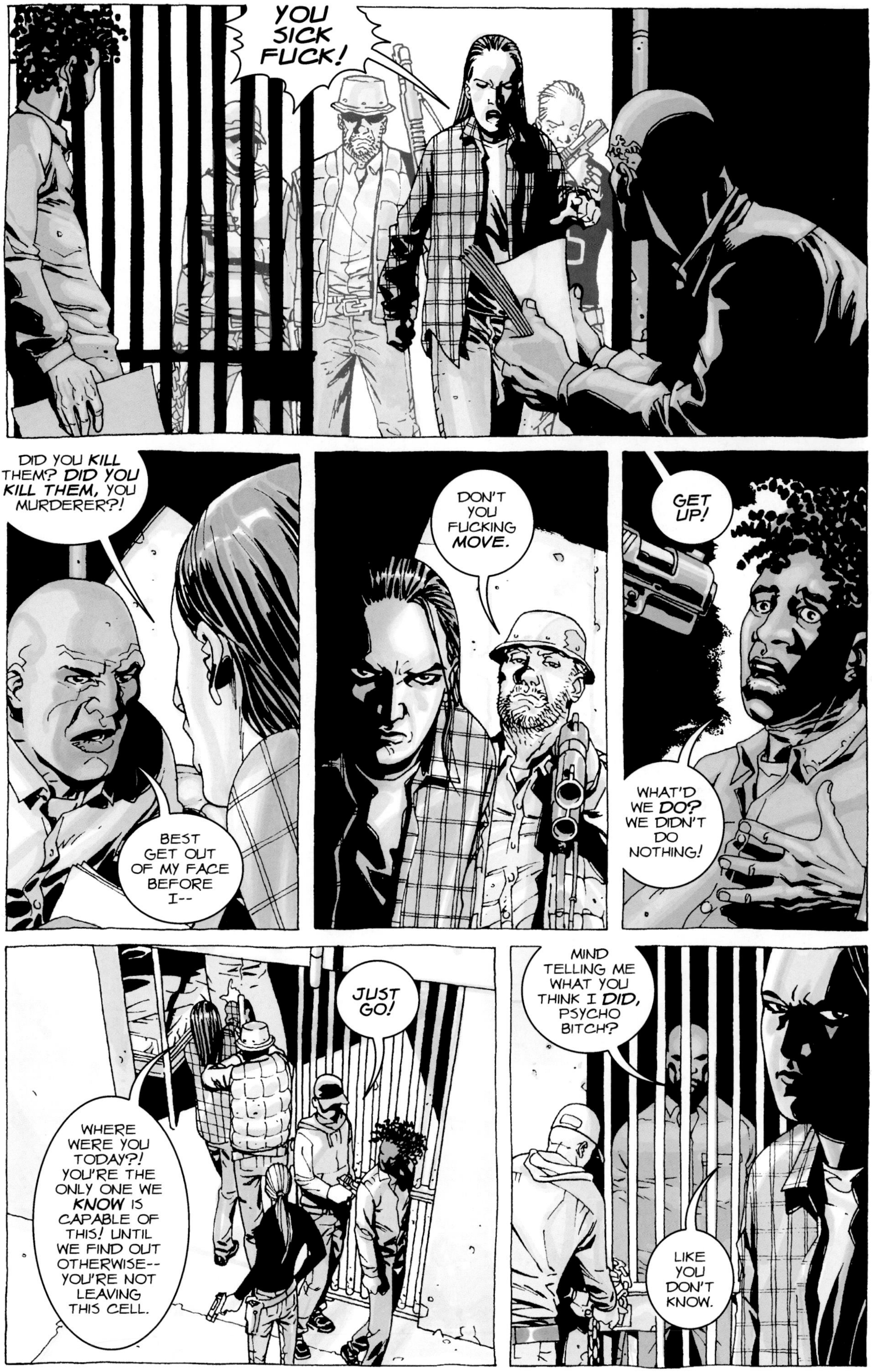
YOU SICK FUCK!
DID YOU **KILL** THEM? ***DID YOU KILL THEM,*** YOU MURDERER?!
BEST GET OUT OF MY FACE BEFORE I--
DON'T YOU FUCKING ***MOVE.***
GET UP!
WHAT'D WE ***DO?*** WE DIDN'T DO NOTHING!
JUST GO!
WHERE WERE YOU TODAY?! YOU'RE THE ONLY ONE WE ***KNOW*** IS CAPABLE OF THIS! UNTIL WE FIND OUT OTHERWISE-- YOU'RE NOT LEAVING THIS CELL.
MIND TELLING ME WHAT YOU THINK I ***DID,*** PSYCHO BITCH?
LIKE YOU DON'T KNOW.

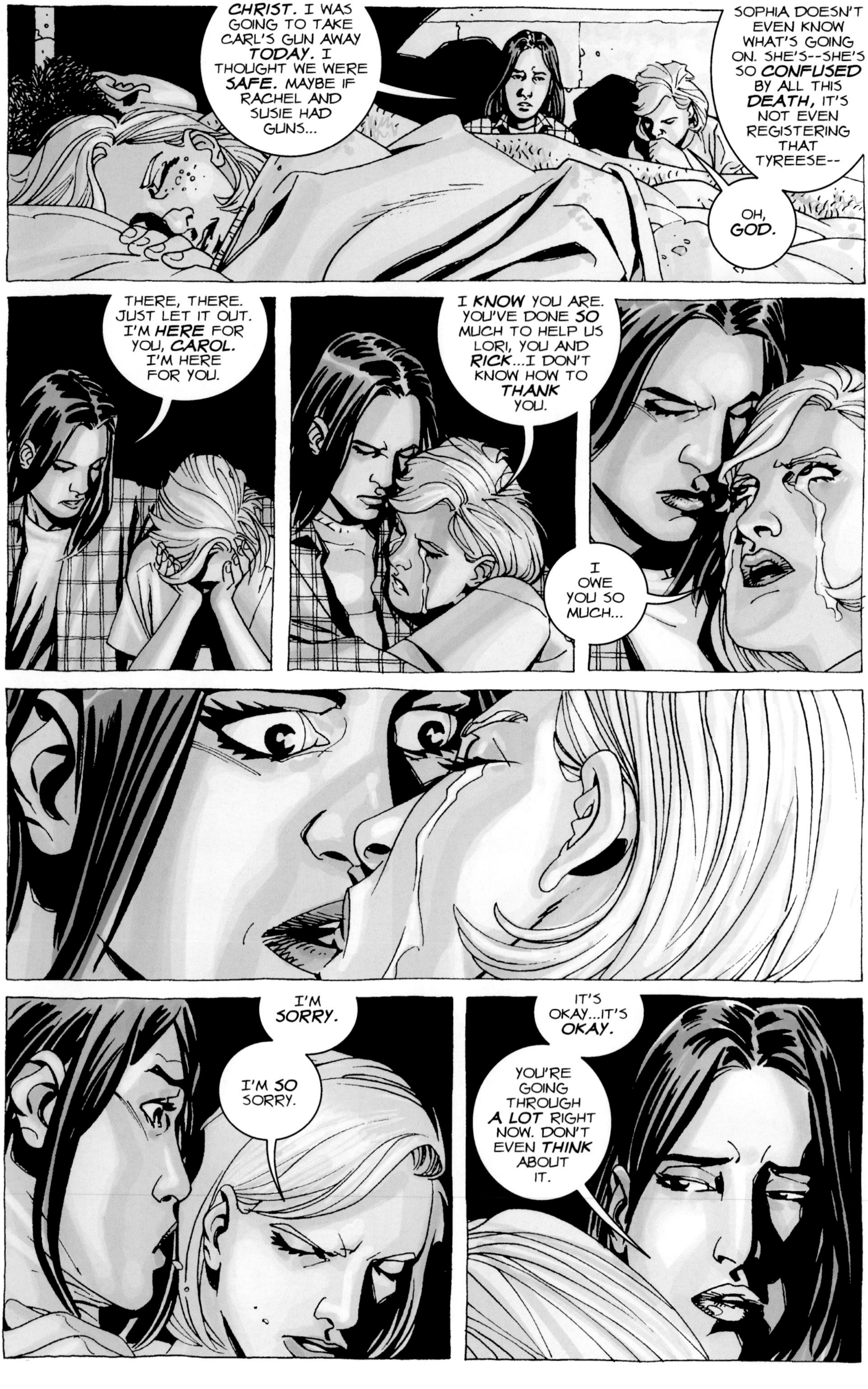
CHRIST. I WAS GOING TO TAKE CARL'S GUN AWAY TODAY. I THOUGHT WE WERE SAFE. MAYBE IF RACHEL AND SUSIE HAD GUNS...
SOPHIA DOESN'T EVEN KNOW WHAT'S GOING ON. SHE'S--SHE'S SO CONFUSED BY ALL THIS DEATH, IT'S NOT EVEN REGISTERING THAT TYREESE--
OH, GOD.
THERE, THERE. JUST LET IT OUT. I'M HERE FOR YOU, CAROL. I'M HERE FOR YOU.
I KNOW YOU ARE. YOU'VE DONE SO MUCH TO HELP US LORI, YOU AND RICK...I DON'T KNOW HOW TO THANK YOU.
I OWE YOU SO MUCH...
I'M SORRY.
I'M SO SORRY.
IT'S OKAY...IT'S OKAY.
YOU'RE GOING THROUGH A LOT RIGHT NOW. DON'T EVEN THINK ABOUT IT.

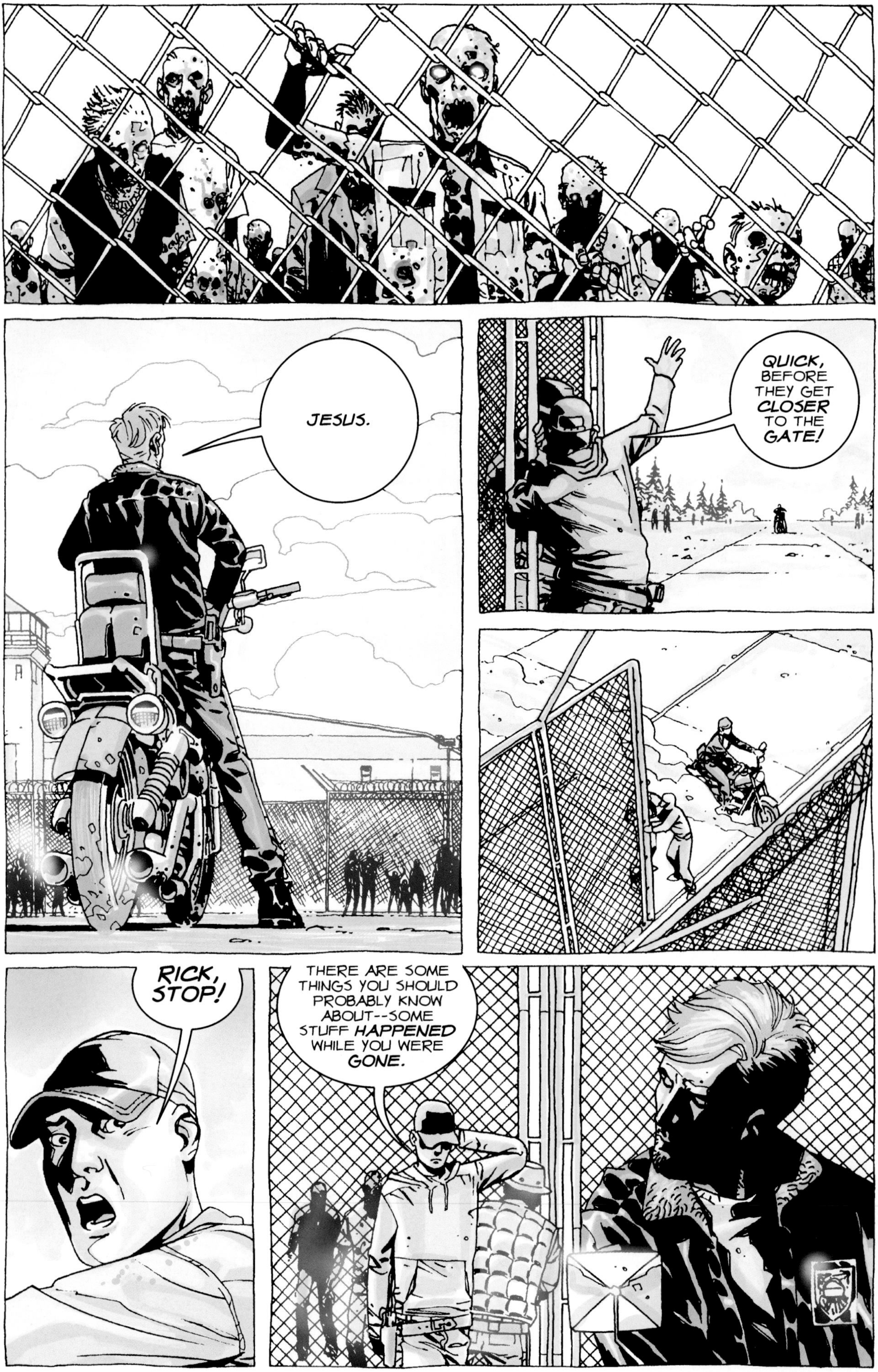

JESUS.
QUICK, BEFORE THEY GET CLOSER TO THE GATE!
RICK, STOP!
THERE ARE SOME THINGS YOU SHOULD PROBABLY KNOW ABOUT--SOME STUFF HAPPENED WHILE YOU WERE GONE.

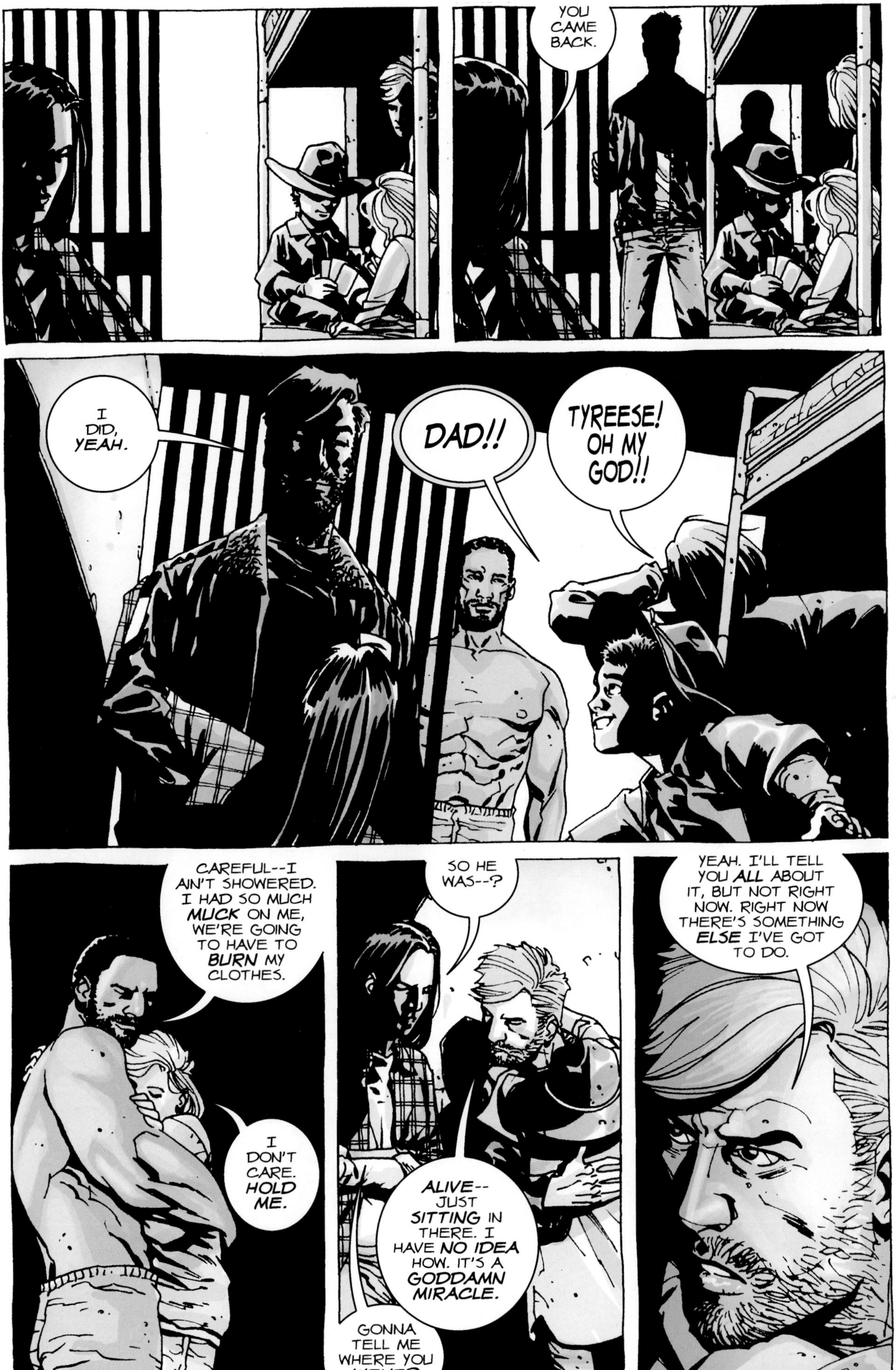
YOU CAME BACK.
I DID, YEAH.
DAD!!
TYREESE! OH MY GOD!!
CAREFUL--I AIN'T SHOWERED. I HAD SO MUCH MUCK ON ME, WE'RE GOING TO HAVE TO BURN MY CLOTHES.
I DON'T CARE. HOLD ME.
SO HE WAS--?
ALIVE--JUST SITTING IN THERE. I HAVE NO IDEA HOW. IT'S A GODDAMN MIRACLE.
GONNA TELL ME WHERE YOU WENT?
YEAH. I'LL TELL YOU ALL ABOUT IT, BUT NOT RIGHT NOW. RIGHT NOW THERE'S SOMETHING ELSE I'VE GOT TO DO.

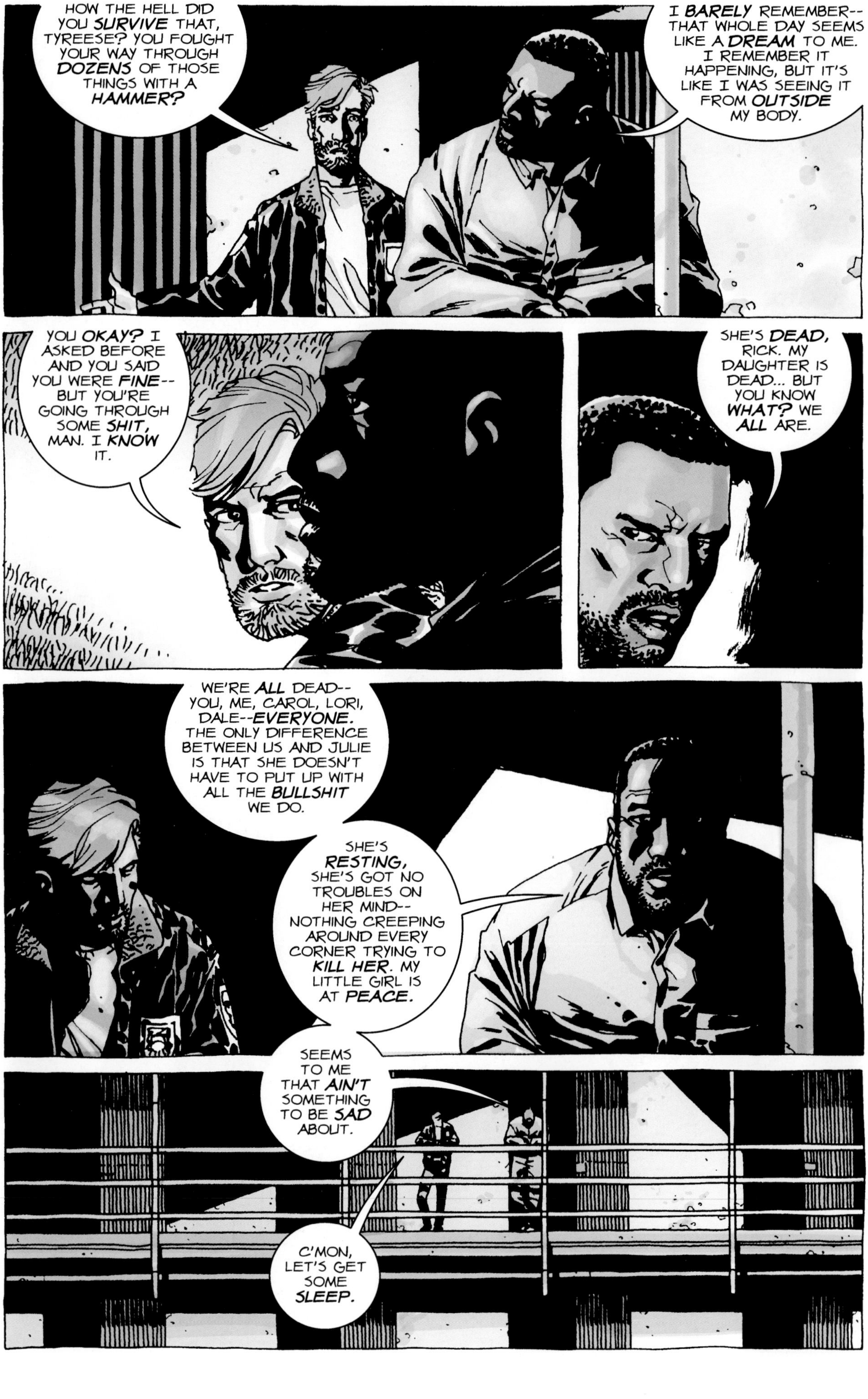
HOW THE HELL DID YOU SURVIVE THAT, TYREESE? YOU FOUGHT YOUR WAY THROUGH DOZENS OF THOSE THINGS WITH A HAMMER?
I BARELY REMEMBER-- THAT WHOLE DAY SEEMS LIKE A DREAM TO ME. I REMEMBER IT HAPPENING, BUT IT'S LIKE I WAS SEEING IT FROM OUTSIDE MY BODY.
YOU OKAY? I ASKED BEFORE AND YOU SAID YOU WERE FINE-- BUT YOU'RE GOING THROUGH SOME SHIT, MAN. I KNOW IT.
SHE'S DEAD, RICK. MY DAUGHTER IS DEAD... BUT YOU KNOW WHAT? WE ALL ARE.
WE'RE ALL DEAD-- YOU, ME, CAROL, LORI, DALE--EVERYONE. THE ONLY DIFFERENCE BETWEEN US AND JULIE IS THAT SHE DOESN'T HAVE TO PUT UP WITH ALL THE BULLSHIT WE DO.
SHE'S RESTING, SHE'S GOT NO TROUBLES ON HER MIND-- NOTHING CREEPING AROUND EVERY CORNER TRYING TO KILL HER. MY LITTLE GIRL IS AT PEACE.
SEEMS TO ME THAT AIN'T SOMETHING TO BE SAD ABOUT.
C'MON, LET'S GET SOME SLEEP.

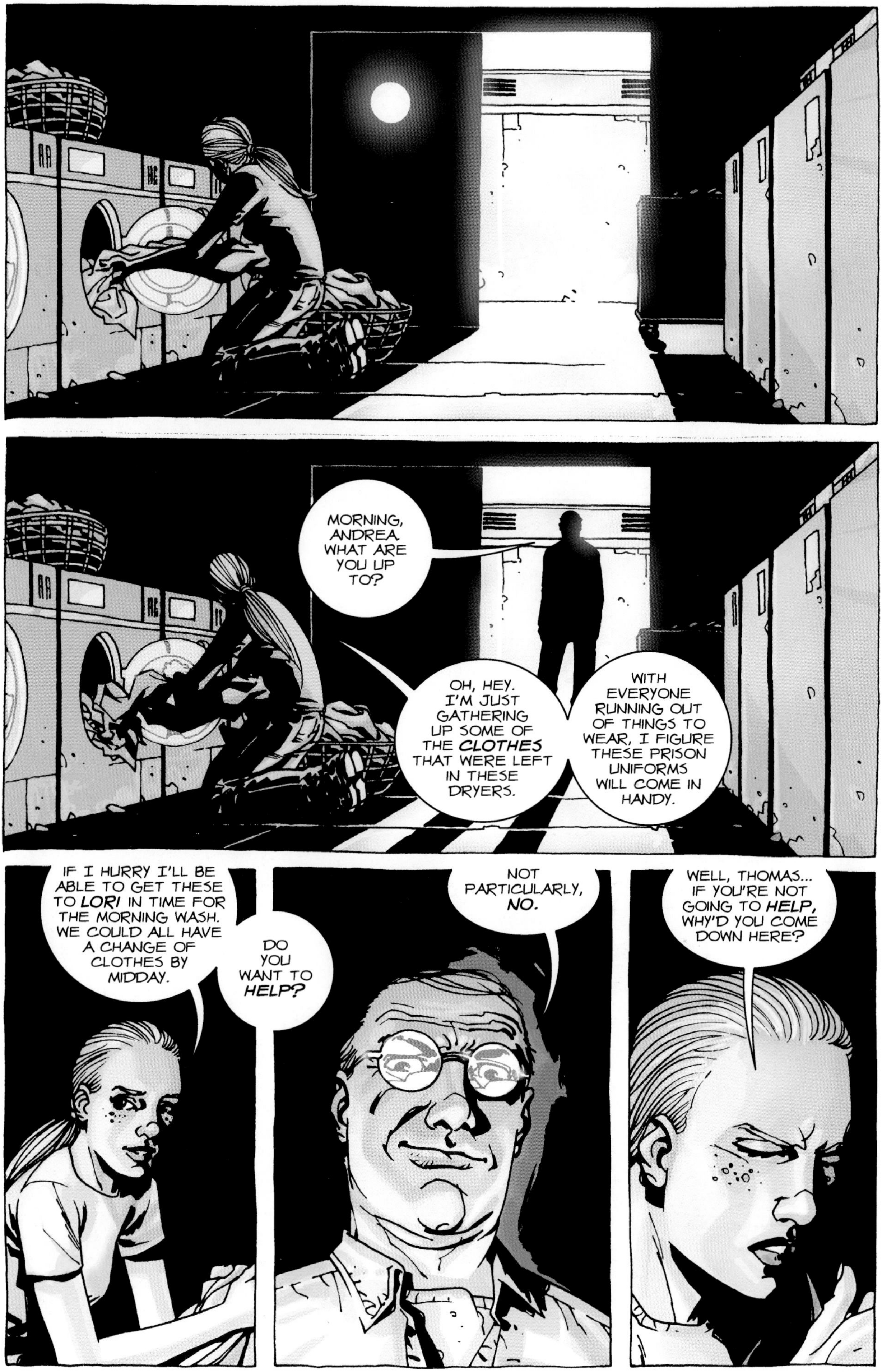
MORNING, ANDREA WHAT ARE YOU UP TO?
OH, HEY. I'M JUST GATHERING UP SOME OF THE CLOTHES THAT WERE LEFT IN THESE DRYERS.
WITH EVERYONE RUNNING OUT OF THINGS TO WEAR, I FIGURE THESE PRISON UNIFORMS WILL COME IN HANDY.
IF I HURRY I'LL BE ABLE TO GET THESE TO LORI IN TIME FOR THE MORNING WASH. WE COULD ALL HAVE A CHANGE OF CLOTHES BY MIDDAY.
DO YOU WANT TO HELP?
NOT PARTICULARLY, NO.
WELL, THOMAS... IF YOU'RE NOT GOING TO HELP, WHY'D YOU COME DOWN HERE?

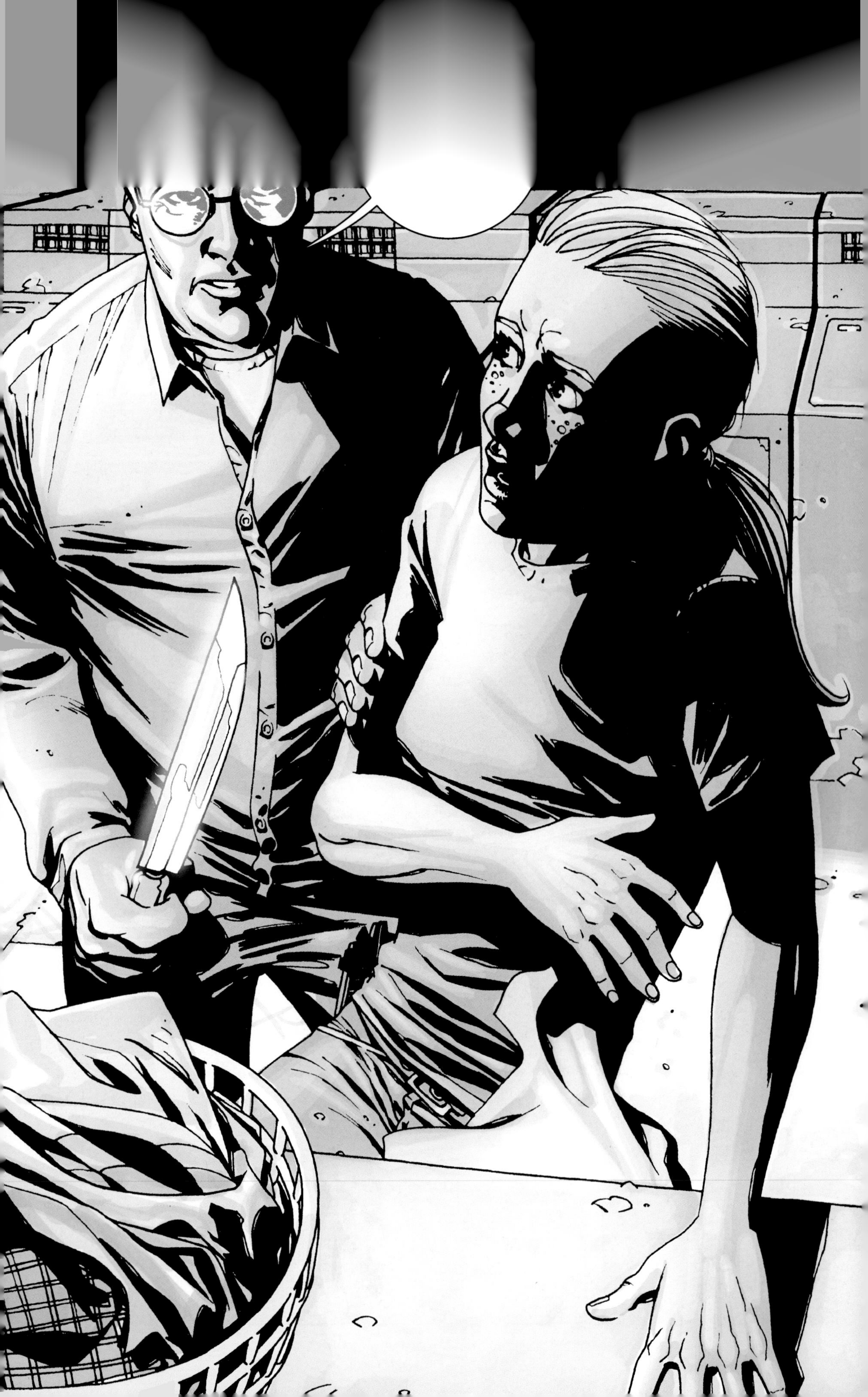

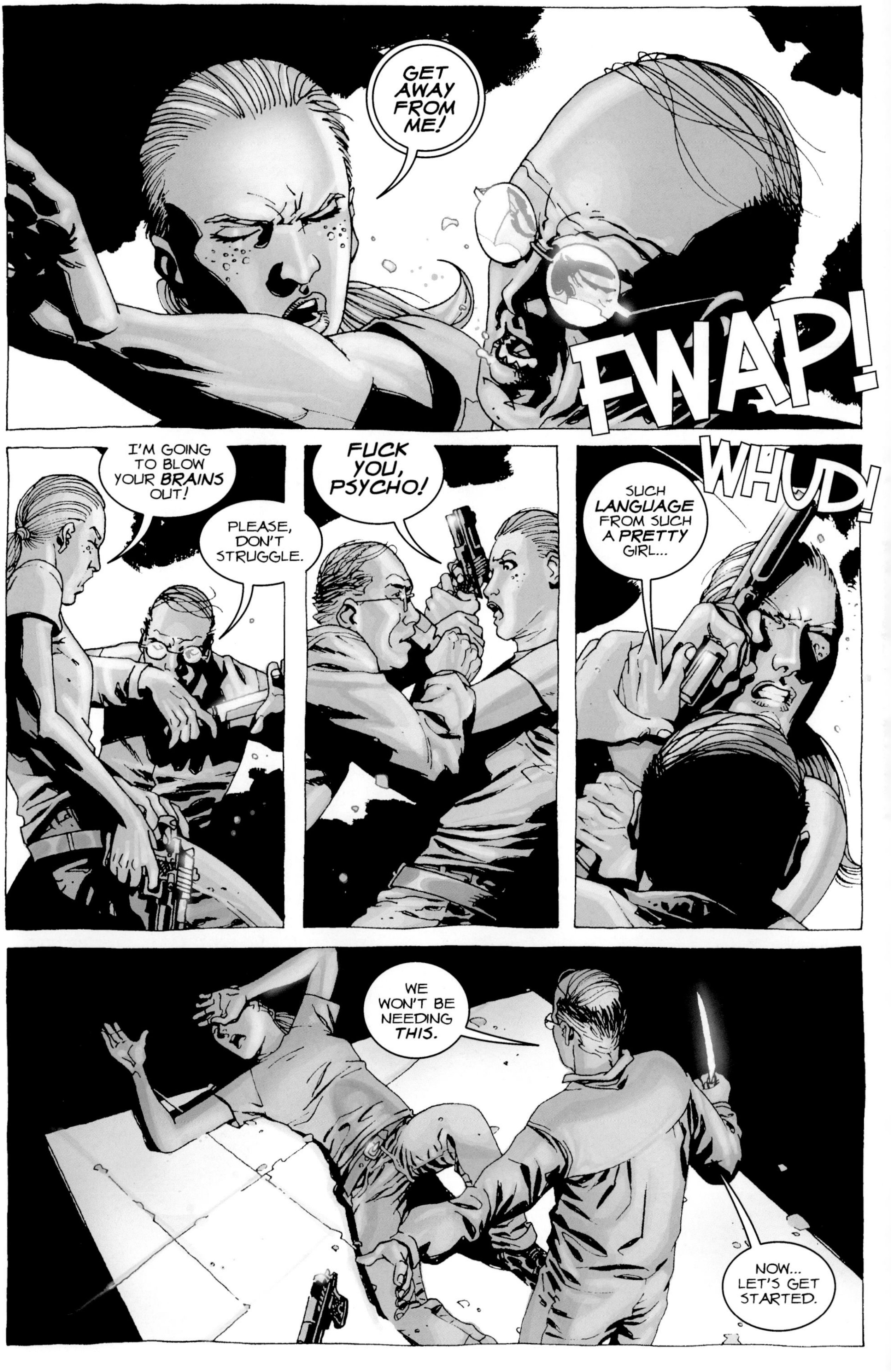
GET AWAY FROM ME!
FWAP!
I'M GOING TO BLOW YOUR BRAINS OUT!
PLEASE, DON'T STRUGGLE.
FUCK YOU, PSYCHO!
WHUD!
SUCH LANGUAGE FROM SUCH A PRETTY GIRL...
WE WON'T BE NEEDING THIS.
NOW... LET'S GET STARTED.

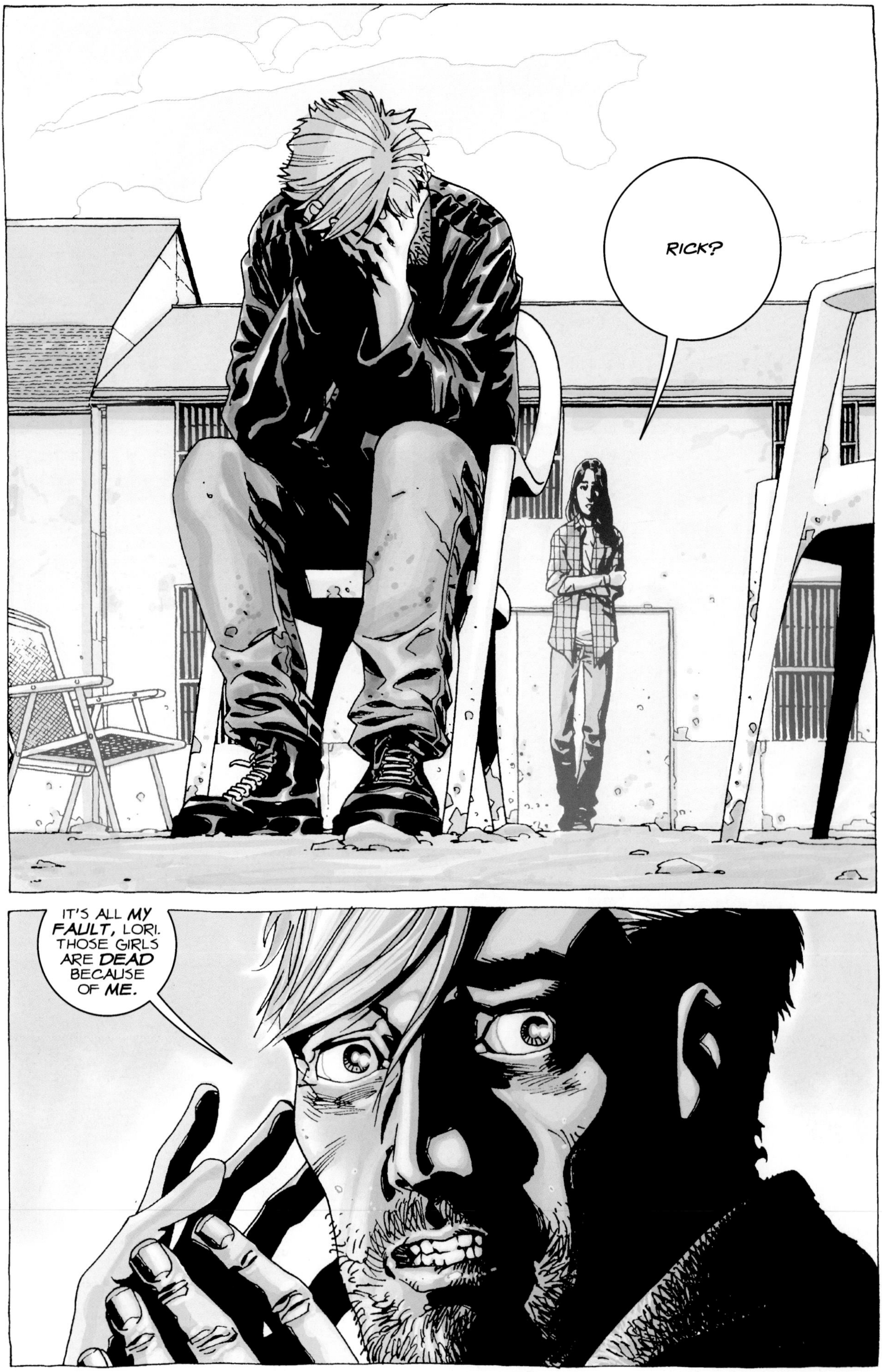
RICK?
IT'S ALL MY FAULT, LORI. THOSE GIRLS ARE DEAD BECAUSE OF ME.

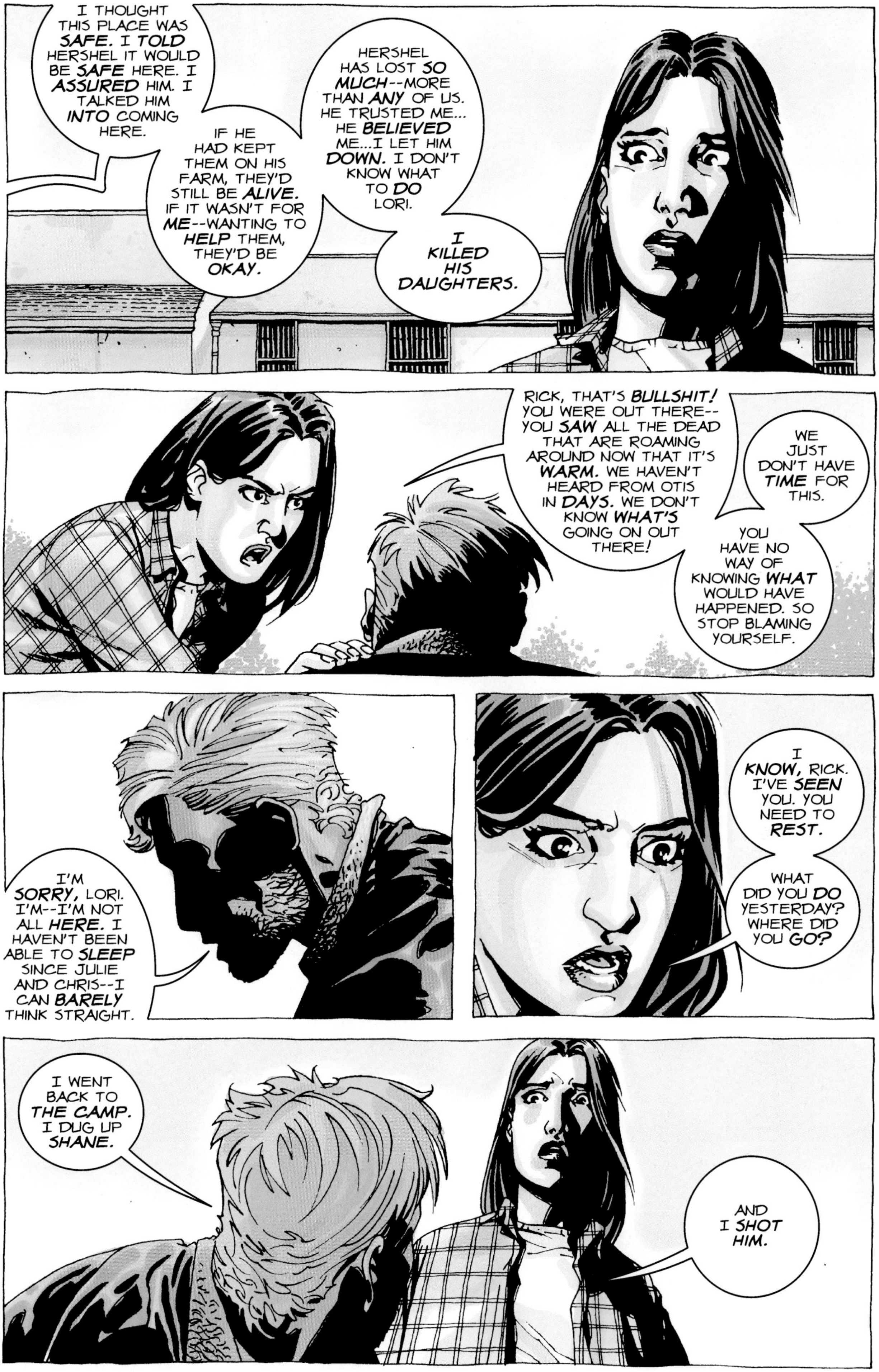
I THOUGHT THIS PLACE WAS SAFE. I TOLD HERSHEL IT WOULD BE SAFE HERE. I ASSURED HIM. I TALKED HIM INTO COMING HERE.
IF HE HAD KEPT THEM ON HIS FARM, THEY'D STILL BE ALIVE. IF IT WASN'T FOR ME--WANTING TO HELP THEM, THEY'D BE OKAY.
HERSHEL HAS LOST SO MUCH--MORE THAN ANY OF US. HE TRUSTED ME... HE BELIEVED ME...I LET HIM DOWN. I DON'T KNOW WHAT TO DO LORI.
I KILLED HIS DAUGHTERS.
RICK, THAT'S BULLSHIT! YOU WERE OUT THERE--YOU SAW ALL THE DEAD THAT ARE ROAMING AROUND NOW THAT IT'S WARM. WE HAVEN'T HEARD FROM OTIS IN DAYS. WE DON'T KNOW WHAT'S GOING ON OUT THERE!
WE JUST DON'T HAVE TIME FOR THIS.
YOU HAVE NO WAY OF KNOWING WHAT WOULD HAVE HAPPENED. SO STOP BLAMING YOURSELF.
I'M SORRY, LORI. I'M--I'M NOT ALL HERE. I HAVEN'T BEEN ABLE TO SLEEP SINCE JULIE AND CHRIS--I CAN BARELY THINK STRAIGHT.
I KNOW, RICK. I'VE SEEN YOU. YOU NEED TO REST.
WHAT DID YOU DO YESTERDAY? WHERE DID YOU GO?
I WENT BACK TO THE CAMP. I DUG UP SHANE.
AND I SHOT HIM.

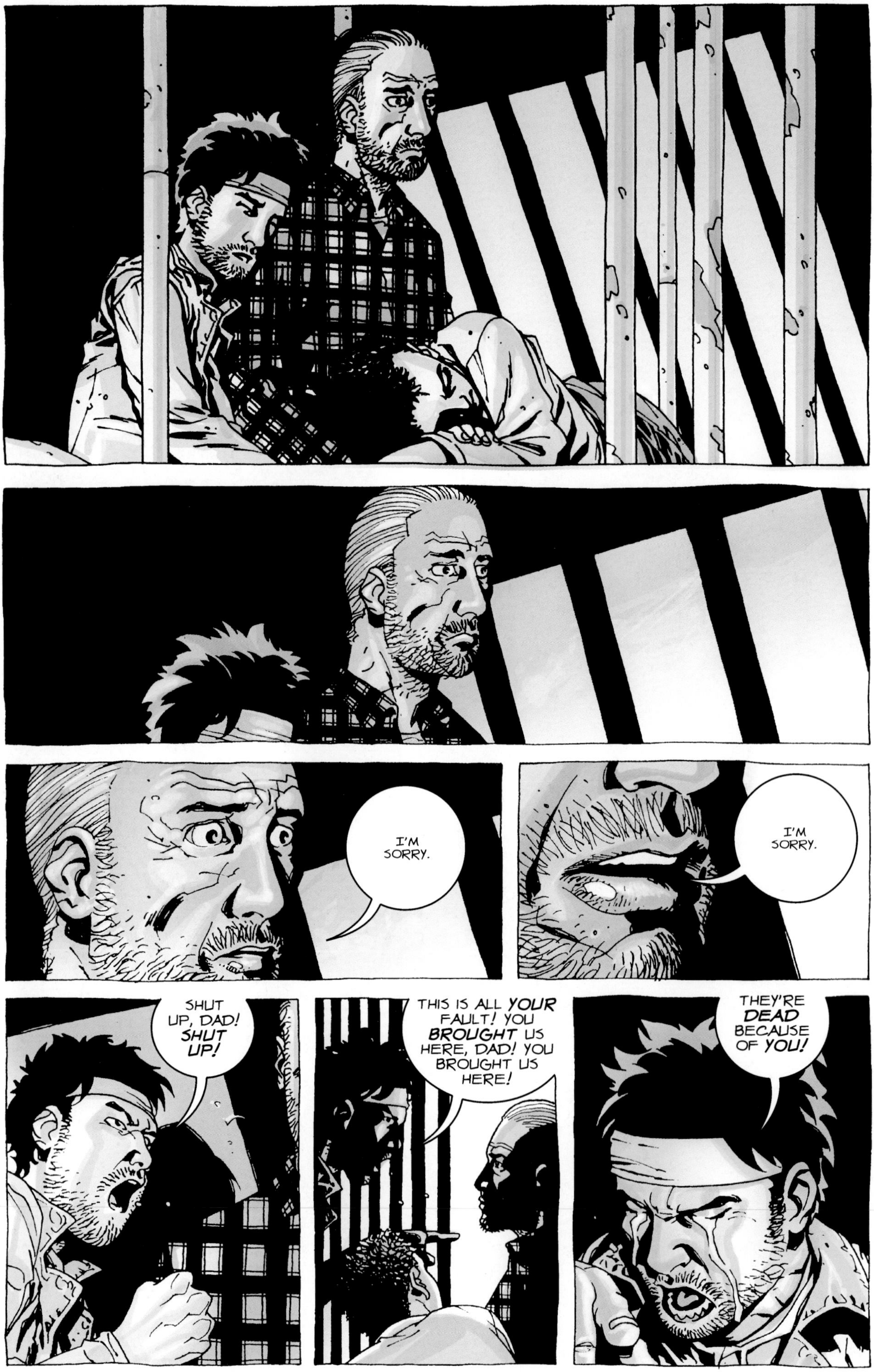
I'M SORRY.
I'M SORRY.
SHUT UP, DAD! SHUT UP!
THIS IS ALL YOUR FAULT! YOU BROUGHT US HERE, DAD! YOU BROUGHT US HERE!
THEY'RE DEAD BECAUSE OF YOU!

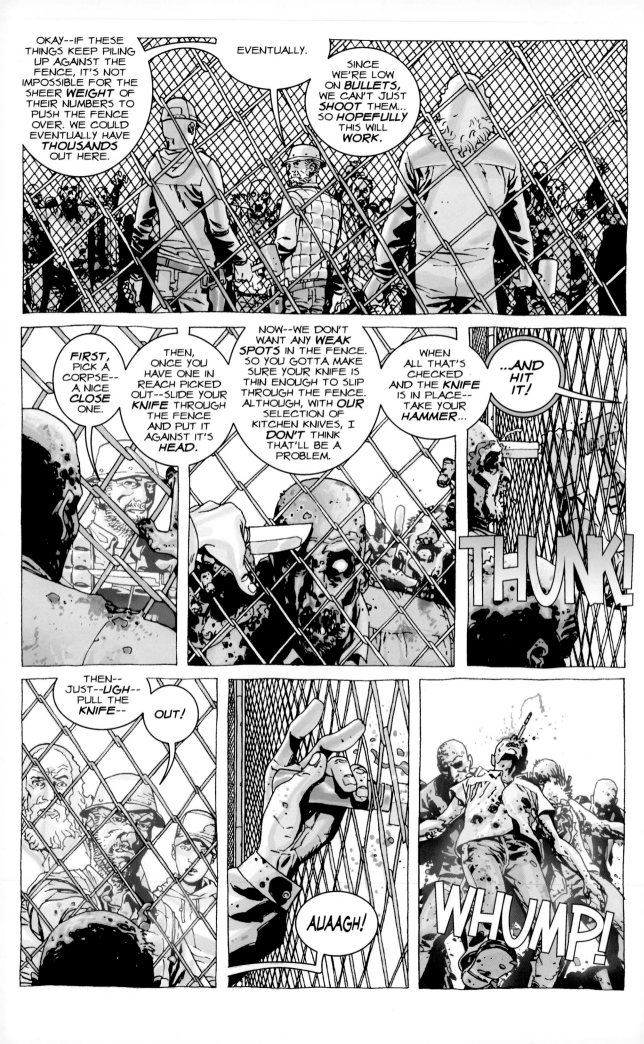

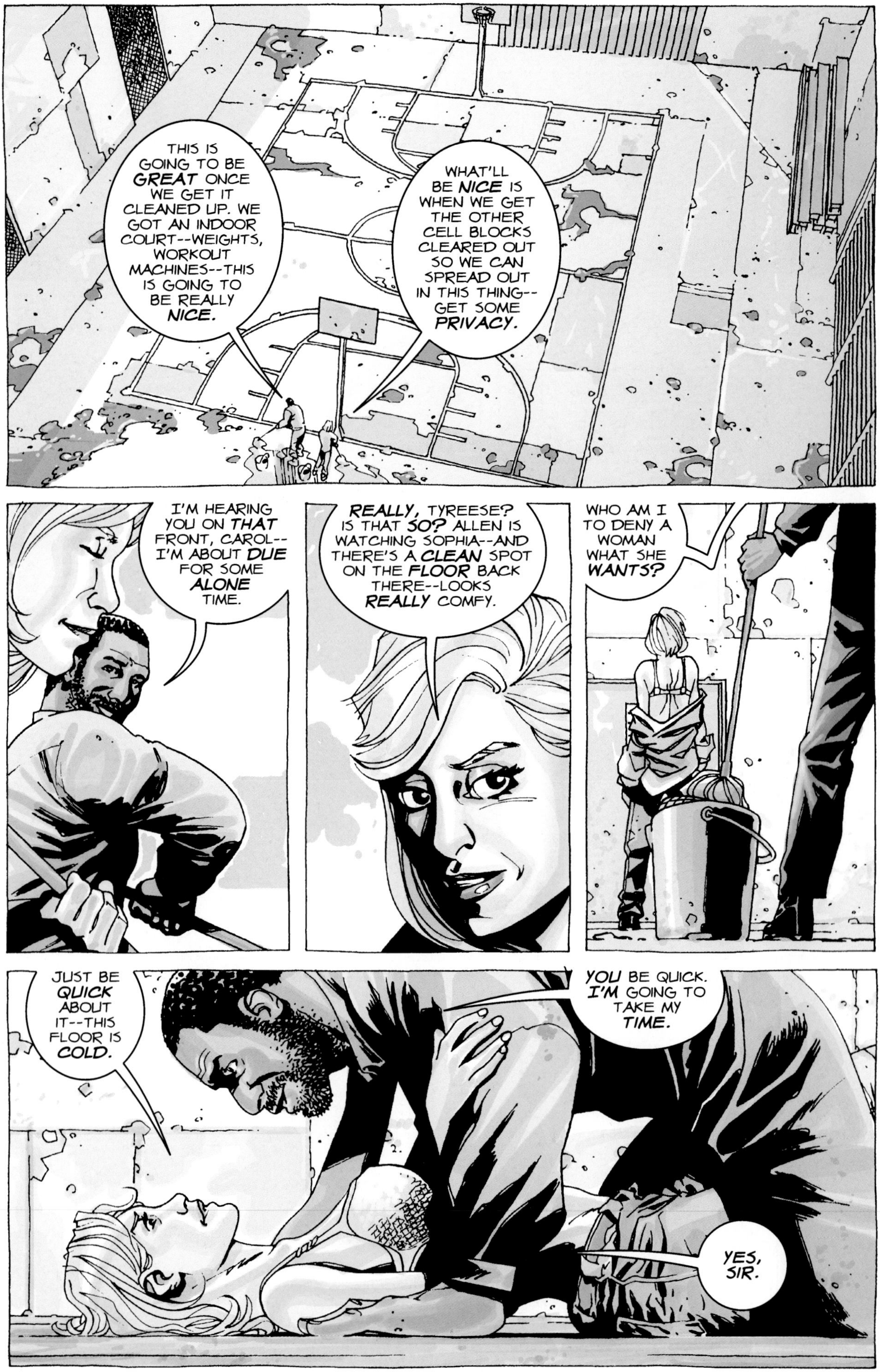
THIS IS GOING TO BE GREAT ONCE WE GET IT CLEANED UP. WE GOT AN INDOOR COURT--WEIGHTS, WORKOUT MACHINES--THIS IS GOING TO BE REALLY NICE.
WHAT'LL BE NICE IS WHEN WE GET THE OTHER CELL BLOCKS CLEARED OUT SO WE CAN SPREAD OUT IN THIS THING--GET SOME PRIVACY.
I'M HEARING YOU ON THAT FRONT, CAROL--I'M ABOUT DUE FOR SOME ALONE TIME.
REALLY, TYREESE? IS THAT SO? ALLEN IS WATCHING SOPHIA--AND THERE'S A CLEAN SPOT ON THE FLOOR BACK THERE--LOOKS REALLY COMFY.
WHO AM I TO DENY A WOMAN WHAT SHE WANTS?
JUST BE QUICK ABOUT IT--THIS FLOOR IS COLD.
YOU BE QUICK. I'M GOING TO TAKE MY TIME.
YES, SIR.

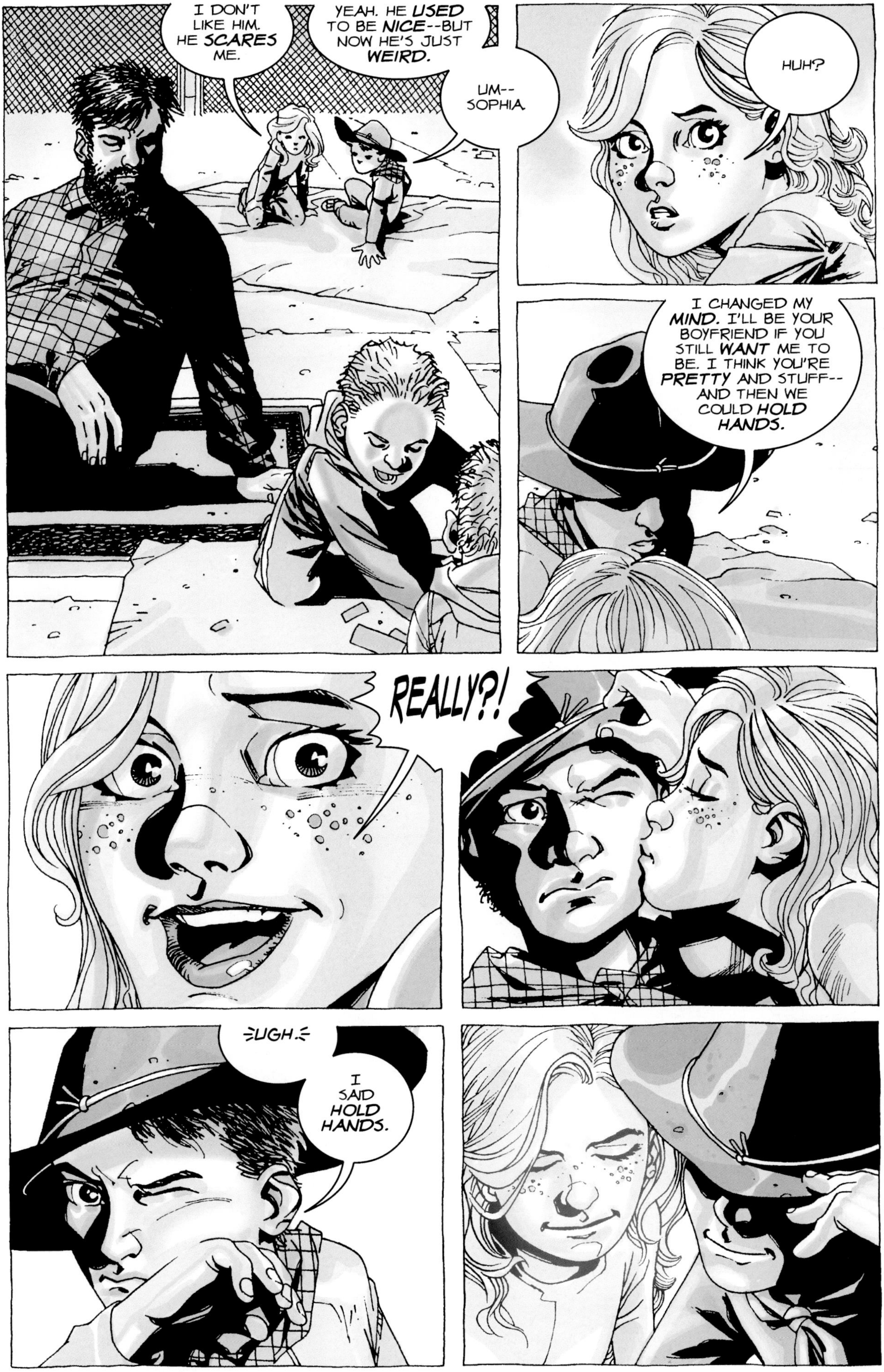
I DON'T LIKE HIM. HE SCARES ME.
YEAH. HE USED TO BE NICE--BUT NOW HE'S JUST WEIRD.
UM-- SOPHIA.
HUH?
I CHANGED MY MIND. I'LL BE YOUR BOYFRIEND IF YOU STILL WANT ME TO BE. I THINK YOU'RE PRETTY AND STUFF-- AND THEN WE COULD HOLD HANDS.
REALLY?!
UGH.
I SAID HOLD HANDS.

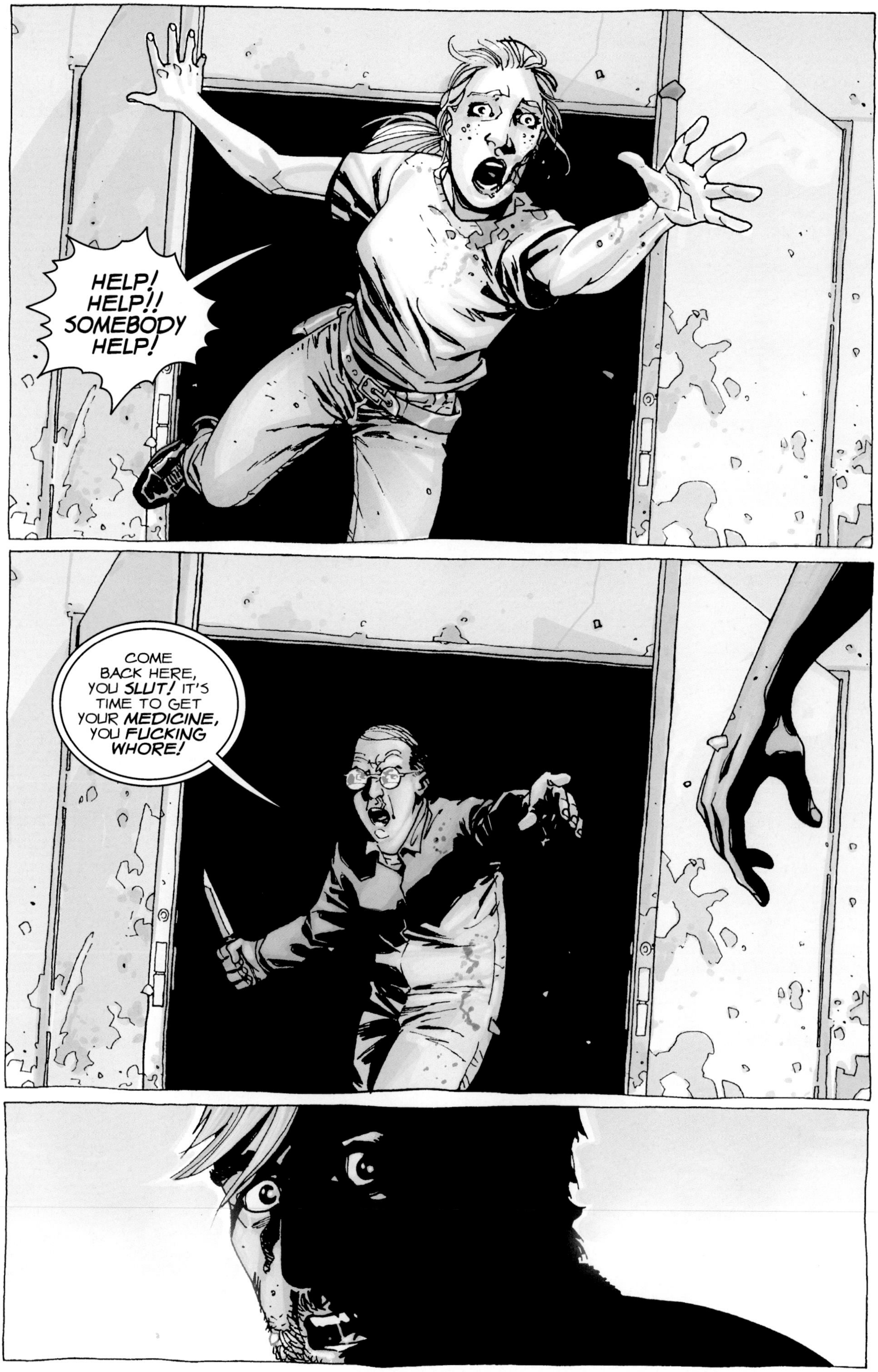
HELP! HELP!! SOMEBODY HELP!
COME BACK HERE, YOU SLUT! IT'S TIME TO GET YOUR MEDICINE, YOU FUCKING WHORE!

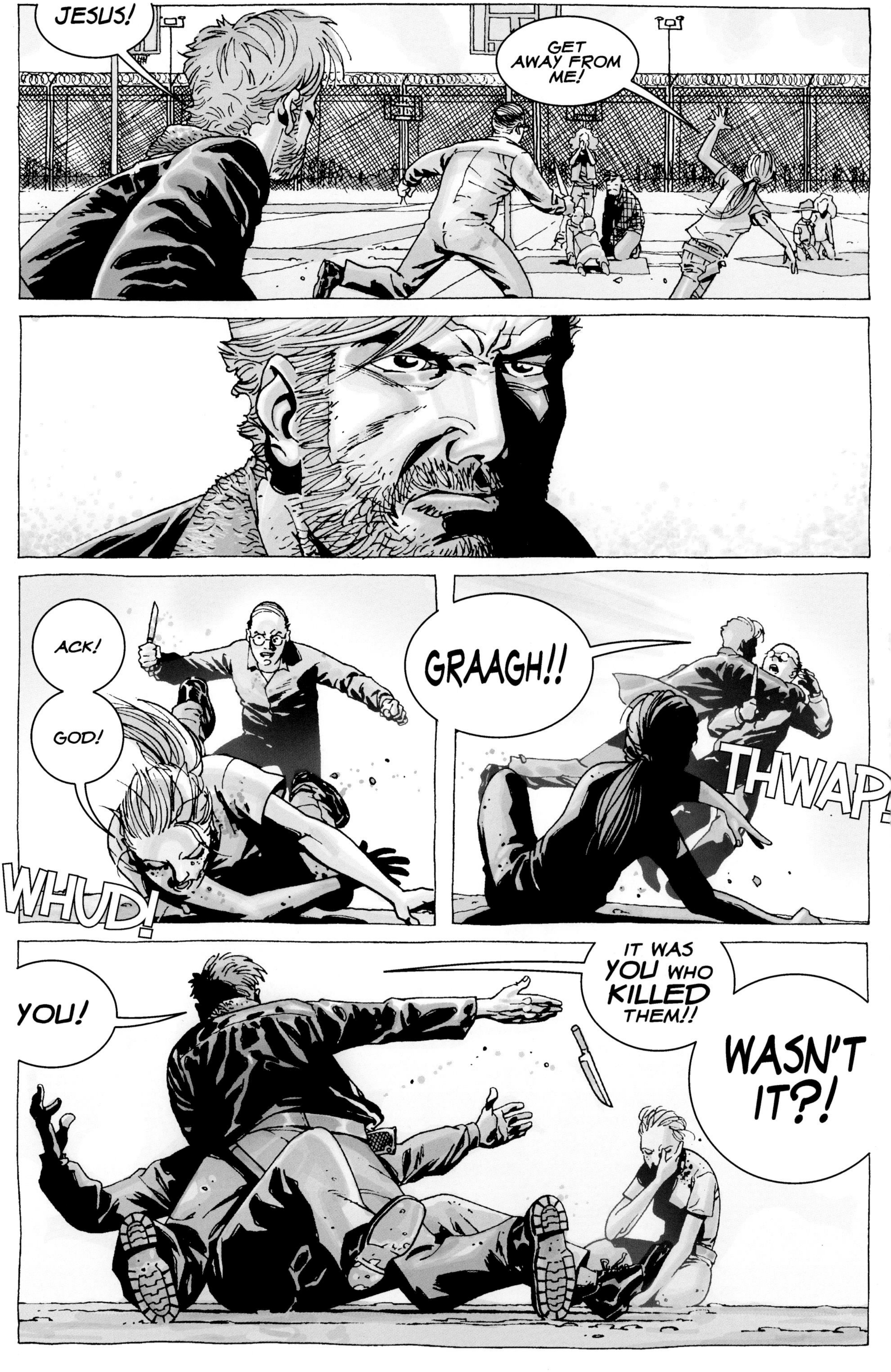
JESUS!
GET AWAY FROM ME!
ACK!
GOD!
WHUD!
GRAAGH!!
THWAP!
YOU!
IT WAS YOU WHO KILLED THEM!!
WASN'T IT?!

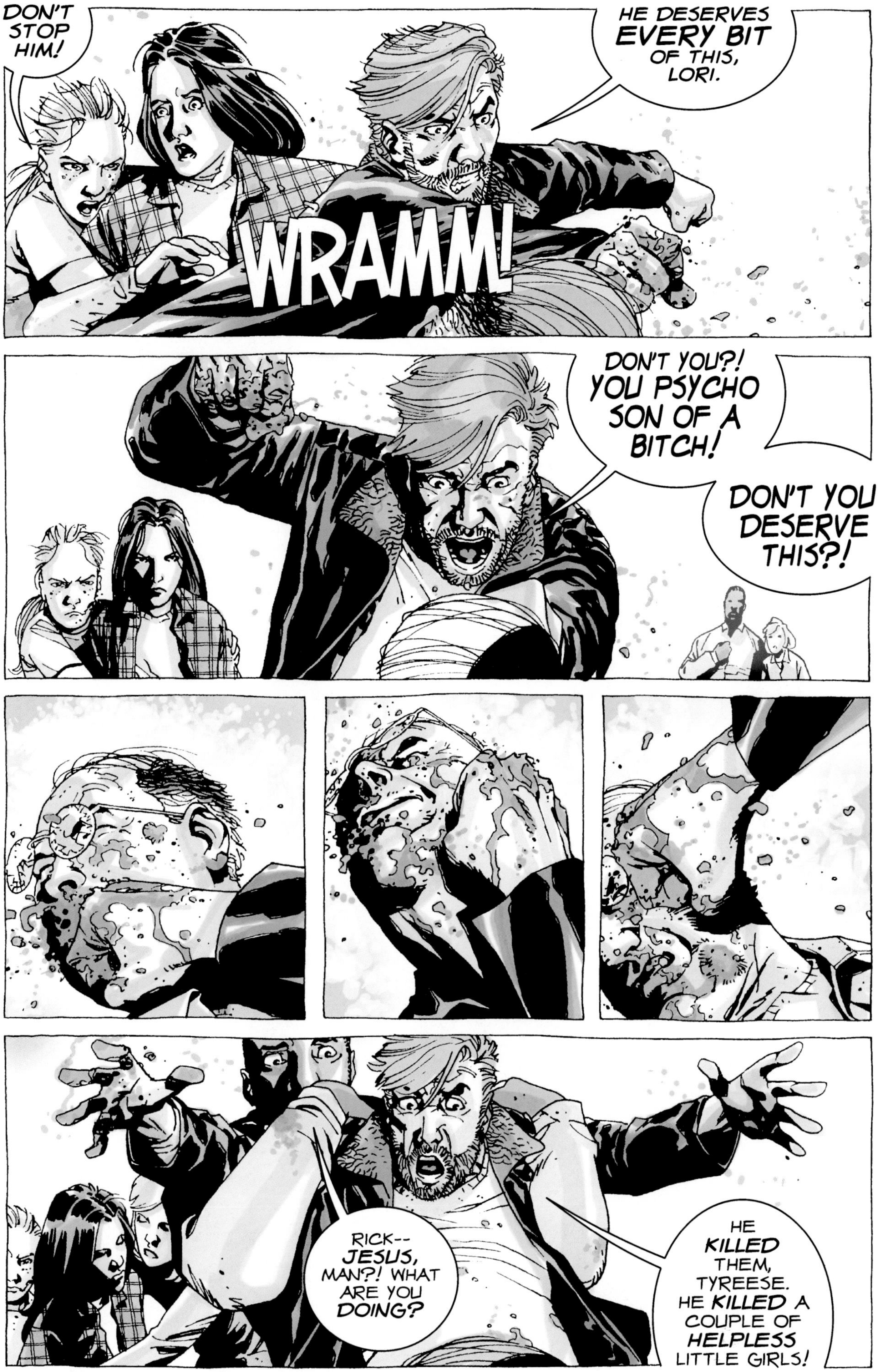
DON'T STOP HIM!
HE DESERVES EVERY BIT OF THIS, LORI.
WRAMM!
DON'T YOU?! YOU PSYCHO SON OF A BITCH!
DON'T YOU DESERVE THIS?!
RICK-- JESUS, MAN?! WHAT ARE YOU DOING?
HE KILLED THEM, TYREESE. HE KILLED A COUPLE OF HELPLESS LITTLE GIRLS!

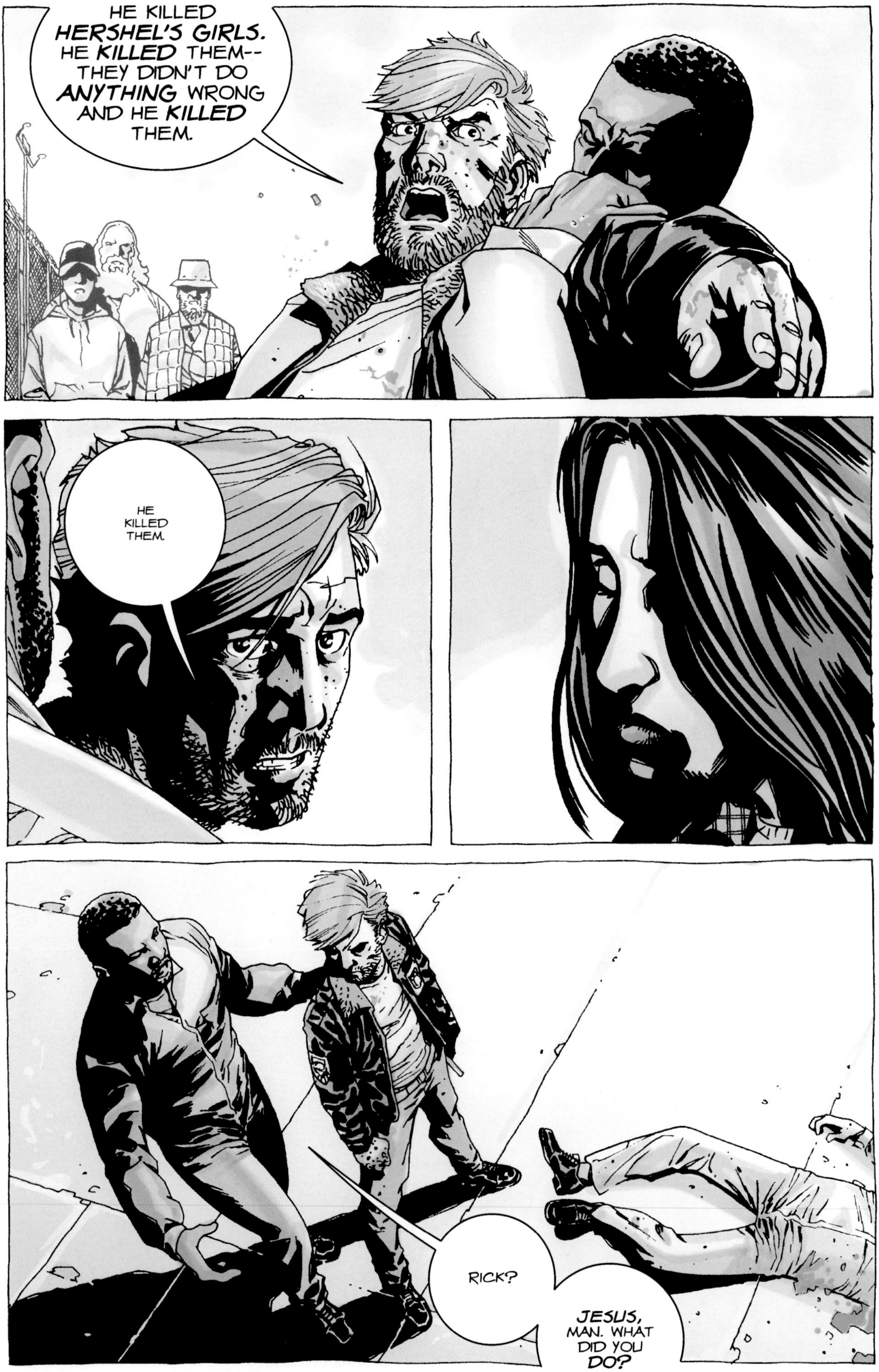
HE KILLED HERSHEL'S GIRLS. HE KILLED THEM-- THEY DIDN'T DO ANYTHING WRONG AND HE KILLED THEM.
HE KILLED THEM.
RICK?
JESUS, MAN. WHAT DID YOU DO?

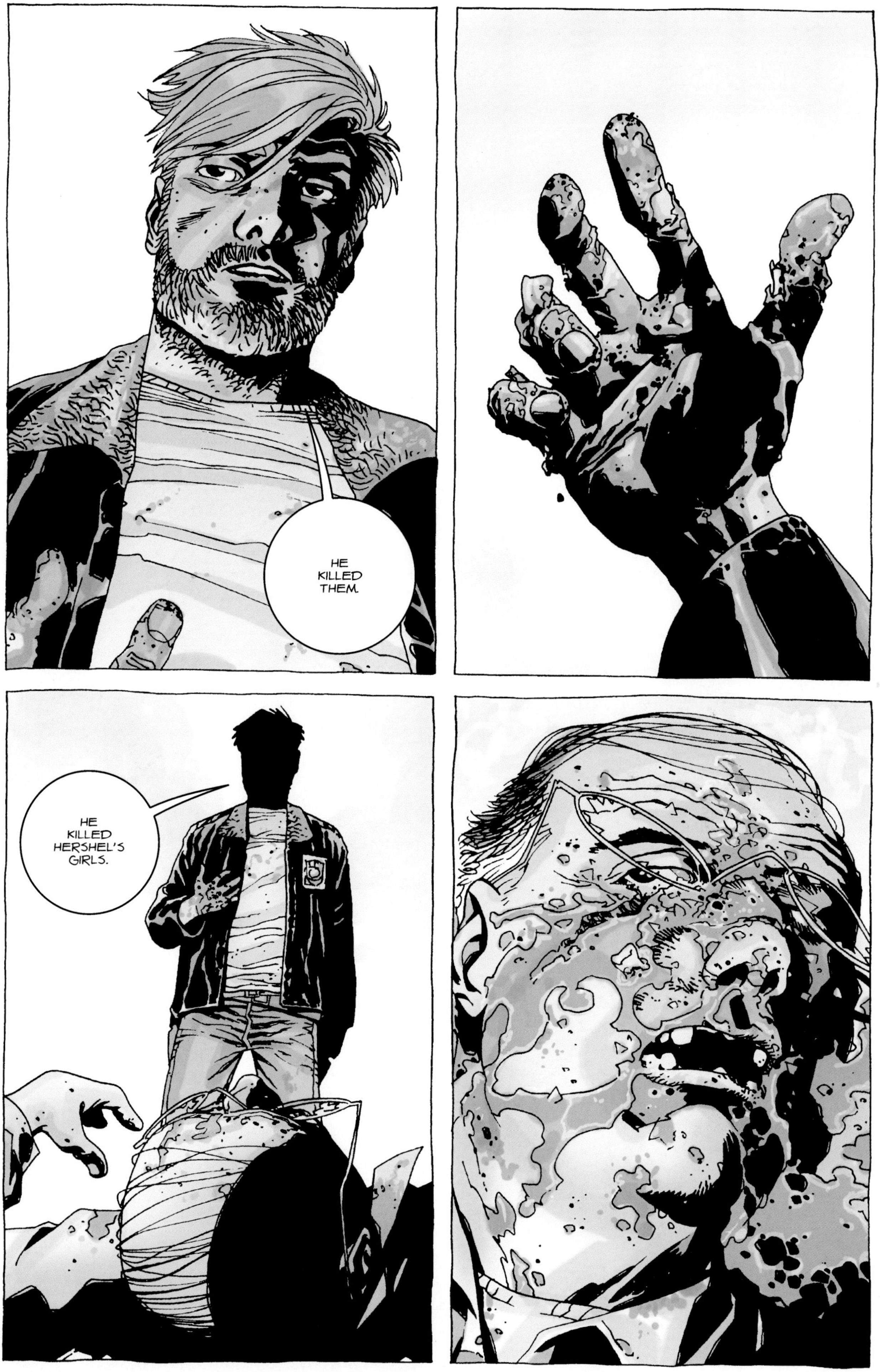
HE KILLED THEM.
HE KILLED HERSHEL'S GIRLS.

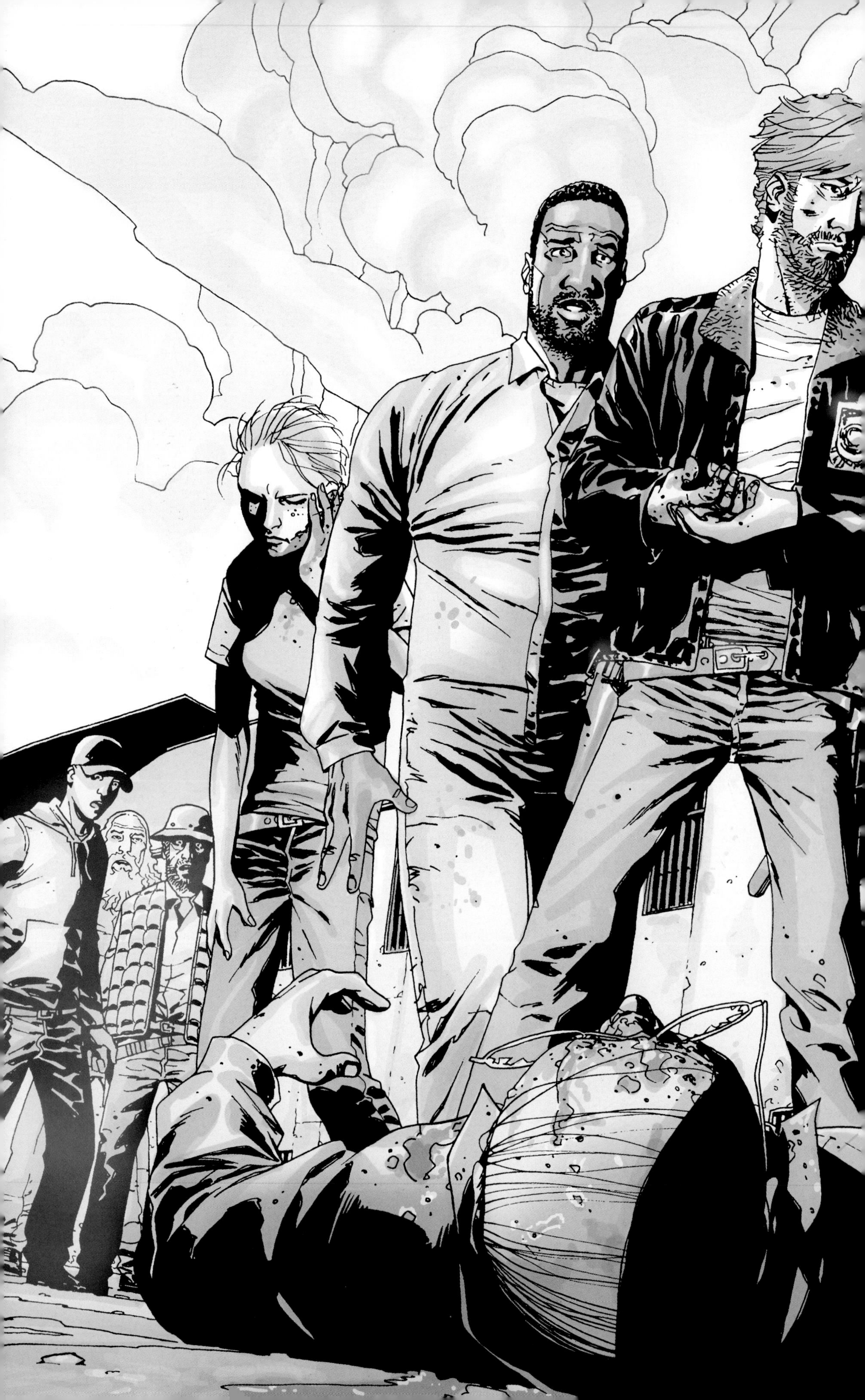

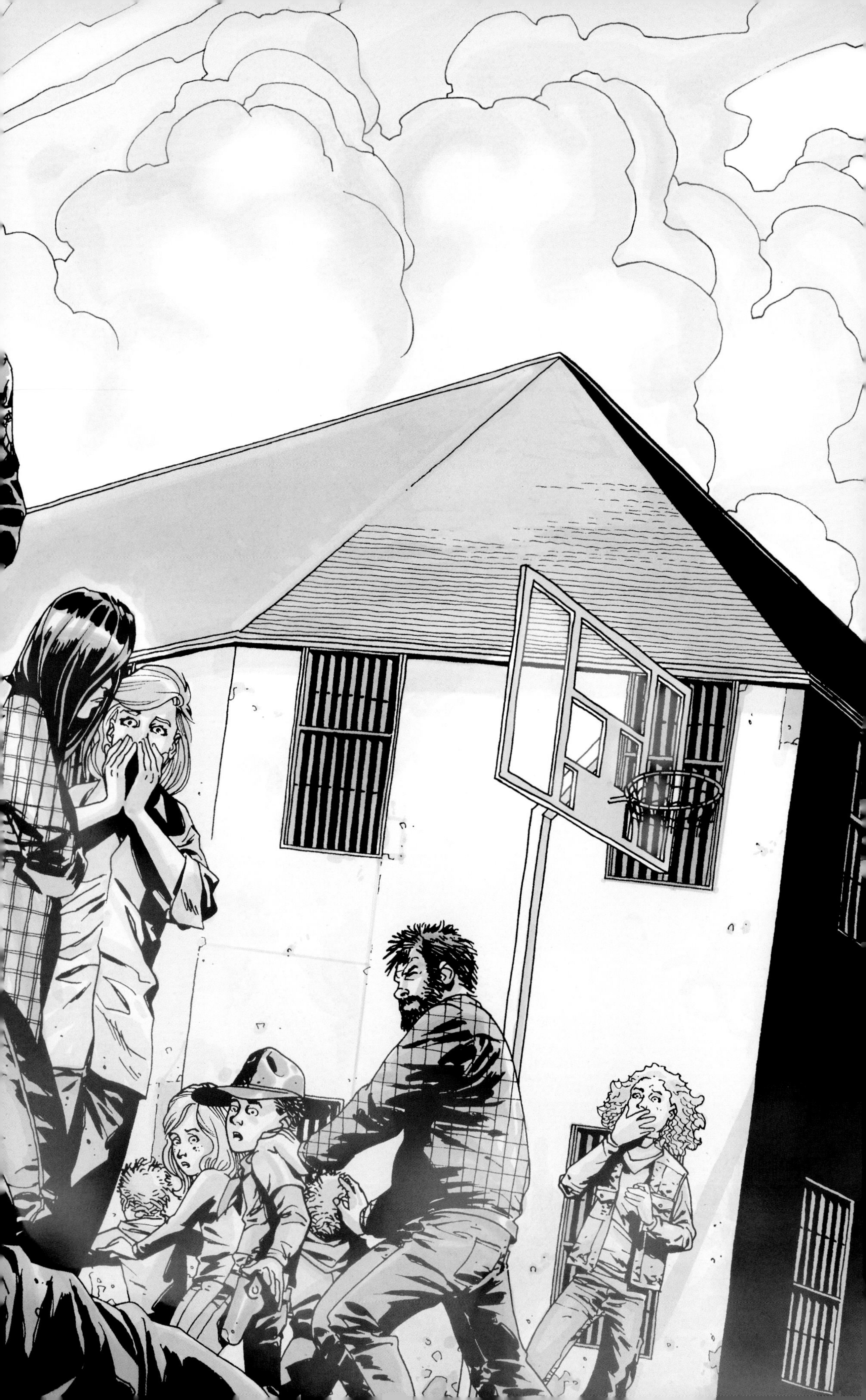

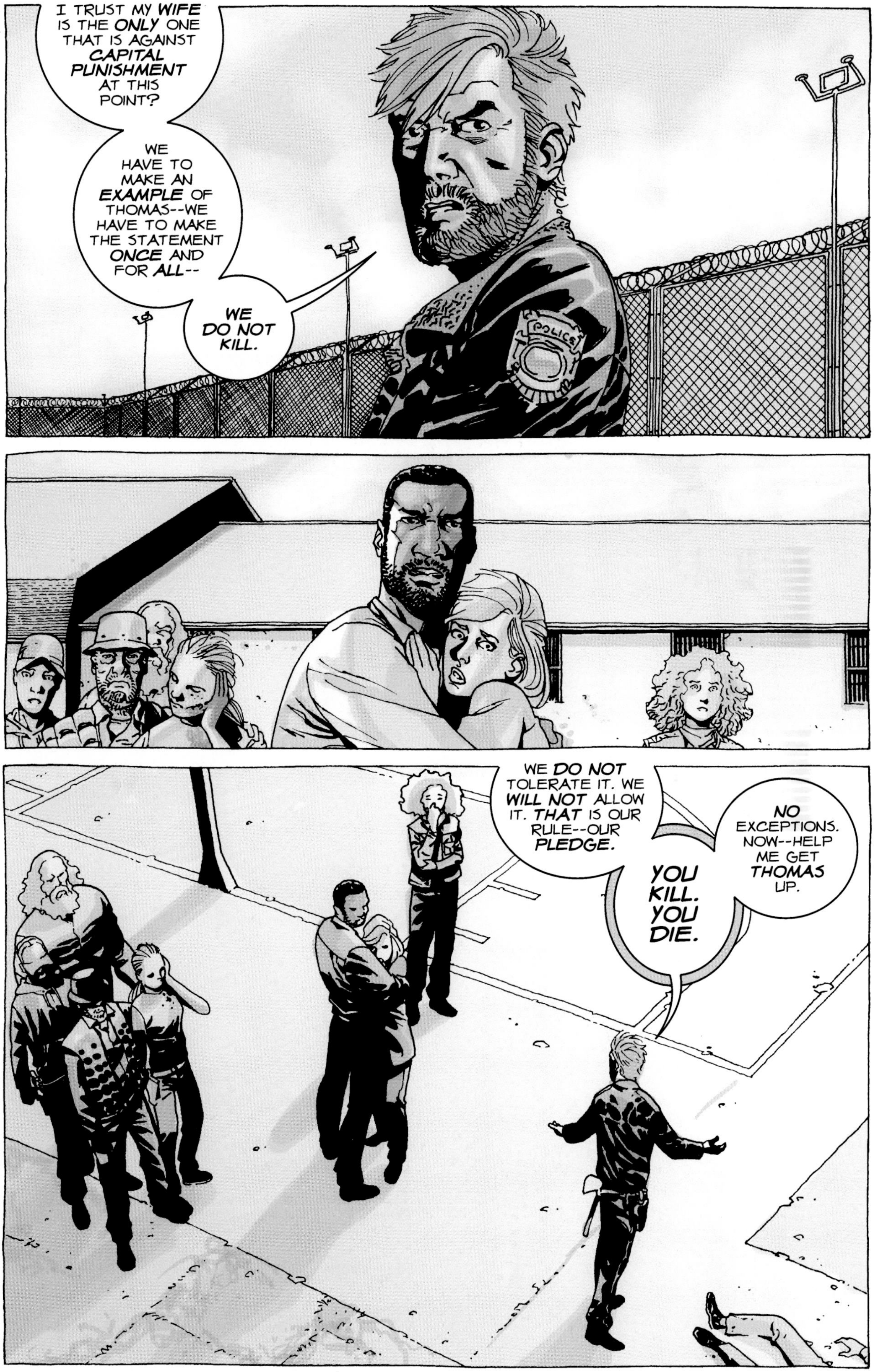
I TRUST MY WIFE IS THE ONLY ONE THAT IS AGAINST CAPITAL PUNISHMENT AT THIS POINT?
WE HAVE TO MAKE AN EXAMPLE OF THOMAS--WE HAVE TO MAKE THE STATEMENT ONCE AND FOR ALL--
WE DO NOT KILL.
WE DO NOT TOLERATE IT. WE WILL NOT ALLOW IT. THAT IS OUR RULE--OUR PLEDGE.
YOU KILL. YOU DIE.
NO EXCEPTIONS. NOW--HELP ME GET THOMAS UP.
POLICE

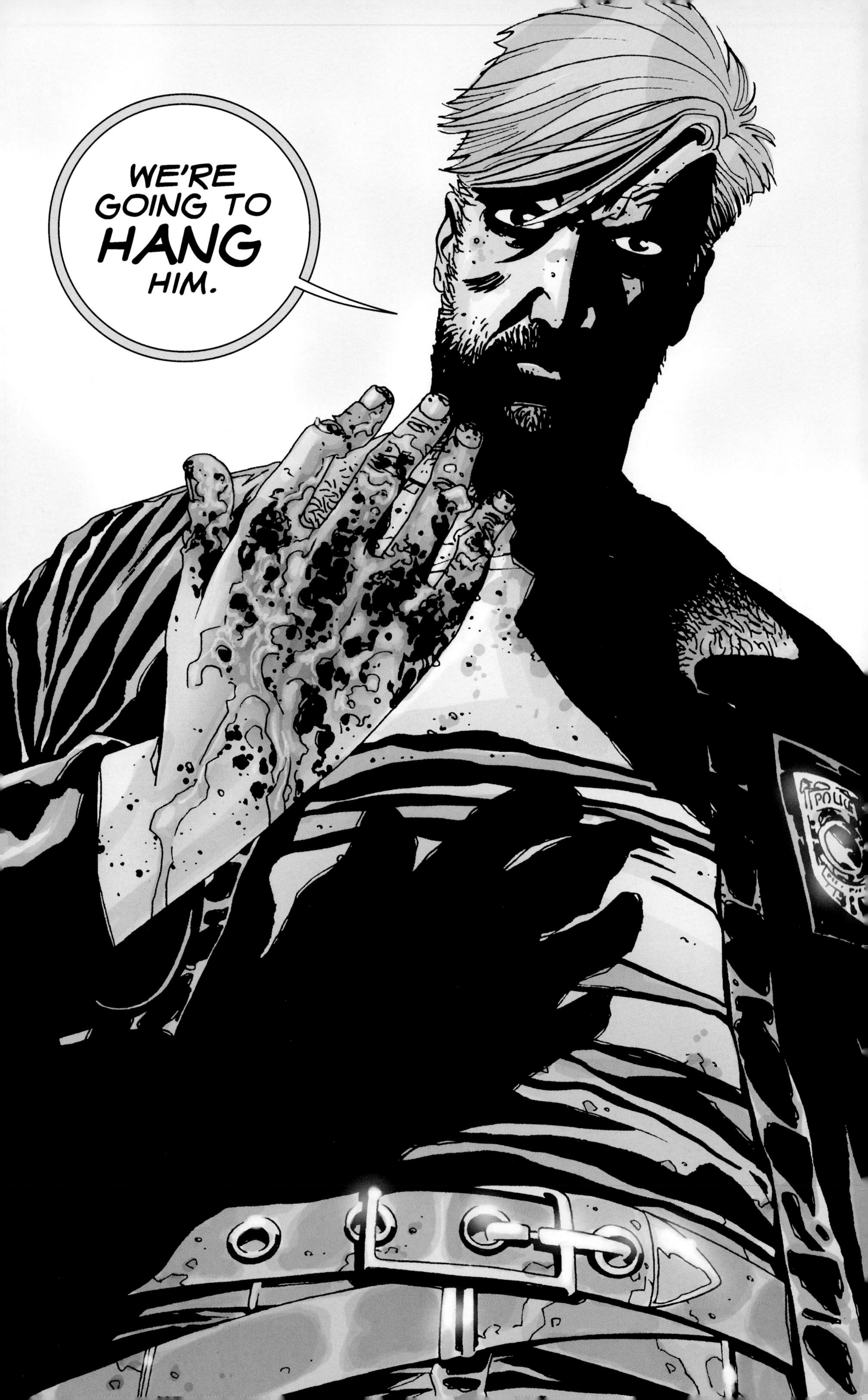
WE'RE GOING TO HANG HIM.

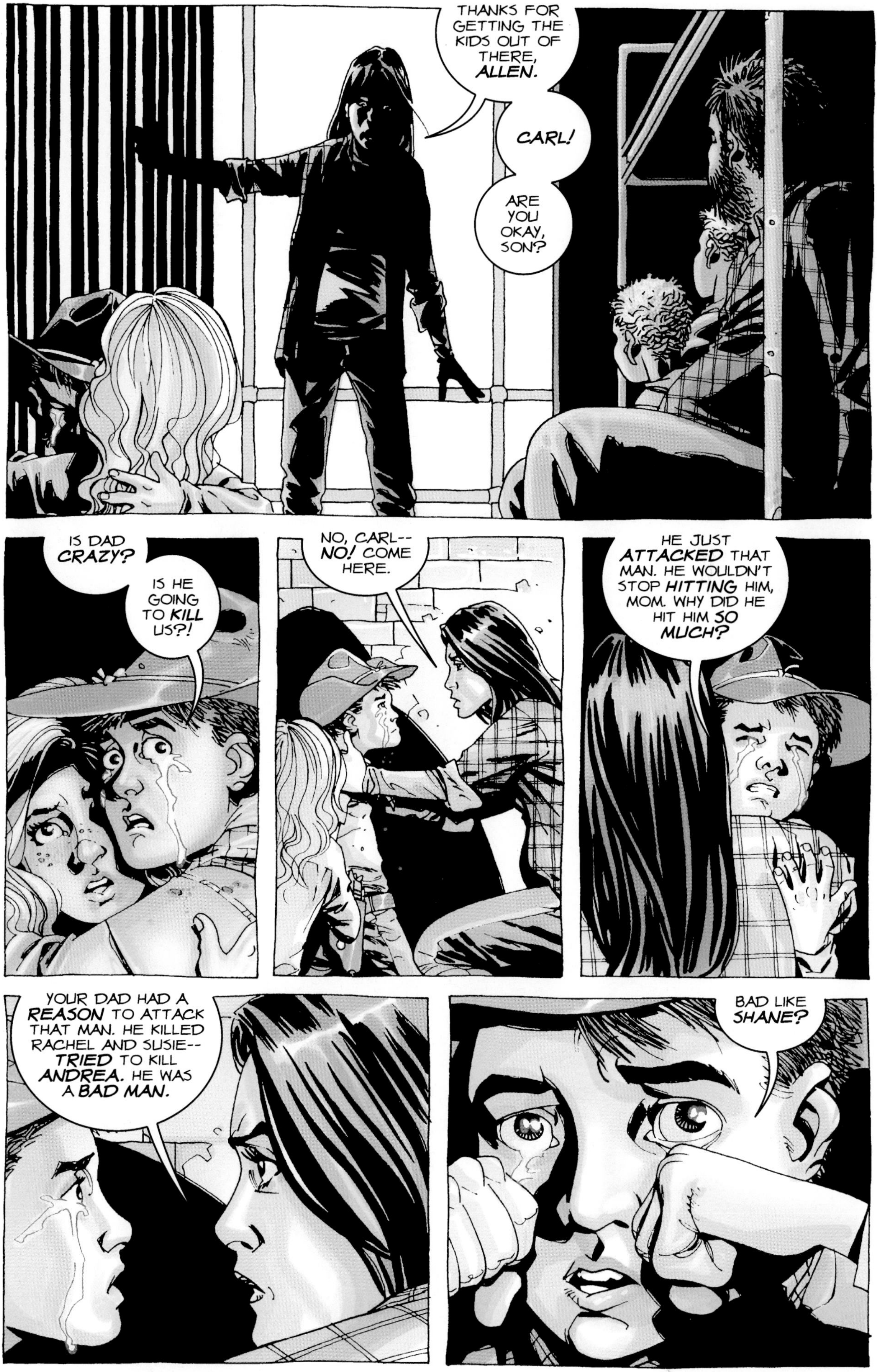
THANKS FOR GETTING THE KIDS OUT OF THERE, ALLEN.
CARL!
ARE YOU OKAY, SON?
IS DAD CRAZY?
IS HE GOING TO KILL US?!
NO, CARL-- NO! COME HERE.
HE JUST ATTACKED THAT MAN. HE WOULDN'T STOP HITTING HIM, MOM. WHY DID HE HIT HIM SO MUCH?
YOUR DAD HAD A REASON TO ATTACK THAT MAN. HE KILLED RACHEL AND SUSIE-- TRIED TO KILL ANDREA. HE WAS A BAD MAN.
BAD LIKE SHANE?

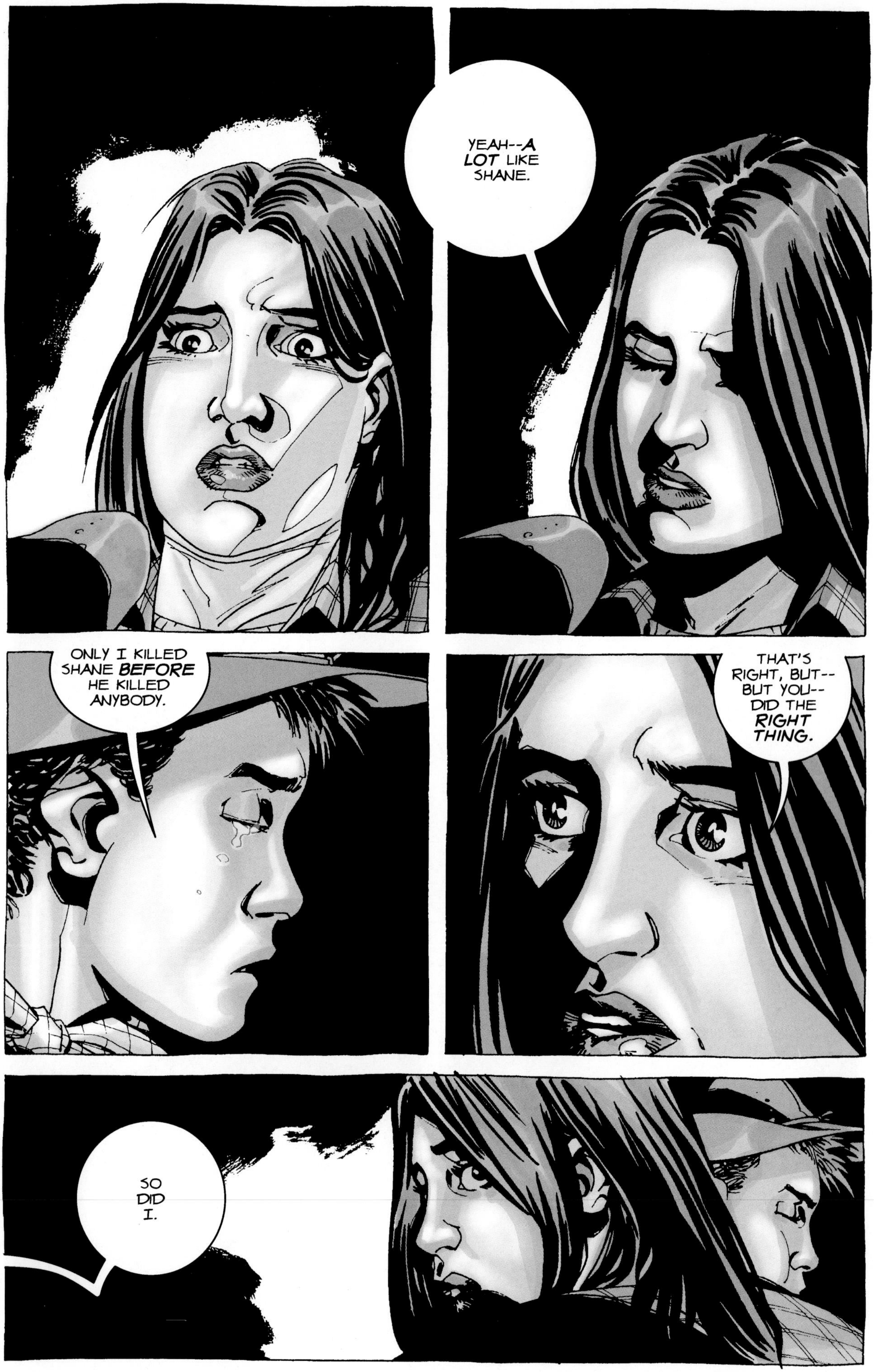
YEAH--A LOT LIKE SHANE.
ONLY I KILLED SHANE BEFORE HE KILLED ANYBODY.
THAT'S RIGHT, BUT-- BUT YOU-- DID THE RIGHT THING.
SO DID I.

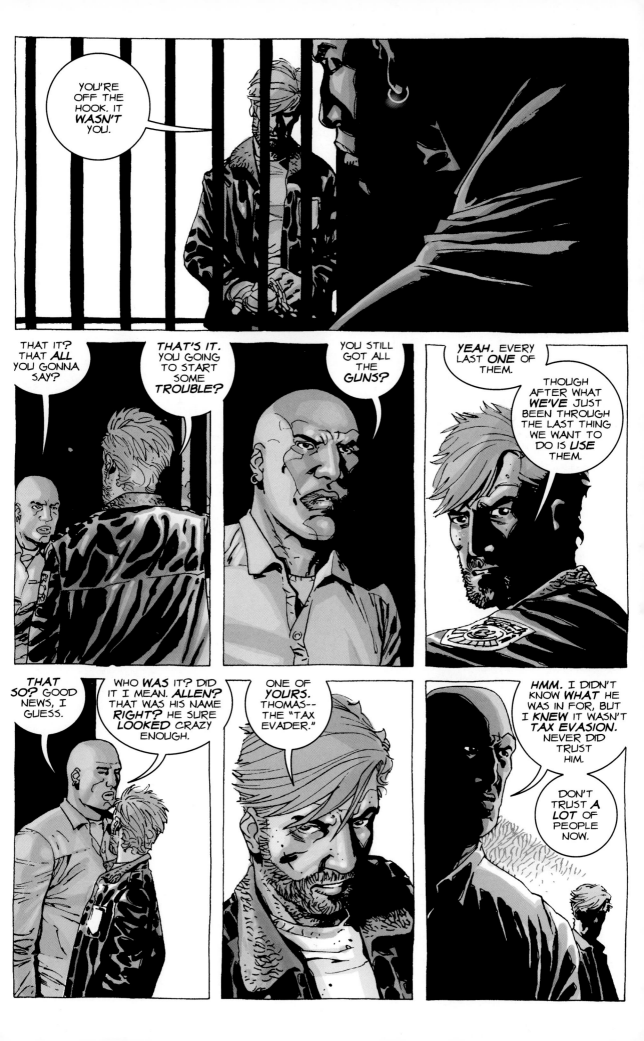

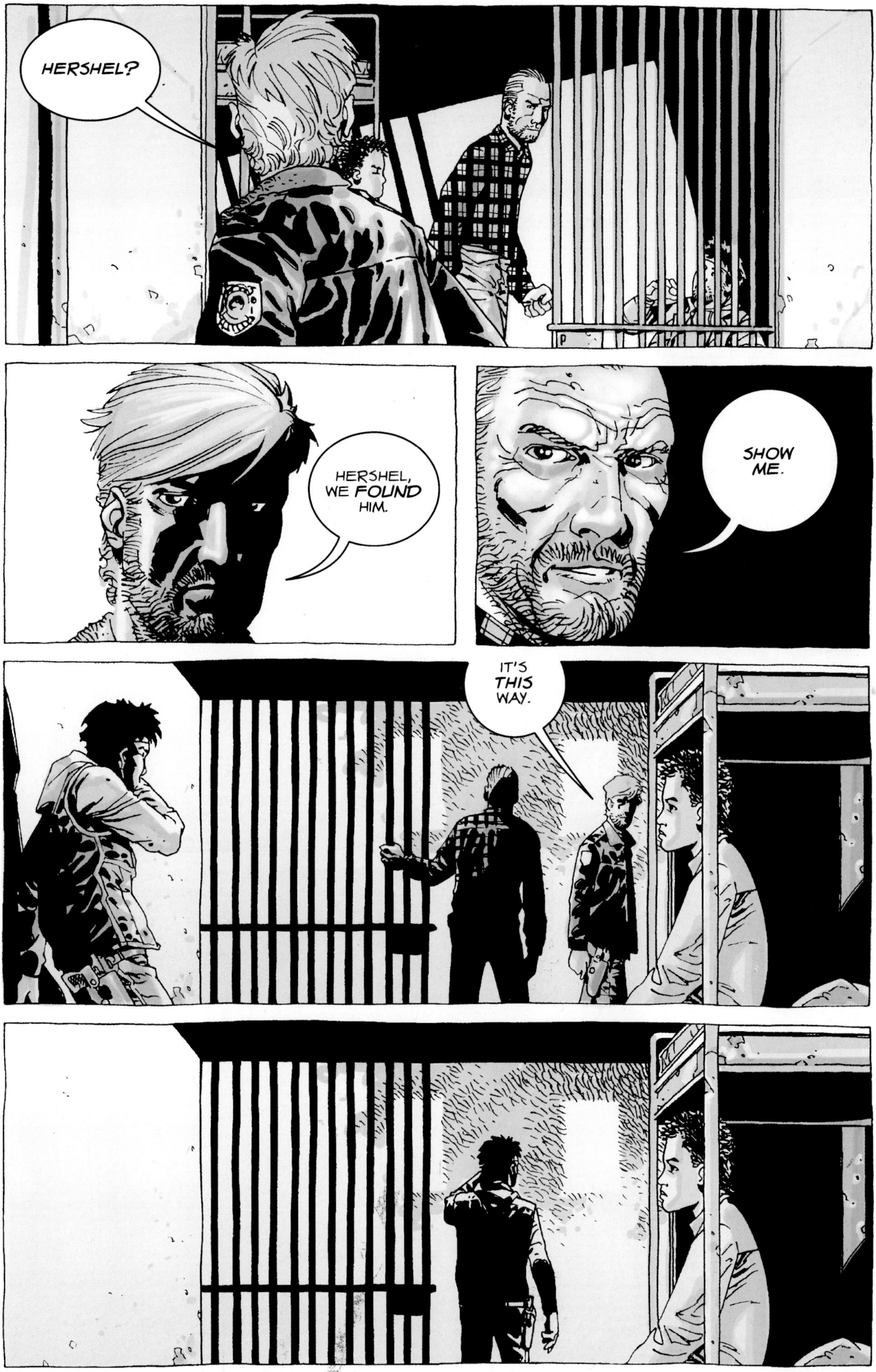
HERSHEL?
HERSHEL, WE FOUND HIM.
SHOW ME.
IT'S THIS WAY.

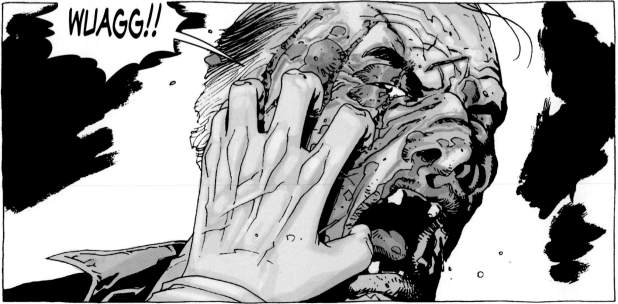

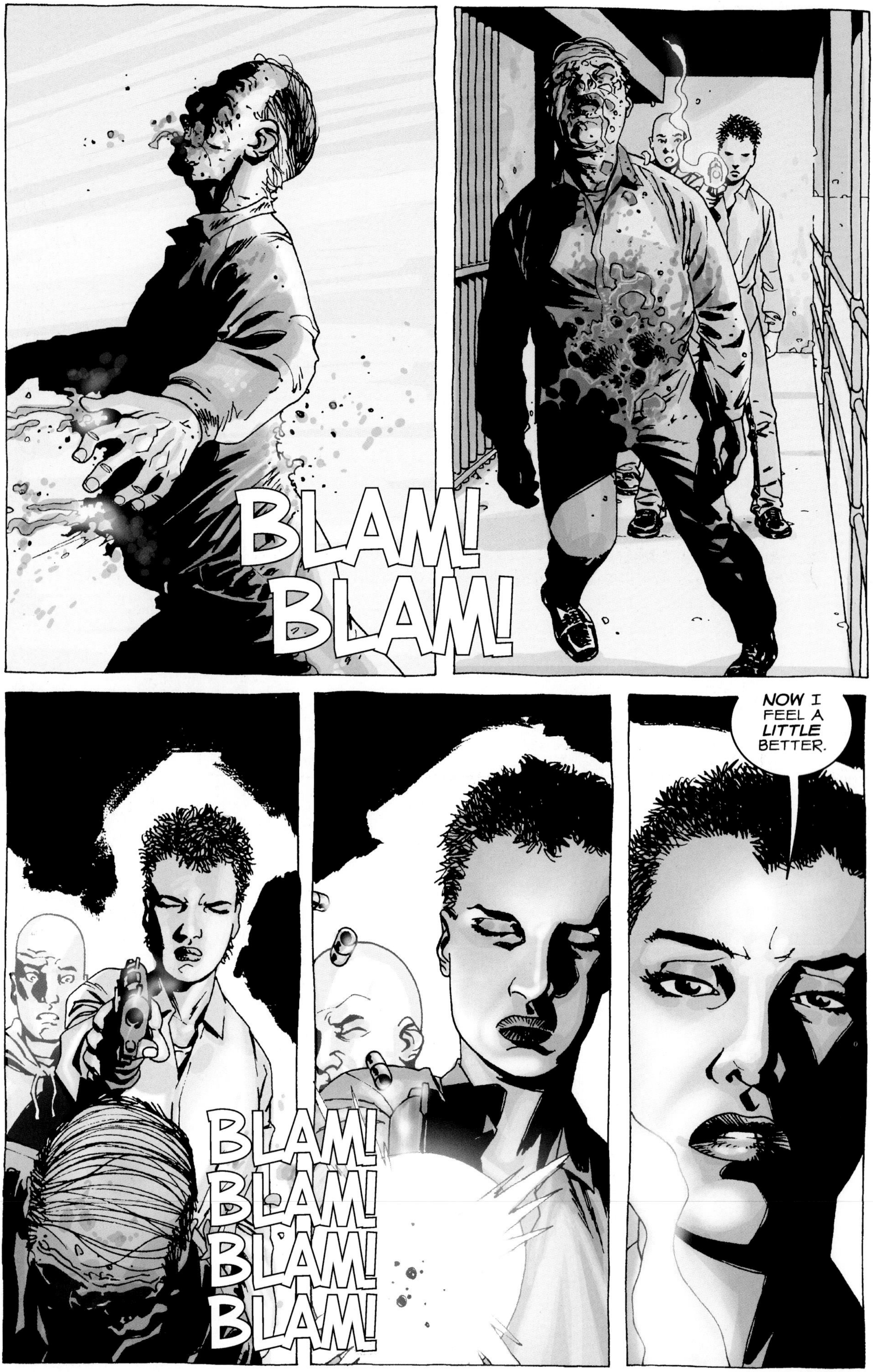
BLAM!
BLAM!
BLAM!
BLAM!
BLAM!
BLAM!
NOW I FEEL A LITTLE BETTER.

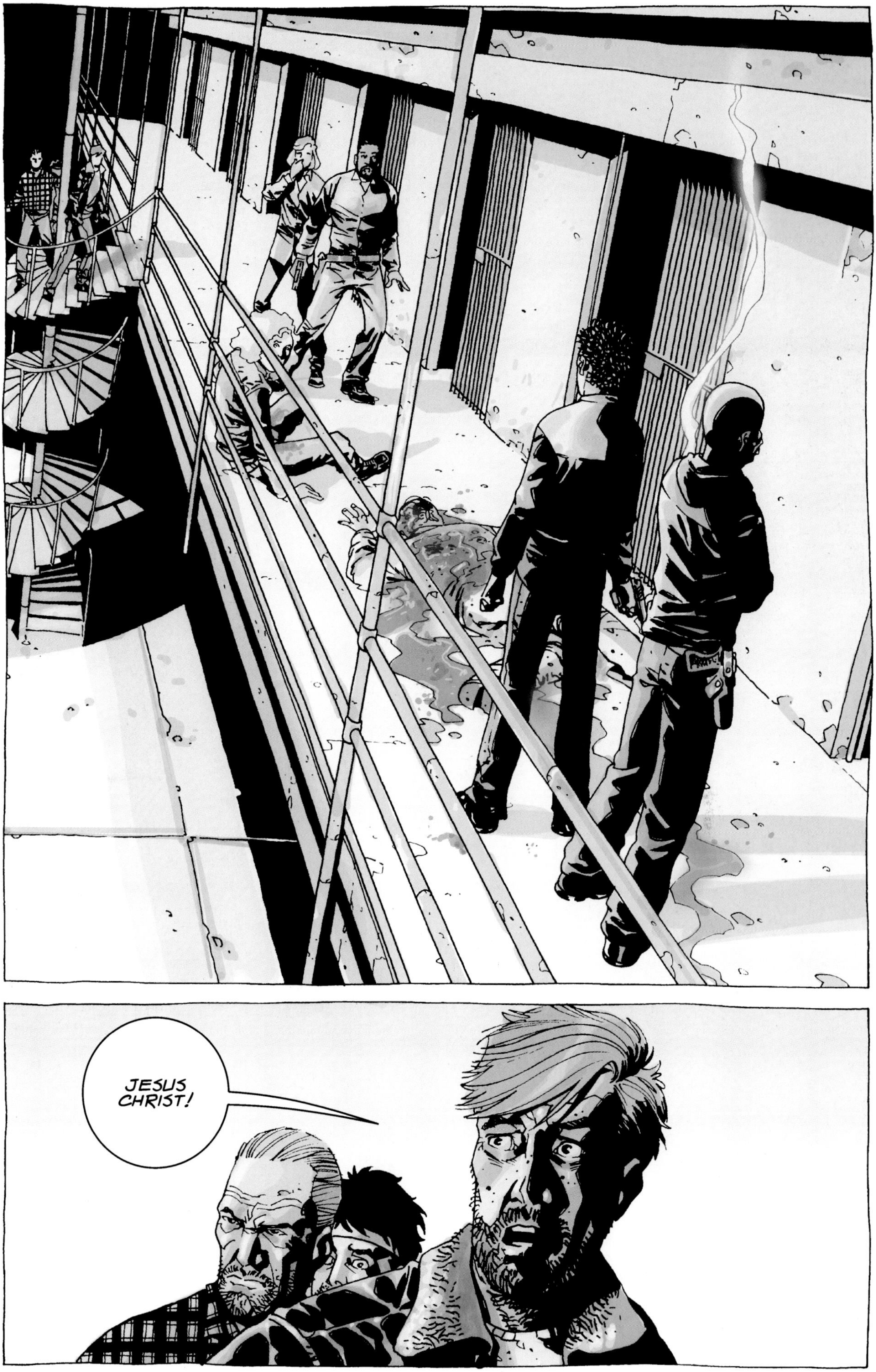
JESUS CHRIST!

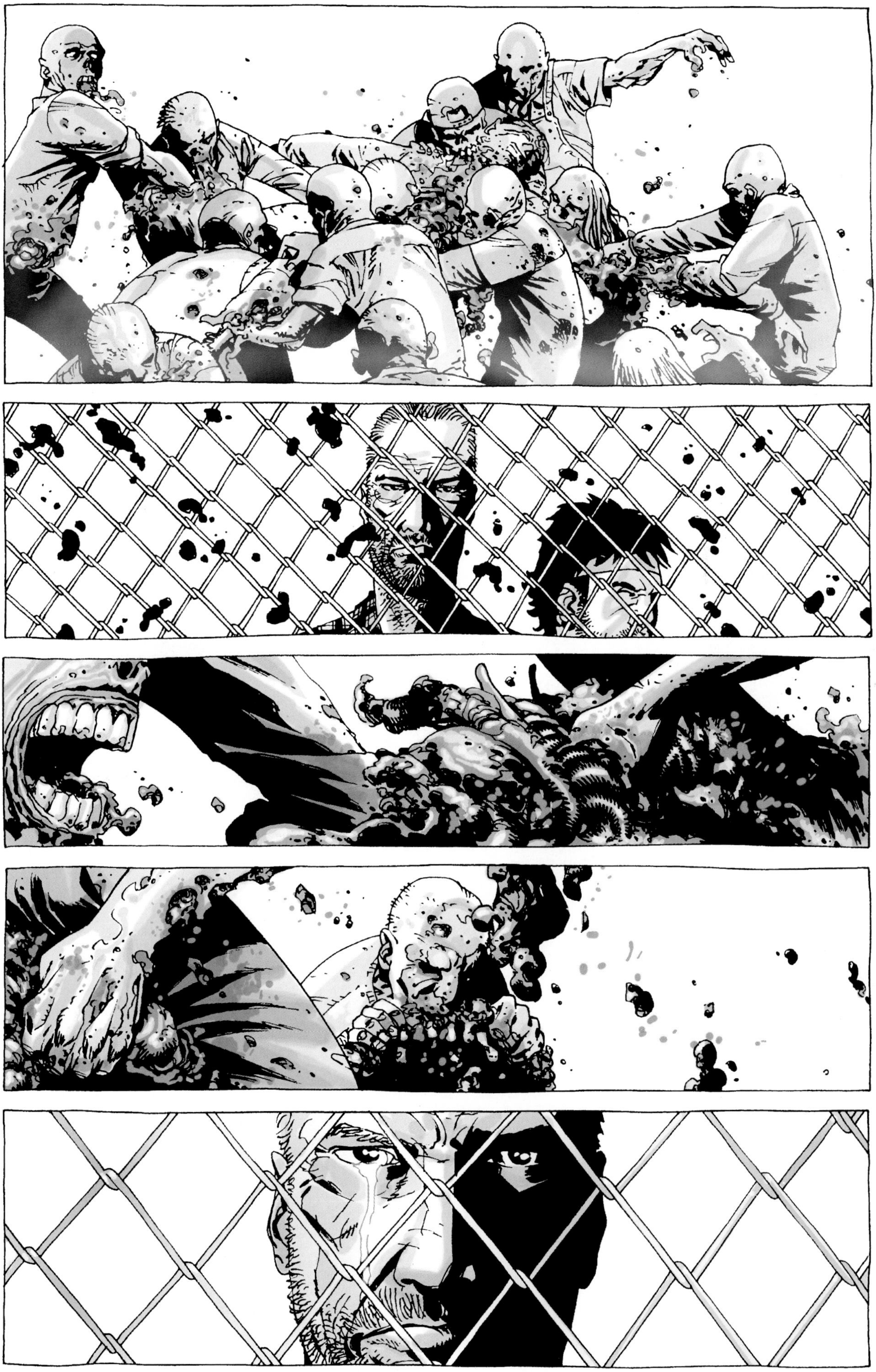

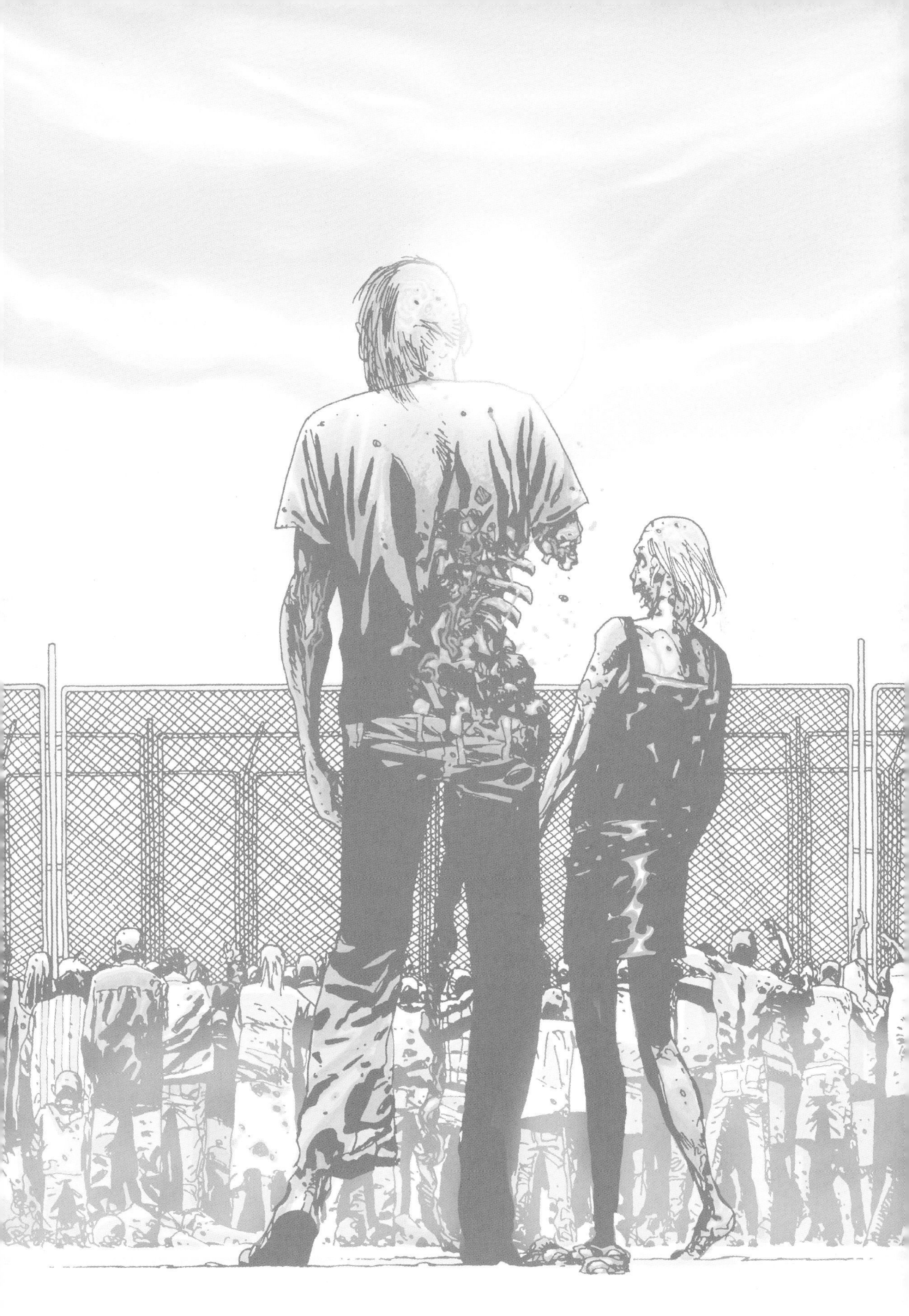

Chapter Four:
The Heart's Desire

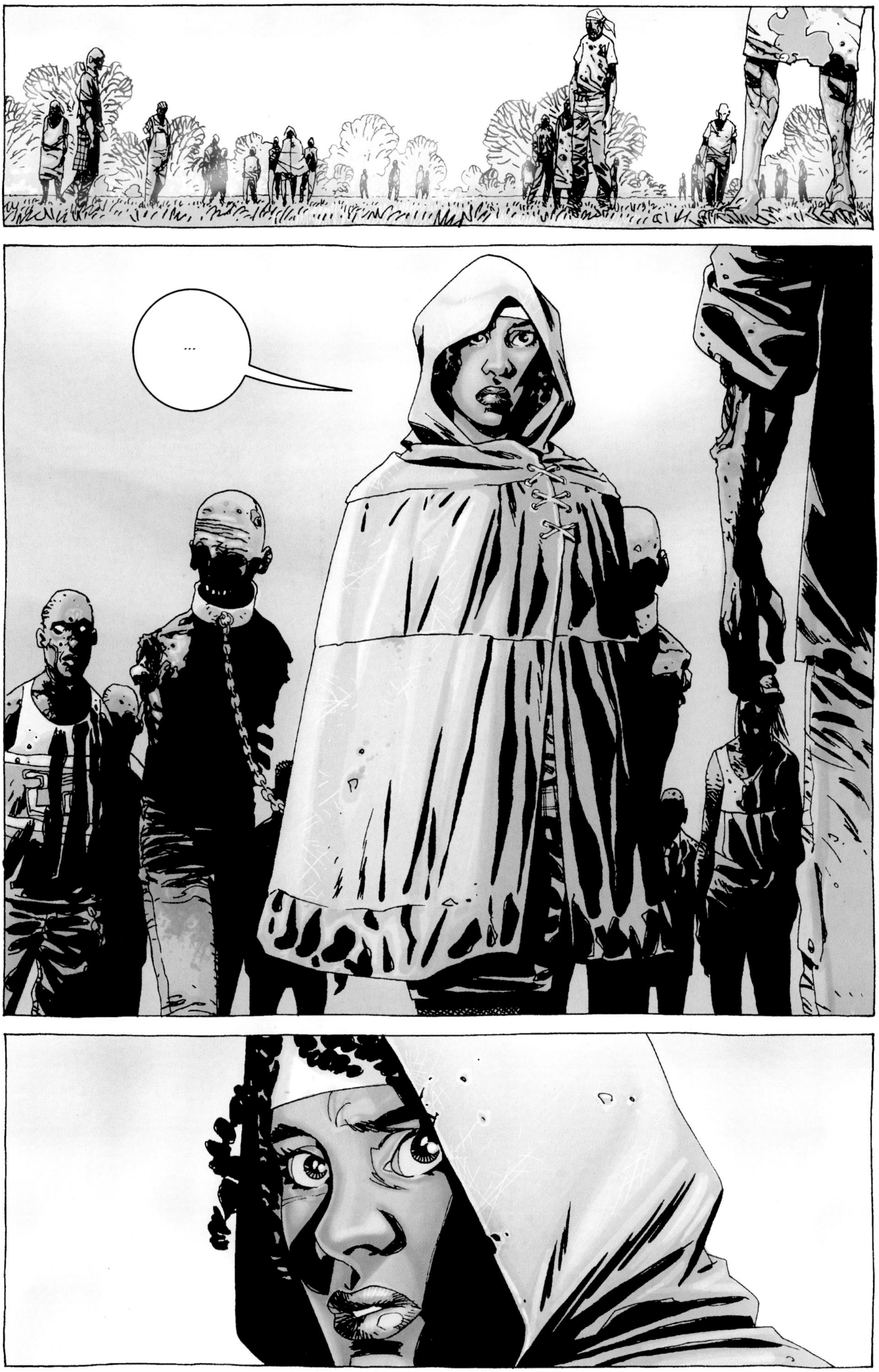
...

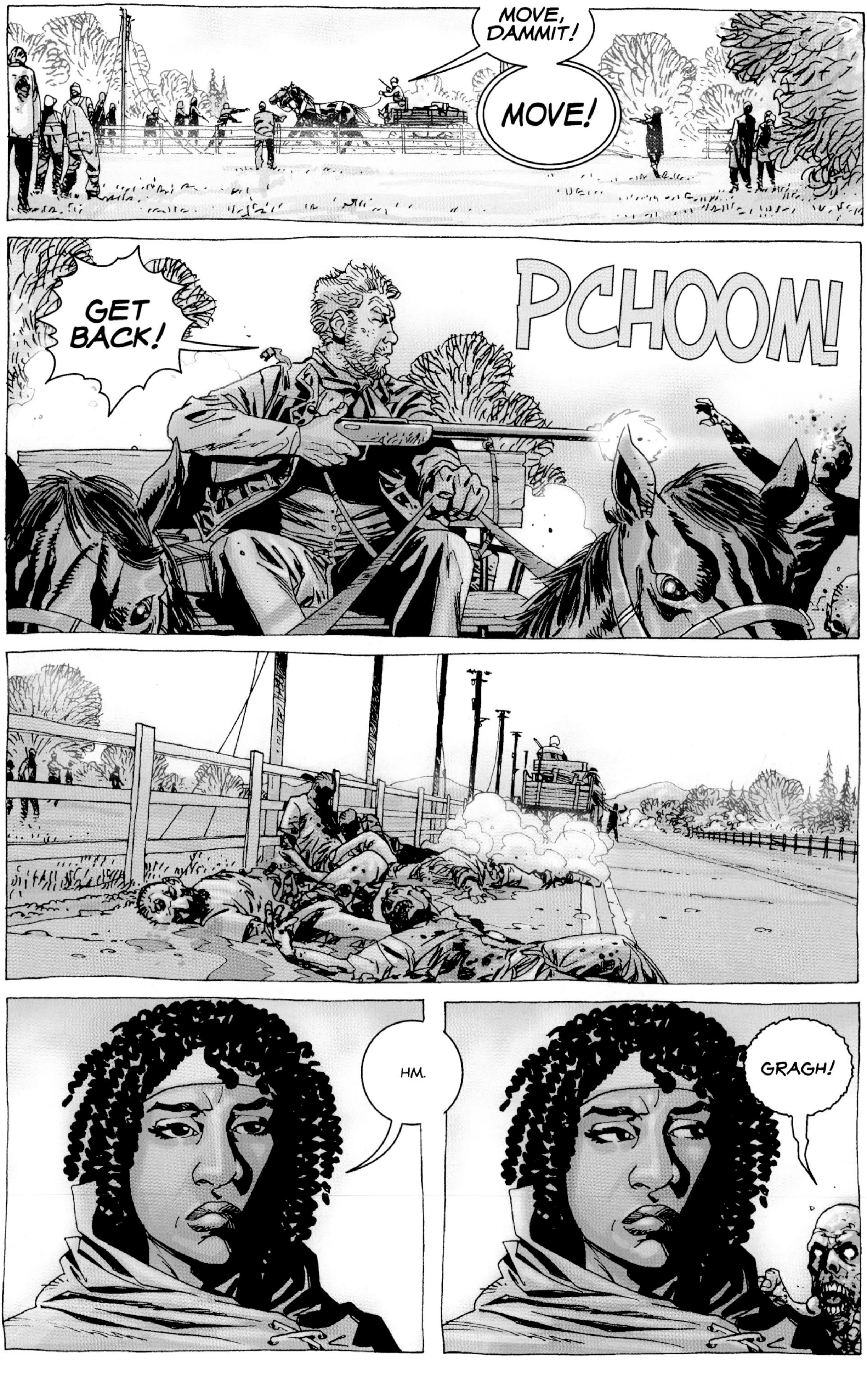
MOVE, DAMMIT!
MOVE!
GET BACK!
PCHOOM!
HM.
GRAGH!

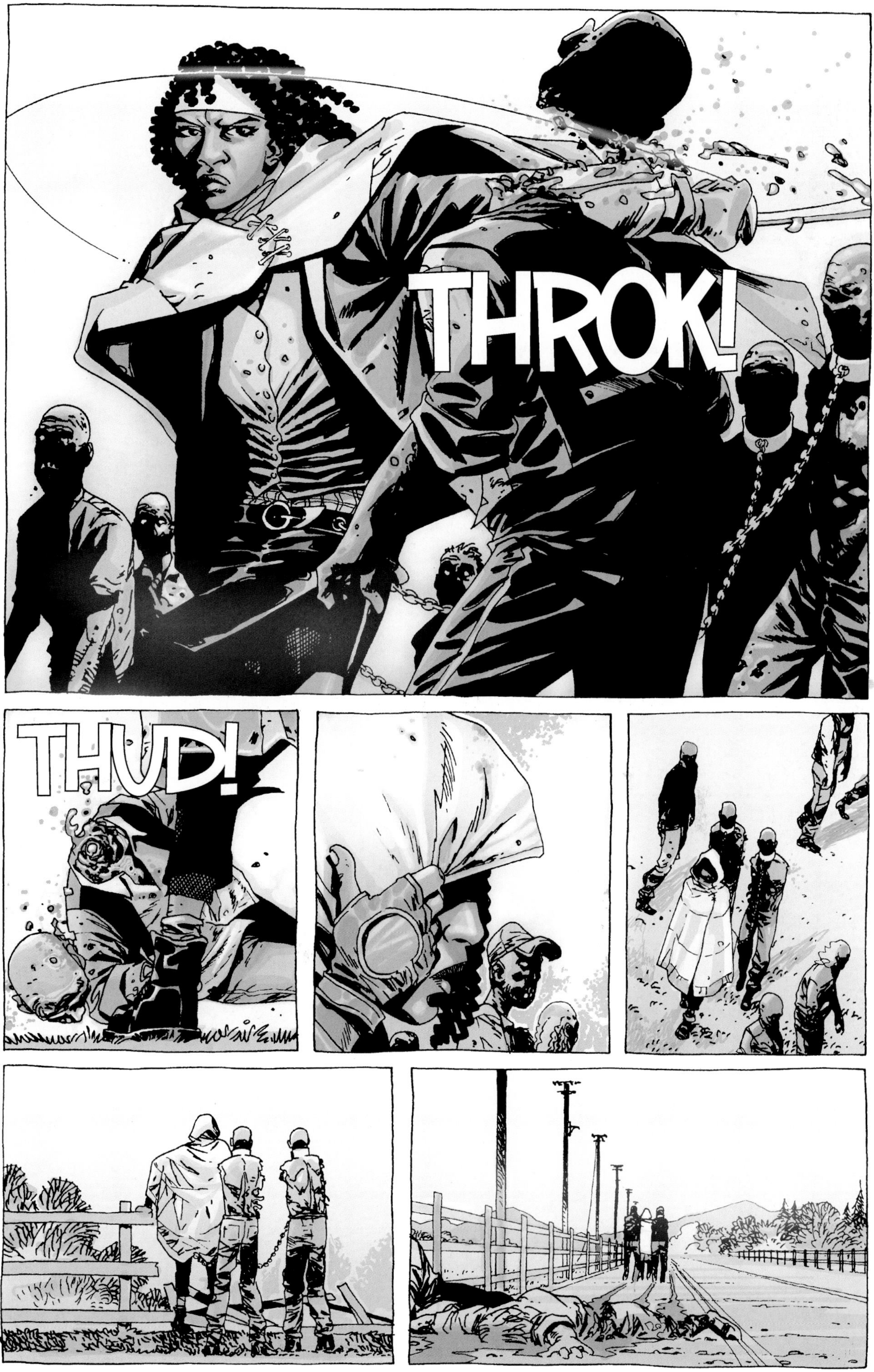
THROK!
THUD!

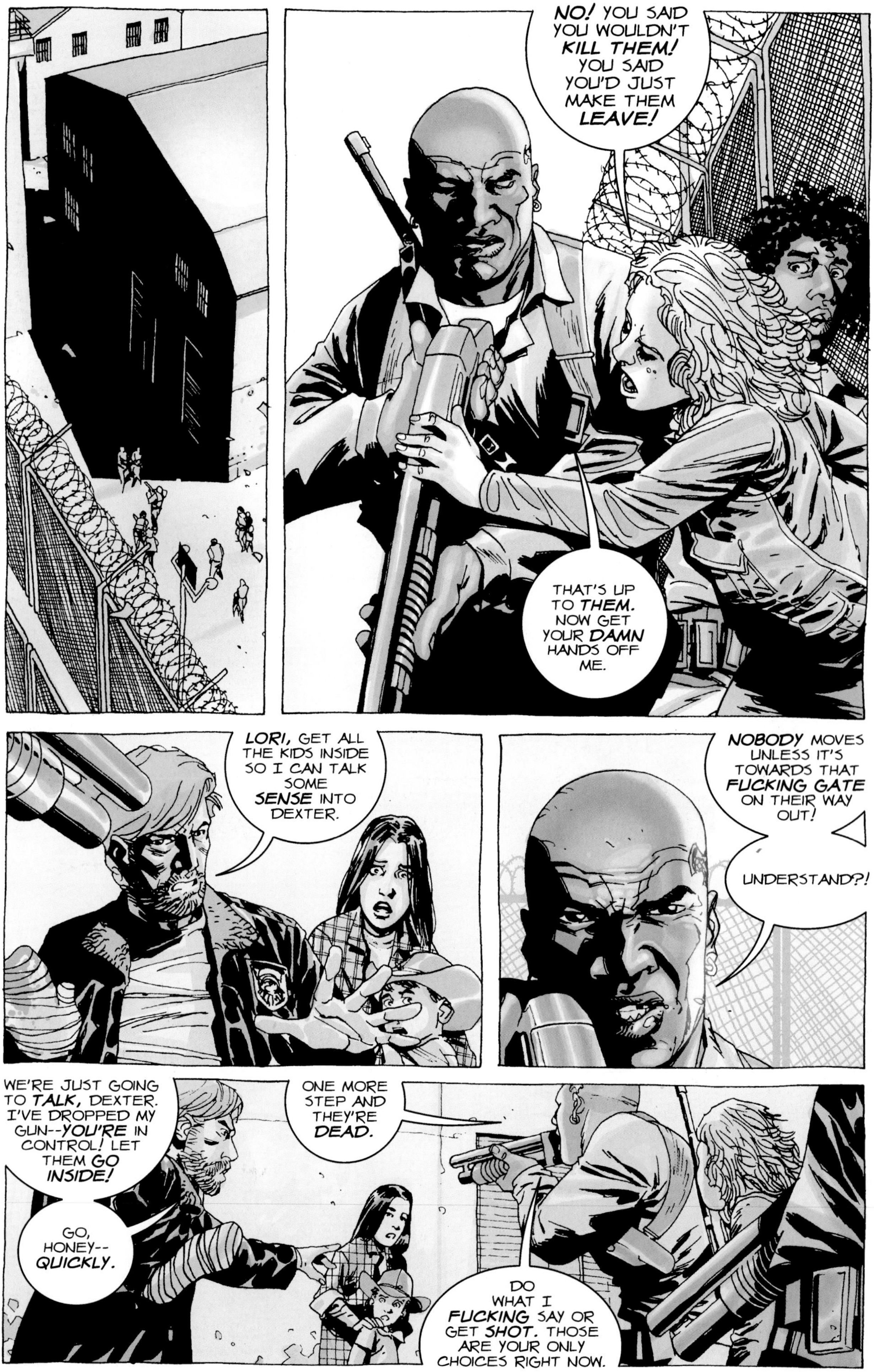
NO! YOU SAID YOU WOULDN'T KILL THEM! YOU SAID YOU'D JUST MAKE THEM LEAVE!
THAT'S UP TO THEM. NOW GET YOUR DAMN HANDS OFF ME.
LORI, GET ALL THE KIDS INSIDE SO I CAN TALK SOME SENSE INTO DEXTER.
NOBODY MOVES UNLESS IT'S TOWARDS THAT FUCKING GATE ON THEIR WAY OUT!
UNDERSTAND?!
WE'RE JUST GOING TO TALK, DEXTER. I'VE DROPPED MY GUN--YOU'RE IN CONTROL! LET THEM GO INSIDE!
GO, HONEY-- QUICKLY.
ONE MORE STEP AND THEY'RE DEAD.
DO WHAT I FUCKING SAY OR GET SHOT. THOSE ARE YOUR ONLY CHOICES RIGHT NOW.

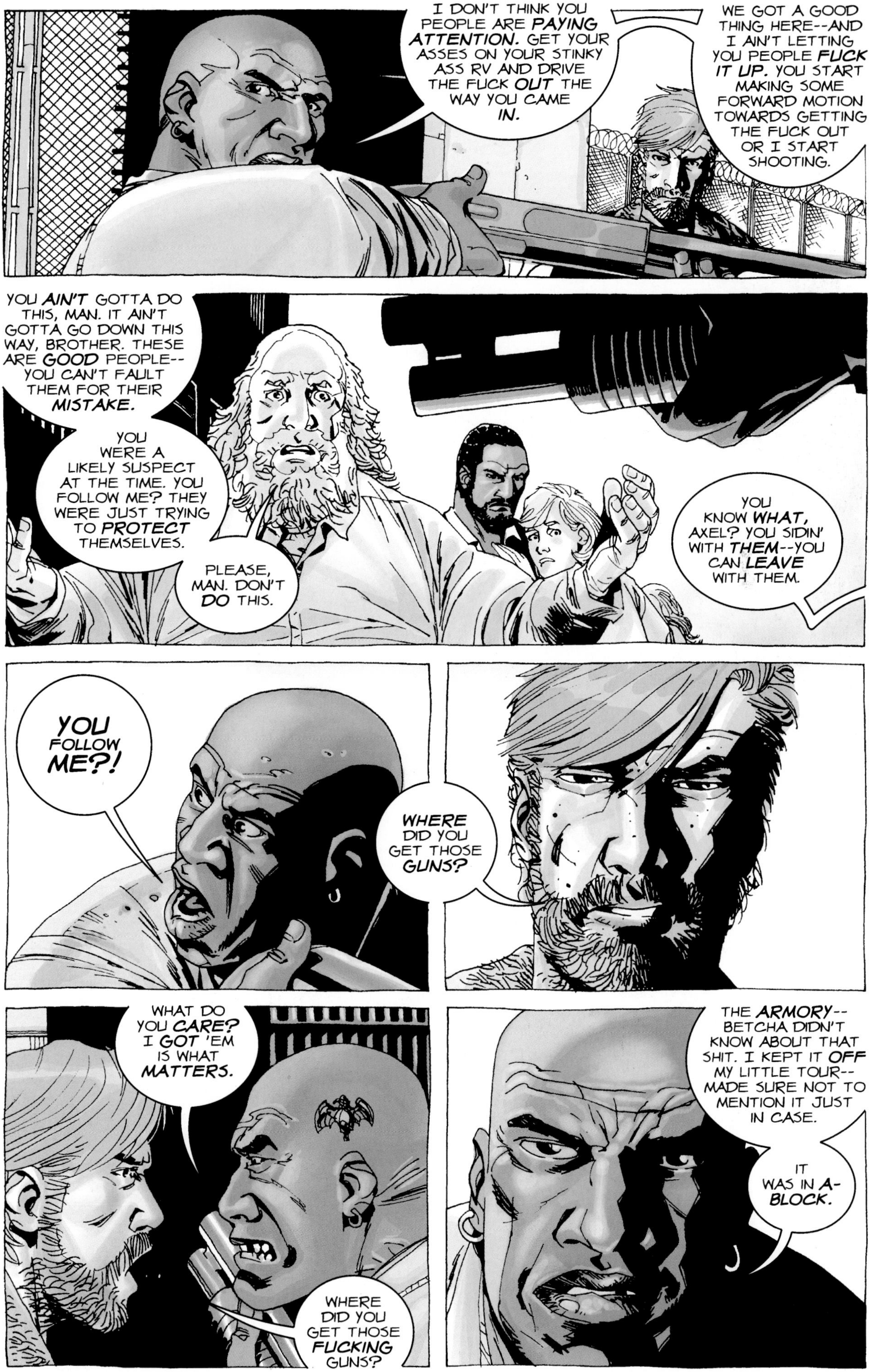
I DON'T THINK YOU PEOPLE ARE PAYING ATTENTION. GET YOUR ASSES ON YOUR STINKY ASS RV AND DRIVE THE FUCK OUT THE WAY YOU CAME IN.
WE GOT A GOOD THING HERE--AND I AIN'T LETTING YOU PEOPLE FUCK IT UP. YOU START MAKING SOME FORWARD MOTION TOWARDS GETTING THE FUCK OUT OR I START SHOOTING.
YOU AIN'T GOTTA DO THIS, MAN. IT AIN'T GOTTA GO DOWN THIS WAY, BROTHER. THESE ARE GOOD PEOPLE-- YOU CAN'T FAULT THEM FOR THEIR MISTAKE.
YOU WERE A LIKELY SUSPECT AT THE TIME. YOU FOLLOW ME? THEY WERE JUST TRYING TO PROTECT THEMSELVES.
PLEASE, MAN. DON'T DO THIS.
YOU KNOW WHAT, AXEL? YOU SIDIN' WITH THEM--YOU CAN LEAVE WITH THEM.
YOU FOLLOW ME?!
WHERE DID YOU GET THOSE GUNS?
WHAT DO YOU CARE? I GOT 'EM IS WHAT MATTERS.
WHERE DID YOU GET THOSE FUCKING GUNS?
THE ARMORY-- BETCHA DIDN'T KNOW ABOUT THAT SHIT. I KEPT IT OFF MY LITTLE TOUR-- MADE SURE NOT TO MENTION IT JUST IN CASE.
IT WAS IN A-BLOCK.

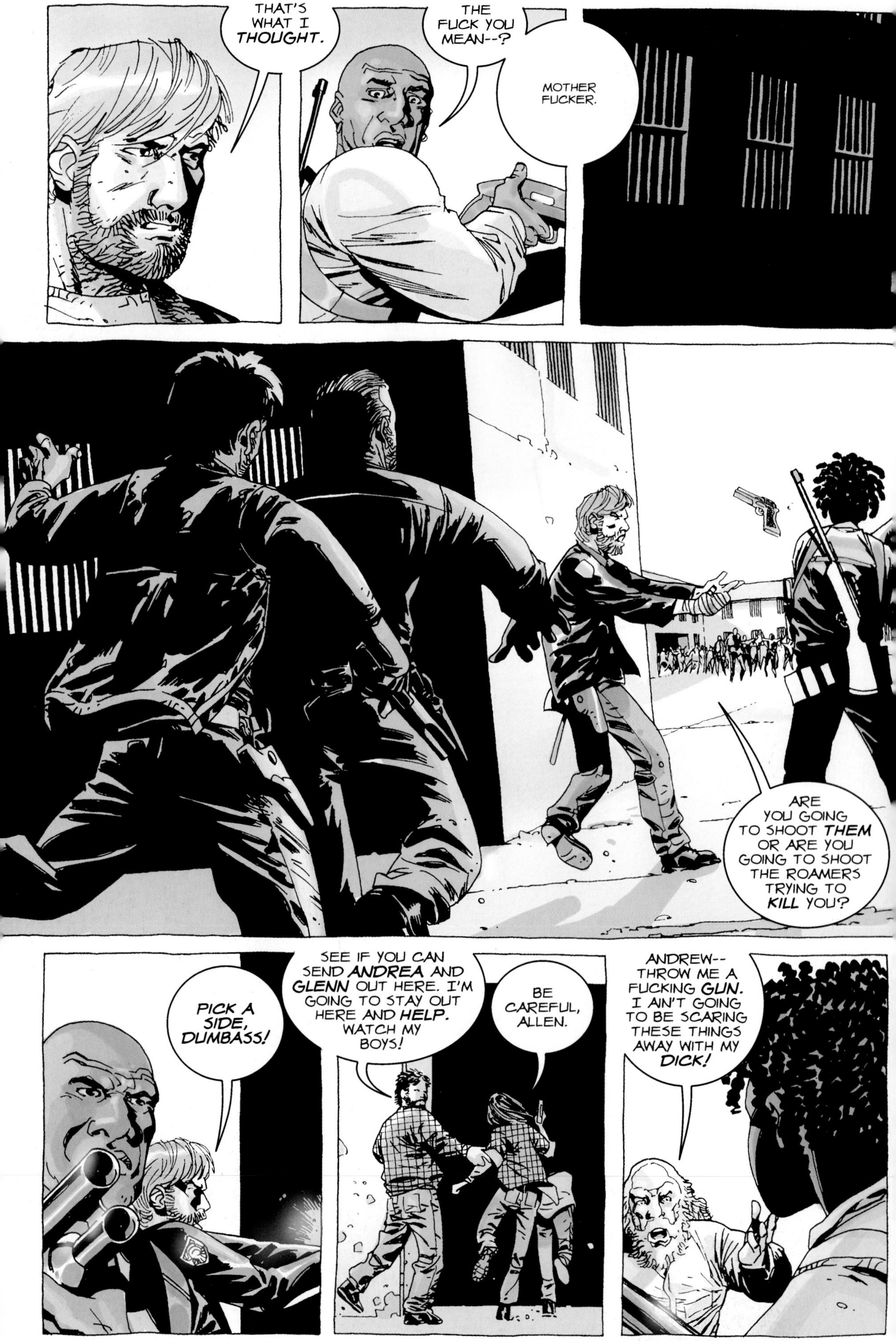
THAT'S WHAT I THOUGHT.
THE FUCK YOU MEAN--?
MOTHER FUCKER.
ARE YOU GOING TO SHOOT THEM OR ARE YOU GOING TO SHOOT THE ROAMERS TRYING TO KILL YOU?
PICK A SIDE, DUMBASS!
SEE IF YOU CAN SEND ANDREA AND GLENN OUT HERE. I'M GOING TO STAY OUT HERE AND HELP. WATCH MY BOYS!
BE CAREFUL, ALLEN.
ANDREW-- THROW ME A FUCKING GUN. I AIN'T GOING TO BE SCARING THESE THINGS AWAY WITH MY DICK!

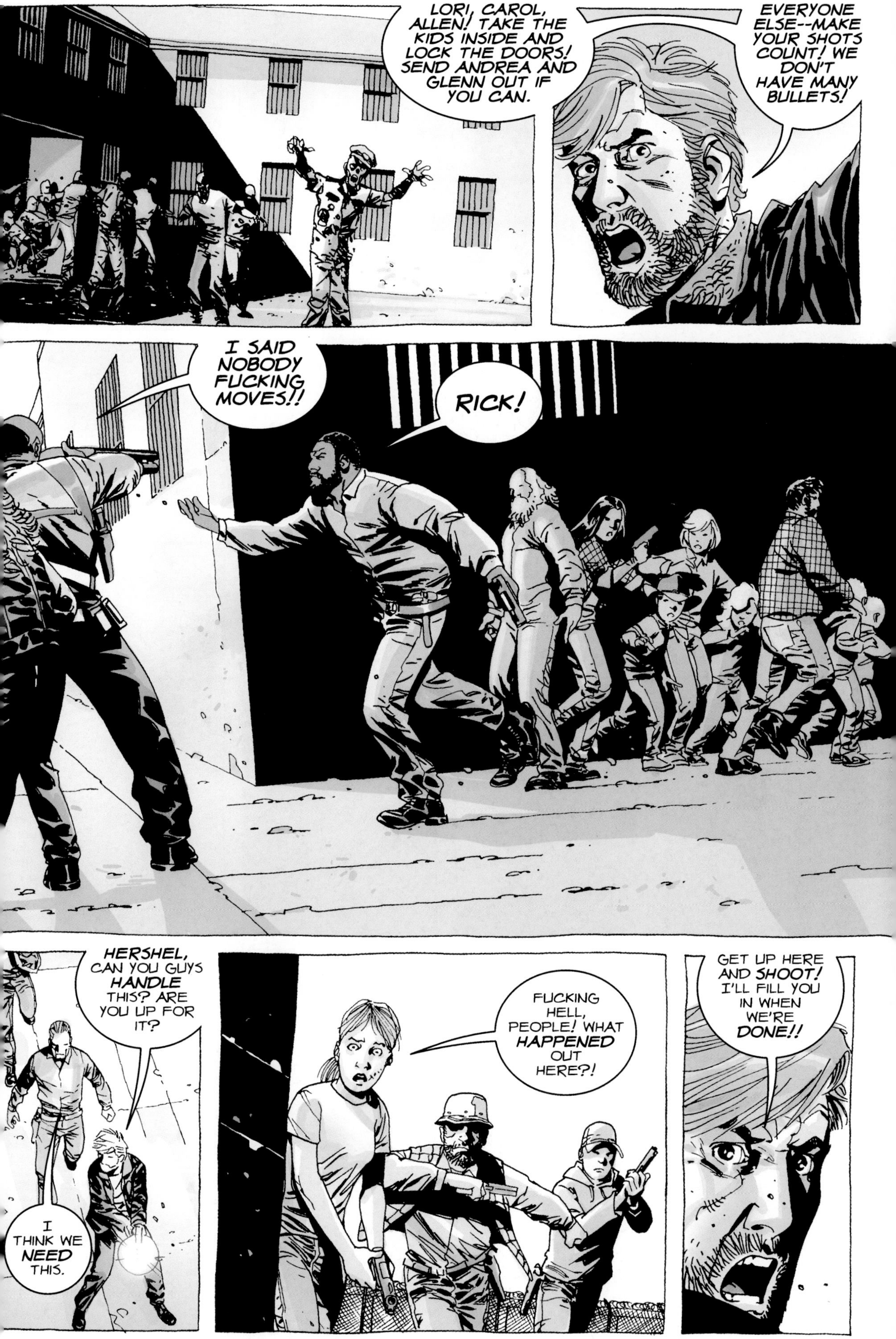
LORI, CAROL, ALLEN! TAKE THE KIDS INSIDE AND LOCK THE DOORS! SEND ANDREA AND GLENN OUT IF YOU CAN.
EVERYONE ELSE--MAKE YOUR SHOTS COUNT! WE DON'T HAVE MANY BULLETS!
I SAID NOBODY FUCKING MOVES!!
RICK!
HERSHEL, CAN YOU GUYS HANDLE THIS? ARE YOU UP FOR IT?
I THINK WE NEED THIS.
FUCKING HELL, PEOPLE! WHAT HAPPENED OUT HERE?!
GET UP HERE AND SHOOT! I'LL FILL YOU IN WHEN WE'RE DONE!!

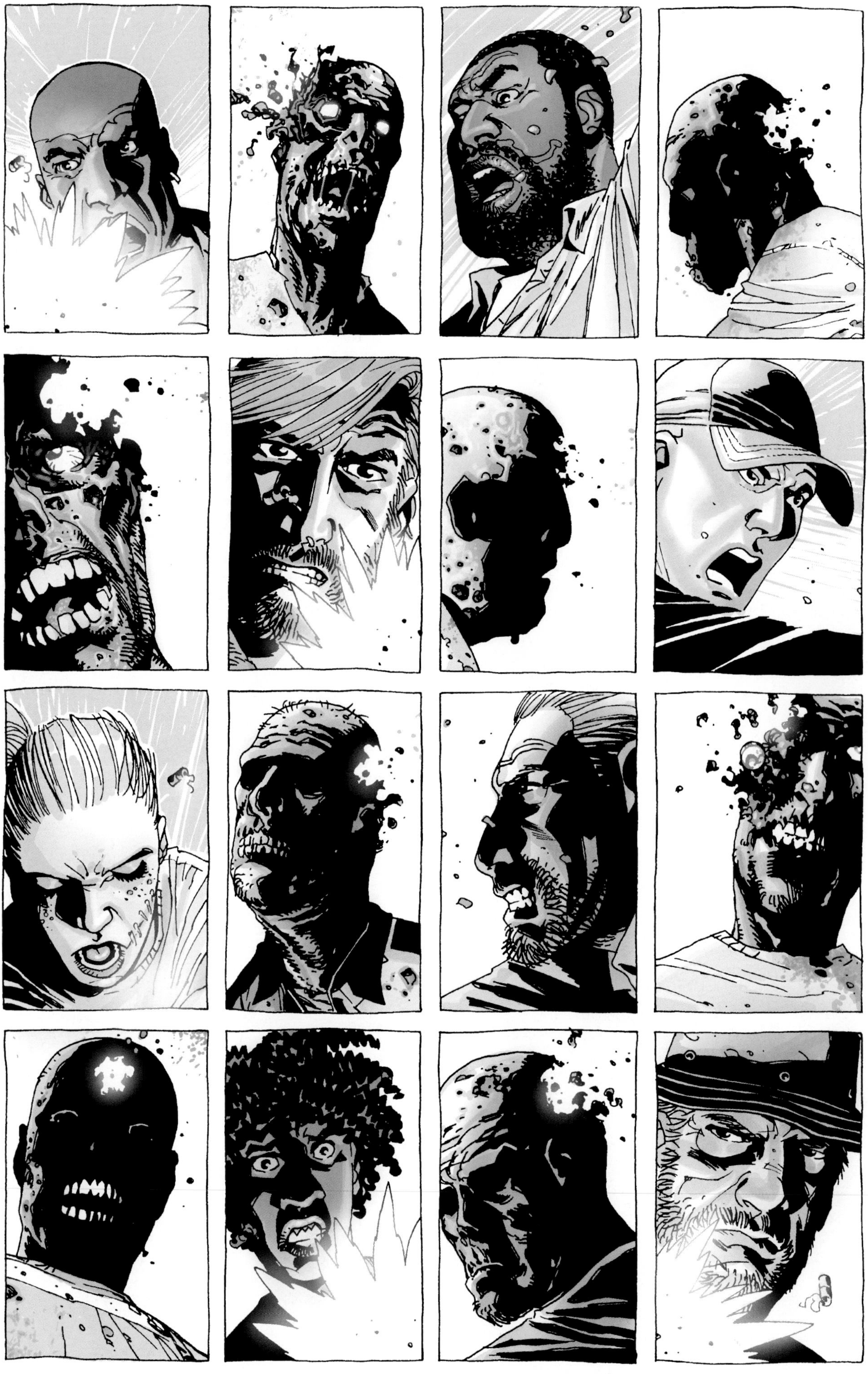

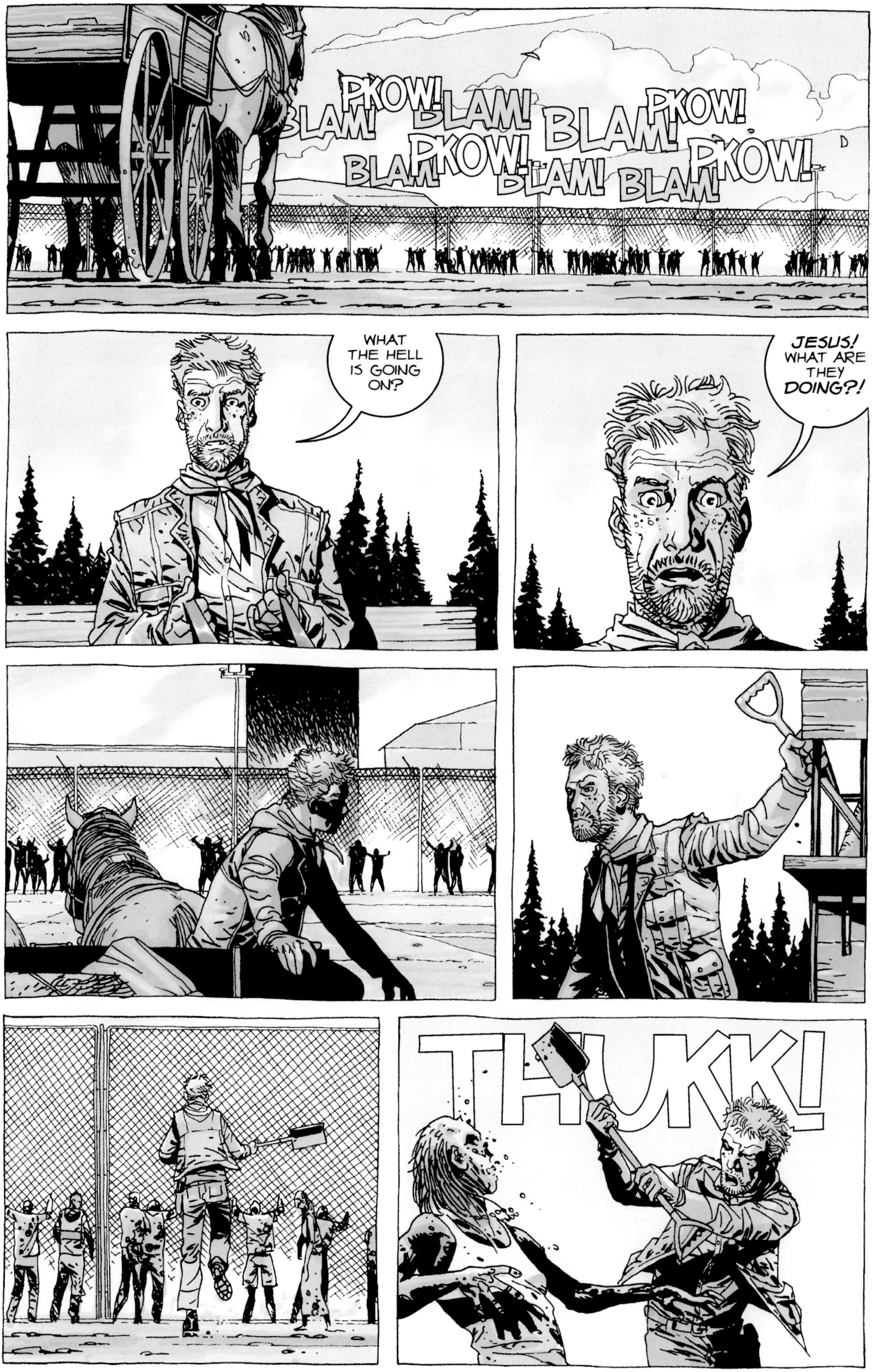
PKOW!
BLAM!
BLAM!
BLAM!
PKOW!
BLAM!
PKOW!
BLAM!
BLAM!
BLAM!
PKOW!
WHAT THE HELL IS GOING ON?
JESUS! WHAT ARE THEY DOING?!
THUKK!

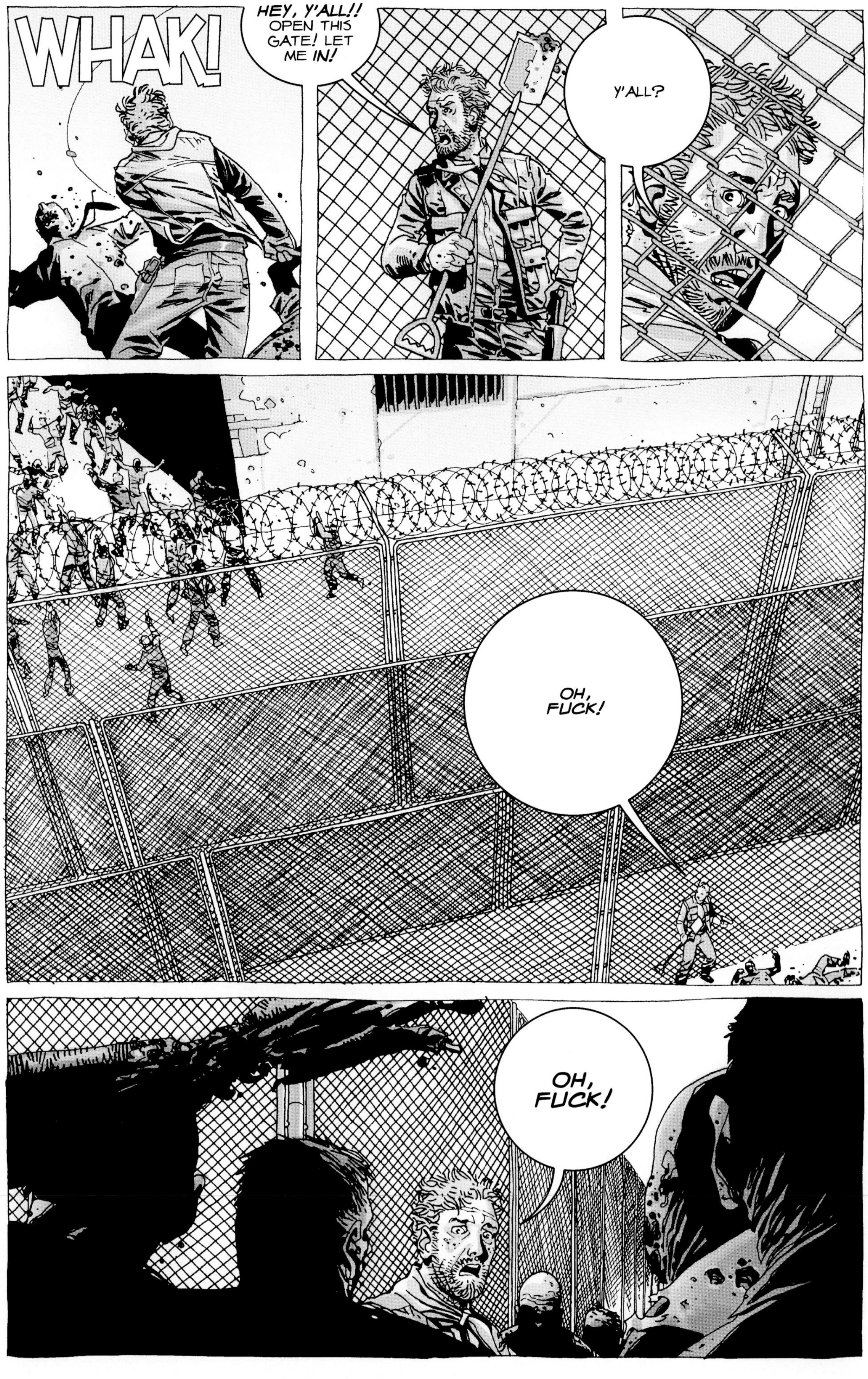
WHAK!
HEY, Y'ALL!! OPEN THIS GATE! LET ME IN!
Y'ALL?
OH, FUCK!
OH, FUCK!

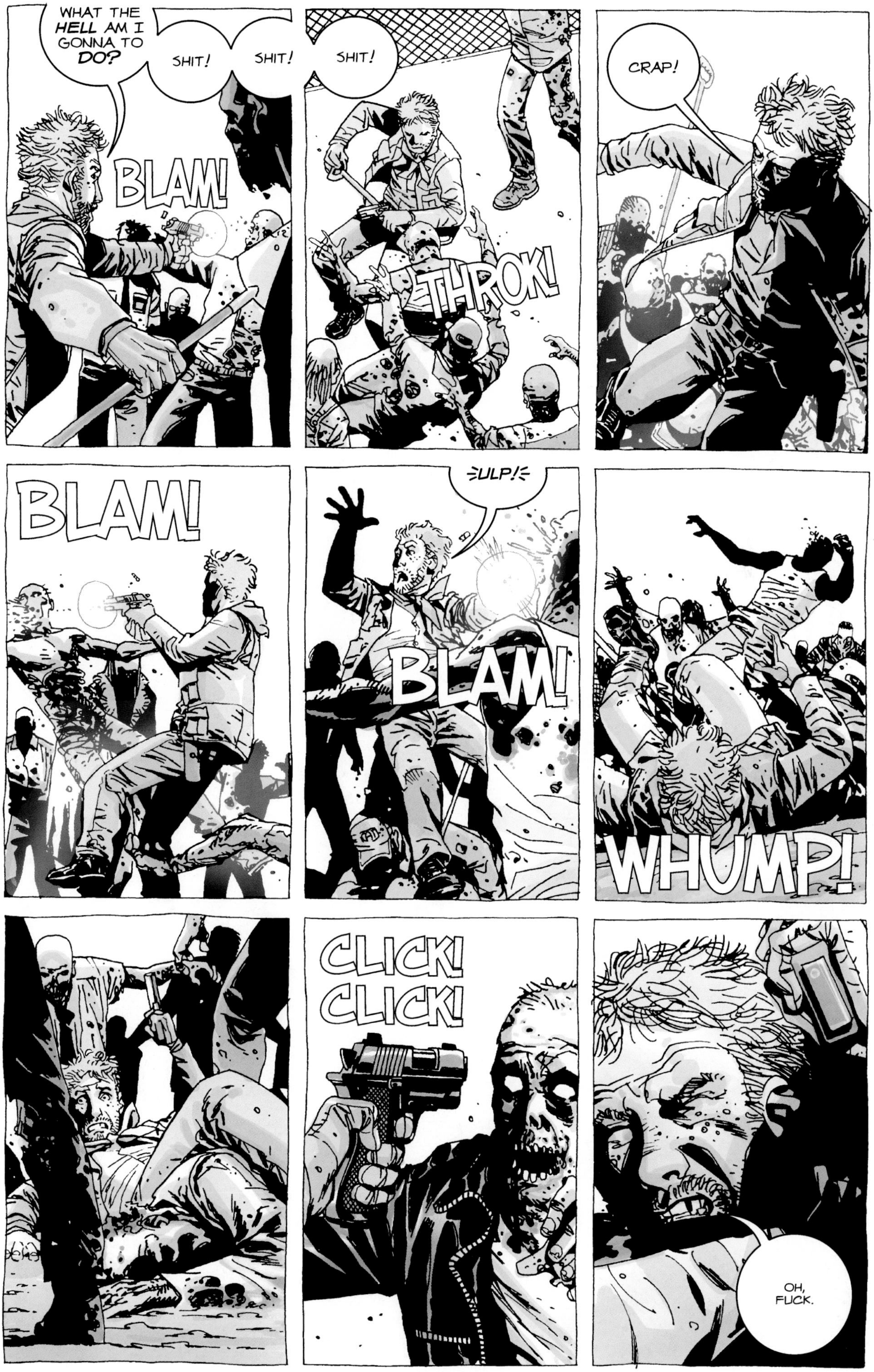
WHAT THE HELL AM I GONNA TO DO?
SHIT!
SHIT!
SHIT!
BLAM!
THROK!
CRAP!
BLAM!
ULP!
BLAM!
WHUMP!
CLICK! CLICK!
OH, FUCK.

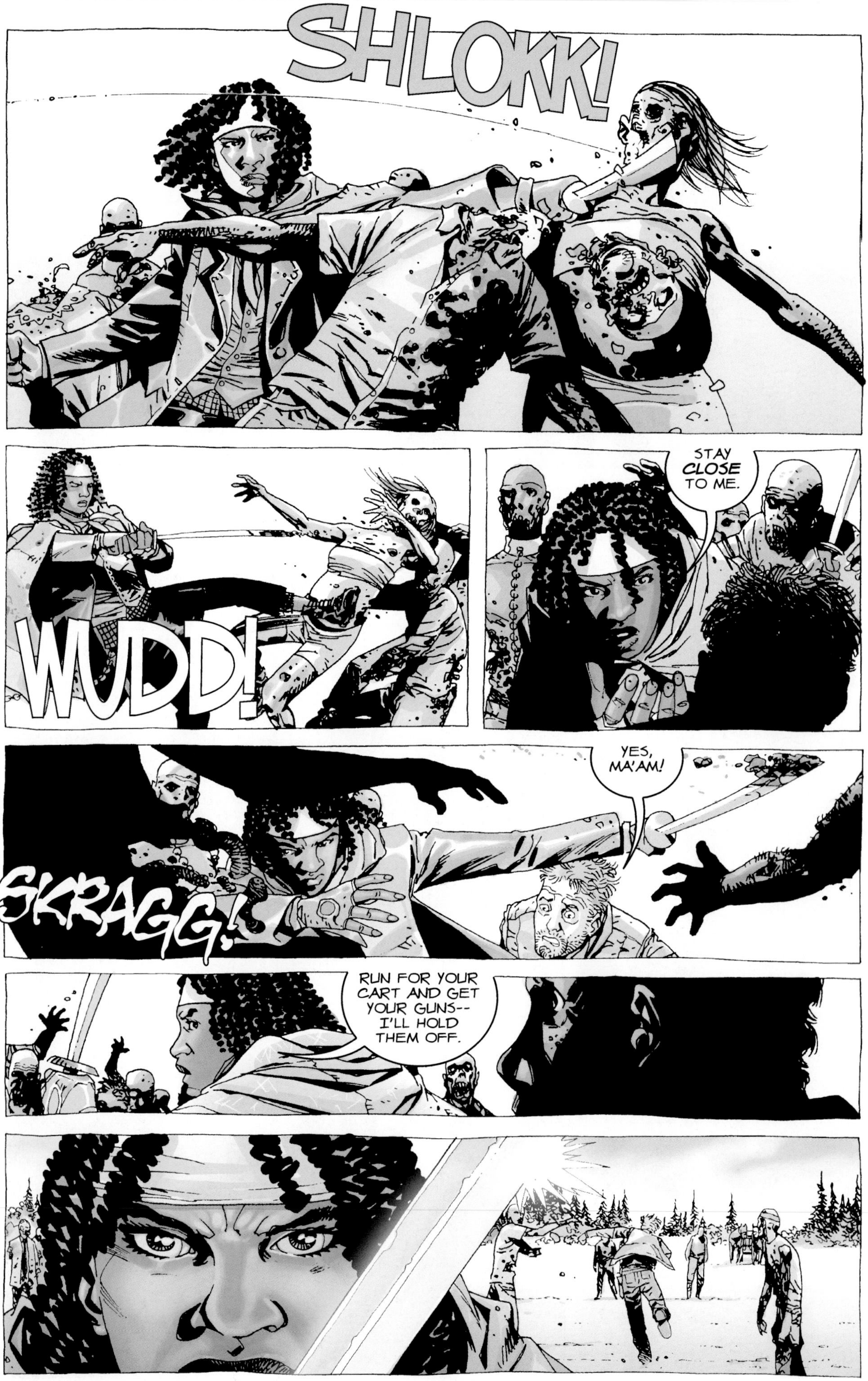
SHLOKK!
WUDD!
STAY CLOSE TO ME.
YES, MA'AM!
SKRAGG!
RUN FOR YOUR CART AND GET YOUR GUNS-- I'LL HOLD THEM OFF.

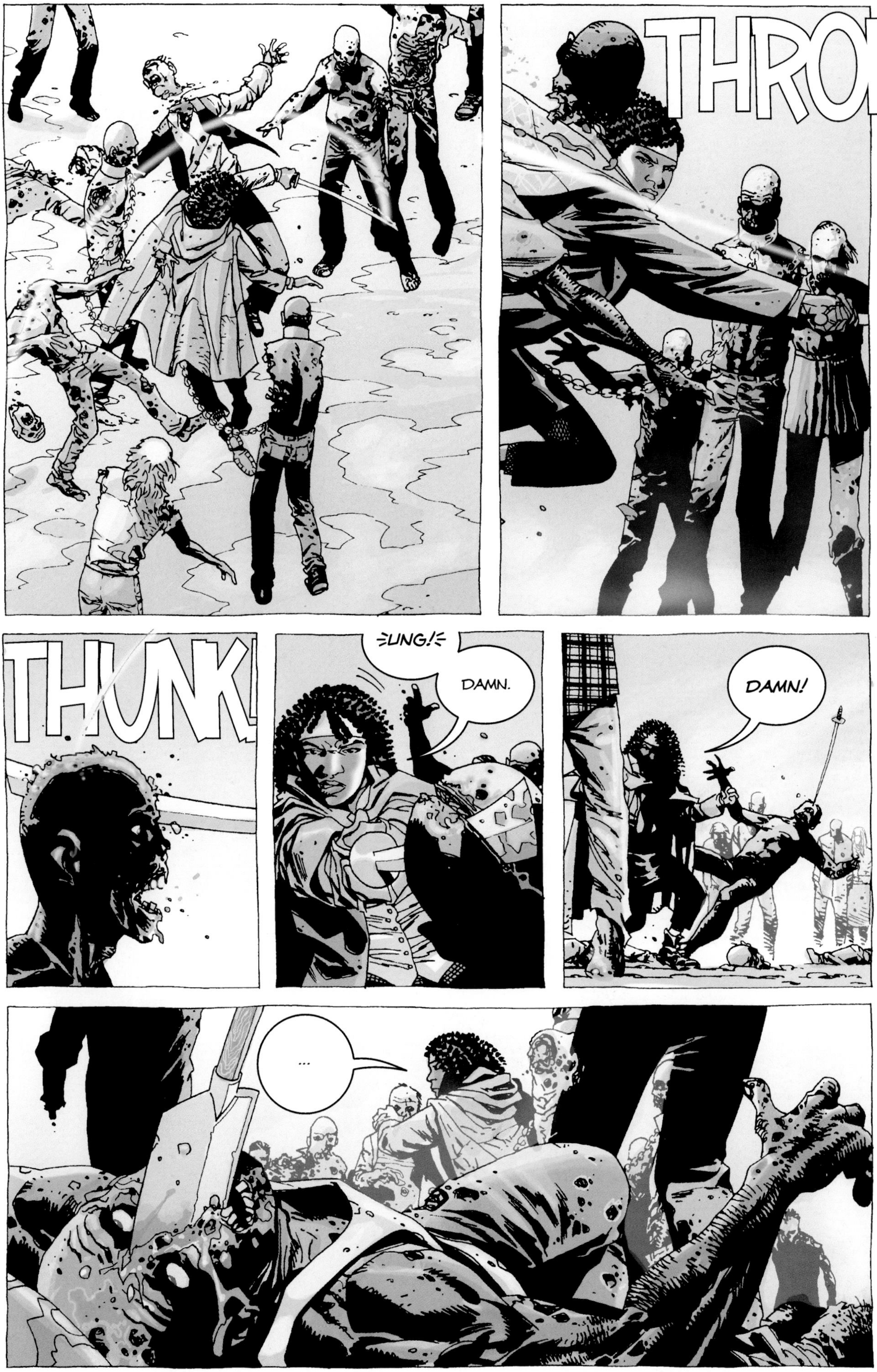
THROK
THUNK
UNG!
DAMN.
DAMN!
...

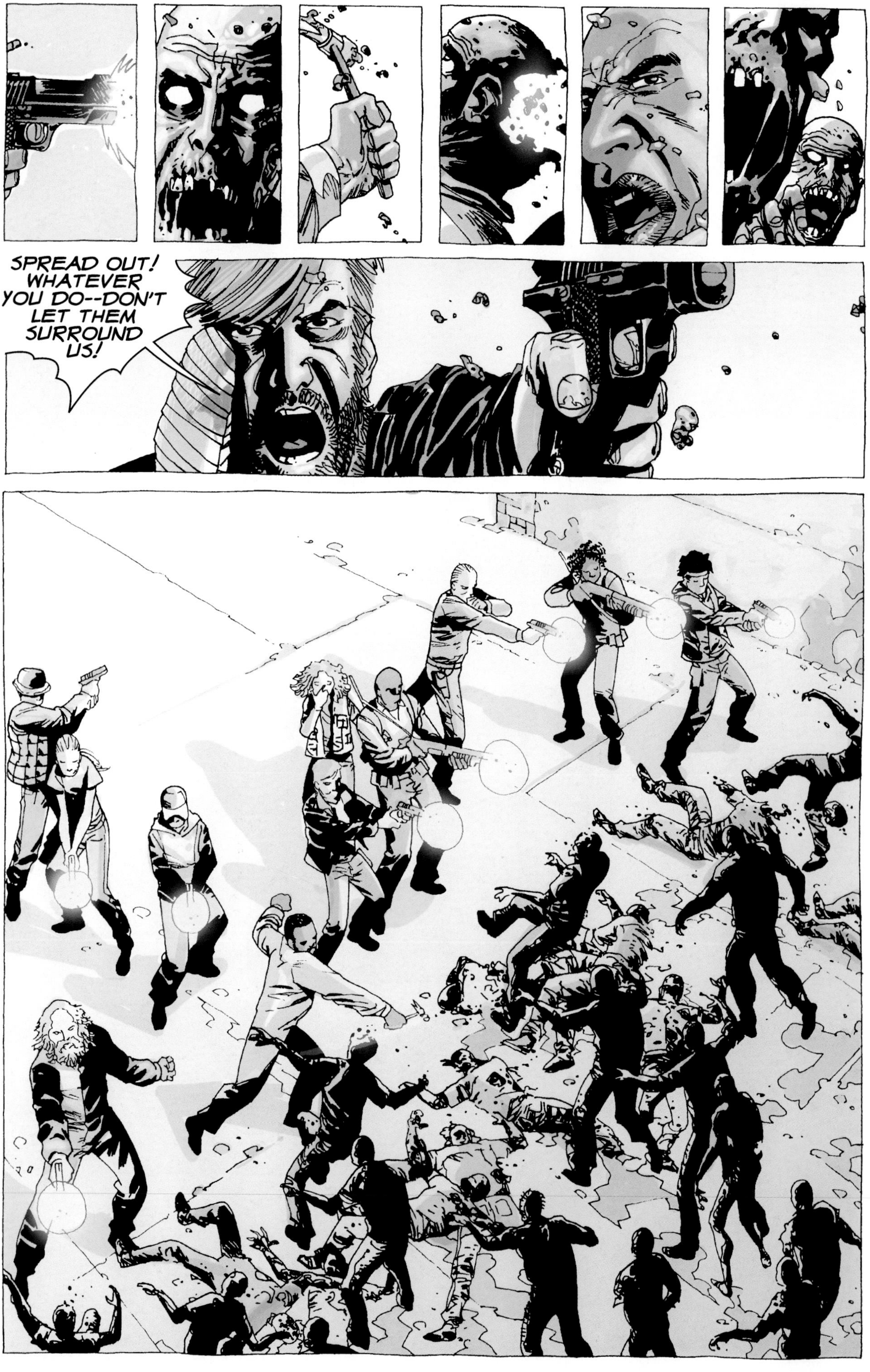
SPREAD OUT! WHATEVER YOU DO--DON'T LET THEM SURROUND US!

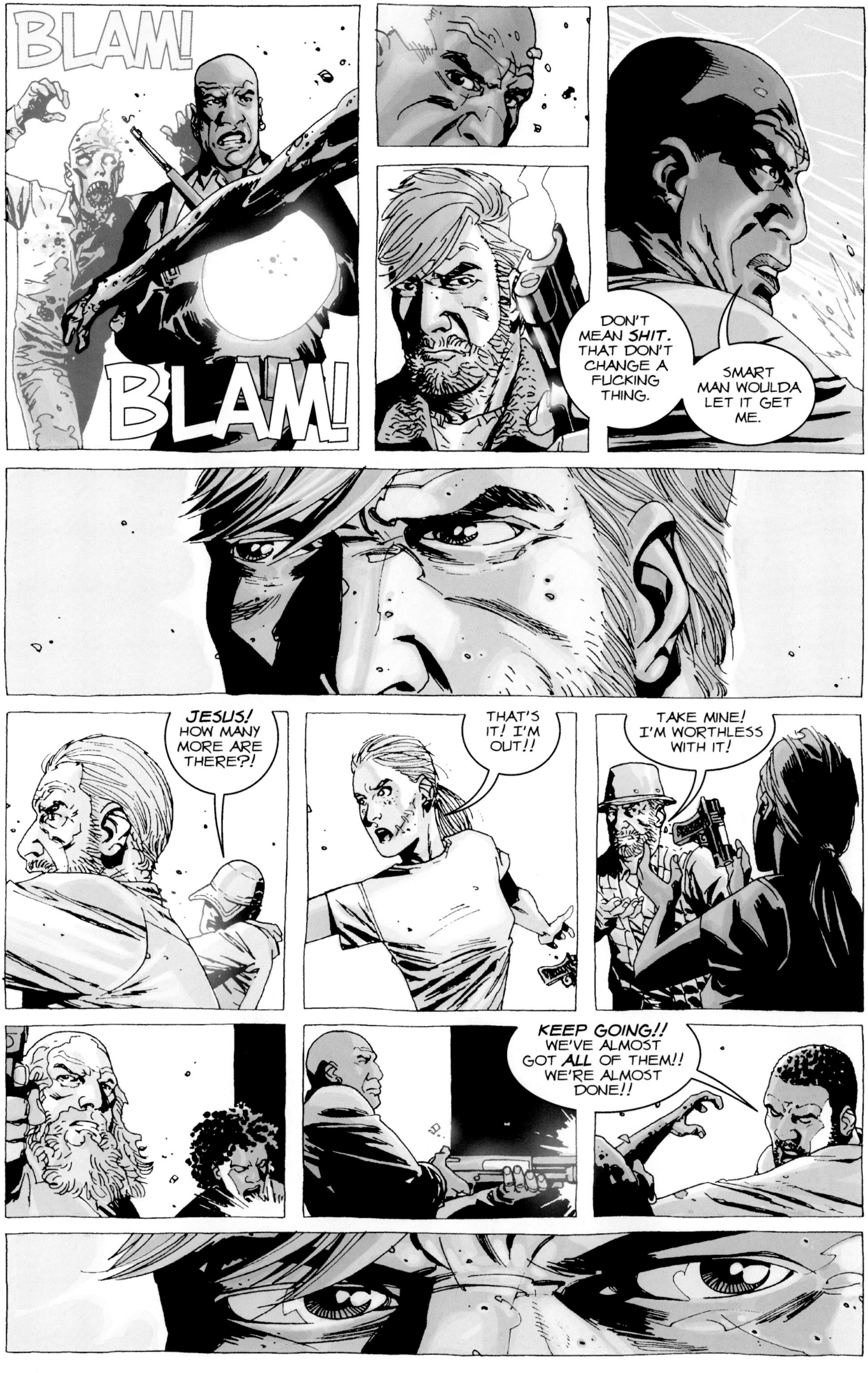
BLAM!
BLAM!
DON'T MEAN SHIT. THAT DON'T CHANGE A FUCKING THING.
SMART MAN WOULDA LET IT GET ME.
JESUS! HOW MANY MORE ARE THERE?!
THAT'S IT! I'M OUT!!
TAKE MINE! I'M WORTHLESS WITH IT!
KEEP GOING!! WE'VE ALMOST GOT ALL OF THEM!! WE'RE ALMOST DONE!!

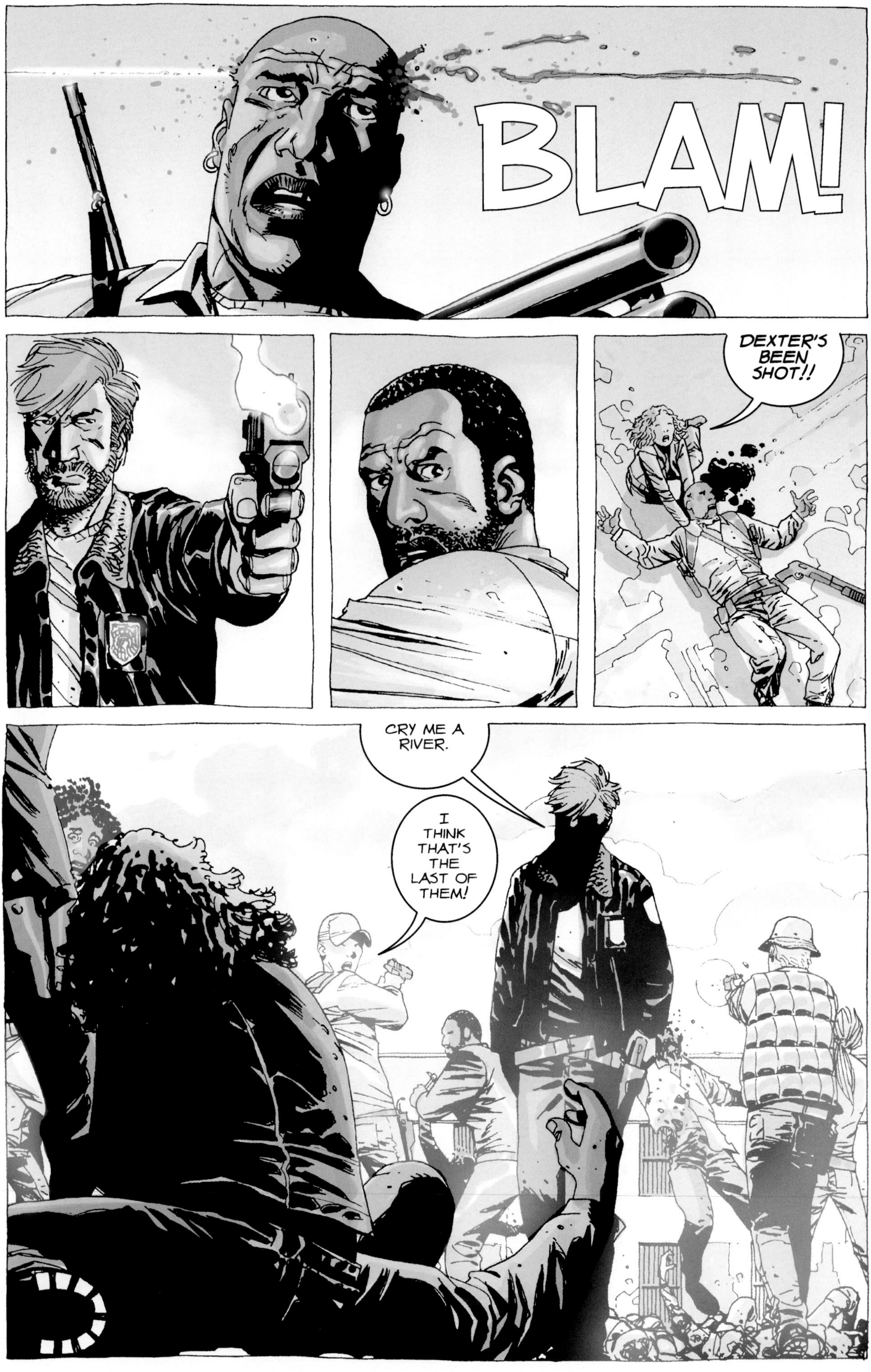
BLAM!
DEXTER'S BEEN SHOT!!
CRY ME A RIVER.
I THINK THAT'S THE LAST OF THEM!

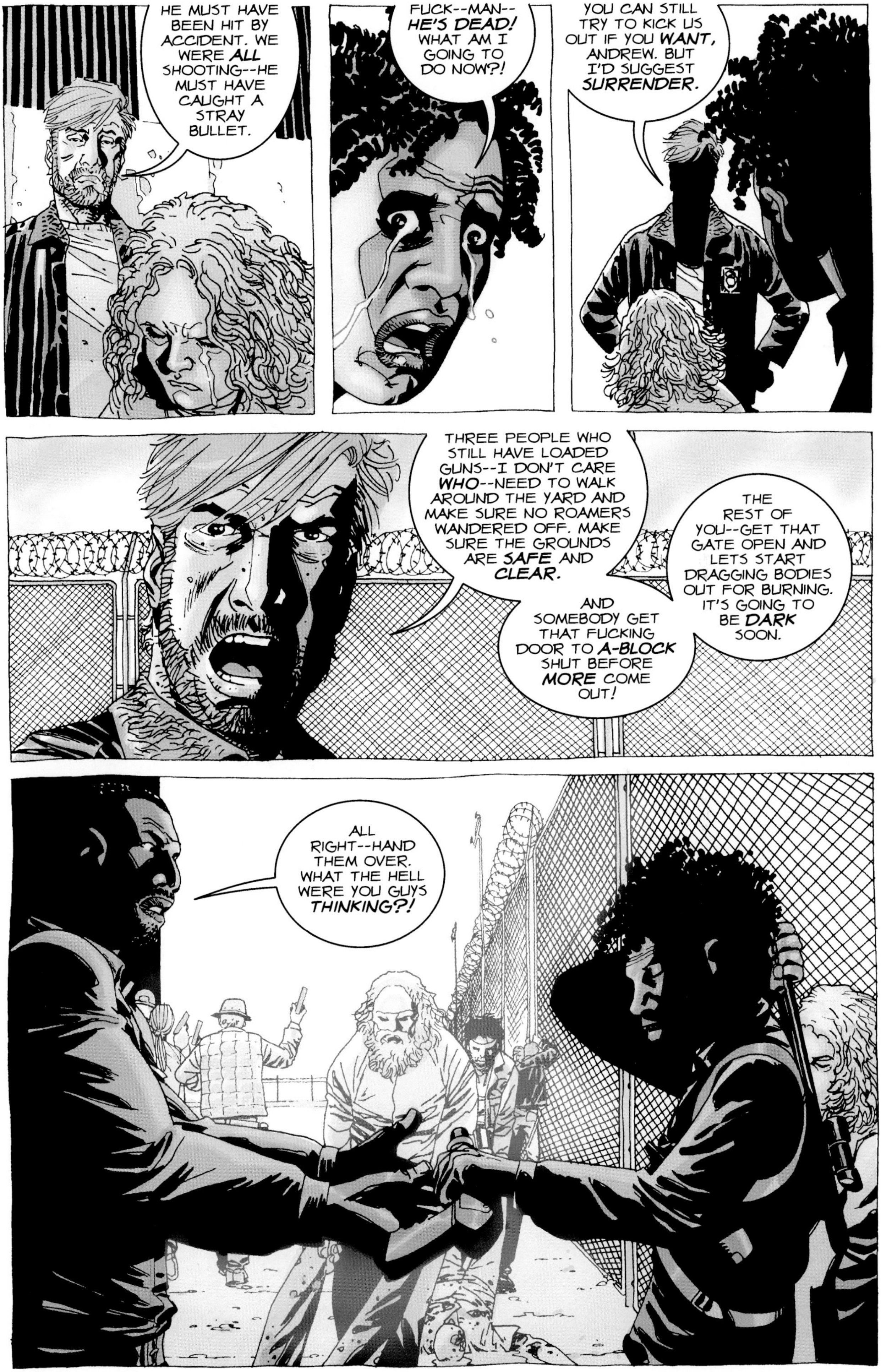
HE MUST HAVE BEEN HIT BY ACCIDENT. WE WERE ALL SHOOTING--HE MUST HAVE CAUGHT A STRAY BULLET.
FUCK--MAN-- HE'S DEAD! WHAT AM I GOING TO DO NOW?!
YOU CAN STILL TRY TO KICK US OUT IF YOU WANT, ANDREW. BUT I'D SUGGEST SURRENDER.
THREE PEOPLE WHO STILL HAVE LOADED GUNS--I DON'T CARE WHO--NEED TO WALK AROUND THE YARD AND MAKE SURE NO ROAMERS WANDERED OFF. MAKE SURE THE GROUNDS ARE SAFE AND CLEAR.
AND SOMEBODY GET THAT FUCKING DOOR TO A-BLOCK SHUT BEFORE MORE COME OUT!
THE REST OF YOU--GET THAT GATE OPEN AND LETS START DRAGGING BODIES OUT FOR BURNING. IT'S GOING TO BE DARK SOON.
ALL RIGHT--HAND THEM OVER. WHAT THE HELL WERE YOU GUYS THINKING?!

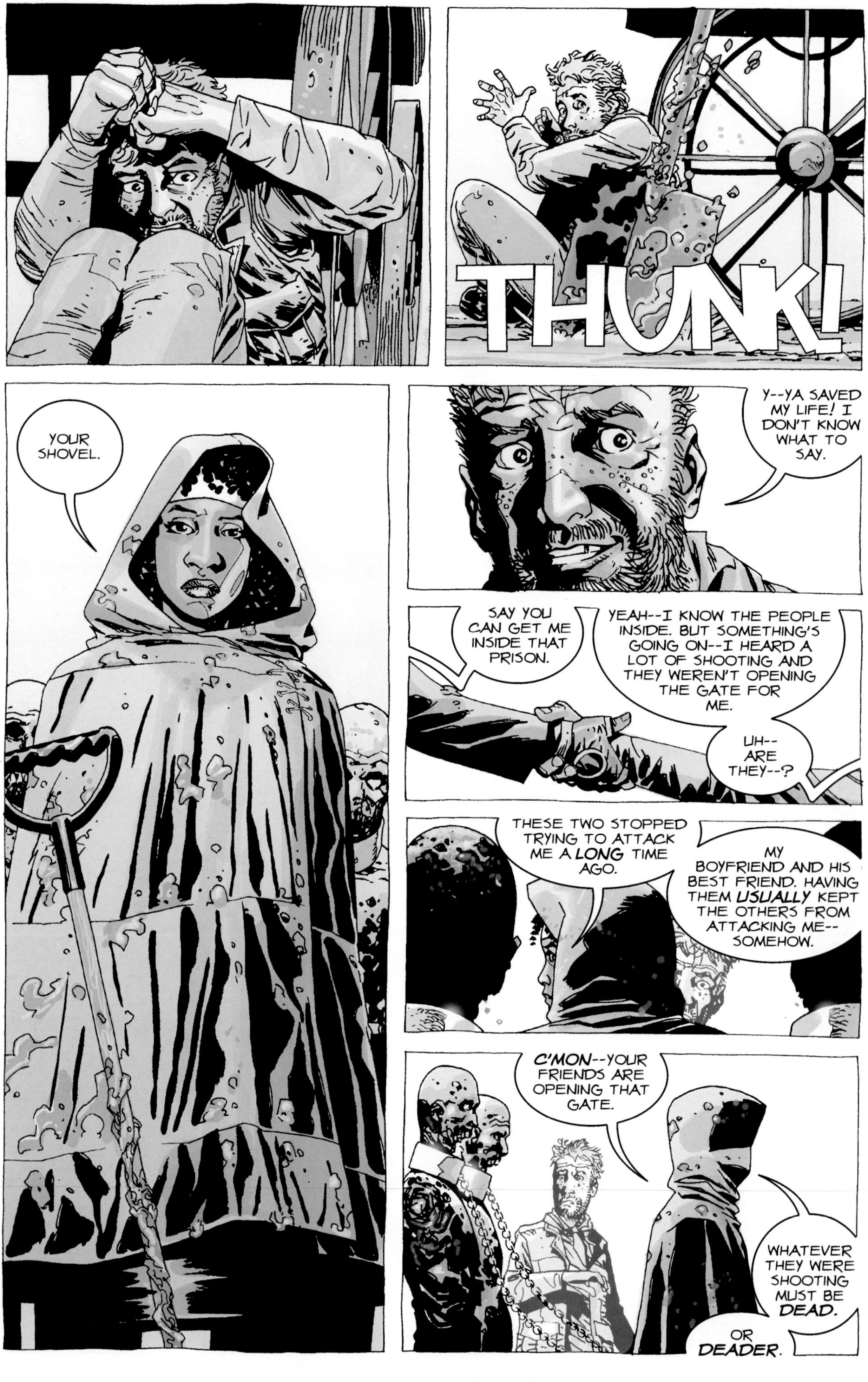
THUNK!
YOUR SHOVEL.
Y--YA SAVED MY LIFE! I DON'T KNOW WHAT TO SAY.
SAY YOU CAN GET ME INSIDE THAT PRISON.
YEAH--I KNOW THE PEOPLE INSIDE. BUT SOMETHING'S GOING ON--I HEARD A LOT OF SHOOTING AND THEY WEREN'T OPENING THE GATE FOR ME.
UH--ARE THEY--?
THESE TWO STOPPED TRYING TO ATTACK ME A **LONG** TIME AGO.
MY BOYFRIEND AND HIS BEST FRIEND. HAVING THEM ***USUALLY*** KEPT THE OTHERS FROM ATTACKING ME--SOMEHOW.
C'MON--YOUR FRIENDS ARE OPENING THAT GATE.
WHATEVER THEY WERE SHOOTING MUST BE ***DEAD.***
OR ***DEADER***.

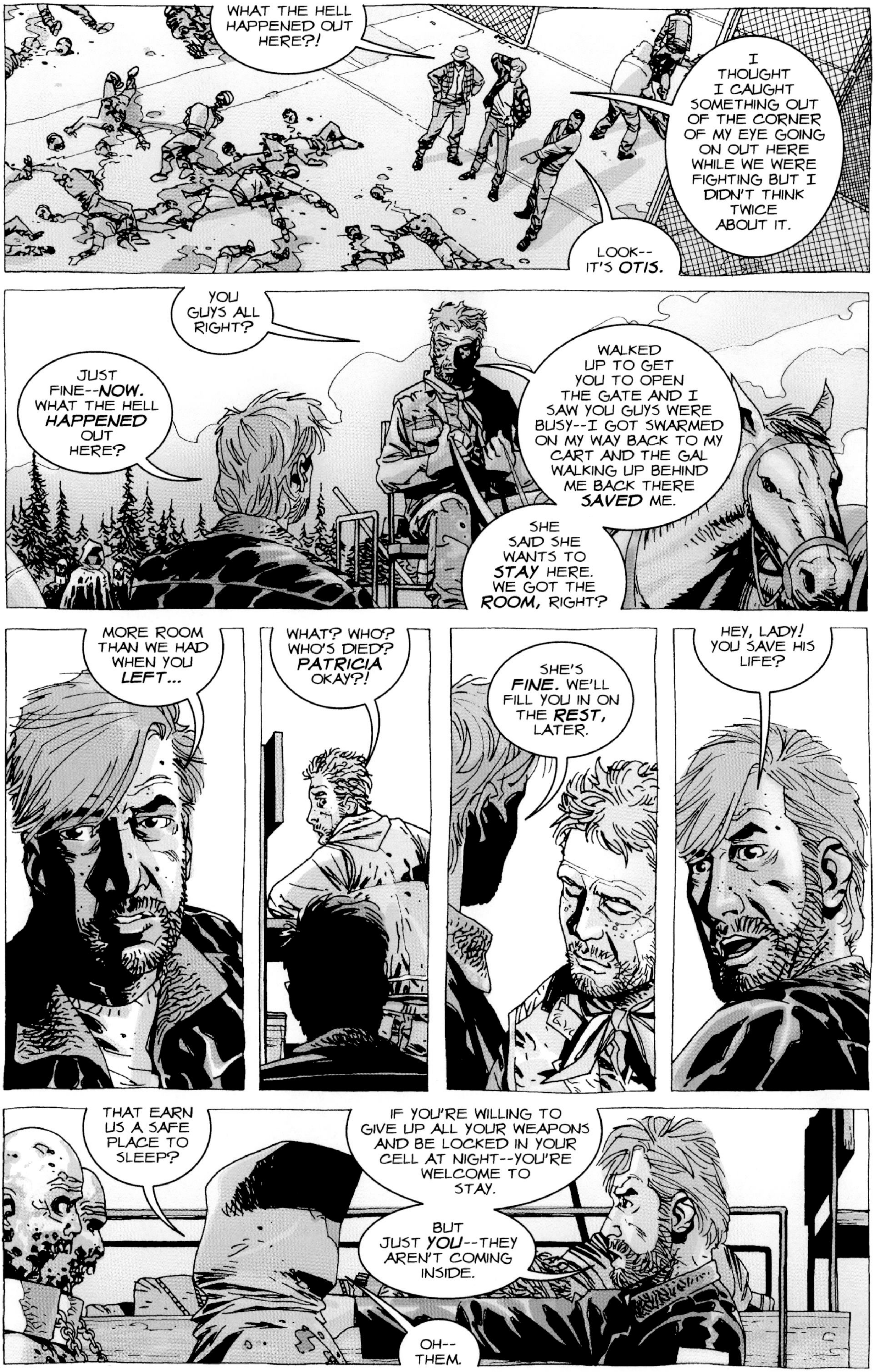
WHAT THE HELL HAPPENED OUT HERE?!
I THOUGHT I CAUGHT SOMETHING OUT OF THE CORNER OF MY EYE GOING ON OUT HERE WHILE WE WERE FIGHTING BUT I DIDN'T THINK TWICE ABOUT IT.
LOOK-- IT'S OTIS.
YOU GUYS ALL RIGHT?
JUST FINE--NOW. WHAT THE HELL HAPPENED OUT HERE?
WALKED UP TO GET YOU TO OPEN THE GATE AND I SAW YOU GUYS WERE BUSY--I GOT SWARMED ON MY WAY BACK TO MY CART AND THE GAL WALKING UP BEHIND ME BACK THERE SAVED ME.
SHE SAID SHE WANTS TO STAY HERE. WE GOT THE ROOM, RIGHT?
MORE ROOM THAN WE HAD WHEN YOU LEFT...
WHAT? WHO? WHO'S DIED? PATRICIA OKAY?!
SHE'S FINE. WE'LL FILL YOU IN ON THE REST, LATER.
HEY, LADY! YOU SAVE HIS LIFE?
THAT EARN US A SAFE PLACE TO SLEEP?
IF YOU'RE WILLING TO GIVE UP ALL YOUR WEAPONS AND BE LOCKED IN YOUR CELL AT NIGHT--YOU'RE WELCOME TO STAY.
BUT JUST YOU--THEY AREN'T COMING INSIDE.
OH-- THEM.

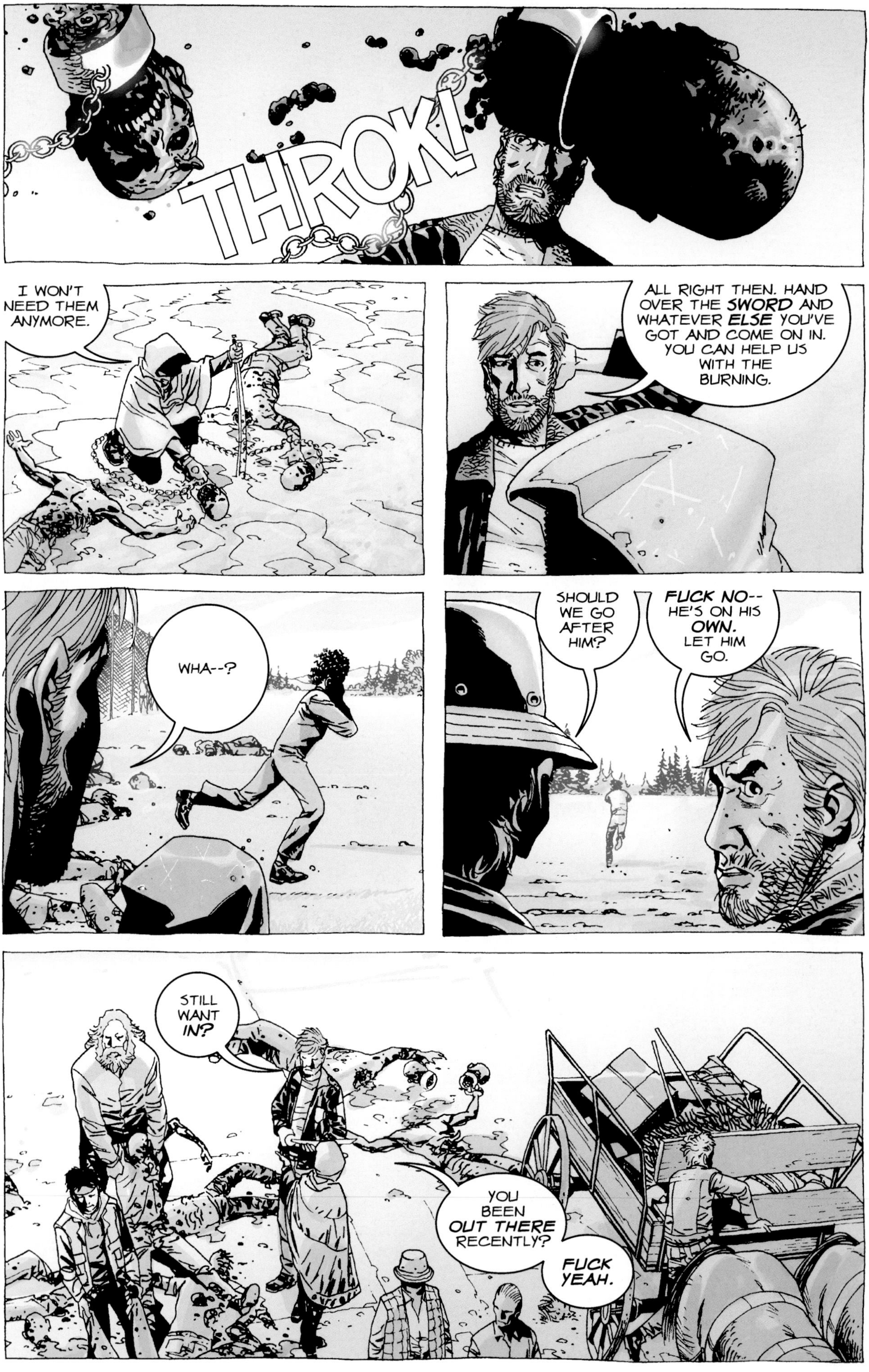
THROK!
I WON'T NEED THEM ANYMORE.
ALL RIGHT THEN. HAND OVER THE SWORD AND WHATEVER ELSE YOU'VE GOT AND COME ON IN. YOU CAN HELP US WITH THE BURNING.
WHA--?
SHOULD WE GO AFTER HIM?
FUCK NO-- HE'S ON HIS OWN. LET HIM GO.
STILL WANT IN?
YOU BEEN OUT THERE RECENTLY?
FUCK YEAH.

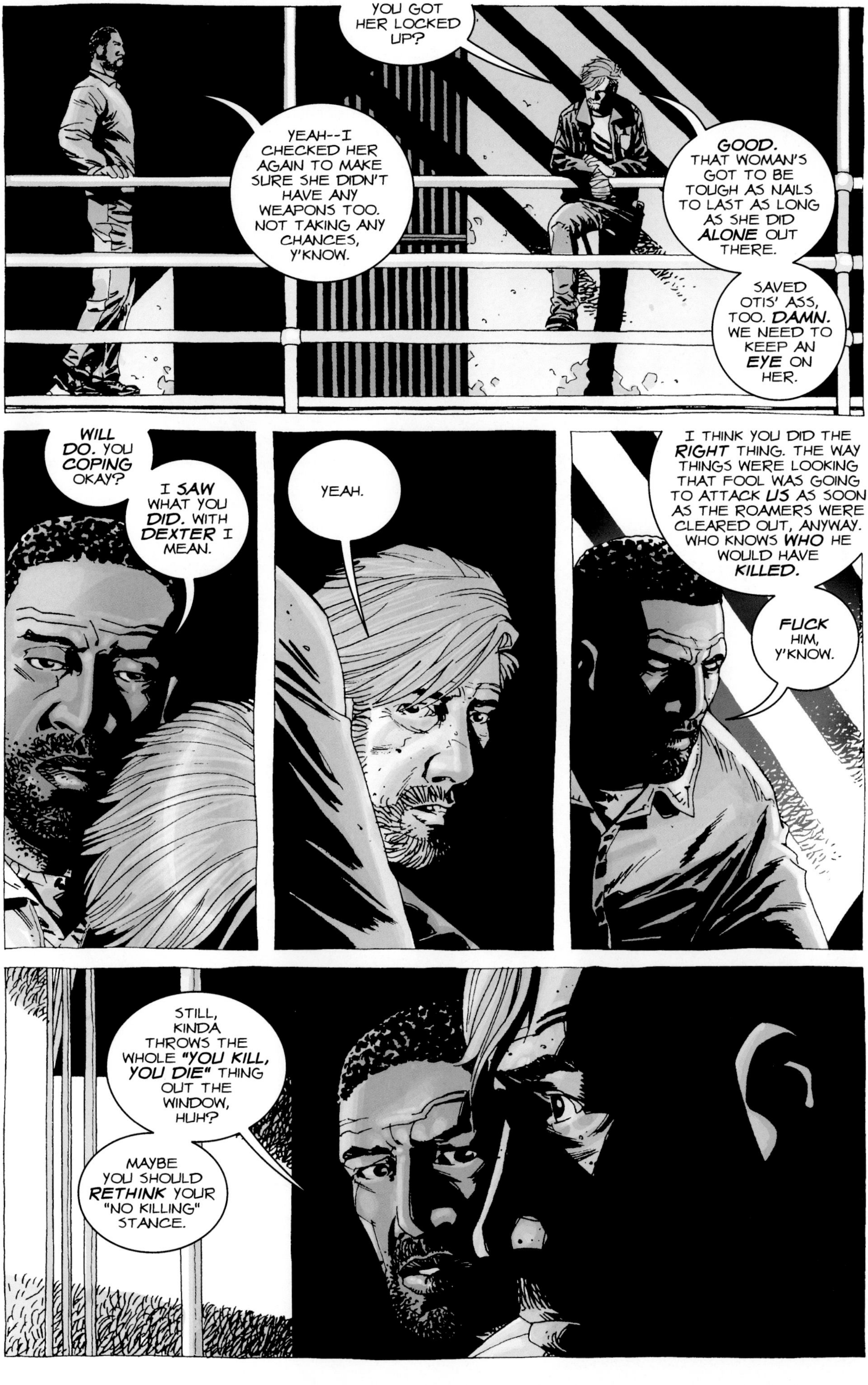
YOU GOT HER LOCKED UP?
YEAH--I CHECKED HER AGAIN TO MAKE SURE SHE DIDN'T HAVE ANY WEAPONS TOO. NOT TAKING ANY CHANCES, Y'KNOW.
GOOD. THAT WOMAN'S GOT TO BE TOUGH AS NAILS TO LAST AS LONG AS SHE DID ALONE OUT THERE.
SAVED OTIS' ASS, TOO. DAMN. WE NEED TO KEEP AN EYE ON HER.
WILL DO. YOU COPING OKAY?
I SAW WHAT YOU DID. WITH DEXTER I MEAN.
YEAH.
I THINK YOU DID THE RIGHT THING. THE WAY THINGS WERE LOOKING THAT FOOL WAS GOING TO ATTACK US AS SOON AS THE ROAMERS WERE CLEARED OUT, ANYWAY. WHO KNOWS WHO HE WOULD HAVE KILLED.
FUCK HIM, Y'KNOW.
STILL, KINDA THROWS THE WHOLE "YOU KILL, YOU DIE" THING OUT THE WINDOW, HUH?
MAYBE YOU SHOULD RETHINK YOUR "NO KILLING" STANCE.

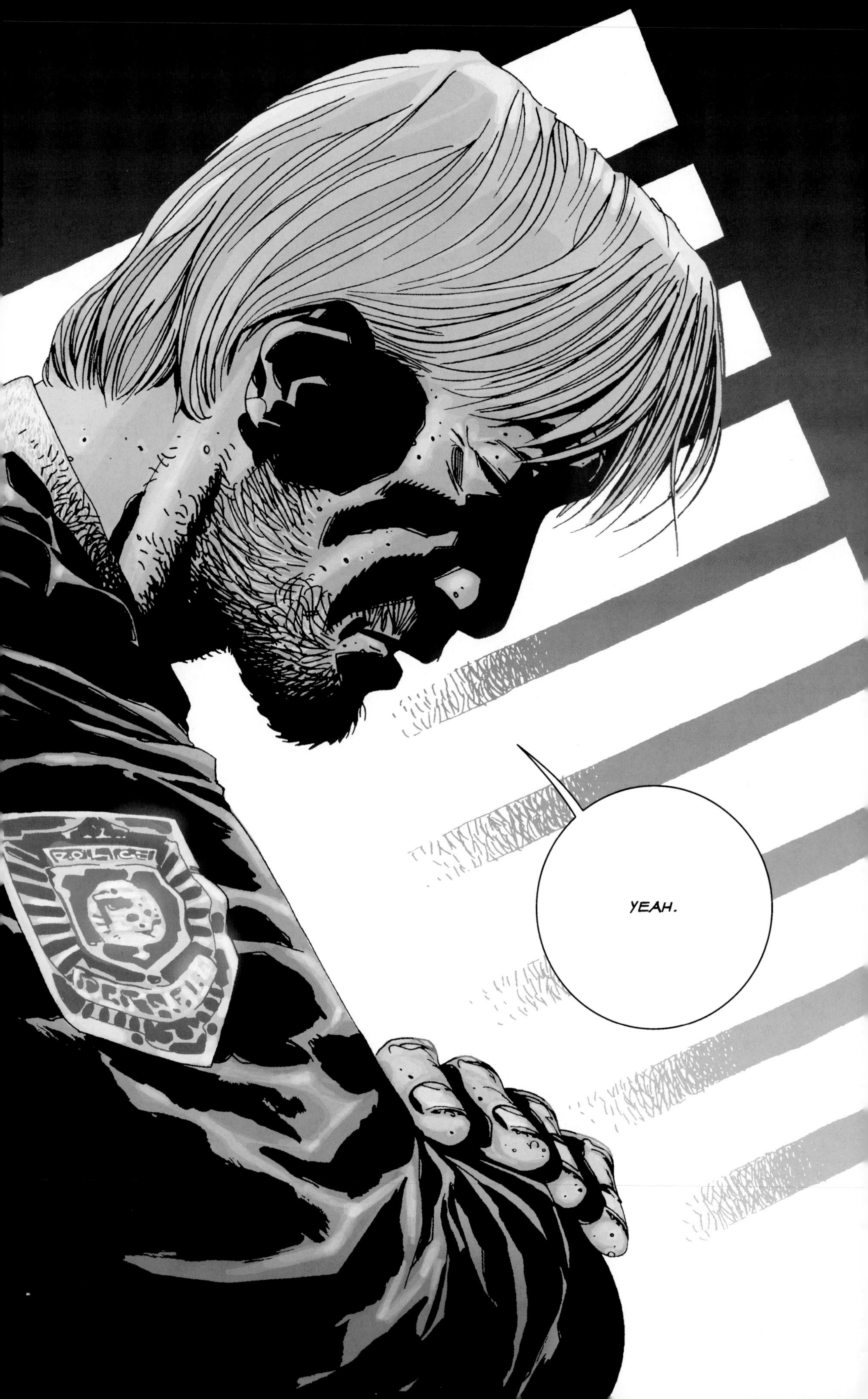
YEAH.

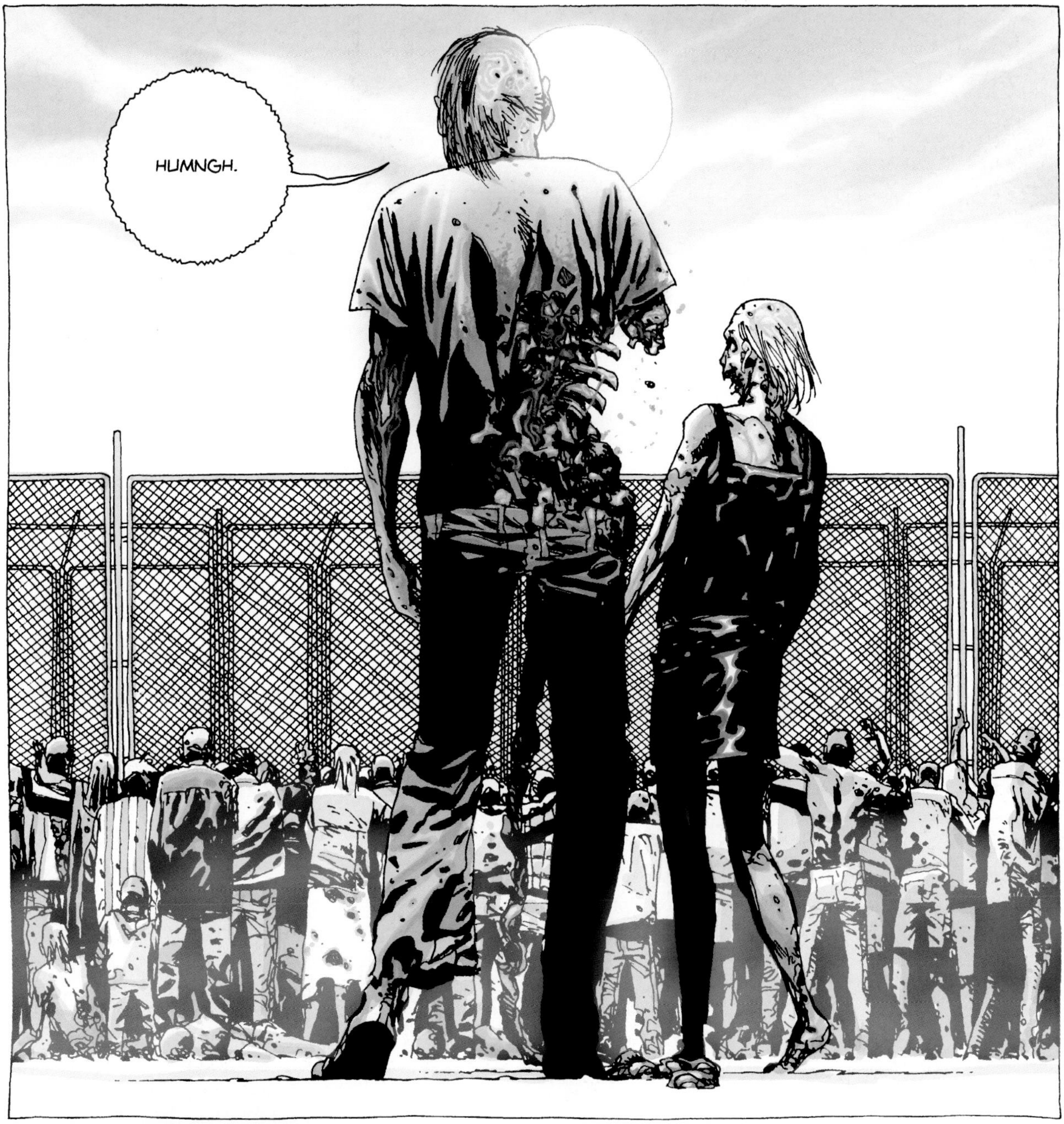
HUMNGH.

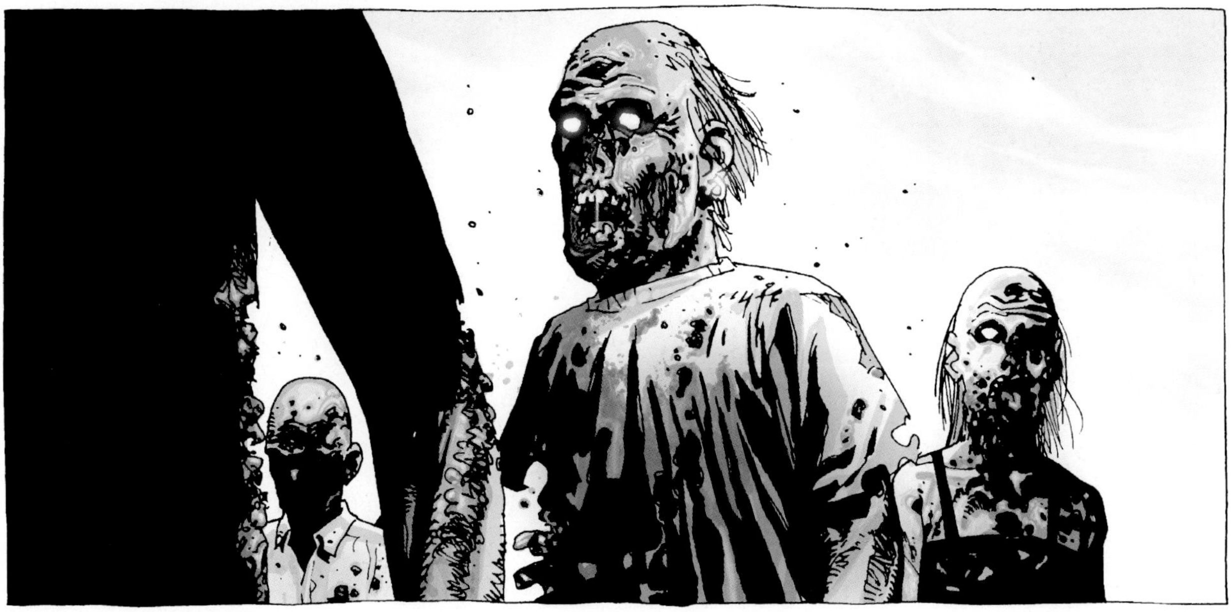

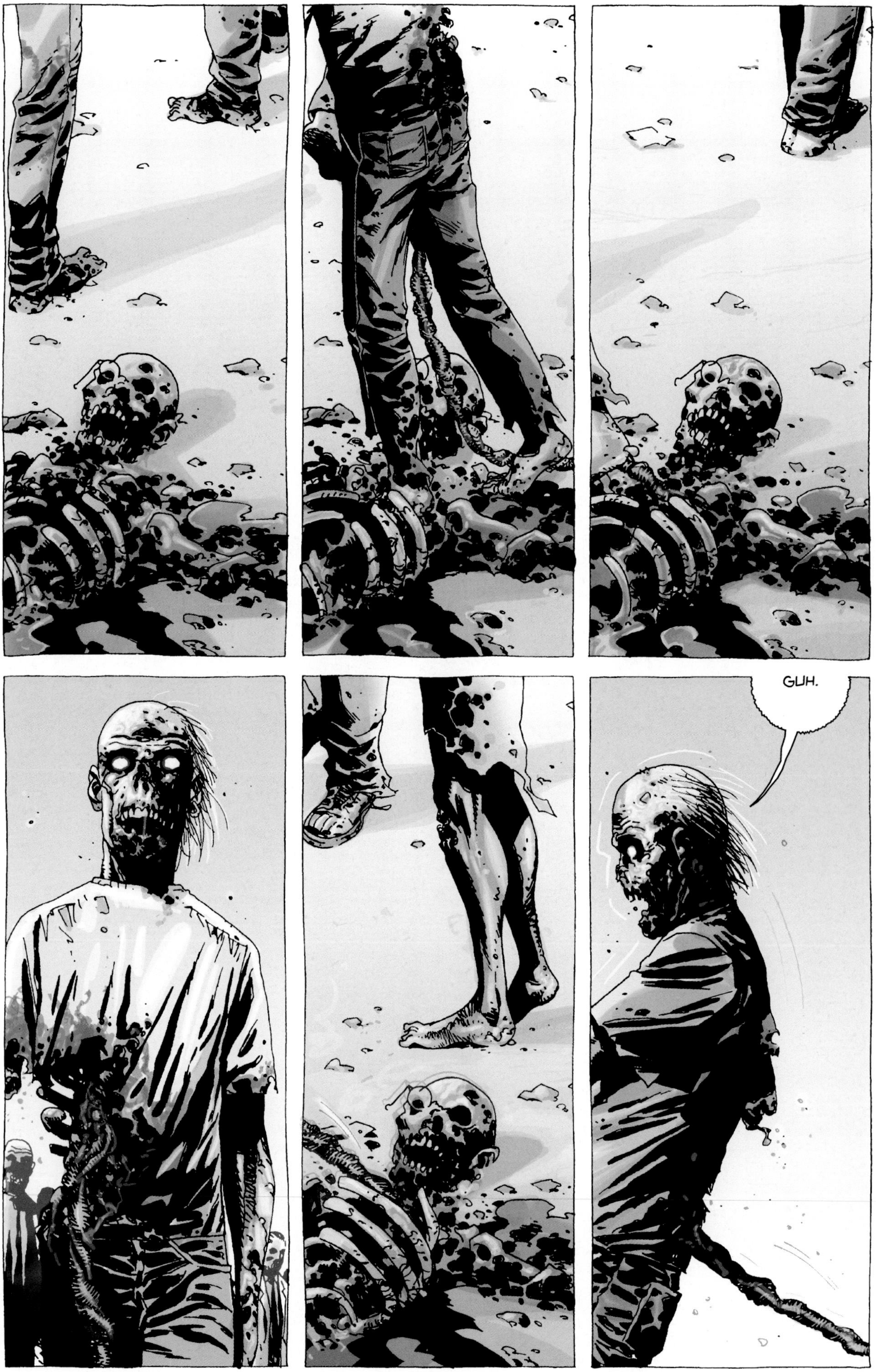
GUH.

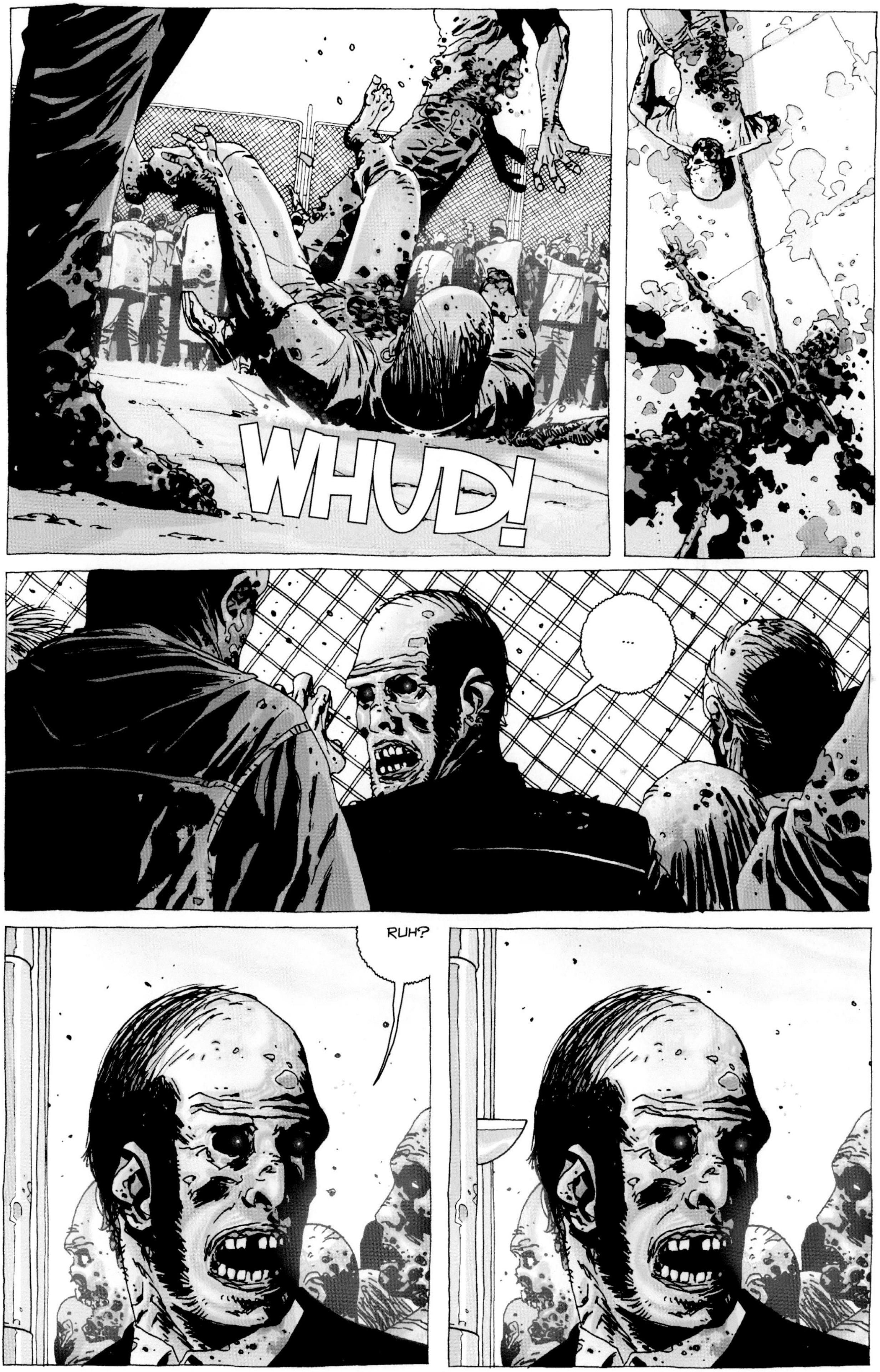
WHUD!
...
RUH?

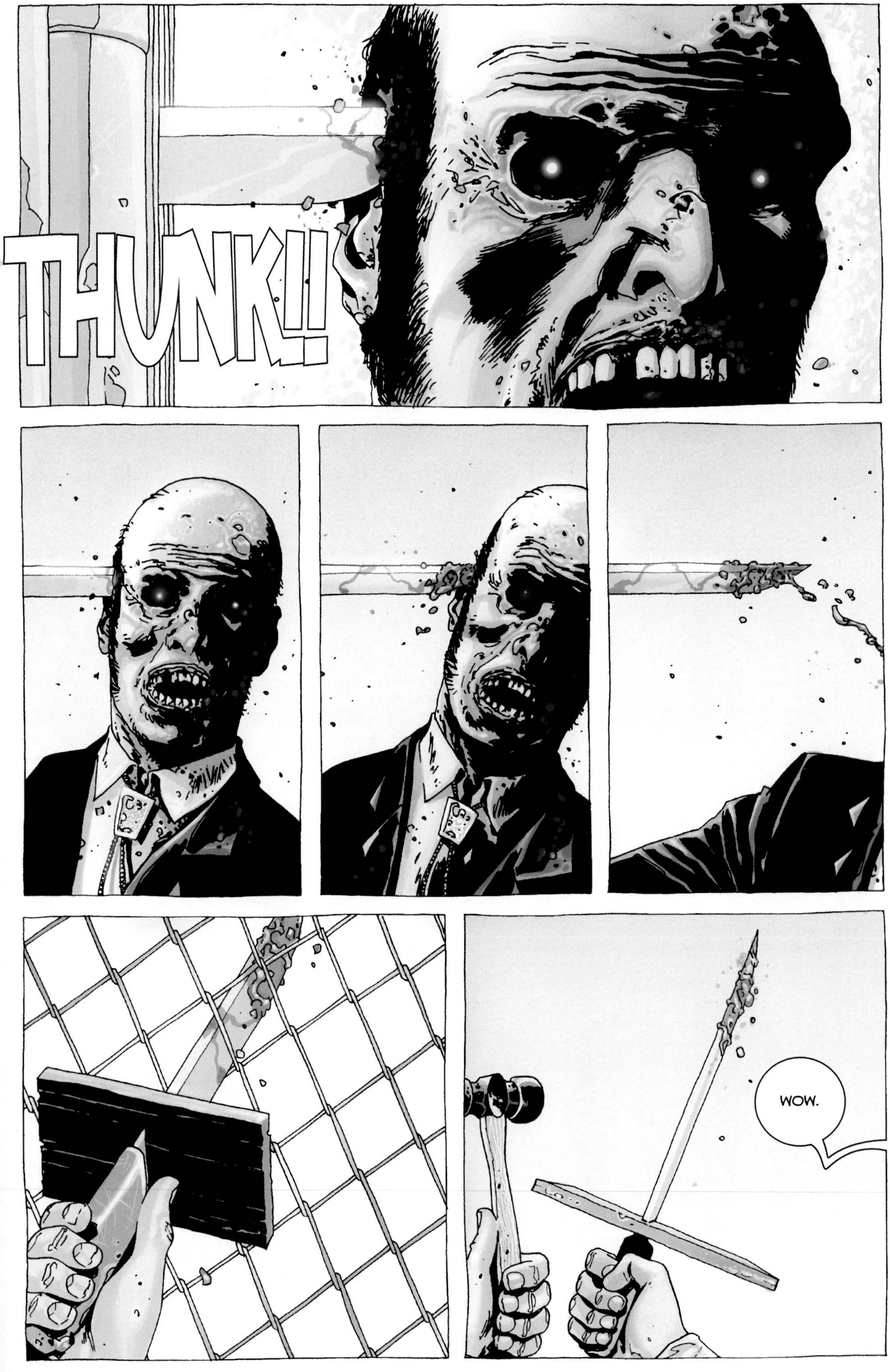
THUNK!!
WOW.

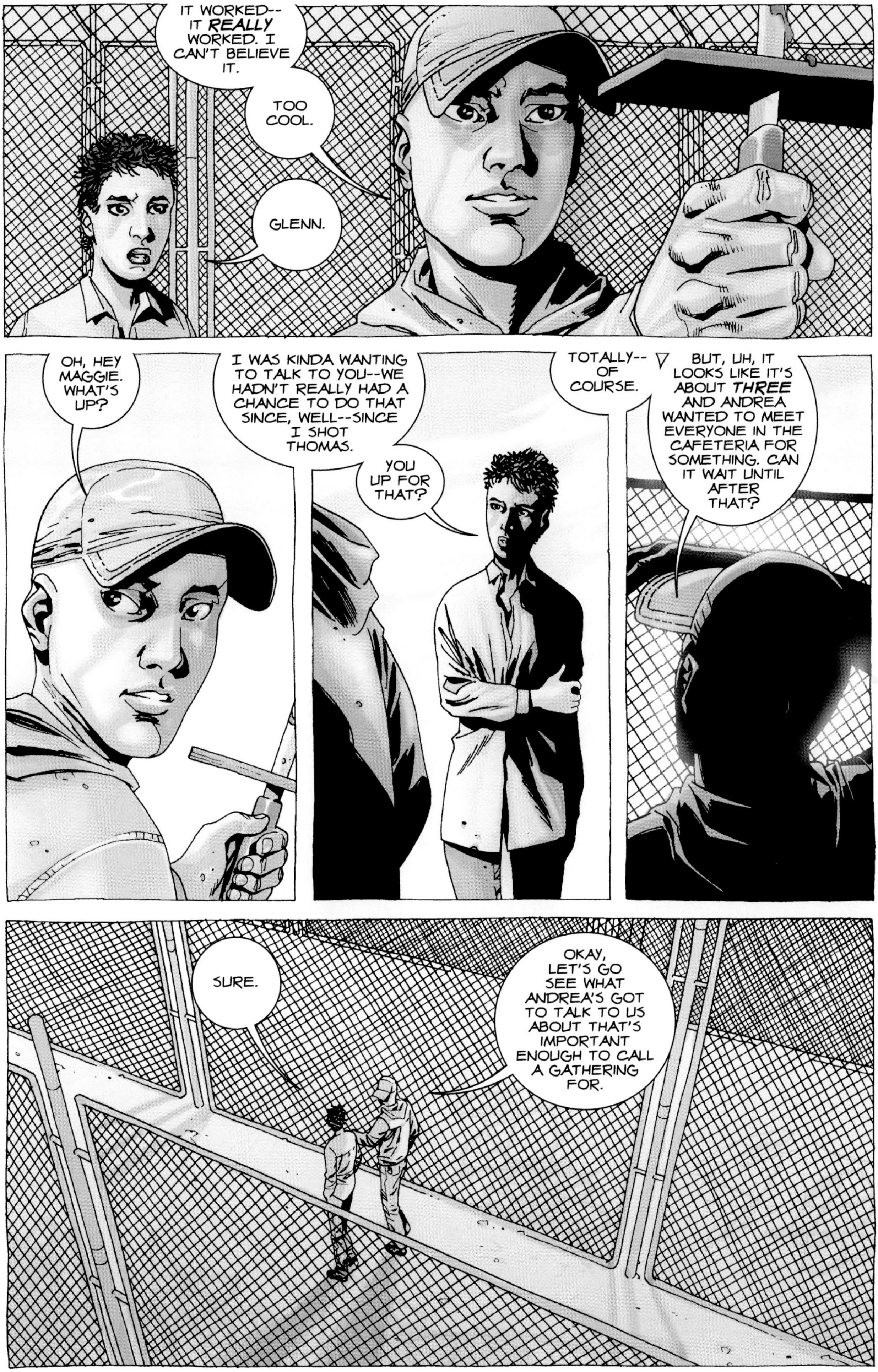
IT WORKED-- IT REALLY WORKED. I CAN'T BELIEVE IT.
TOO COOL.
GLENN.
OH, HEY MAGGIE. WHAT'S UP?
I WAS KINDA WANTING TO TALK TO YOU--WE HADN'T REALLY HAD A CHANCE TO DO THAT SINCE, WELL--SINCE I SHOT THOMAS.
YOU UP FOR THAT?
TOTALLY-- OF COURSE.
BUT, UH, IT LOOKS LIKE IT'S ABOUT THREE AND ANDREA WANTED TO MEET EVERYONE IN THE CAFETERIA FOR SOMETHING. CAN IT WAIT UNTIL AFTER THAT?
SURE.
OKAY, LET'S GO SEE WHAT ANDREA'S GOT TO TALK TO US ABOUT THAT'S IMPORTANT ENOUGH TO CALL A GATHERING FOR.

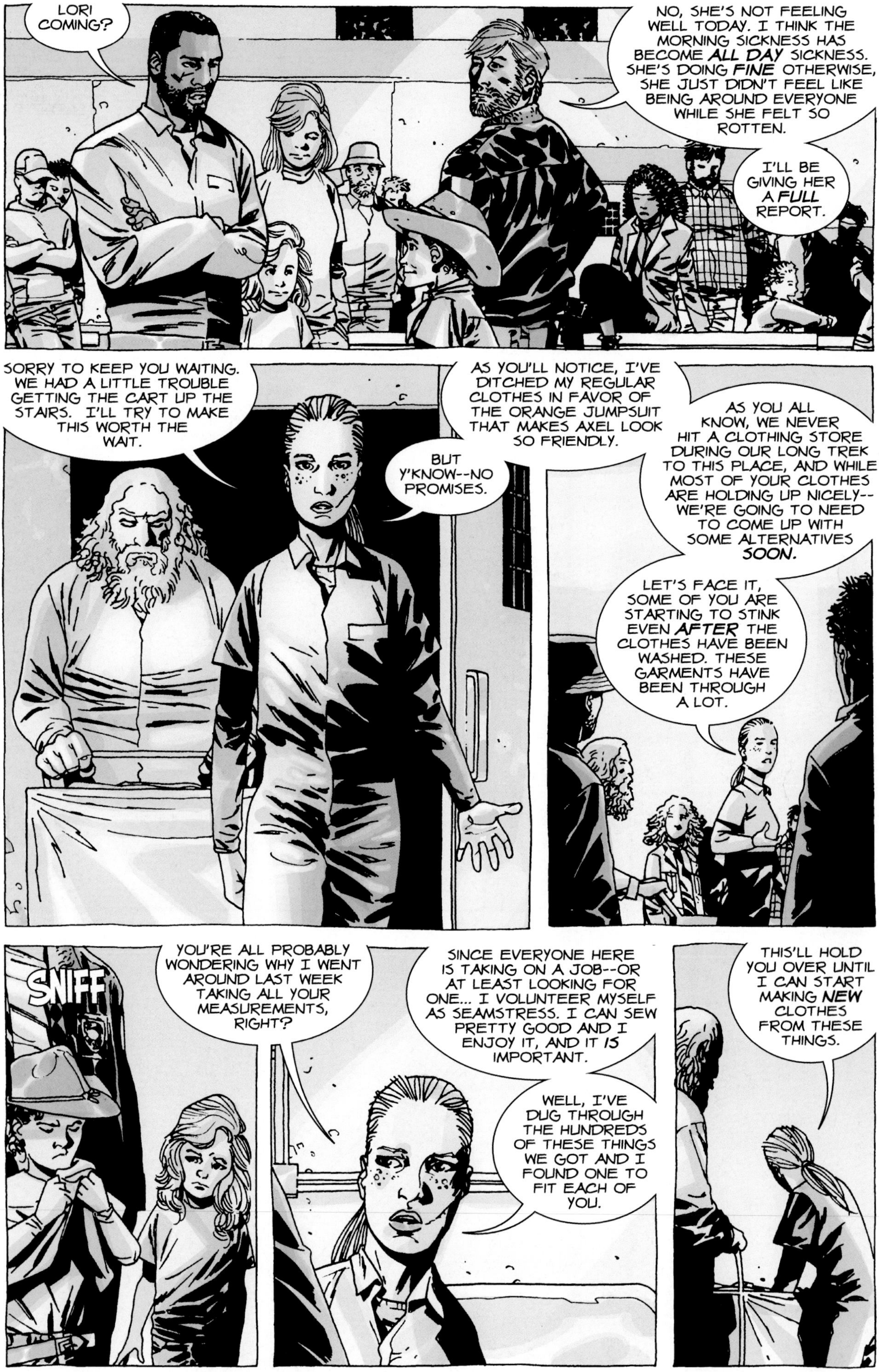
LORI COMING?
NO, SHE'S NOT FEELING WELL TODAY. I THINK THE MORNING SICKNESS HAS BECOME ALL DAY SICKNESS. SHE'S DOING FINE OTHERWISE, SHE JUST DIDN'T FEEL LIKE BEING AROUND EVERYONE WHILE SHE FELT SO ROTTEN.
I'LL BE GIVING HER A FULL REPORT.
SORRY TO KEEP YOU WAITING. WE HAD A LITTLE TROUBLE GETTING THE CART UP THE STAIRS. I'LL TRY TO MAKE THIS WORTH THE WAIT.
BUT Y'KNOW--NO PROMISES.
AS YOU'LL NOTICE, I'VE DITCHED MY REGULAR CLOTHES IN FAVOR OF THE ORANGE JUMPSUIT THAT MAKES AXEL LOOK SO FRIENDLY.
AS YOU ALL KNOW, WE NEVER HIT A CLOTHING STORE DURING OUR LONG TREK TO THIS PLACE, AND WHILE MOST OF YOUR CLOTHES ARE HOLDING UP NICELY--WE'RE GOING TO NEED TO COME UP WITH SOME ALTERNATIVES SOON.
LET'S FACE IT, SOME OF YOU ARE STARTING TO STINK EVEN AFTER THE CLOTHES HAVE BEEN WASHED. THESE GARMENTS HAVE BEEN THROUGH A LOT.
SNIFF
YOU'RE ALL PROBABLY WONDERING WHY I WENT AROUND LAST WEEK TAKING ALL YOUR MEASUREMENTS, RIGHT?
SINCE EVERYONE HERE IS TAKING ON A JOB--OR AT LEAST LOOKING FOR ONE... I VOLUNTEER MYSELF AS SEAMSTRESS. I CAN SEW PRETTY GOOD AND I ENJOY IT, AND IT IS IMPORTANT.
WELL, I'VE DUG THROUGH THE HUNDREDS OF THESE THINGS WE GOT AND I FOUND ONE TO FIT EACH OF YOU.
THIS'LL HOLD YOU OVER UNTIL I CAN START MAKING NEW CLOTHES FROM THESE THINGS.

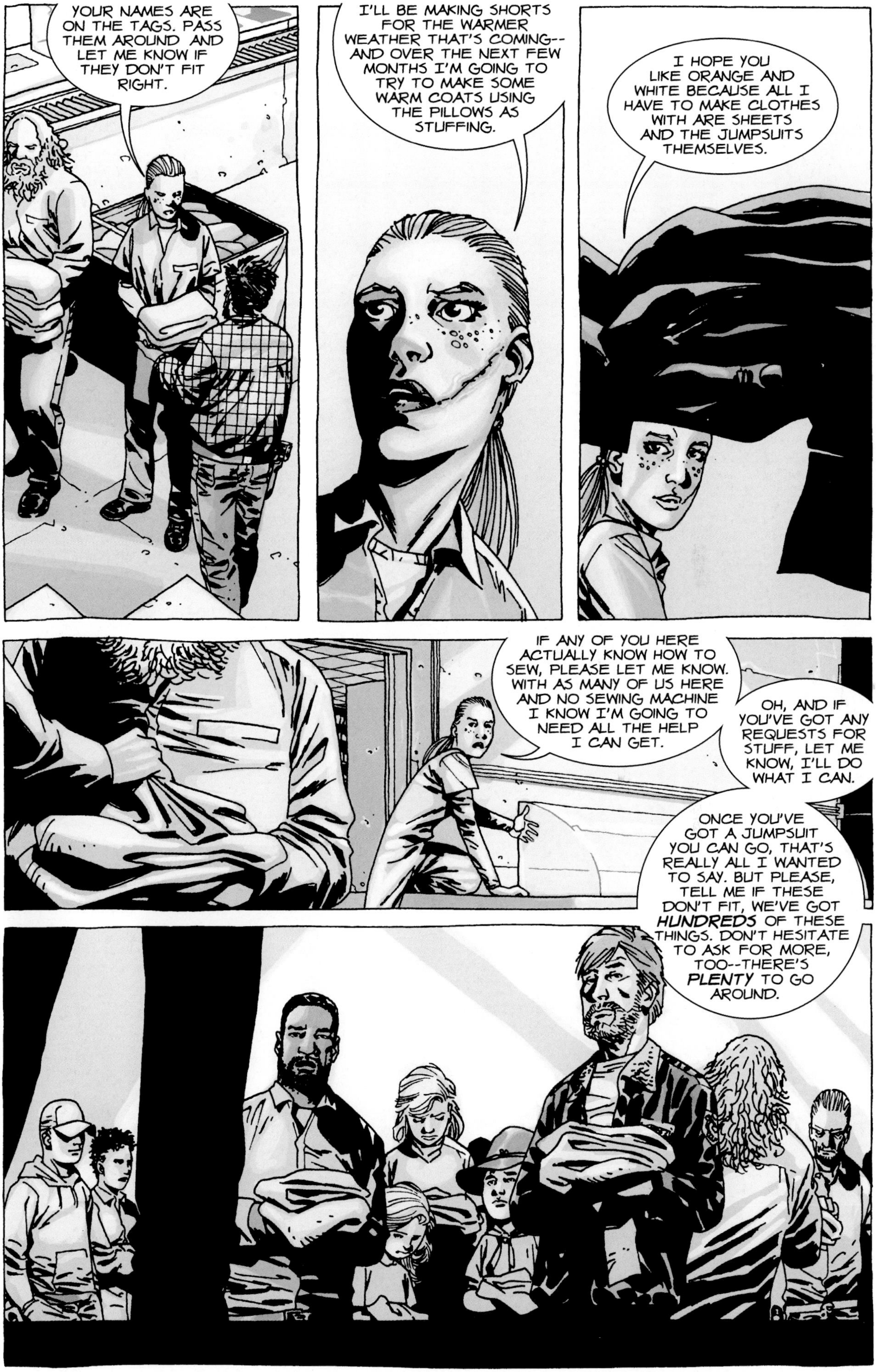
YOUR NAMES ARE ON THE TAGS. PASS THEM AROUND AND LET ME KNOW IF THEY DON'T FIT RIGHT.
I'LL BE MAKING SHORTS FOR THE WARMER WEATHER THAT'S COMING-- AND OVER THE NEXT FEW MONTHS I'M GOING TO TRY TO MAKE SOME WARM COATS USING THE PILLOWS AS STUFFING.
I HOPE YOU LIKE ORANGE AND WHITE BECAUSE ALL I HAVE TO MAKE CLOTHES WITH ARE SHEETS AND THE JUMPSUITS THEMSELVES.
IF ANY OF YOU HERE ACTUALLY KNOW HOW TO SEW, PLEASE LET ME KNOW. WITH AS MANY OF US HERE AND NO SEWING MACHINE I KNOW I'M GOING TO NEED ALL THE HELP I CAN GET.
OH, AND IF YOU'VE GOT ANY REQUESTS FOR STUFF, LET ME KNOW, I'LL DO WHAT I CAN.
ONCE YOU'VE GOT A JUMPSUIT YOU CAN GO, THAT'S REALLY ALL I WANTED TO SAY. BUT PLEASE, TELL ME IF THESE DON'T FIT, WE'VE GOT *HUNDREDS* OF THESE THINGS. DON'T HESITATE TO ASK FOR MORE, TOO--THERE'S *PLENTY* TO GO AROUND.

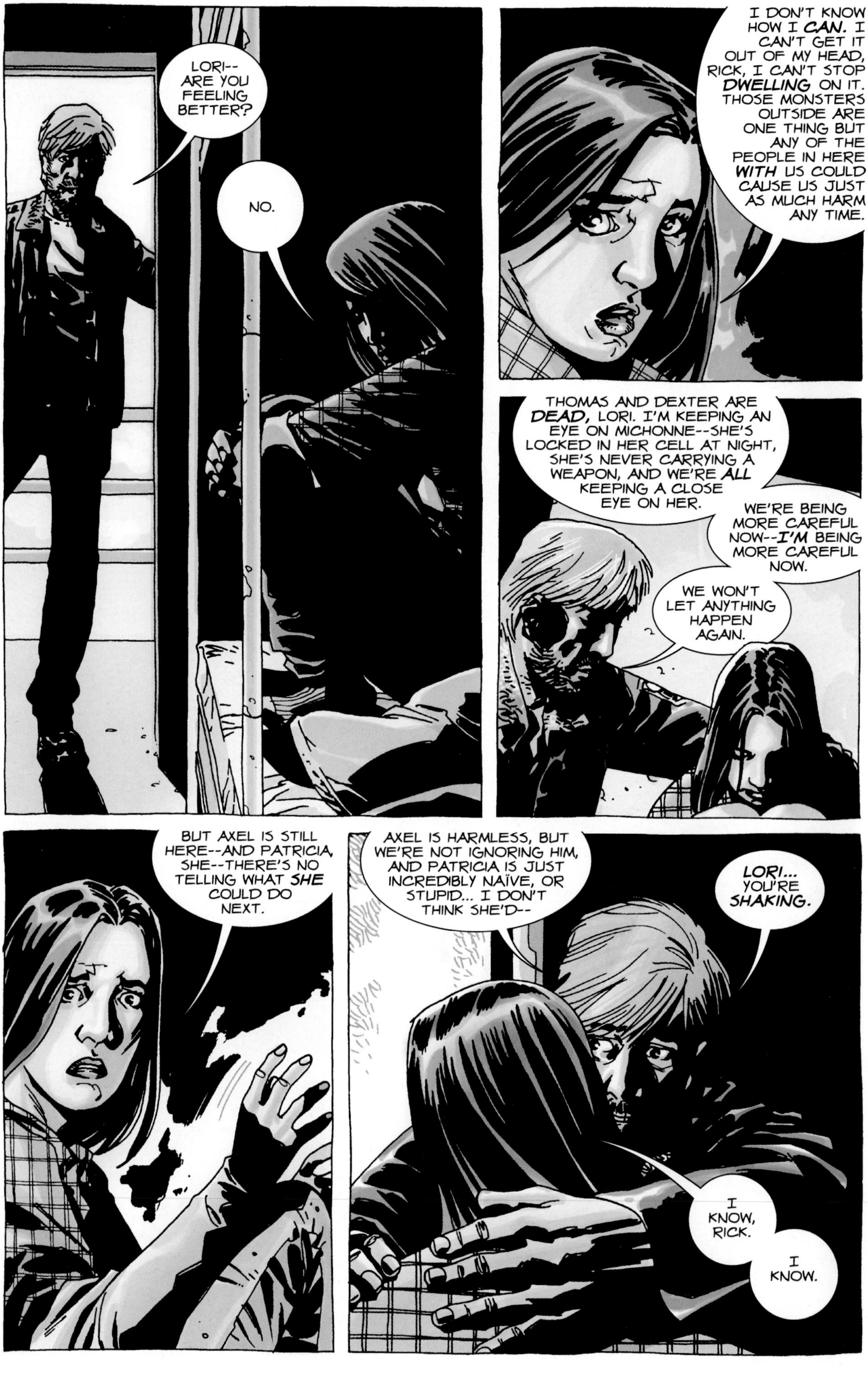

LORI-- ARE YOU FEELING BETTER?
NO.
I DON'T KNOW HOW I CAN. I CAN'T GET IT OUT OF MY HEAD, RICK, I CAN'T STOP DWELLING ON IT. THOSE MONSTERS OUTSIDE ARE ONE THING BUT ANY OF THE PEOPLE IN HERE WITH US COULD CAUSE US JUST AS MUCH HARM ANY TIME.
THOMAS AND DEXTER ARE DEAD, LORI. I'M KEEPING AN EYE ON MICHONNE--SHE'S LOCKED IN HER CELL AT NIGHT, SHE'S NEVER CARRYING A WEAPON, AND WE'RE ALL KEEPING A CLOSE EYE ON HER.
WE'RE BEING MORE CAREFUL NOW--I'M BEING MORE CAREFUL NOW.
WE WON'T LET ANYTHING HAPPEN AGAIN.
BUT AXEL IS STILL HERE--AND PATRICIA, SHE--THERE'S NO TELLING WHAT SHE COULD DO NEXT.
AXEL IS HARMLESS, BUT WE'RE NOT IGNORING HIM, AND PATRICIA IS JUST INCREDIBLY NAÏVE, OR STUPID... I DON'T THINK SHE'D--
LORI... YOU'RE SHAKING.
I KNOW, RICK.
I KNOW.

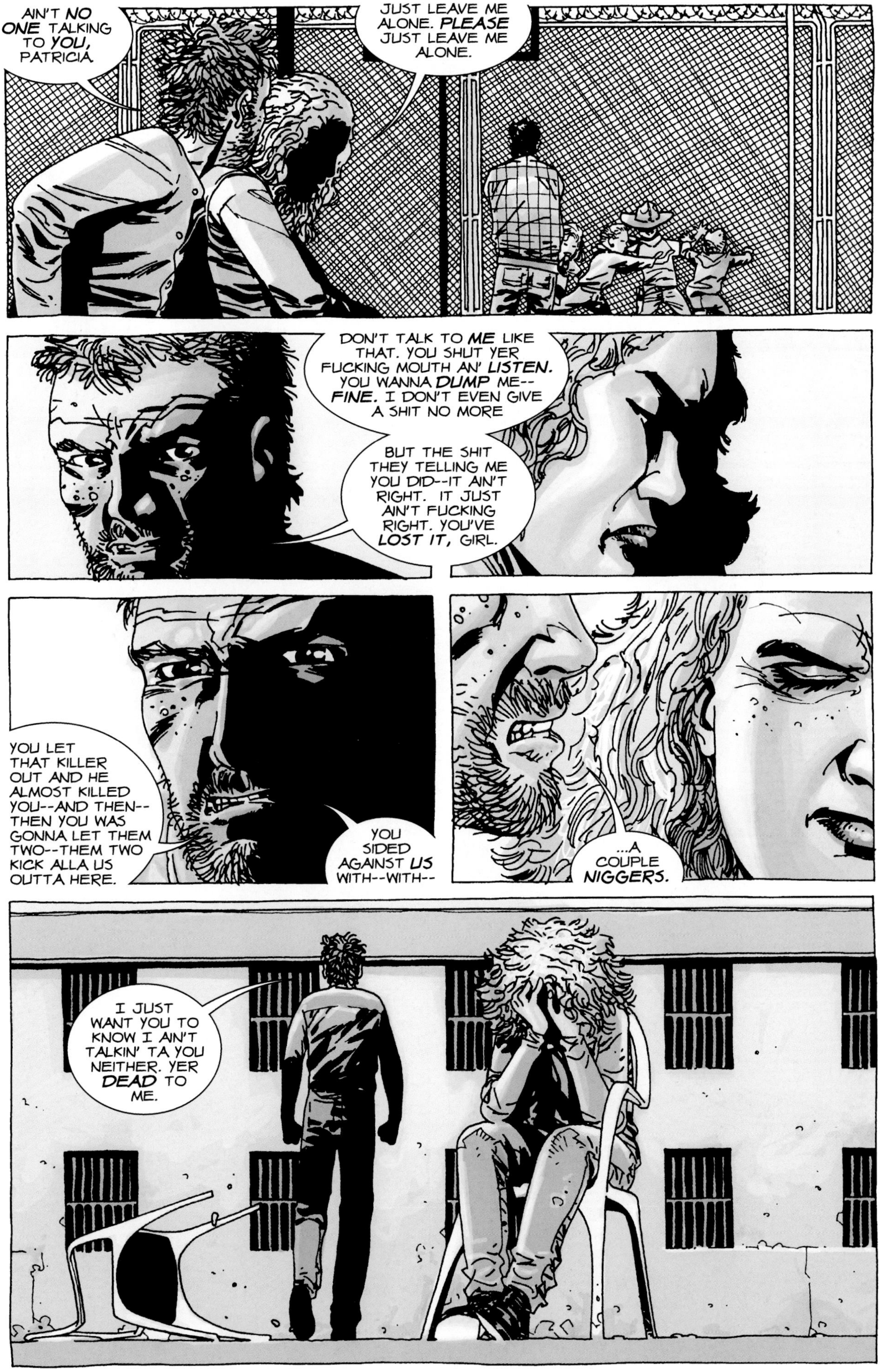
AIN'T NO ONE TALKING TO YOU, PATRICIA.
JUST LEAVE ME ALONE. PLEASE JUST LEAVE ME ALONE.
DON'T TALK TO ME LIKE THAT. YOU SHUT YER FUCKING MOUTH AN' LISTEN. YOU WANNA DUMP ME-- FINE. I DON'T EVEN GIVE A SHIT NO MORE
BUT THE SHIT THEY TELLING ME YOU DID--IT AIN'T RIGHT. IT JUST AIN'T FUCKING RIGHT. YOU'VE LOST IT, GIRL.
YOU LET THAT KILLER OUT AND HE ALMOST KILLED YOU--AND THEN--THEN YOU WAS GONNA LET THEM TWO--THEM TWO KICK ALLA US OUTTA HERE.
YOU SIDED AGAINST US WITH--WITH--
...A COUPLE NIGGERS.
I JUST WANT YOU TO KNOW I AIN'T TALKIN' TA YOU NEITHER. YER DEAD TO ME.

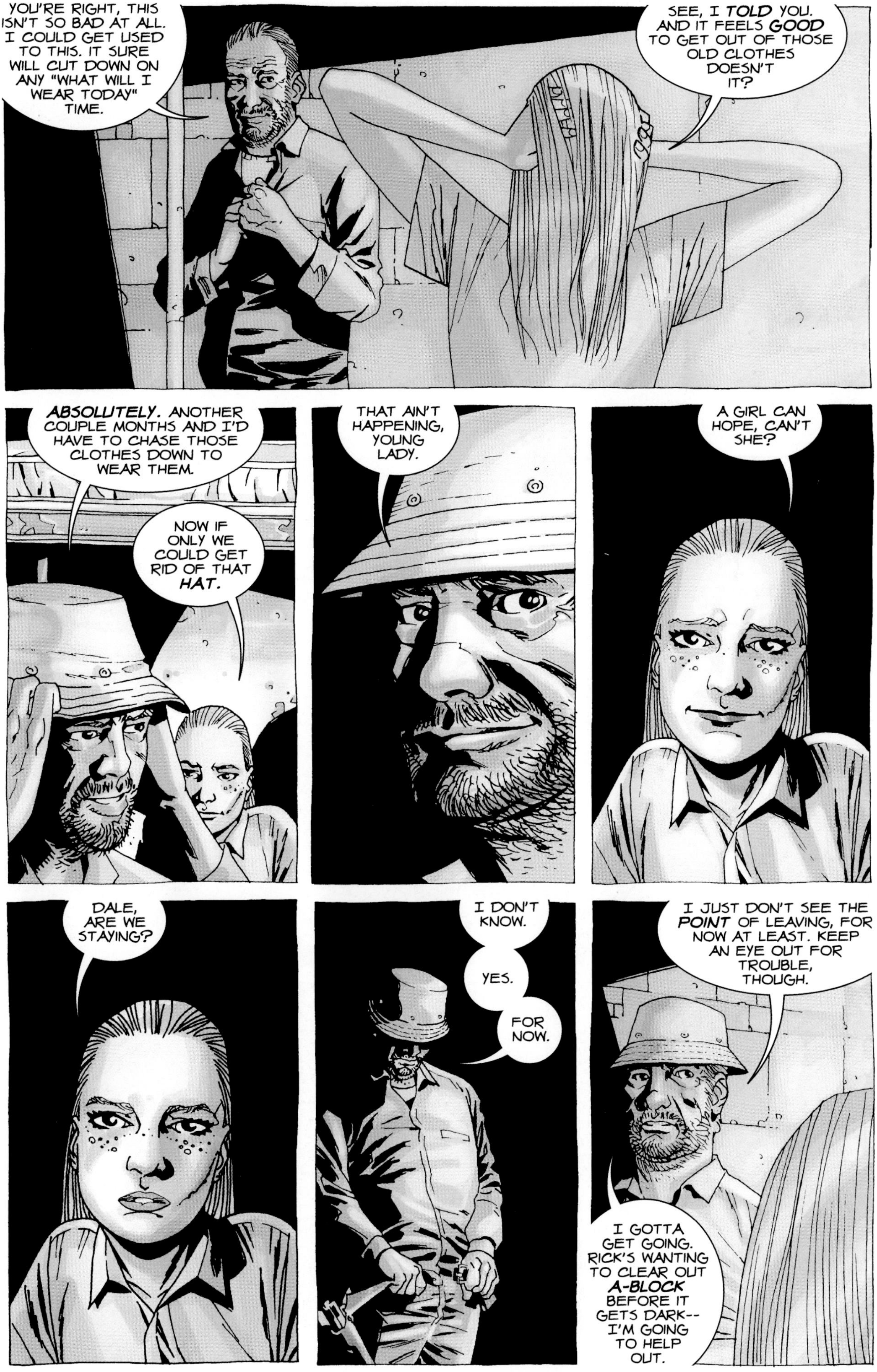
YOU'RE RIGHT, THIS ISN'T SO BAD AT ALL. I COULD GET USED TO THIS. IT SURE WILL CUT DOWN ON ANY "WHAT WILL I WEAR TODAY" TIME.
SEE, I TOLD YOU. AND IT FEELS GOOD TO GET OUT OF THOSE OLD CLOTHES DOESN'T IT?
ABSOLUTELY. ANOTHER COUPLE MONTHS AND I'D HAVE TO CHASE THOSE CLOTHES DOWN TO WEAR THEM.
NOW IF ONLY WE COULD GET RID OF THAT HAT.
THAT AIN'T HAPPENING, YOUNG LADY.
A GIRL CAN HOPE, CAN'T SHE?
DALE, ARE WE STAYING?
I DON'T KNOW.
YES.
FOR NOW.
I JUST DON'T SEE THE POINT OF LEAVING, FOR NOW AT LEAST. KEEP AN EYE OUT FOR TROUBLE, THOUGH.
I GOTTA GET GOING. RICK'S WANTING TO CLEAR OUT A-BLOCK BEFORE IT GETS DARK-- I'M GOING TO HELP OUT.

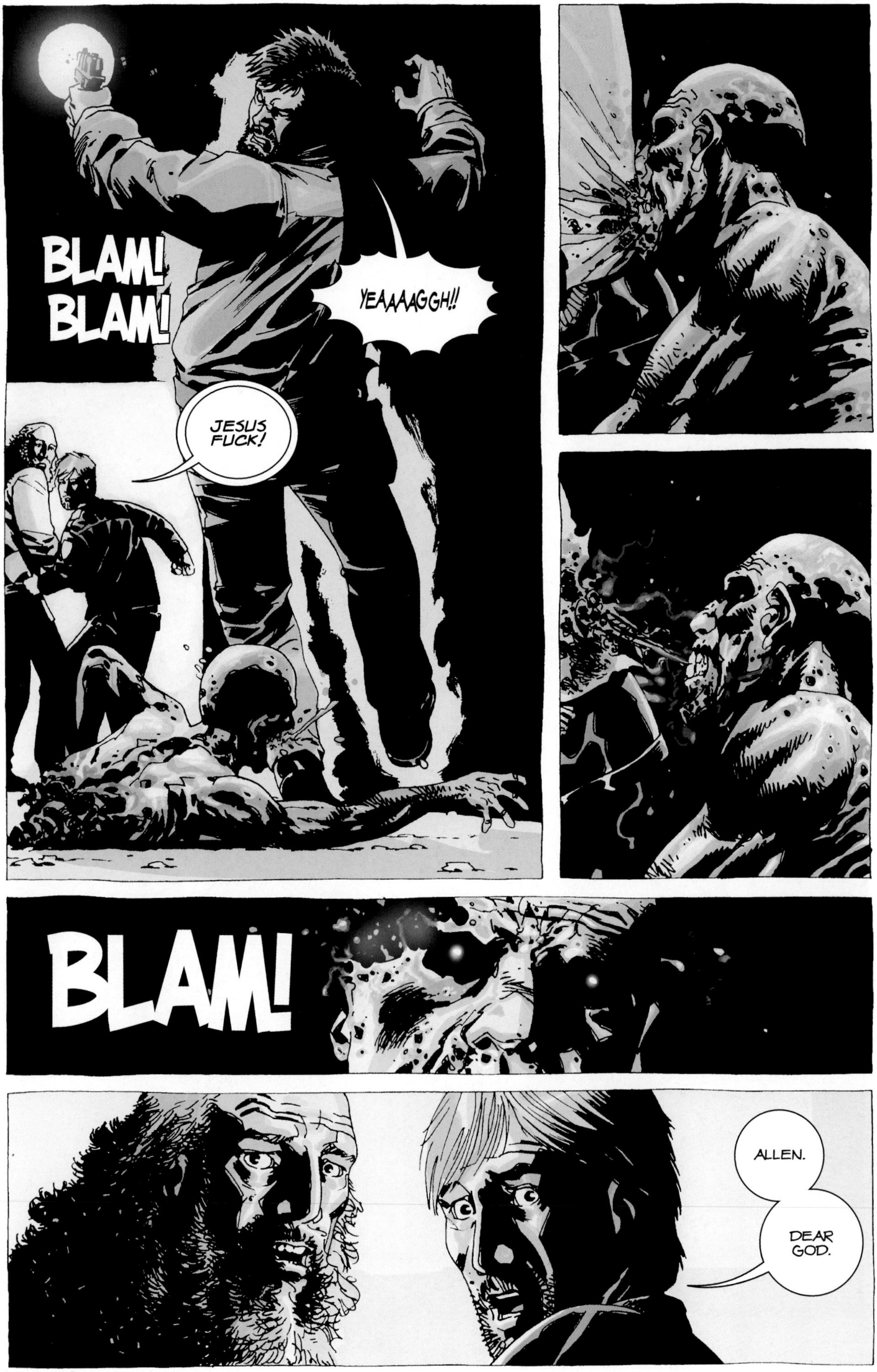
BLAM! BLAM!
YEAAAAGGH!!
JESUS FUCK!
BLAM!
ALLEN.
DEAR GOD.

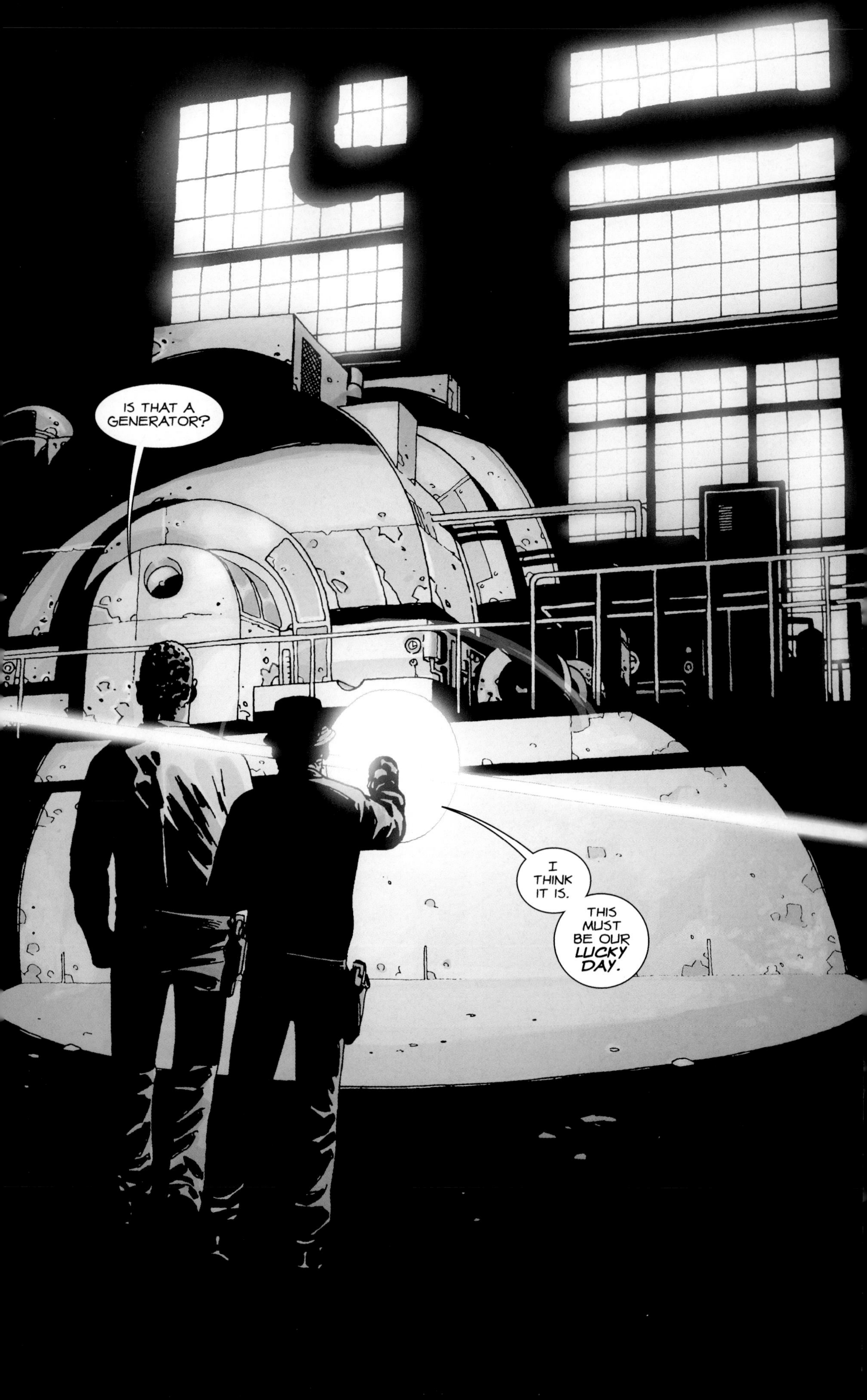
IS THAT A GENERATOR?
I THINK IT IS.
THIS MUST BE OUR LUCKY DAY.

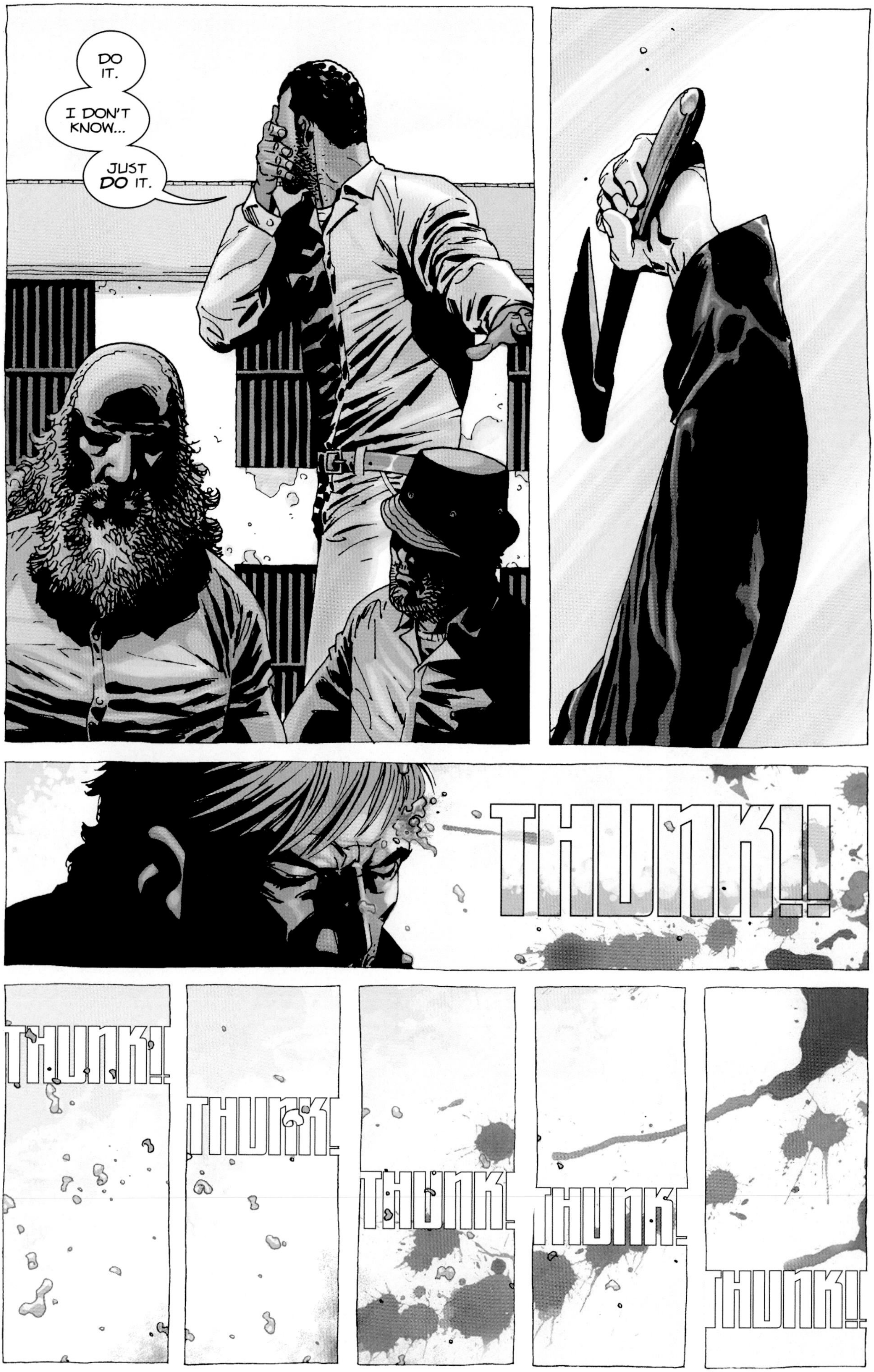
DO IT.
I DON'T KNOW...
JUST DO IT.
THUNK!!
THUNK!!
THUNK!!
THUNK!!
THUNK!!
THUNK!!

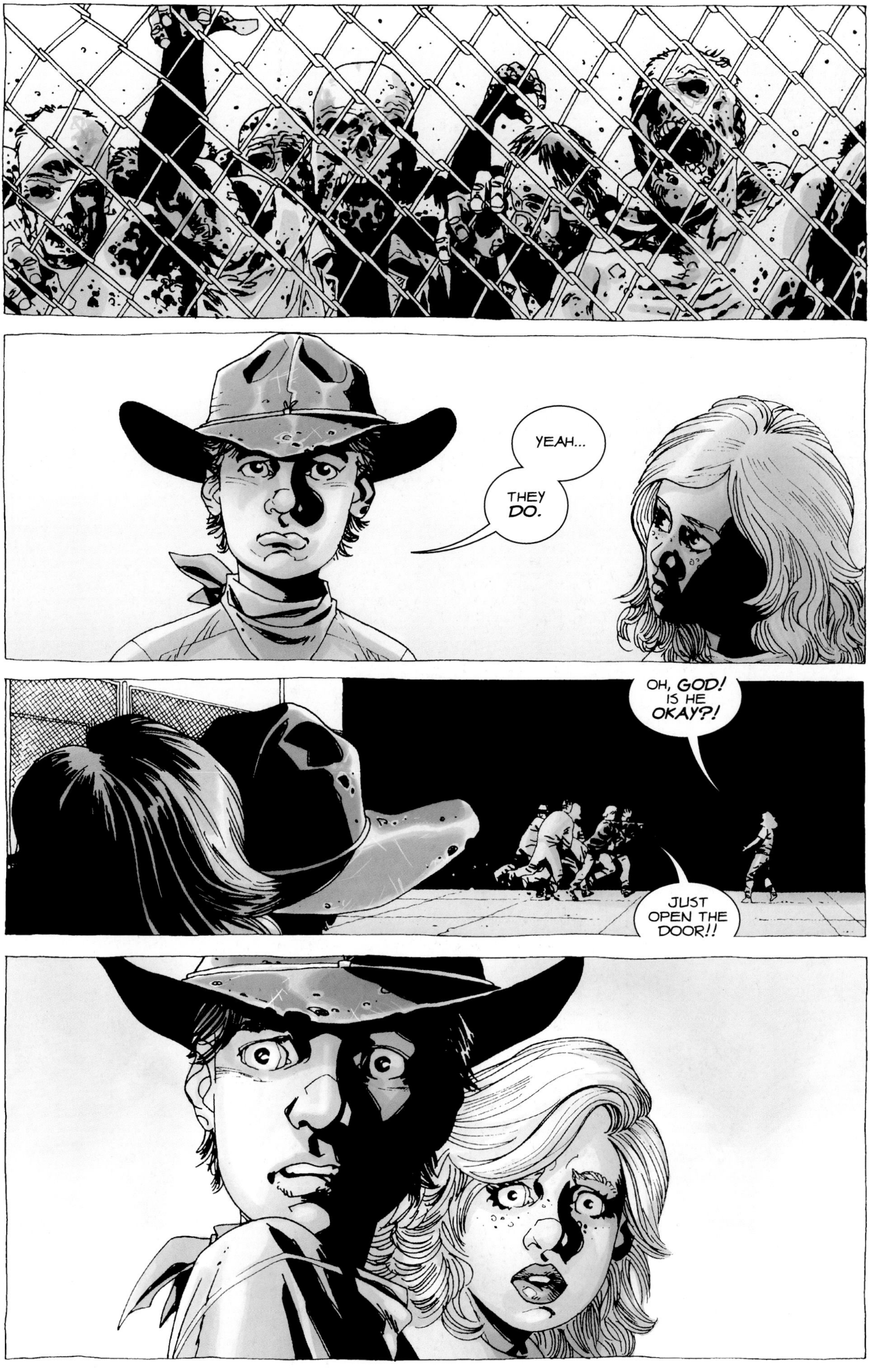
YEAH...
THEY DO.
OH, GOD! IS HE OKAY?!
JUST OPEN THE DOOR!!

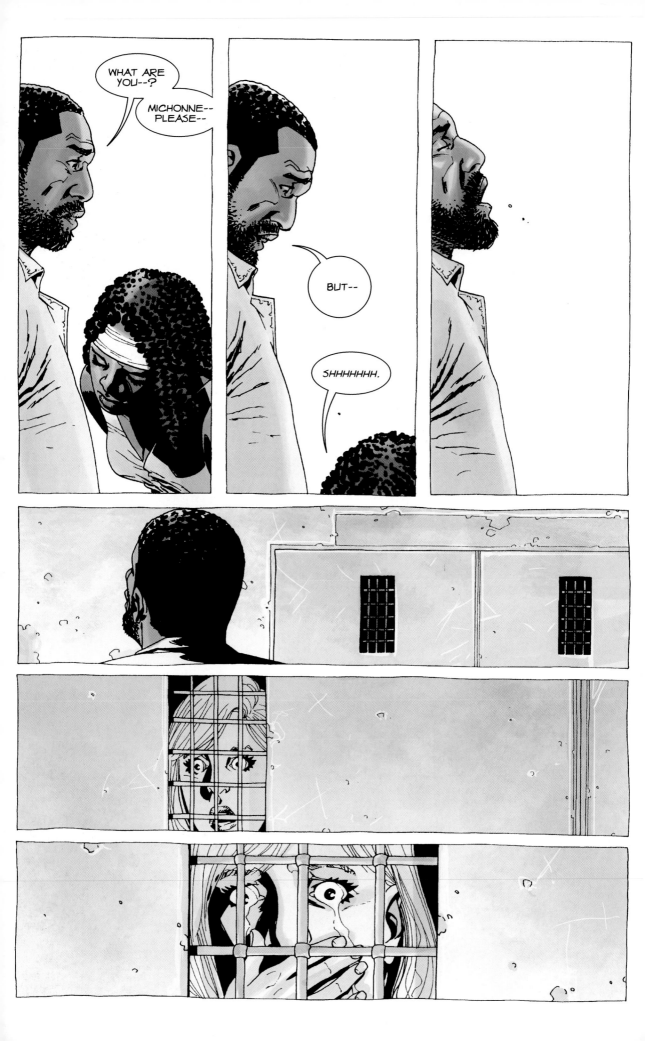

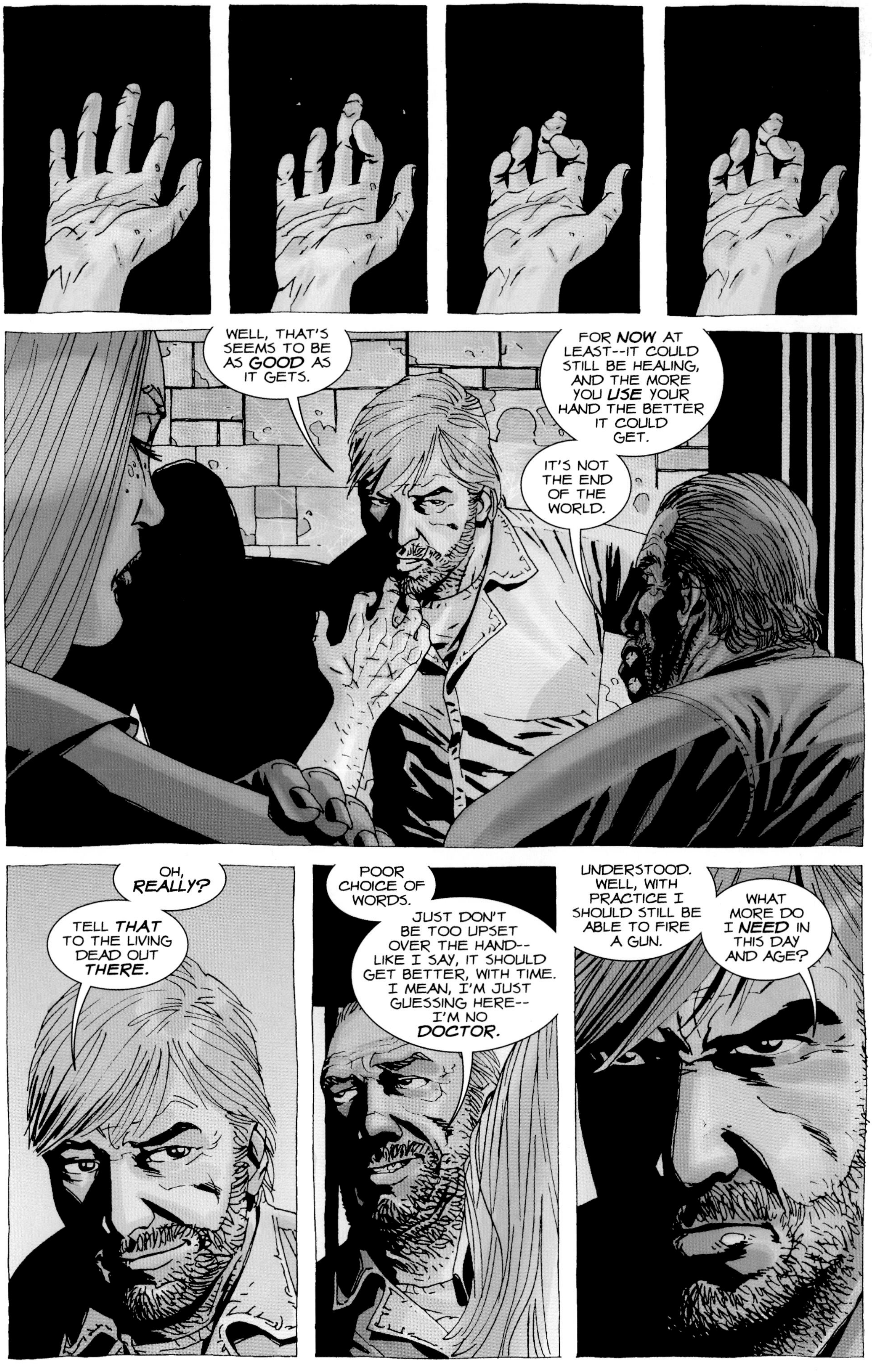

WELL, THAT'S SEEMS TO BE AS GOOD AS IT GETS.
FOR NOW AT LEAST--IT COULD STILL BE HEALING, AND THE MORE YOU USE YOUR HAND THE BETTER IT COULD GET.
IT'S NOT THE END OF THE WORLD.
OH, REALLY?
TELL THAT TO THE LIVING DEAD OUT THERE.
POOR CHOICE OF WORDS.
JUST DON'T BE TOO UPSET OVER THE HAND-- LIKE I SAY, IT SHOULD GET BETTER, WITH TIME. I MEAN, I'M JUST GUESSING HERE-- I'M NO DOCTOR.
UNDERSTOOD. WELL, WITH PRACTICE I SHOULD STILL BE ABLE TO FIRE A GUN.
WHAT MORE DO I NEED IN THIS DAY AND AGE?

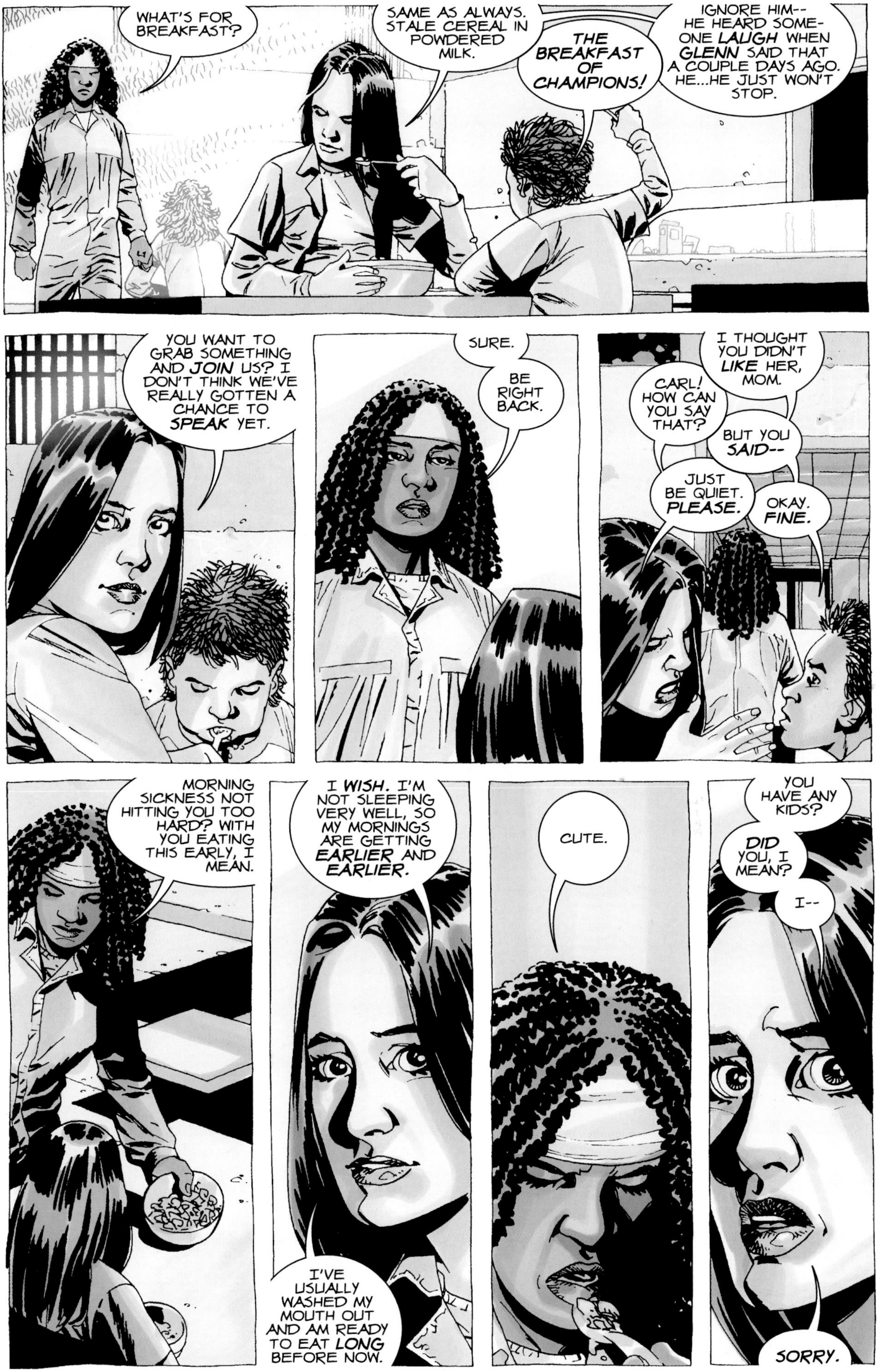
WHAT'S FOR BREAKFAST?
SAME AS ALWAYS. STALE CEREAL IN POWDERED MILK.
THE BREAKFAST OF CHAMPIONS!
IGNORE HIM-- HE HEARD SOMEONE LAUGH WHEN GLENN SAID THAT A COUPLE DAYS AGO. HE...HE JUST WON'T STOP.
YOU WANT TO GRAB SOMETHING AND JOIN US? I DON'T THINK WE'VE REALLY GOTTEN A CHANCE TO SPEAK YET.
SURE.
BE RIGHT BACK.
I THOUGHT YOU DIDN'T LIKE HER, MOM.
CARL! HOW CAN YOU SAY THAT?
BUT YOU SAID--
JUST BE QUIET. PLEASE.
OKAY. FINE.
MORNING SICKNESS NOT HITTING YOU TOO HARD? WITH YOU EATING THIS EARLY, I MEAN.
I WISH. I'M NOT SLEEPING VERY WELL, SO MY MORNINGS ARE GETTING EARLIER AND EARLIER.
I'VE USUALLY WASHED MY MOUTH OUT AND AM READY TO EAT LONG BEFORE NOW.
CUTE.
YOU HAVE ANY KIDS?
DID YOU, I MEAN?
I--
SORRY.

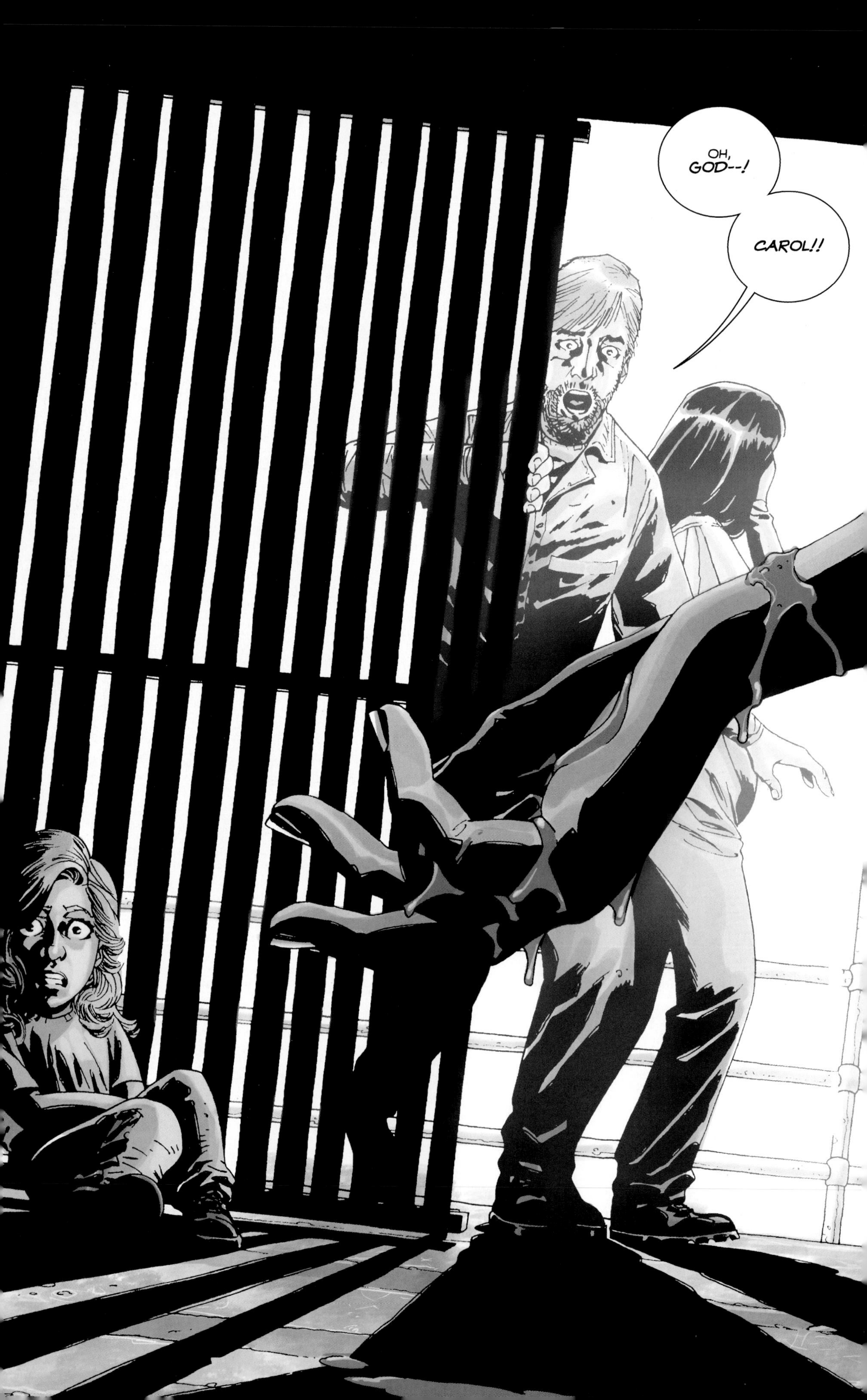
OH, GOD--!
CAROL!!

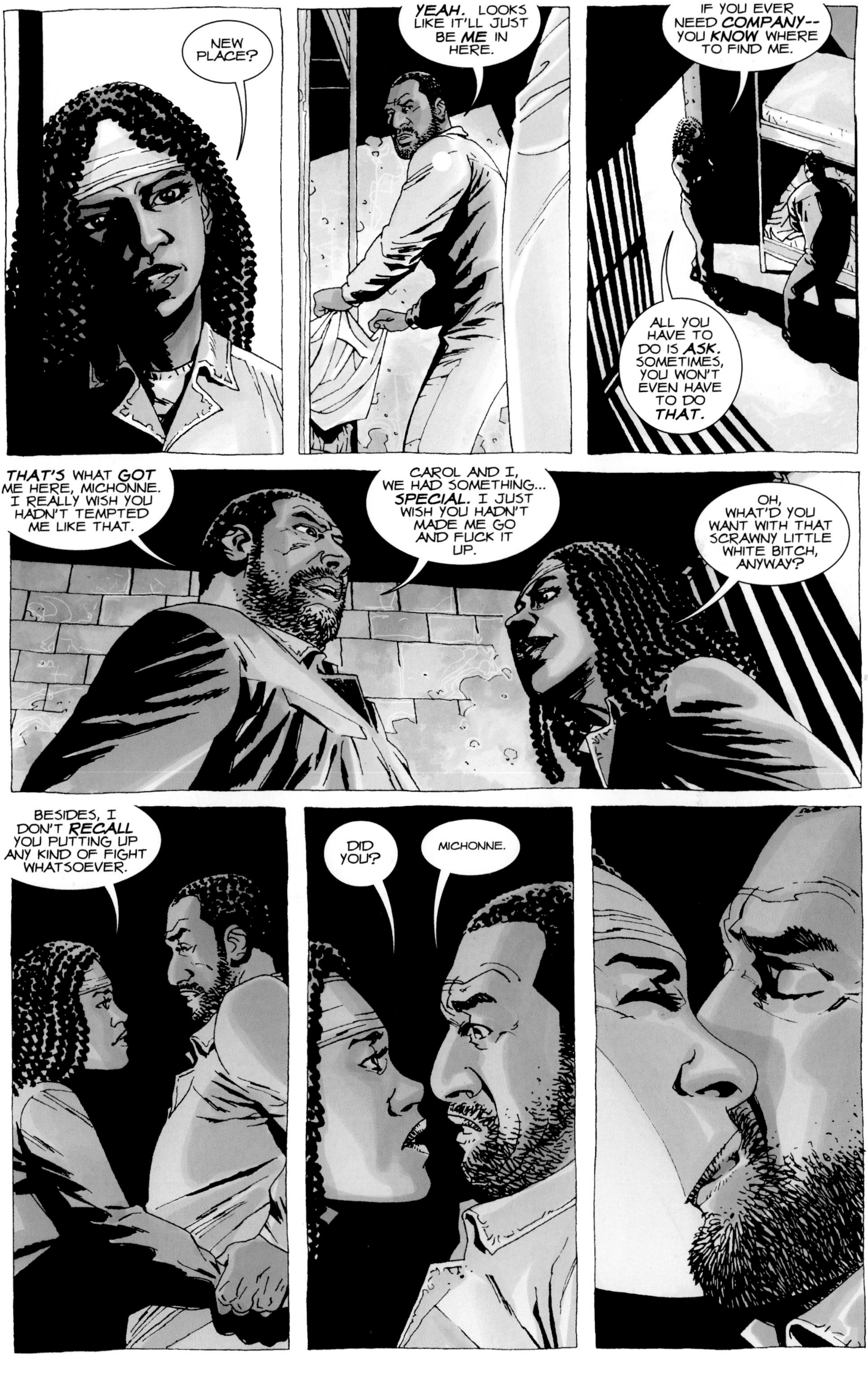
NEW PLACE?
YEAH. LOOKS LIKE IT'LL JUST BE ME IN HERE.
IF YOU EVER NEED COMPANY-- YOU KNOW WHERE TO FIND ME.
ALL YOU HAVE TO DO IS ASK. SOMETIMES, YOU WON'T EVEN HAVE TO DO THAT.
THAT'S WHAT GOT ME HERE, MICHONNE. I REALLY WISH YOU HADN'T TEMPTED ME LIKE THAT.
CAROL AND I, WE HAD SOMETHING... SPECIAL. I JUST WISH YOU HADN'T MADE ME GO AND FUCK IT UP.
OH, WHAT'D YOU WANT WITH THAT SCRAWNY LITTLE WHITE BITCH, ANYWAY?
BESIDES, I DON'T RECALL YOU PUTTING UP ANY KIND OF FIGHT WHATSOEVER.
DID YOU?
MICHONNE.

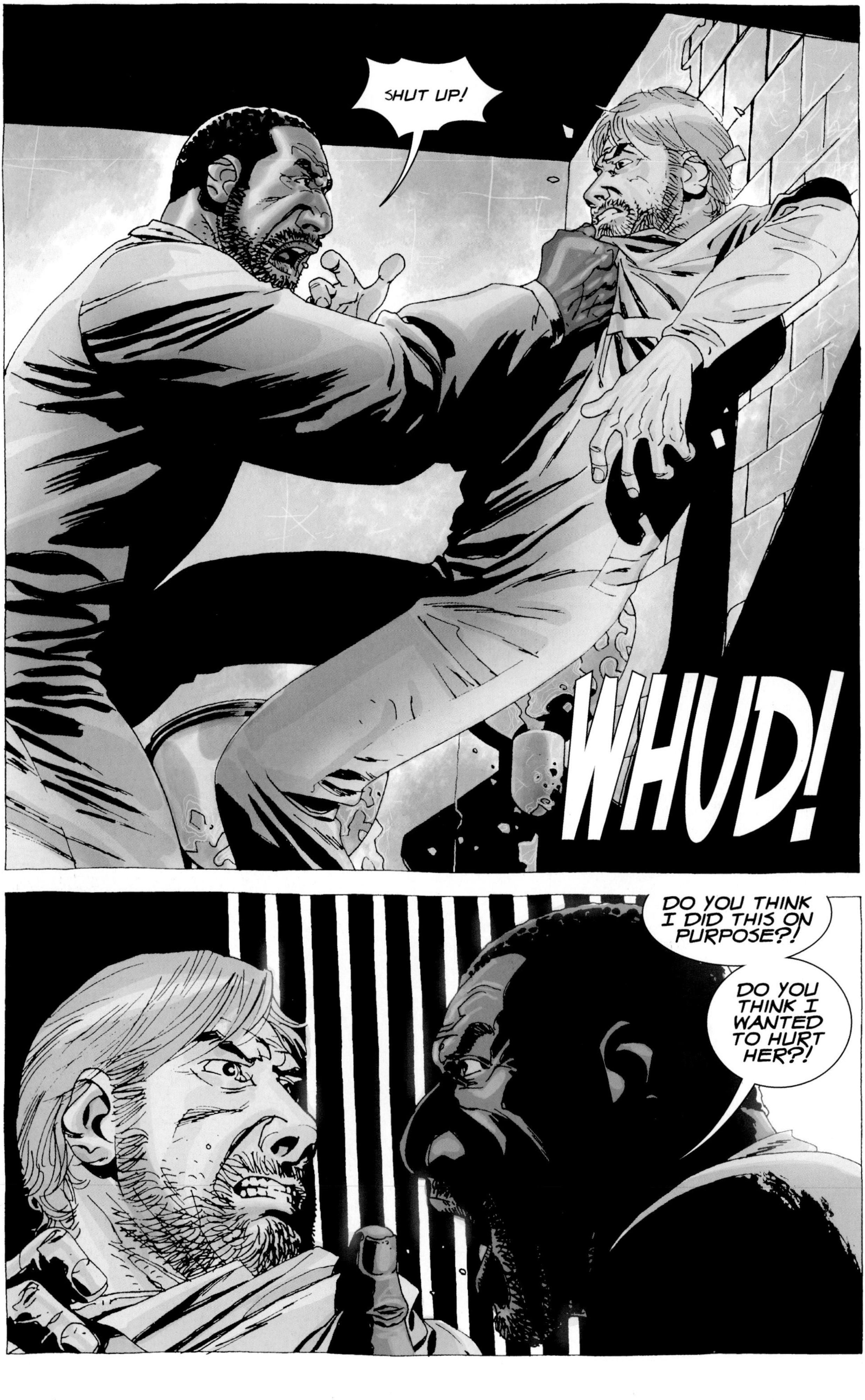
SHUT UP!
WHUD!
DO YOU THINK I DID THIS ON PURPOSE?!
DO YOU THINK I WANTED TO HURT HER?!

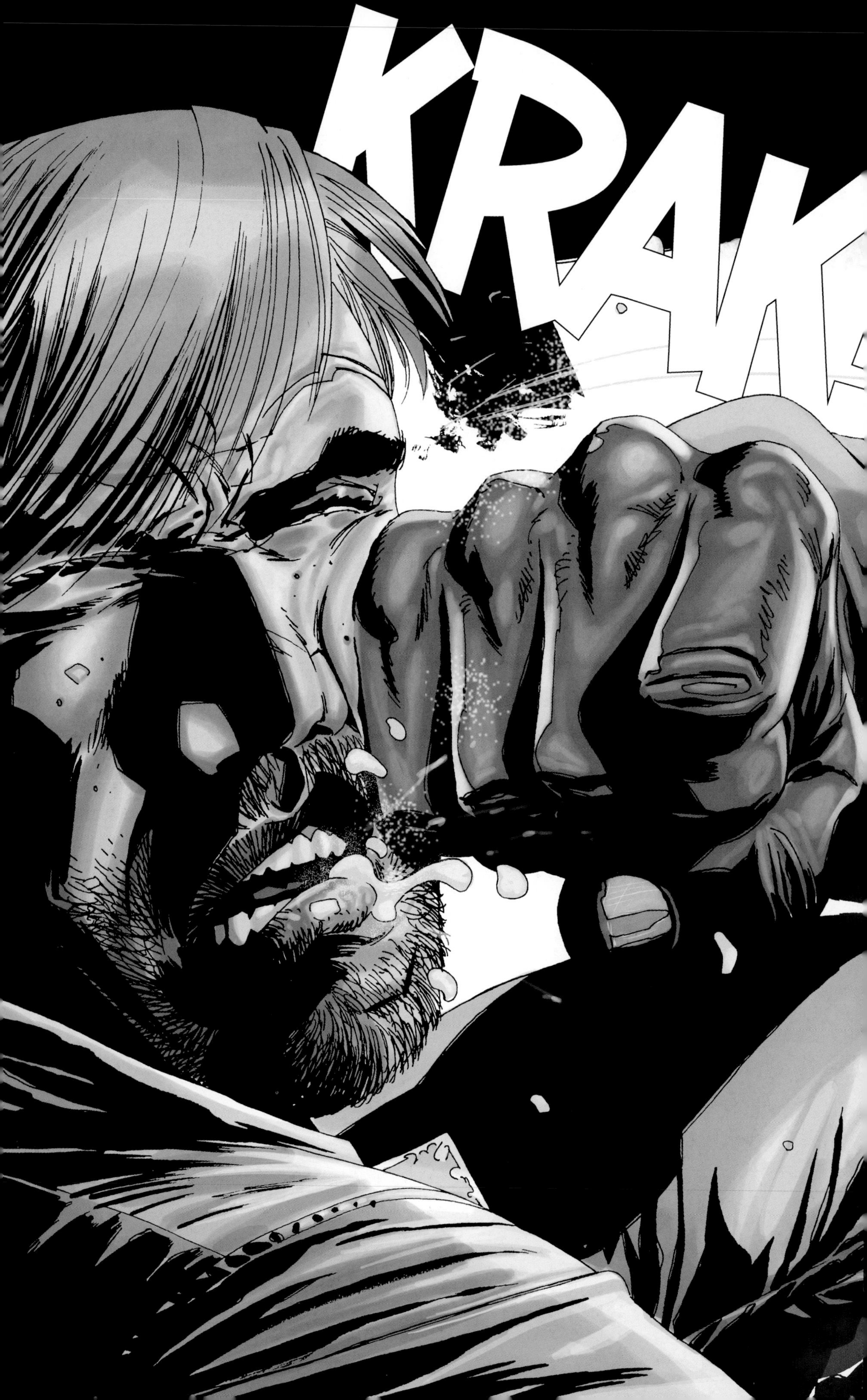
KRAAK

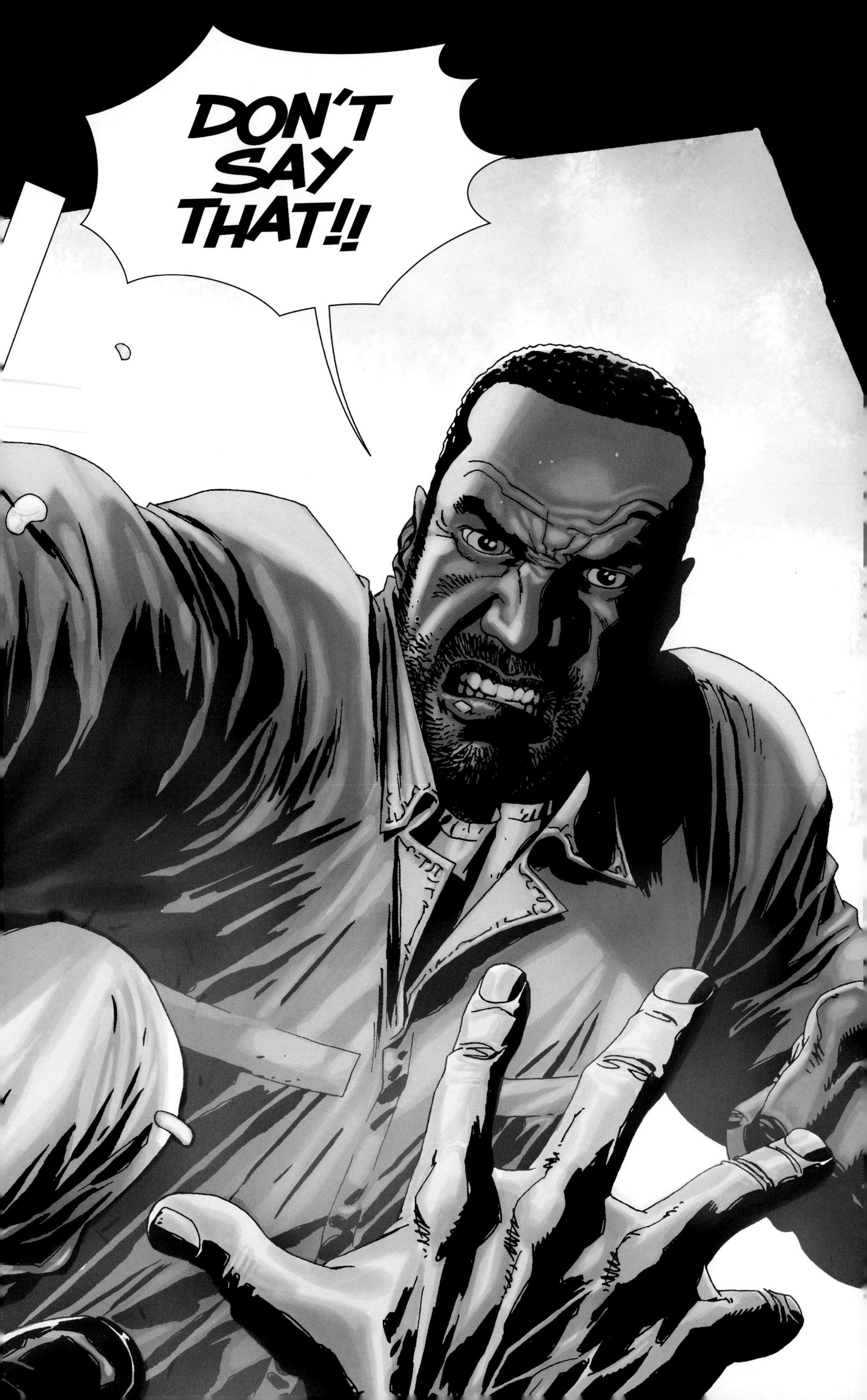
DON'T SAY THAT!!

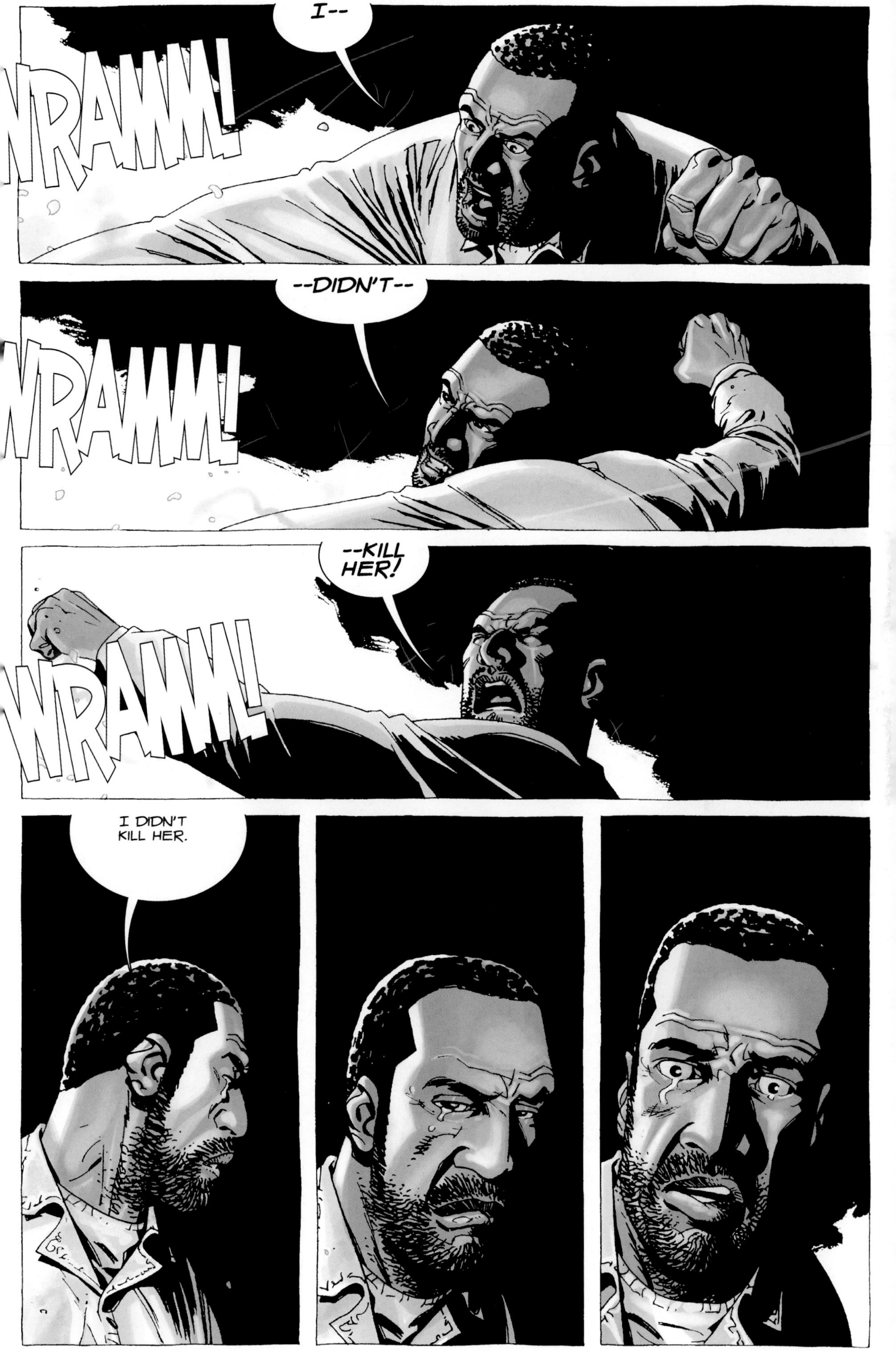
I--
WRAMM!
--DIDN'T--
WRAMM!
--KILL HER!
WRAMM!
I DIDN'T KILL HER.

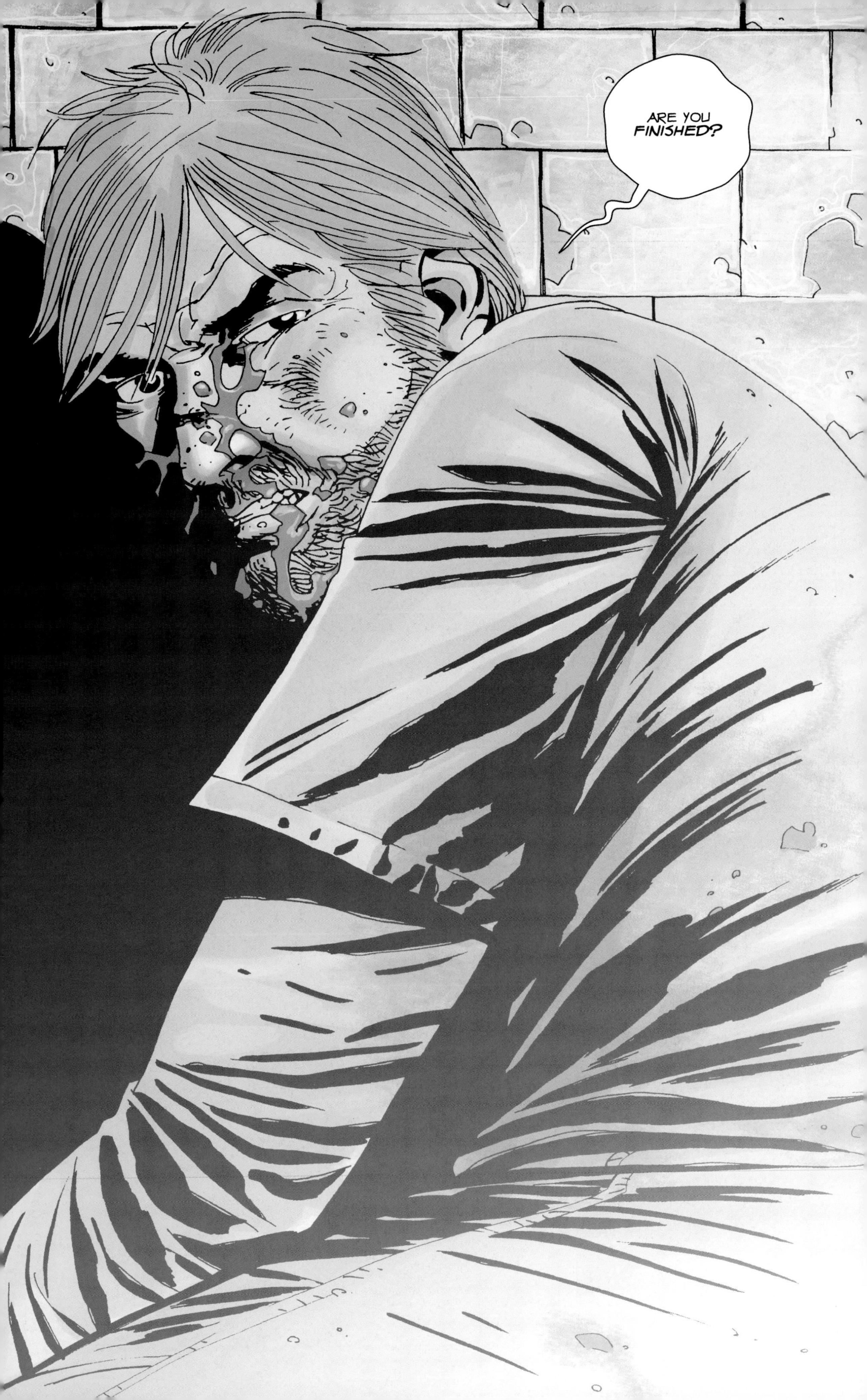
ARE YOU FINISHED?

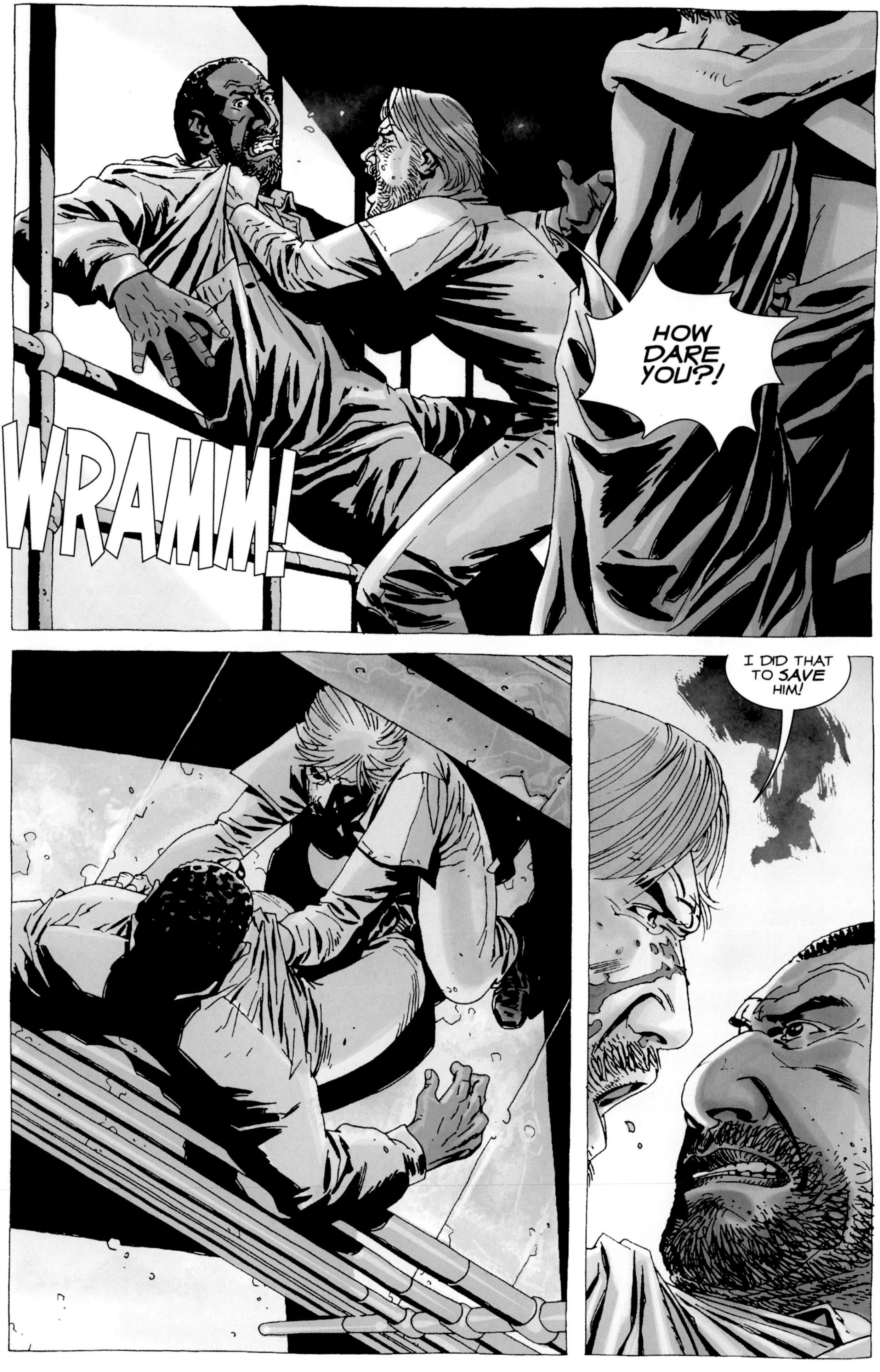
WRAMM!
HOW DARE YOU?!
I DID THAT TO SAVE HIM!

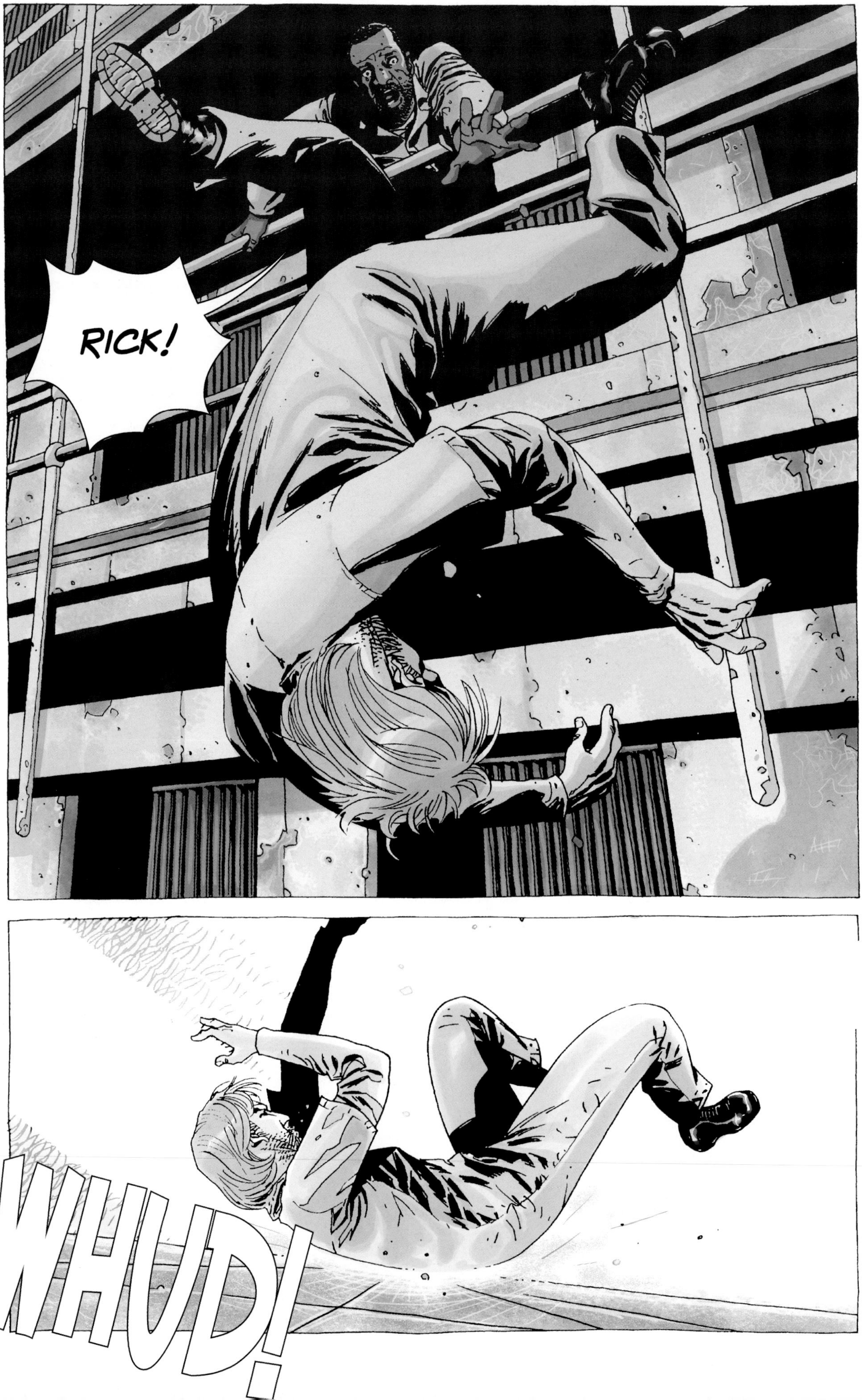
RICK!
WHUD!

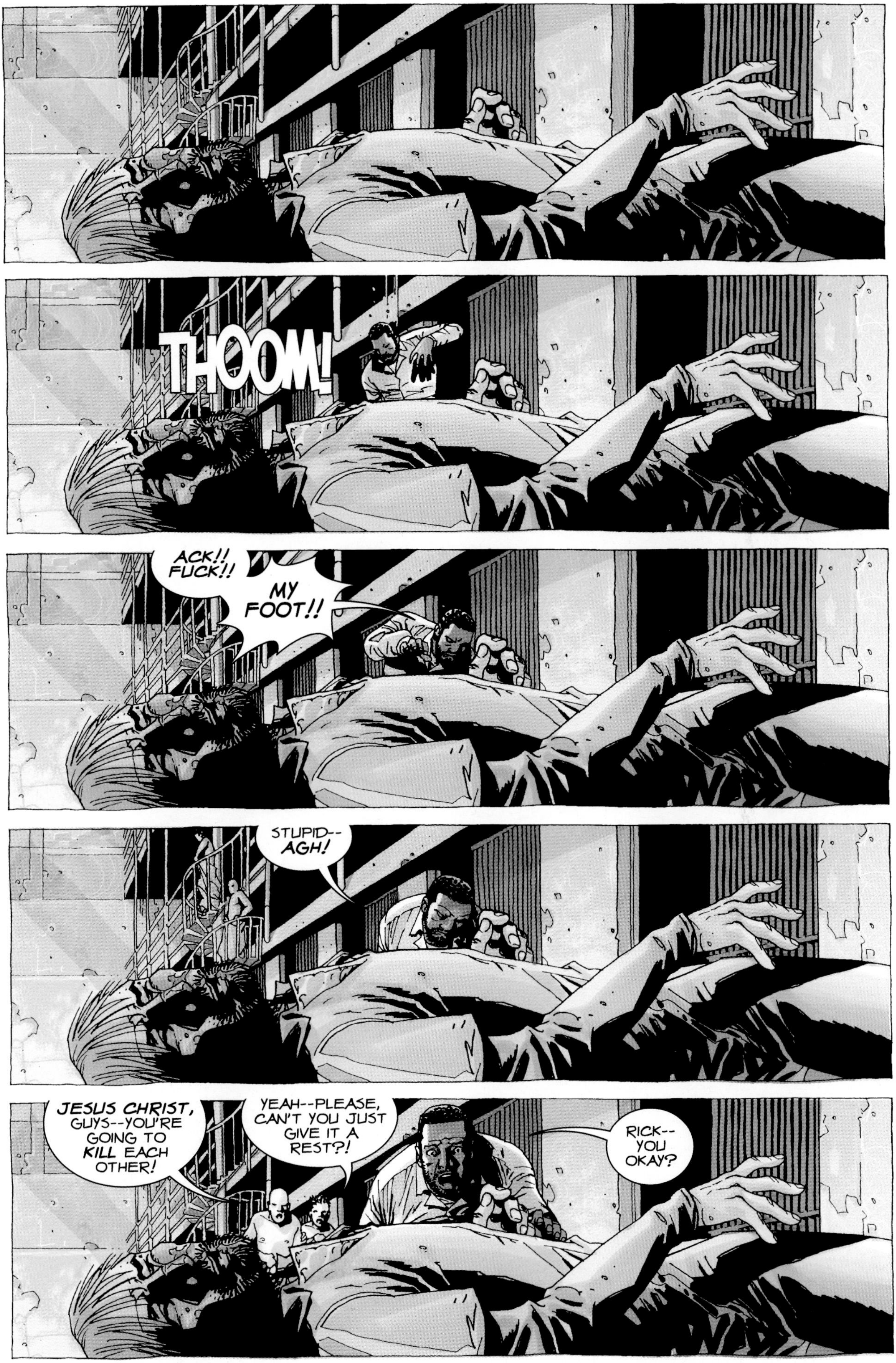
THOOM!
ACK!! FUCK!!
MY FOOT!!
STUPID-- AGH!
JESUS CHRIST, GUYS--YOU'RE GOING TO KILL EACH OTHER!
YEAH--PLEASE, CAN'T YOU JUST GIVE IT A REST?!
RICK-- YOU OKAY?

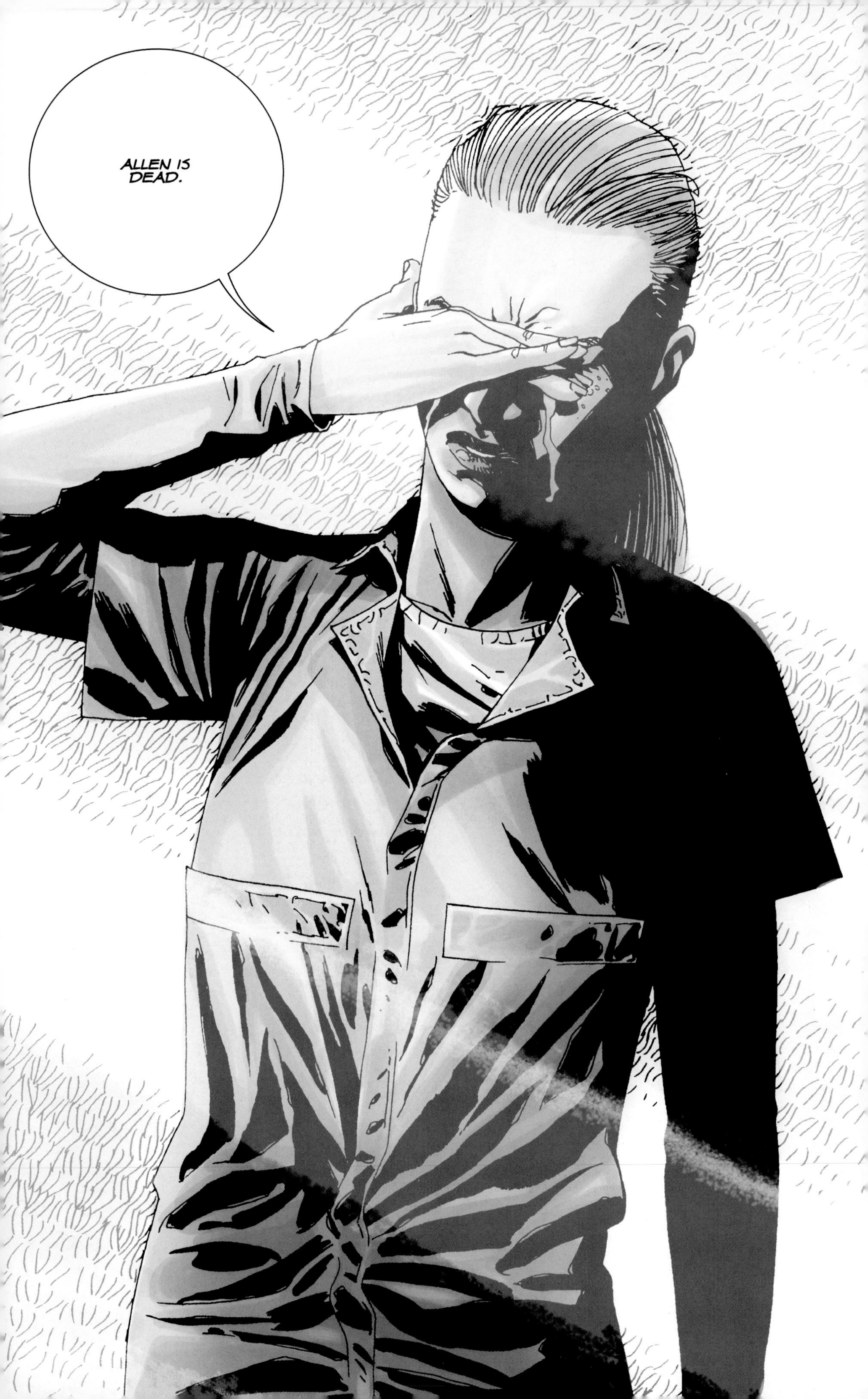
ALLEN IS DEAD.

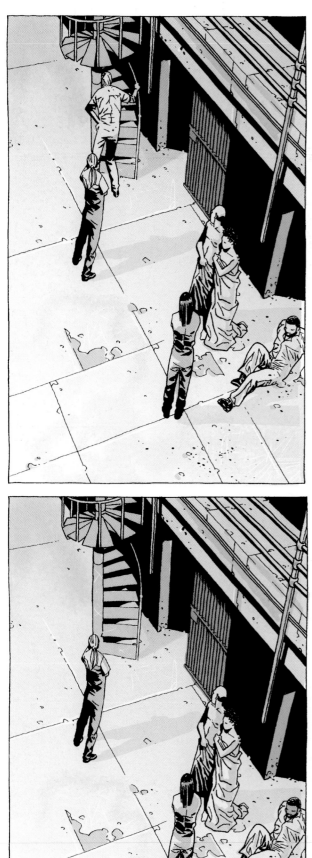

YOU GOING TO TELL ME *EXACTLY* WHAT THE HELL THIS WAS ABOUT?

LATER.

BLAM!

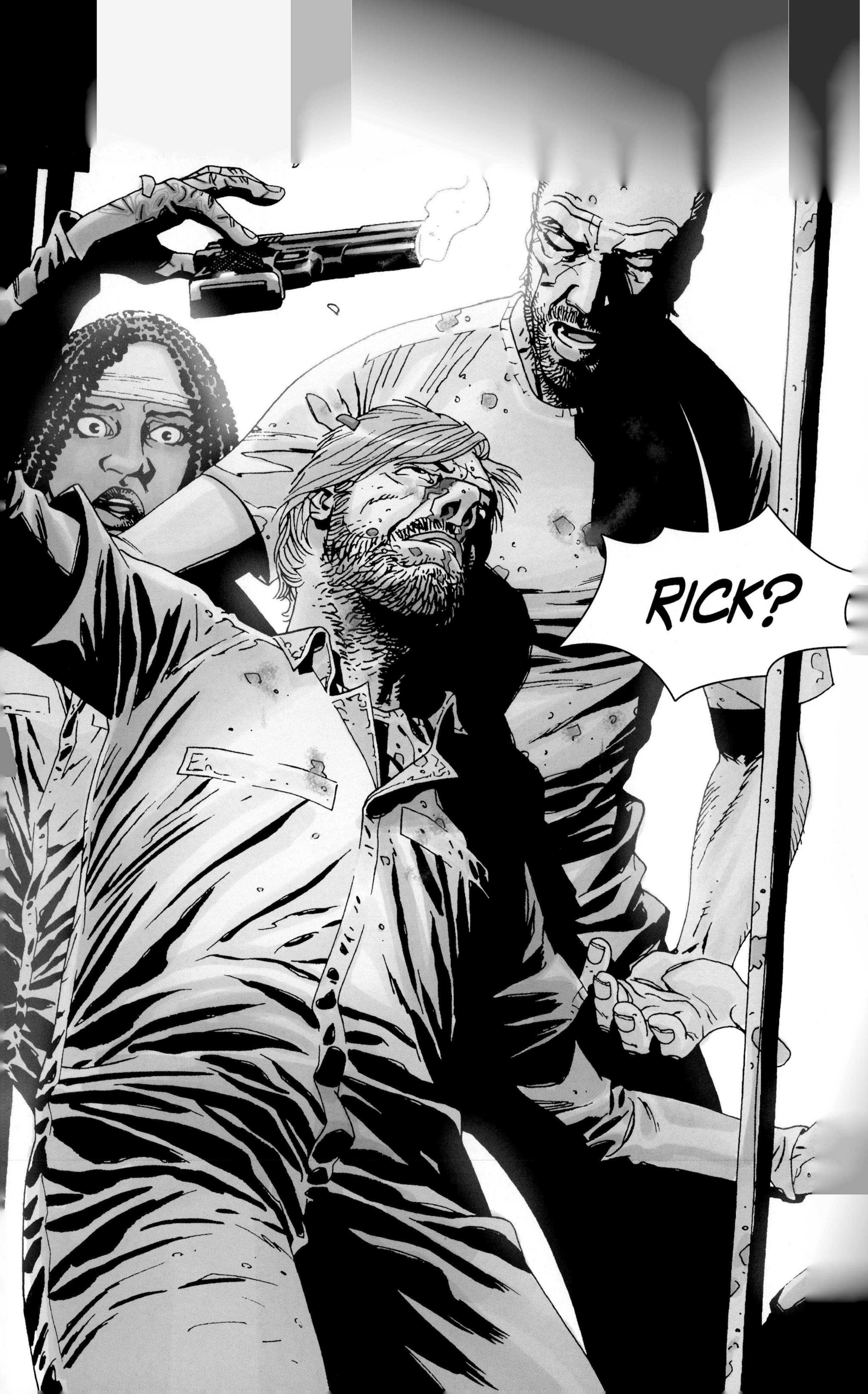
RICK?

RICK?

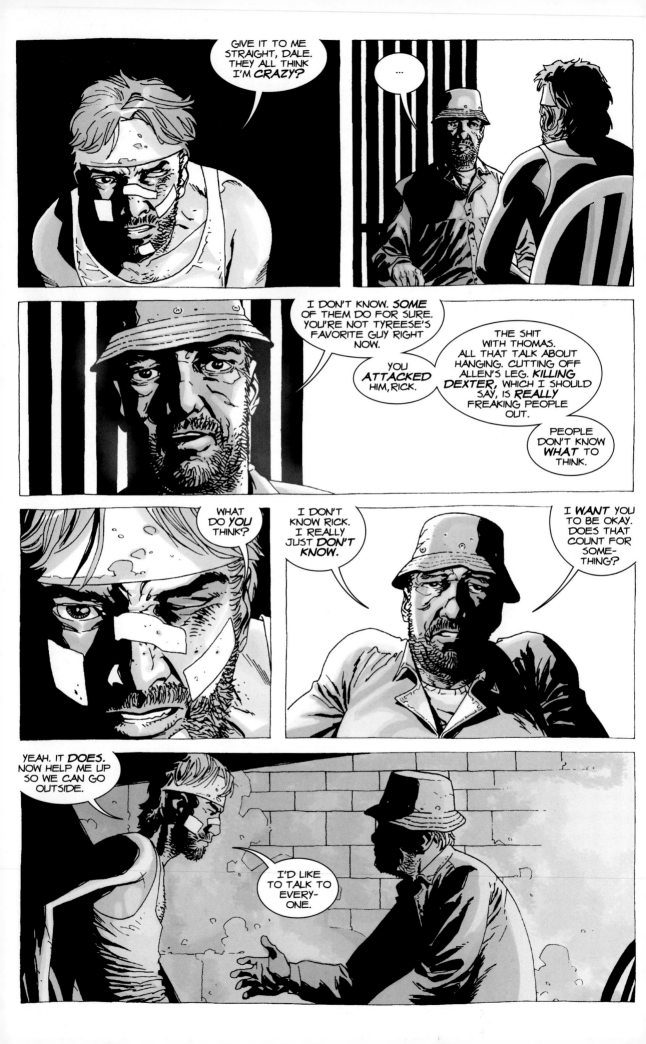

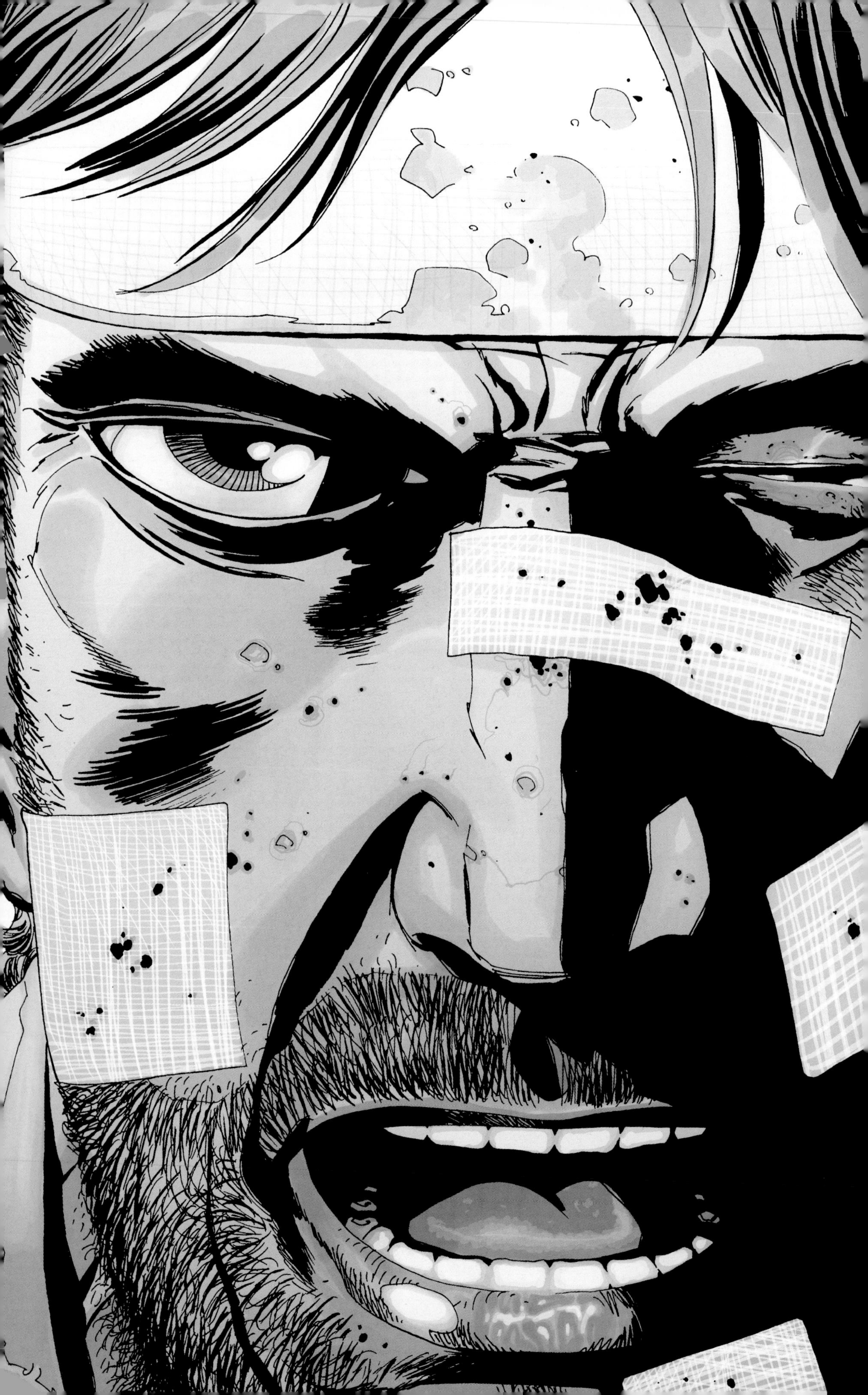

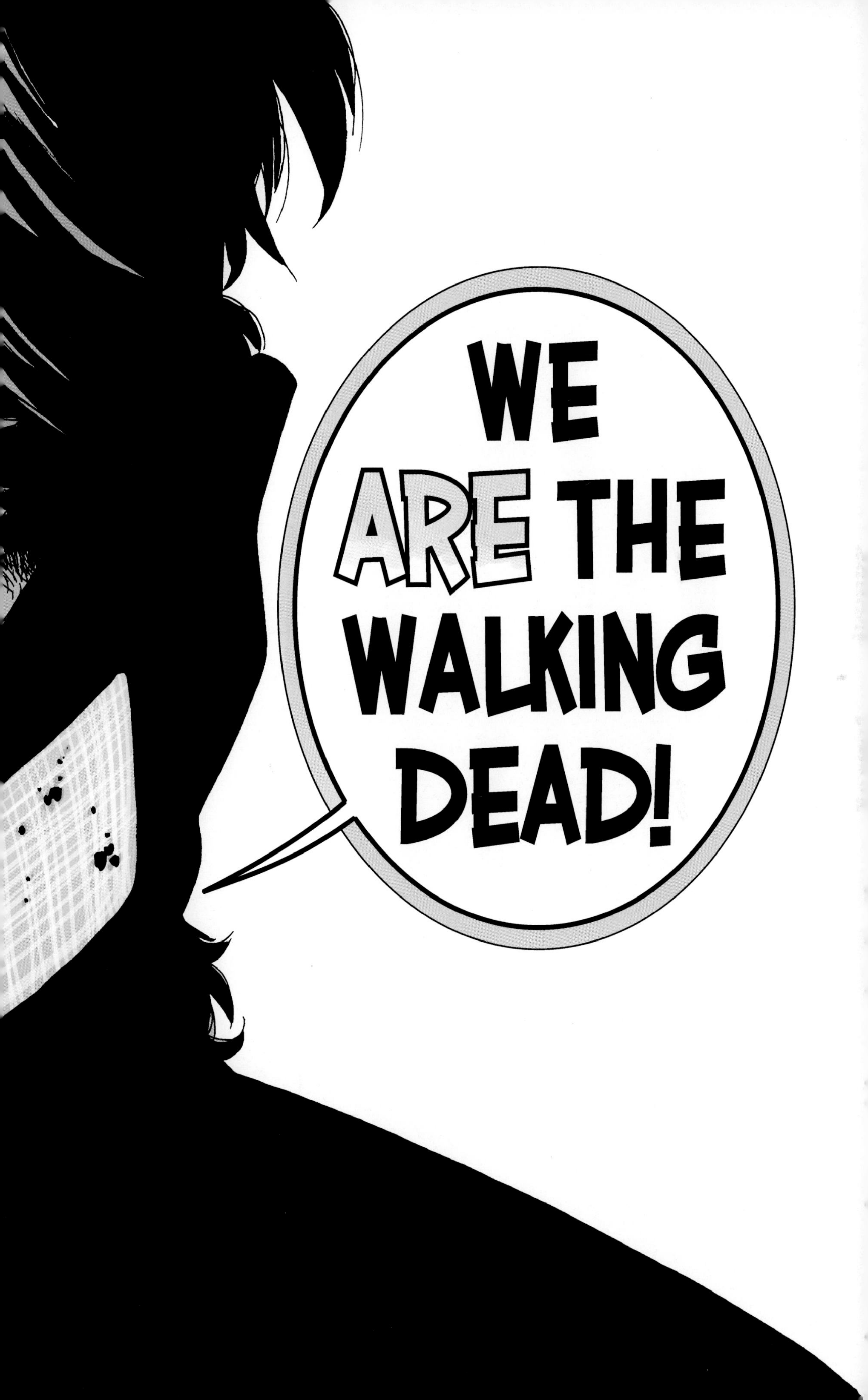
WE ARE THE WALKING DEAD!

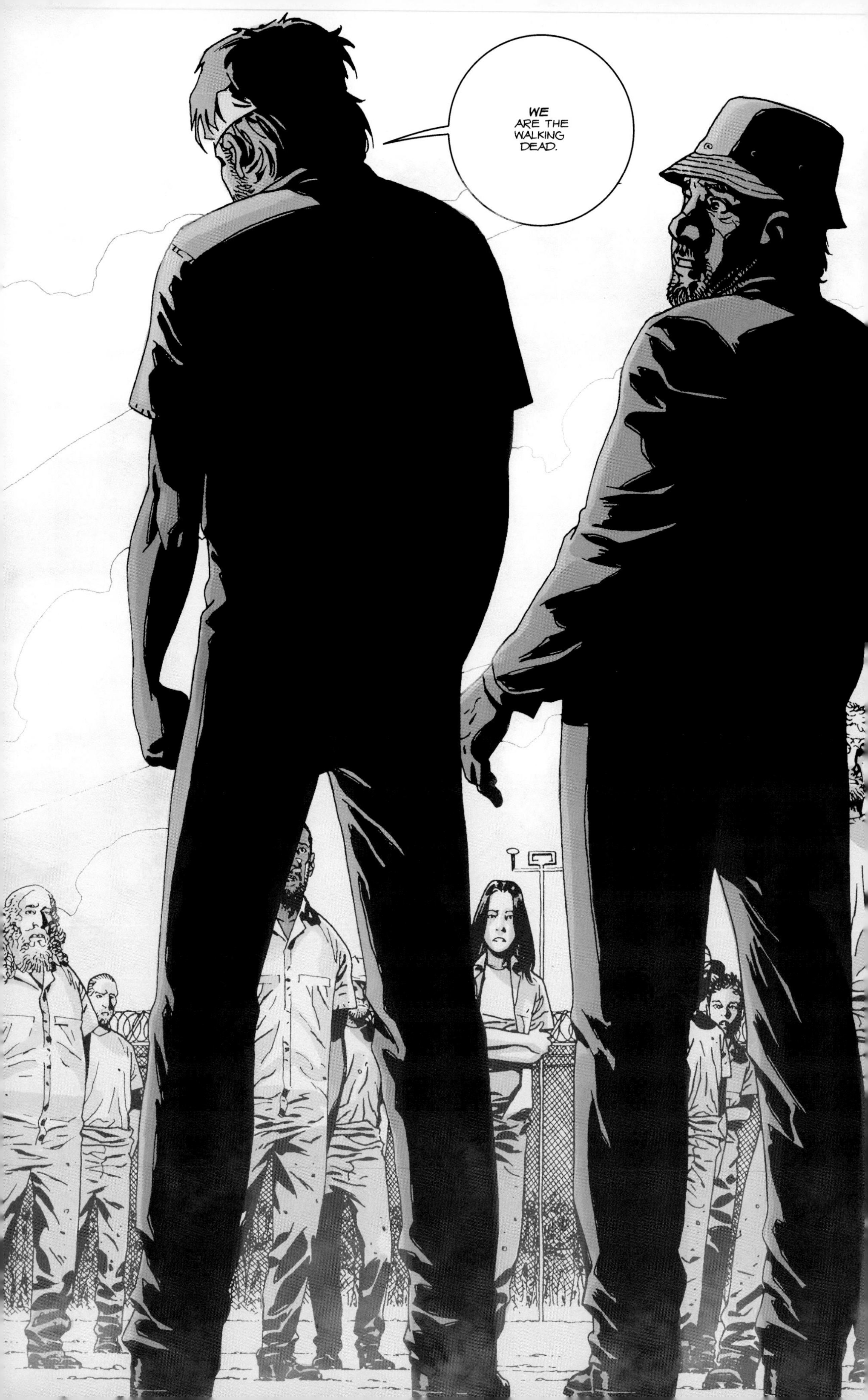
WE ARE THE WALKING DEAD.

to be continued...

Sketchbook

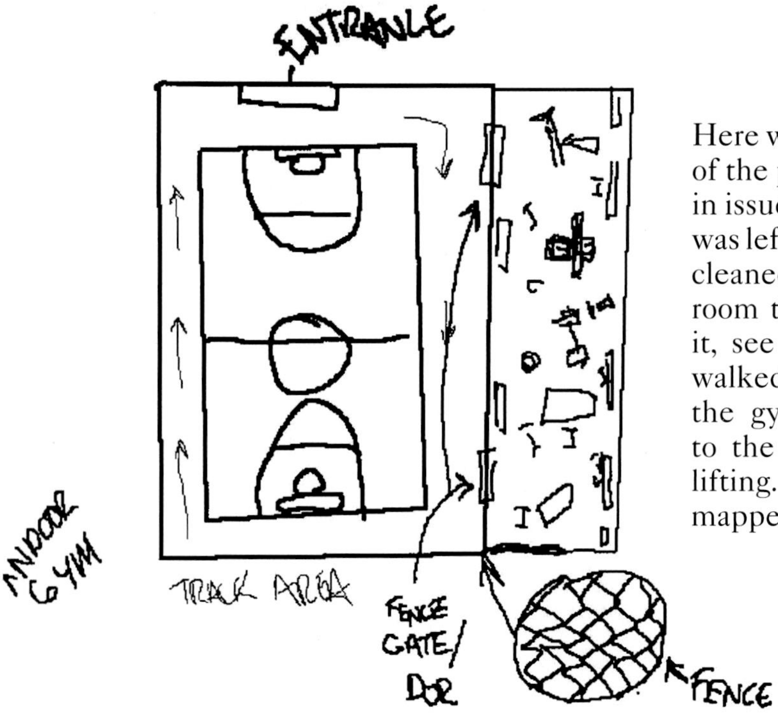

ENTRANCE
INDOOR GYM
TRACK AREA
FENCE GATE/ DOR
FENCE

Here we'll see an overhead layout of the prison gym. This was used in issue 15 or 16 for when Tyreese was left inside and later when they cleaned the place up. The weight room thing is right there next to it, see issue 20 when Michonne walked by Tyreese and Carol in the gym and then walked over to the weight room to do some lifting. See--these things are all mapped out!

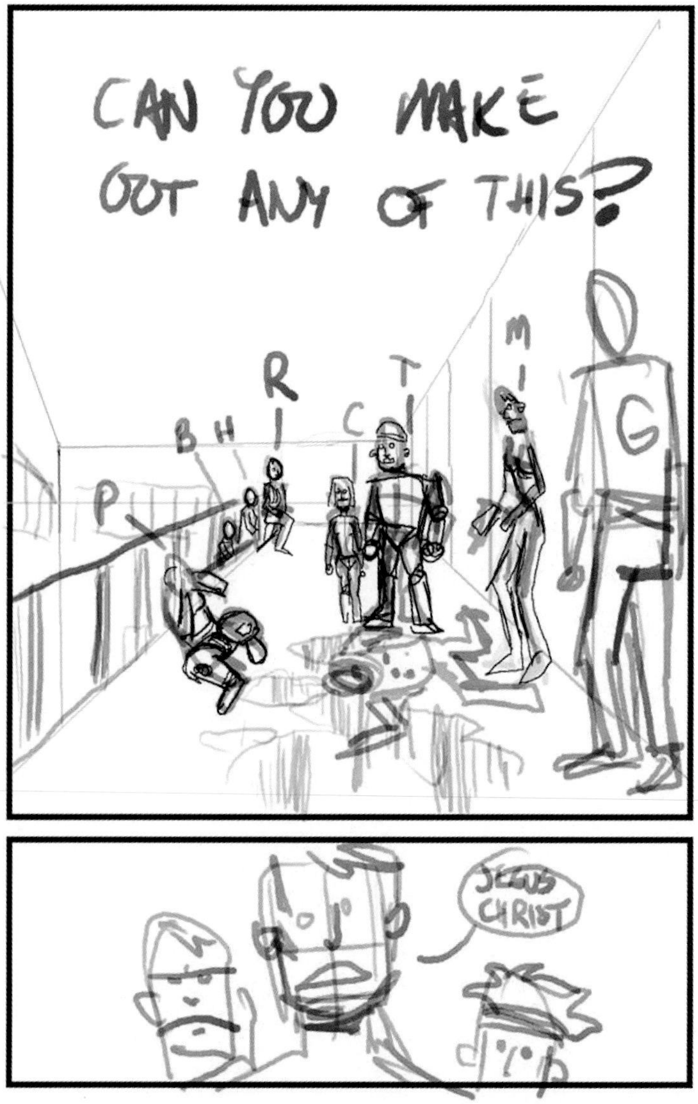

CAN YOU MAKE OUT ANY OF THIS?
JESUS CHRIST

Also on this page is a layout for page 17 of issue 18 (toward the end of what is chapter 3 of this book, actually, about 5 pages from the end). I thought my panel description was a little confusing so I made an even more confusing sketch for Charlie to go off of. As you can see by looking at the final page, Charlie did a bang-up job. He even added a nice little spiral staircase, which I get a real kick out of including in future scripts because Charlie admitted to me that he hates drawing the thing. What was he thinking?

Ah, Michonne.

I had the idea for Michonne long before work on the book started. The lone swordsman with the unarmed zombie pets was something I'd been itching to throw into the book for a long time. I've got big plans for her, so keep your eyes peeled for the Book Three hardcover, or run out to your local comic shop or book seller and grab a copy of The Walking Dead Volume 5 in paperback. She's a very important character in this series.

Since Michonne was appearing on a cover before the issue she appeared in was drawn I had Charlie whip up a quick drawing of her so Tony would know what she looked like for the cover.

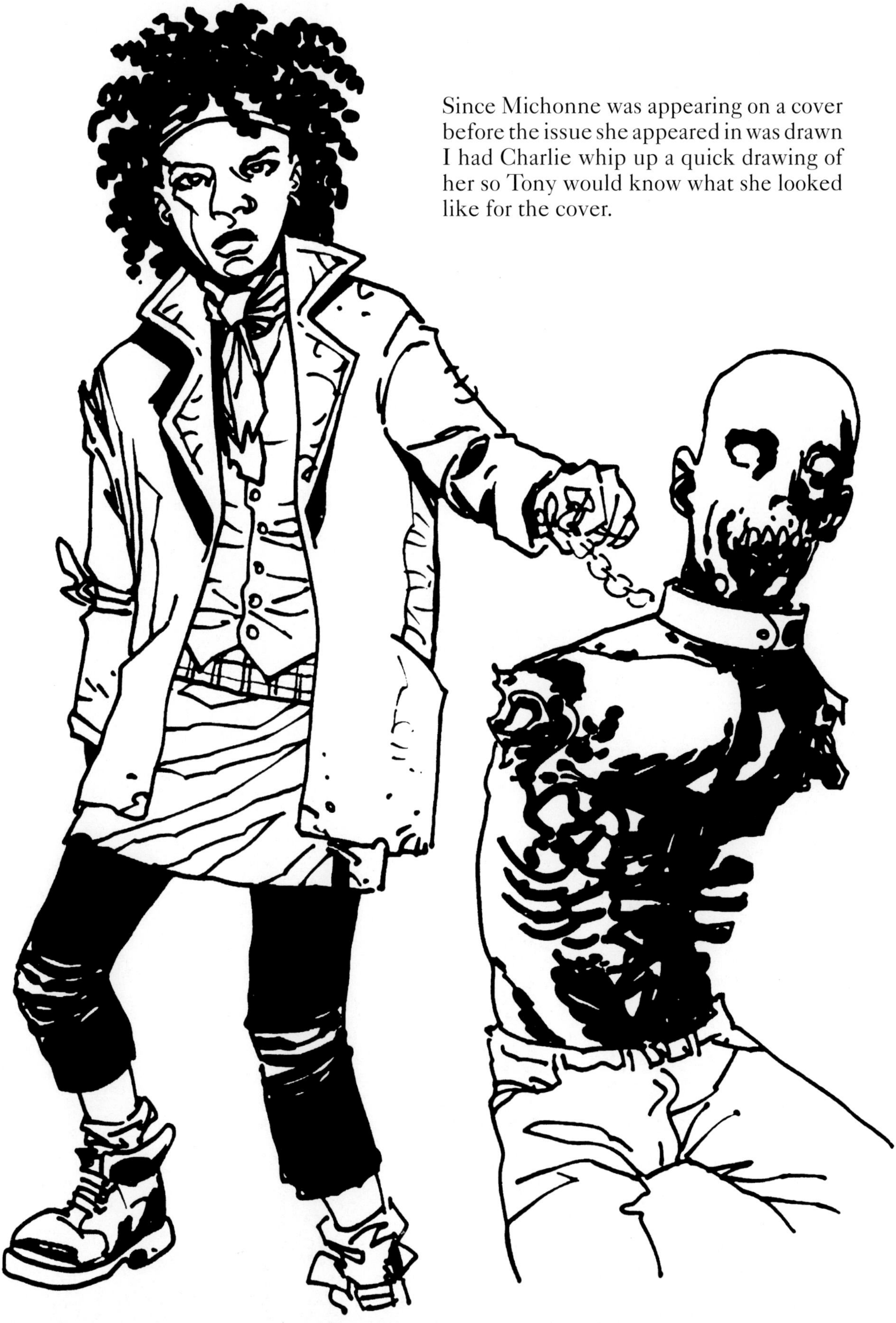

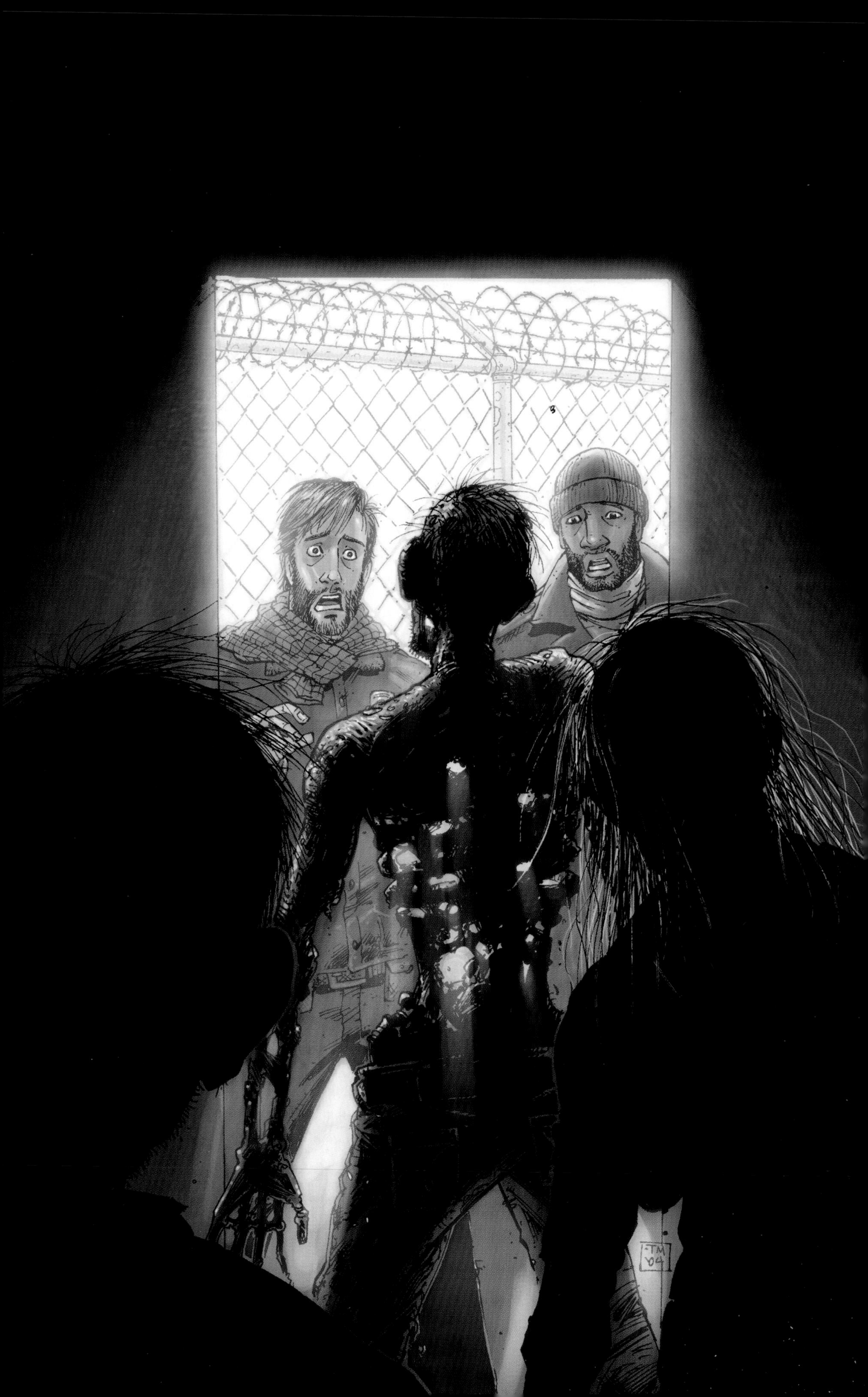

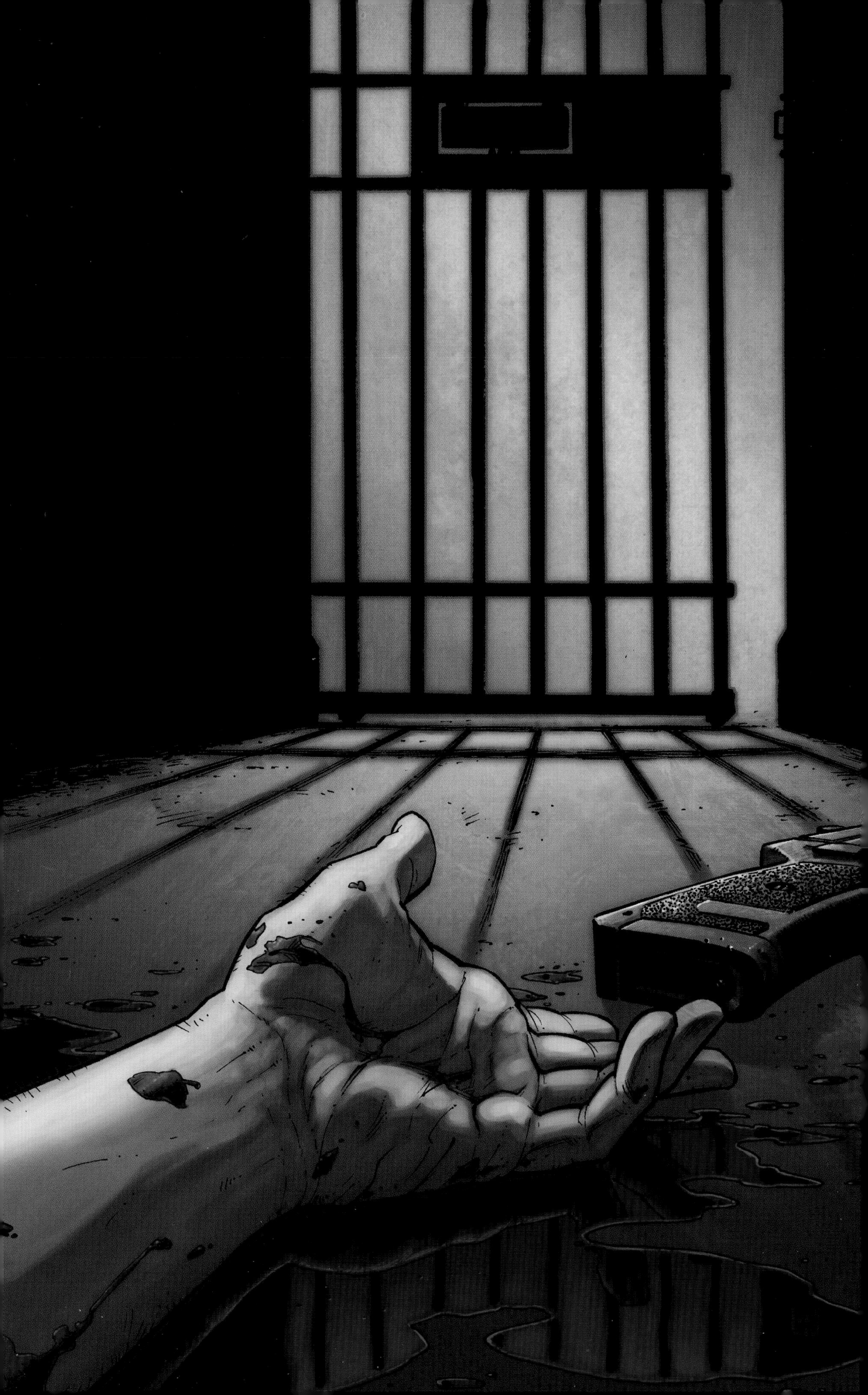

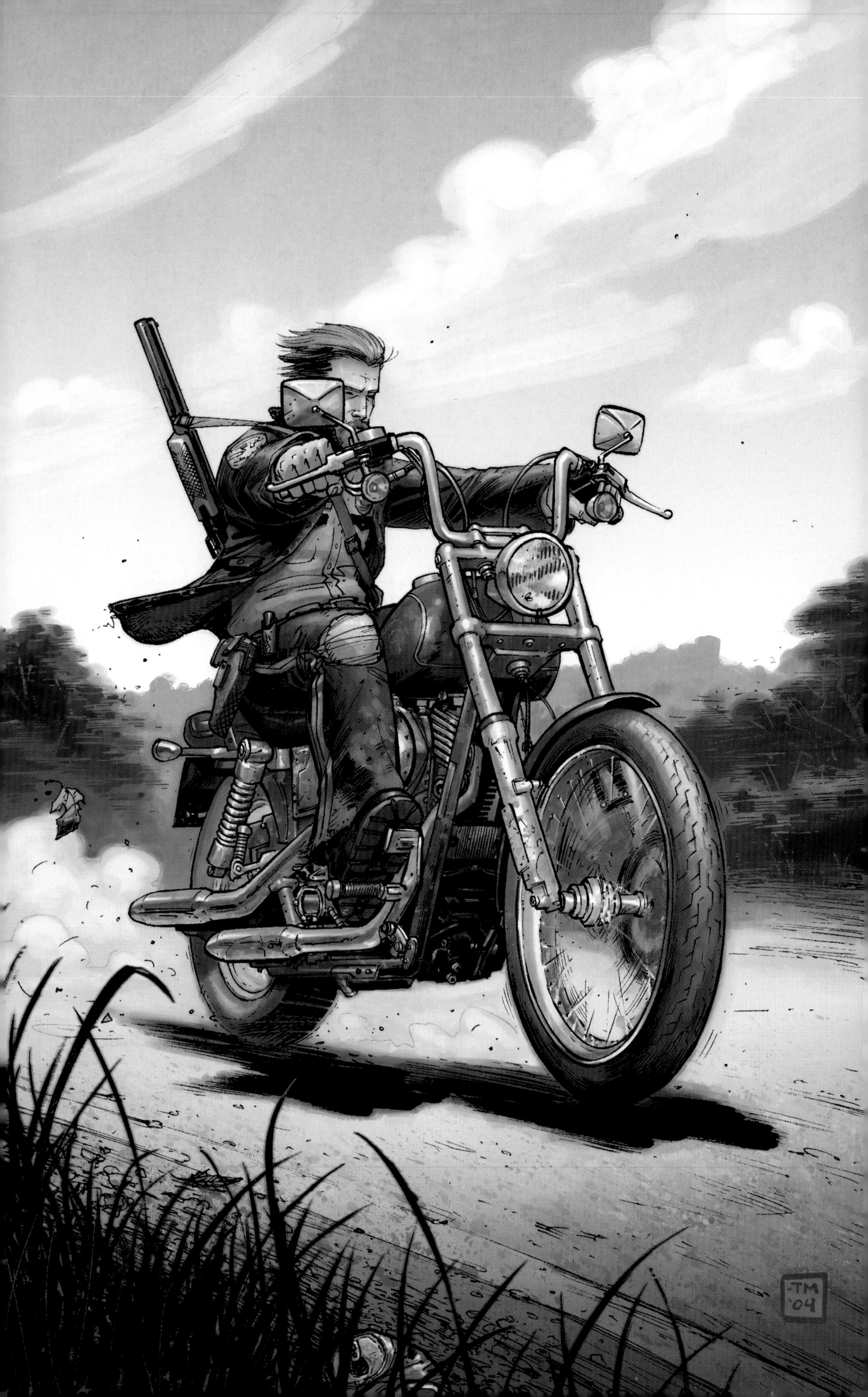
TM
'04

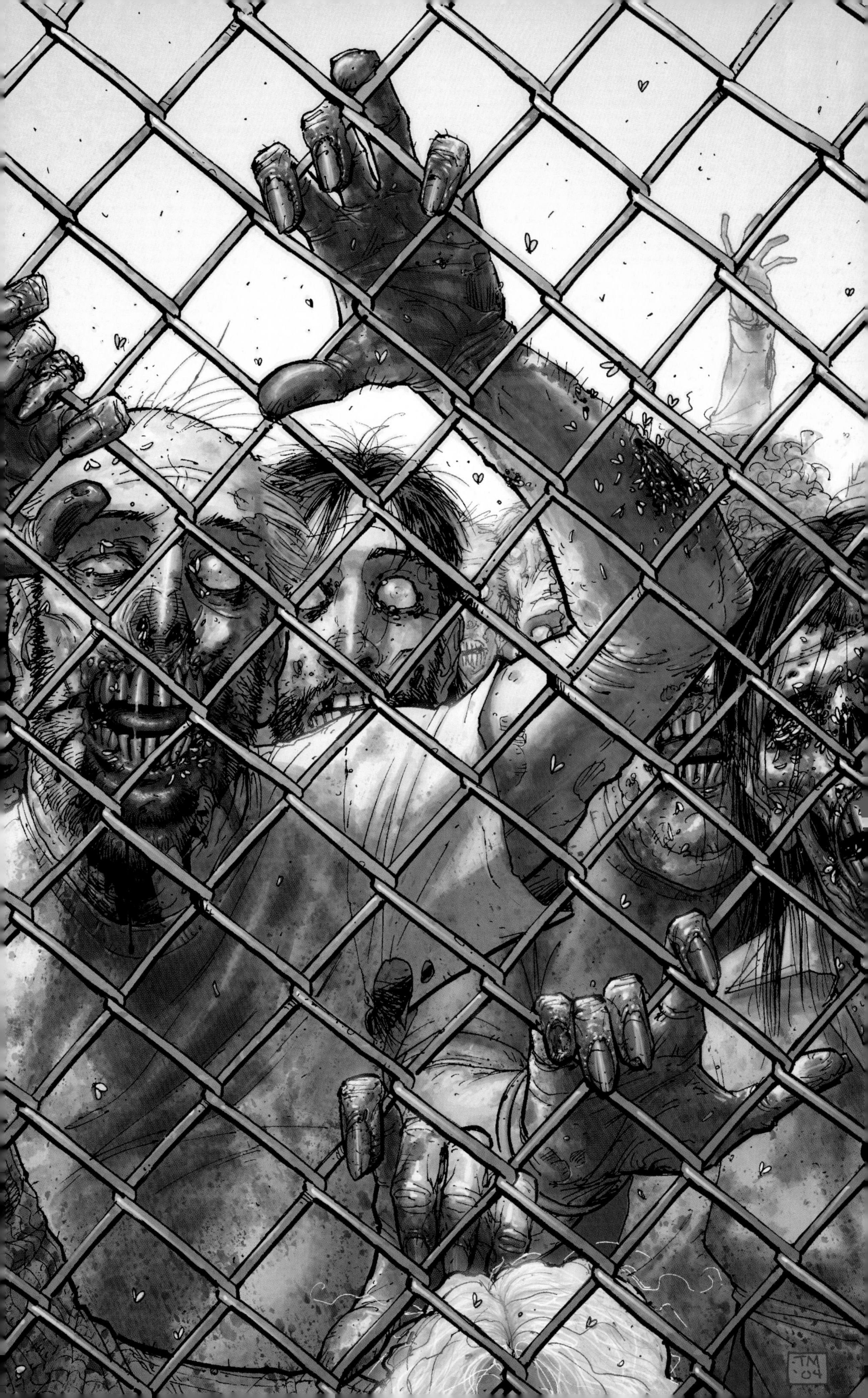

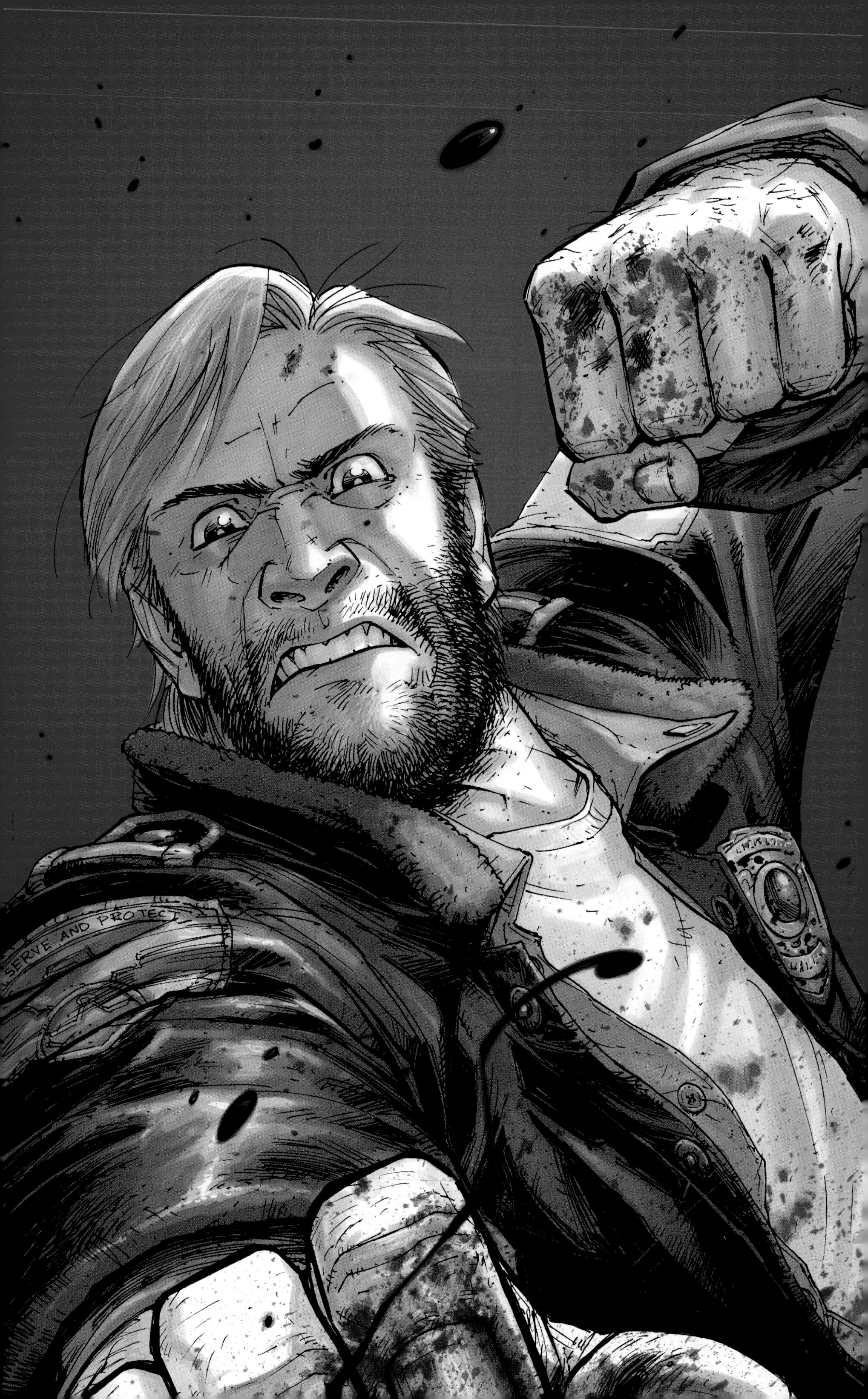
SERVE AND PROTECT

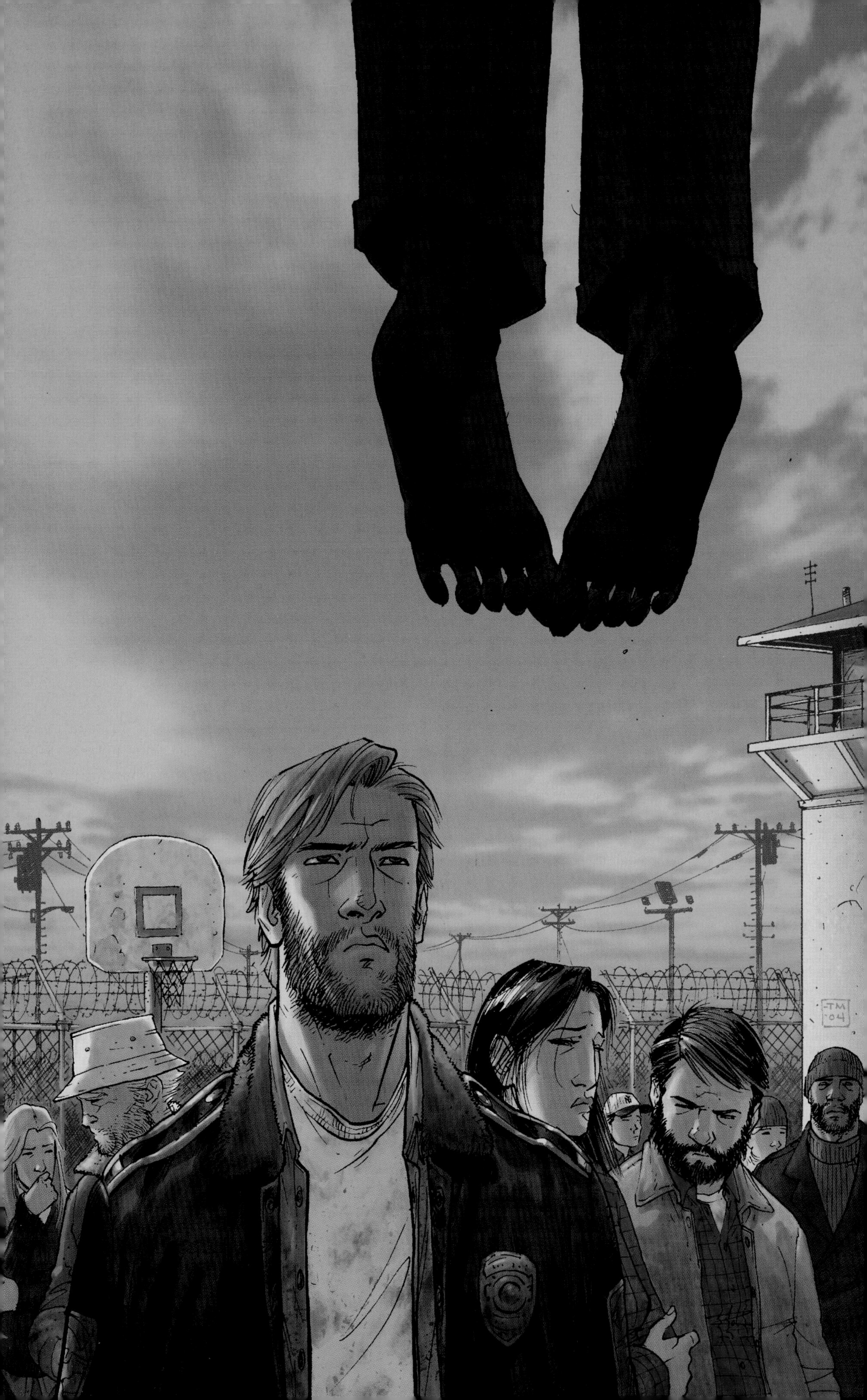
TM '04

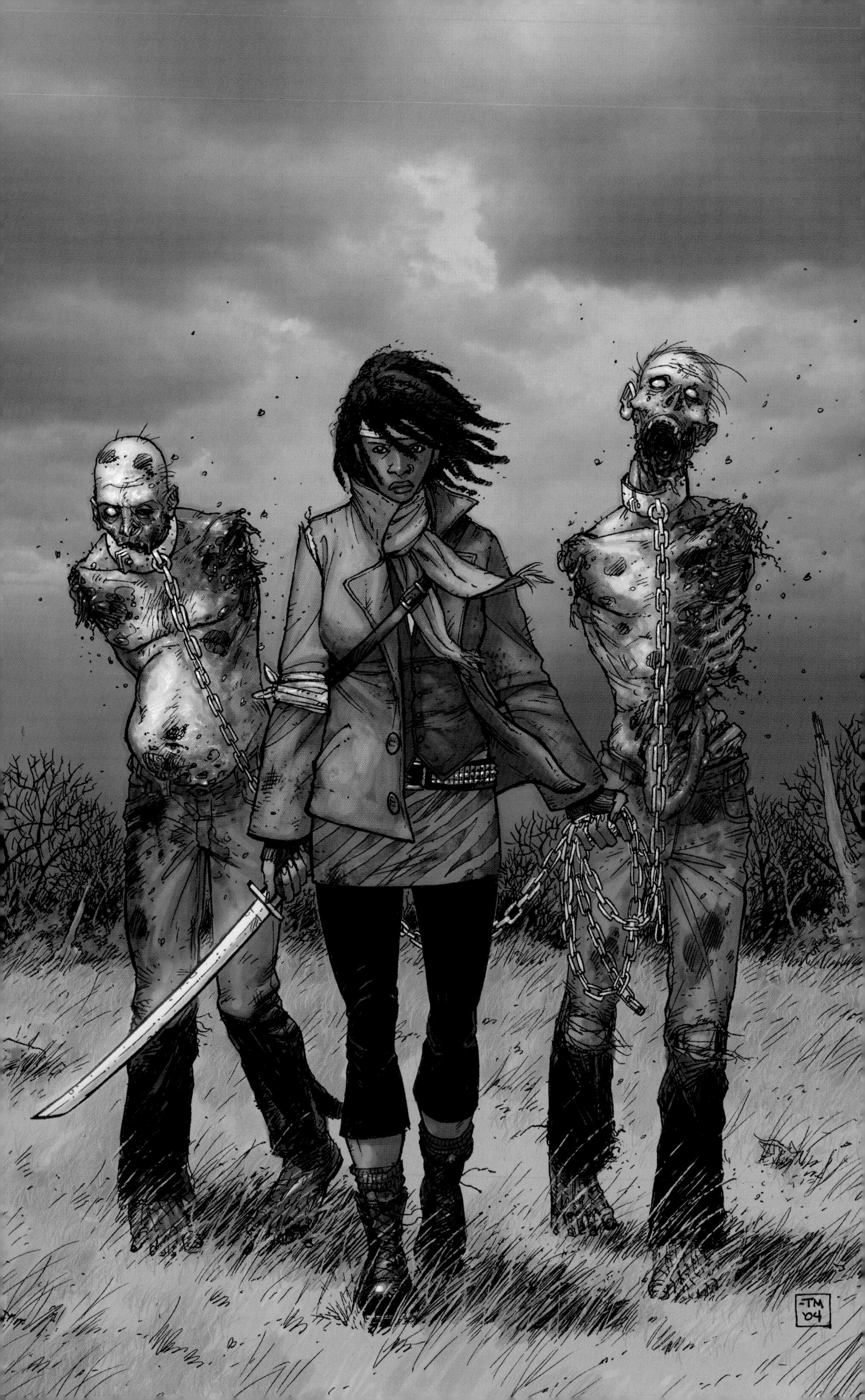
TM
'04

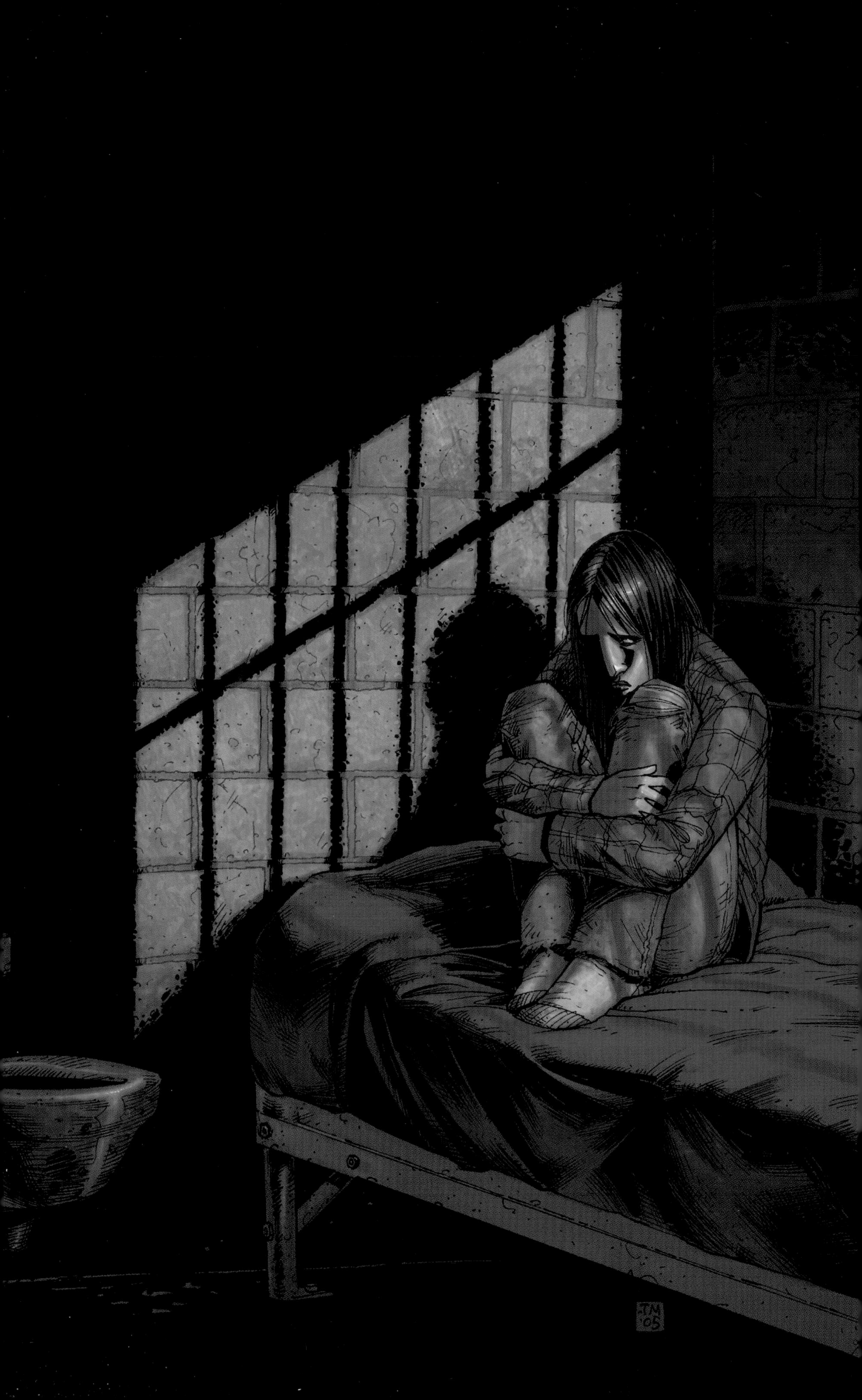
TM '05

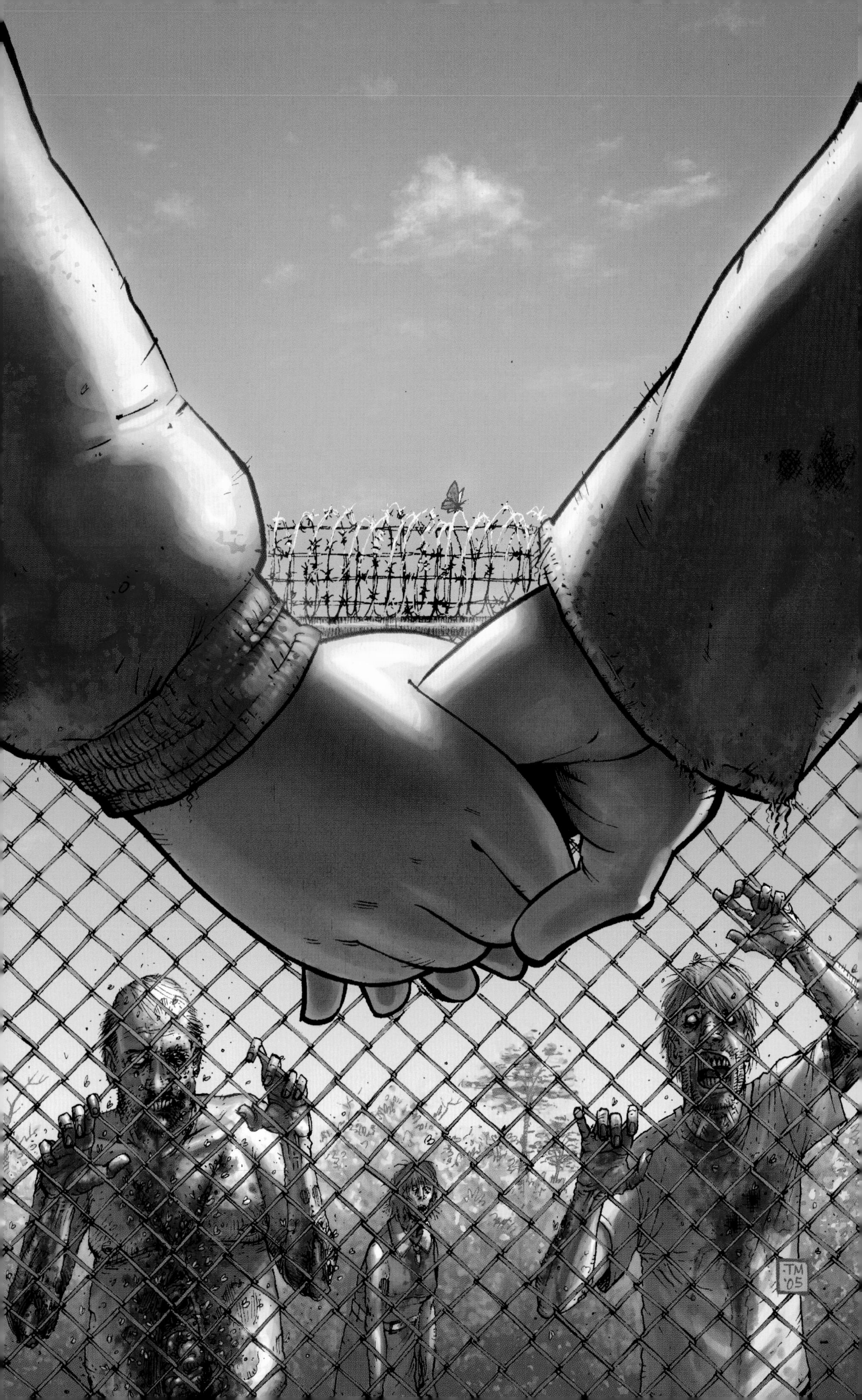
TM
'05

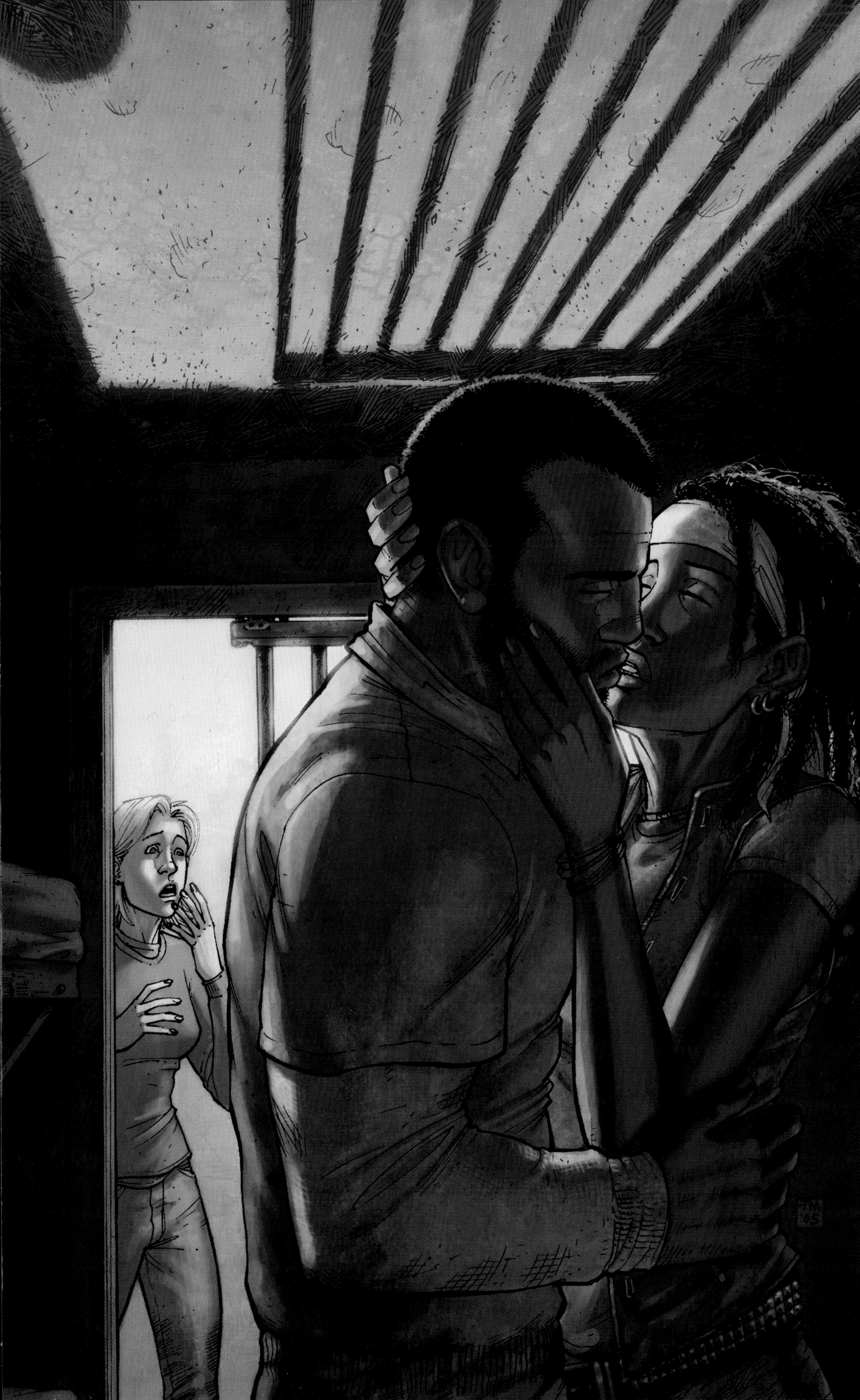

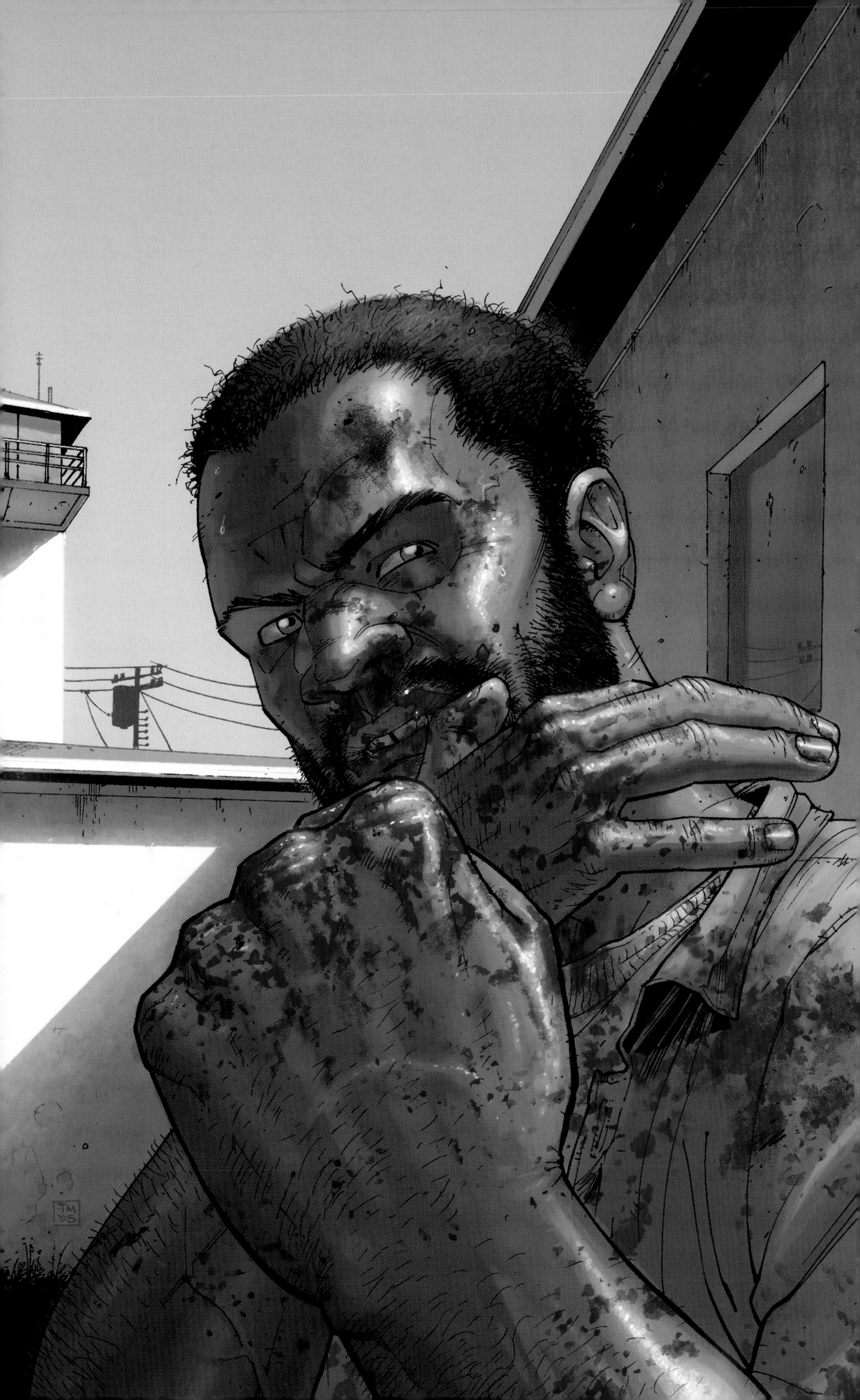

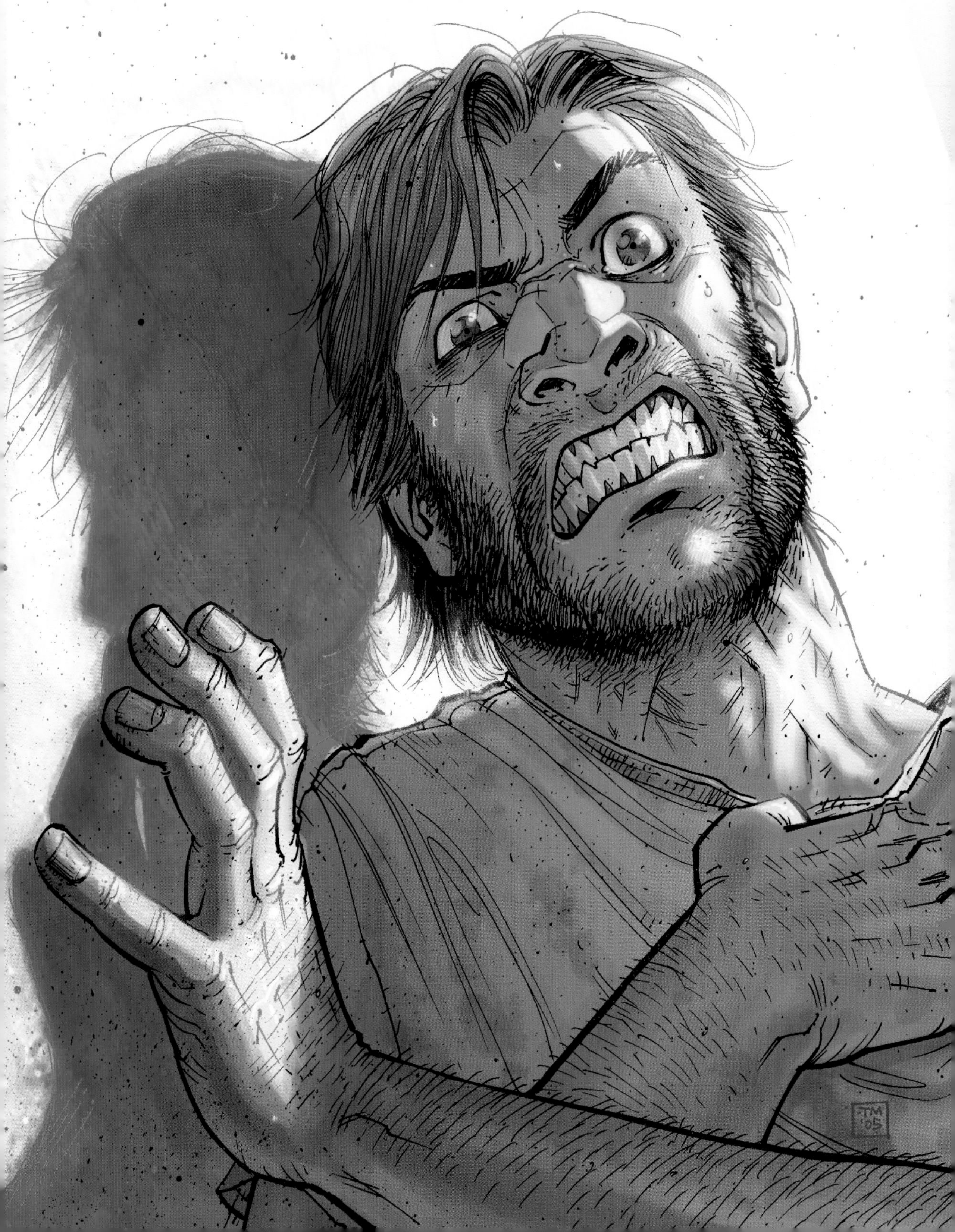

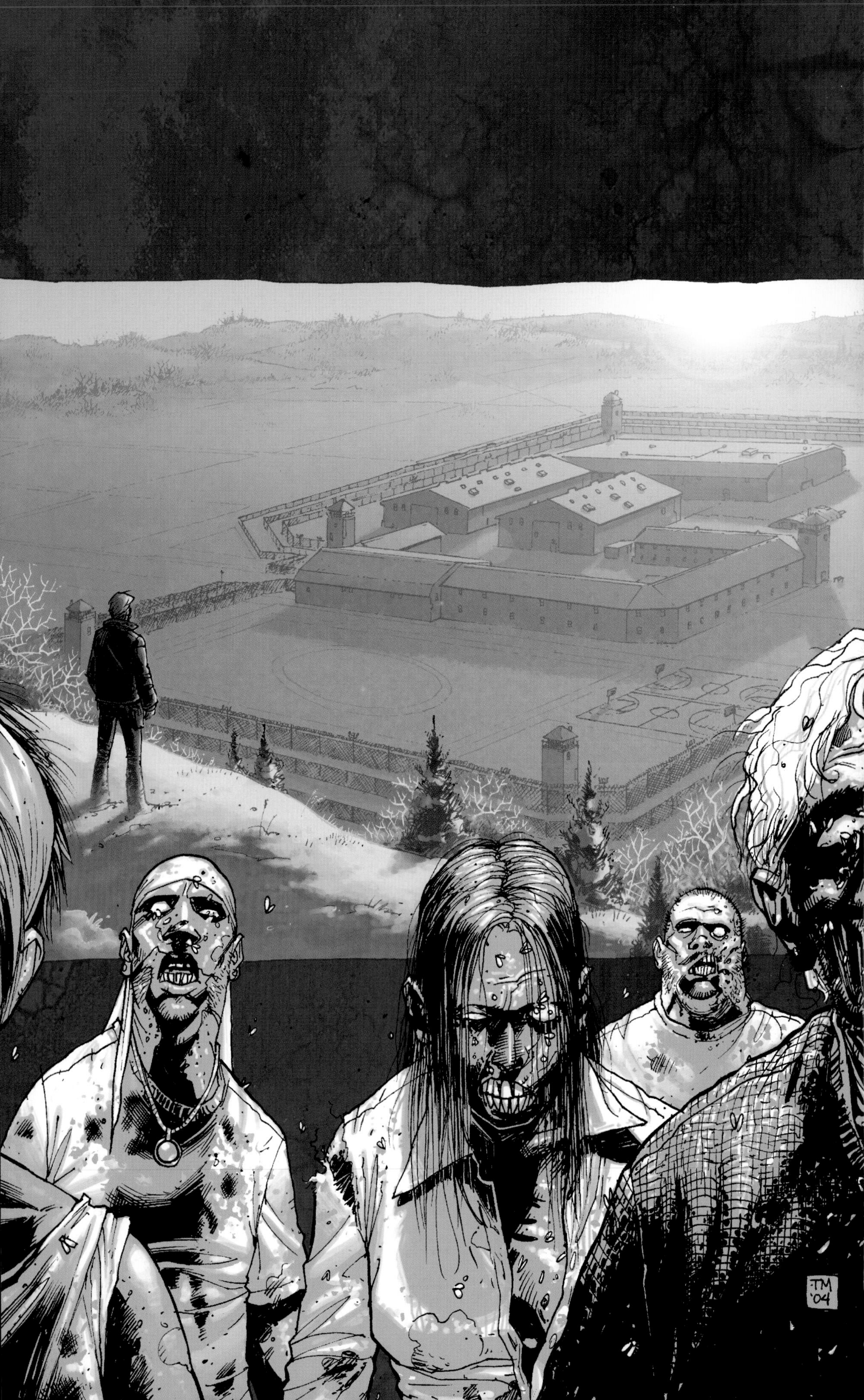
TM
'04

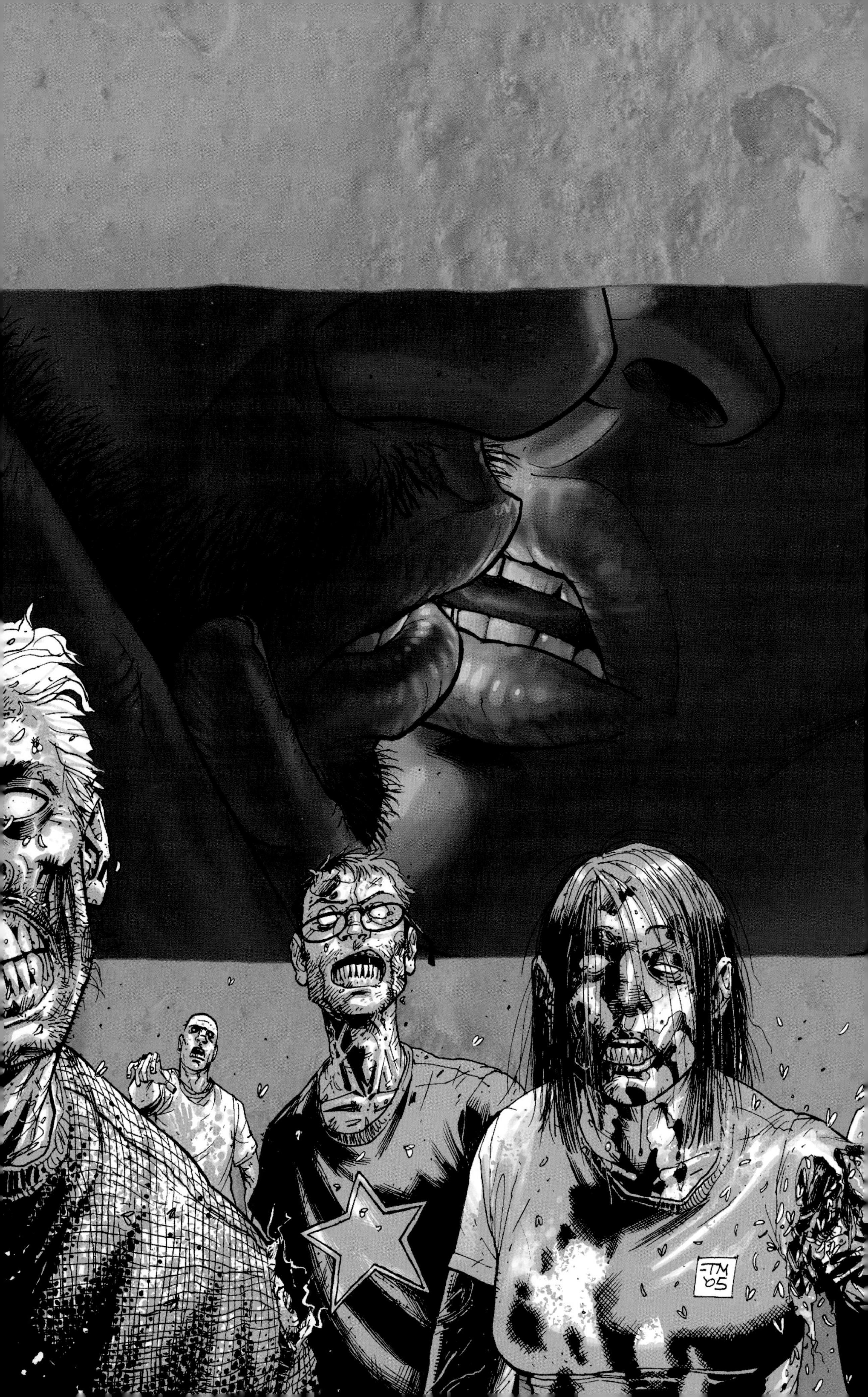
TM
'05

MORE GREAT BOOKS FROM
ROBERT KIRKMAN
& IMAGE COMICS!

BATTLE POPE
VOL. 1: GENESIS TP
ISBN: 978-1-58240-572-8
$12.95
VOL. 2: MAYHEM TP
ISBN: 978-1-58240-529-2
$12.99
VOL. 3: PILLOW TALK TP
ISBN: 978-1-58240-677-0
$12.99
VOL. 4: WRATH OF GOD TP
ISBN: 978-1-58240-751-7
$9.99

BRIT
VOL. 1: OLD SOLDIER TP
ISBN: 978-1-58240-656-5
$14.99

CAPES
VOL. 1:
PUNCHING THE CLOCK TP
ISBN: 978-1-58240-656-5
$17.99

CLOUDFALL
GRAPHIC NOVEL
$6.95

REAPER
GRAPHIC NOVEL
$6.95

TECH JACKET
VOL. 1:
THE BOY FROM EARTH TP
ISBN: 978-1-58240-771-5
FULL COLOR • $14.99

TALES OF THE
REALM
HARDCOVER
ISBN: 978-1-58240-426-0
$34.95
TRADE PAPERBACK
ISBN: 978-1-58240-394-6
$14.95

INVINCIBLE
VOL. 1:
FAMILY MATTERS TP
ISBN: 978-1-58240-711-1
$12.99
VOL. 2:
EIGHT IS ENOUGH TP
ISBN: 978-1-58240-347-2
$12.99
VOL. 3:
PERFECT STRANGERS TP
ISBN: 978-1-58240-915-5
$12.95
VOL. 4:
HEAD OF THE CLASS TP
ISBN: 978-1-58240-440-2
$14.95
VOL. 5:
THE FACTS OF LIFE TP
ISBN: 978-1-58240-554-4
$14.99

VOL. 6:
A DIFFERENT WORLD TP
ISBN: 978-1-58240-579-7
$14.99
VOL. 7:
THREE'S COMPANY TP
ISBN: 978-1-58240-656-5
$14.99
VOL. 8:
MY FAVORITE MARTIAN TP
ISBN: 978-1-58240-656-5
$14.99
ULTIMATE COLLECTION,
VOL. 1 HC
ISBN 978-1-58240-500-1
$34.95
ULTIMATE COLLECTION,
VOL. 2 HC
ISBN: 978-1-58240-594-0
$34.99
ULTIMATE COLLECTION,
VOL. 3 HC
ISBN: 978-1-58240-763-0
$34.99
THE OFFICIAL HANDBOOK
OF THE INVINCIBLE
UNIVERSE TP
ISBN: 978-1-58240-831-6
$12.99

THE WALKING
DEAD
VOL. 1:
DAYS GONE BYE TP
ISBN: 978-1-58240-672-8
$9.99
VOL. 2:
MILES BEHIND US TP
ISBN: 978-1-58240-413-4
$12.95
VOL. 3:
SAFETY BEHIND BARS TP
ISBN: 978-1-58240-487-5
$12.95
VOL. 4:
THE HEART'S DESIRE TP
ISBN: 978-1-58240-530-8
$12.99
VOL. 5:
THE BEST DEFENSE TP
ISBN: 978-1-58240-612-1
$12.99
VOL. 6:
THIS SORROWFUL LIFE TP
ISBN: 978-1-58240-684-8
$12.99
VOL. 7:
THE CALM BEFORE TP
ISBN: 978-1-58240-828-6
$12.99
BOOK ONE HC
ISBN: 978-1-58240-619-0
$29.99
BOOK TWO HC
ISBN: 978-1-58240-759-3
$29.99
BOOK THREE HC
ISBN: 978-1-58240-825-5
$29.99

TO FIND YOUR NEAREST COMIC BOOK STORE, CALL:
1-888-COMIC-BOOK